CONTEMPORARY KOREAN ART

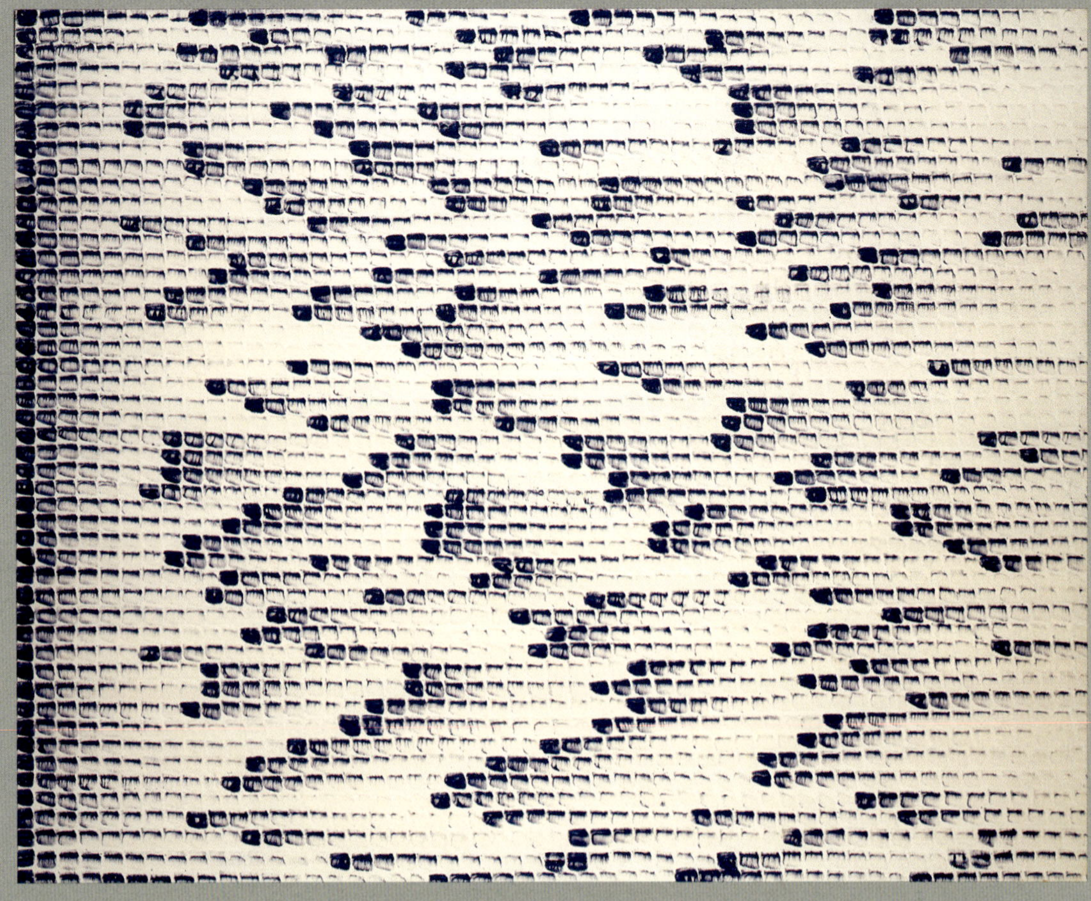

CONTEMPORARY KOREAN ART

TANSAEKHWA AND THE URGENCY OF METHOD *Joan Kee*

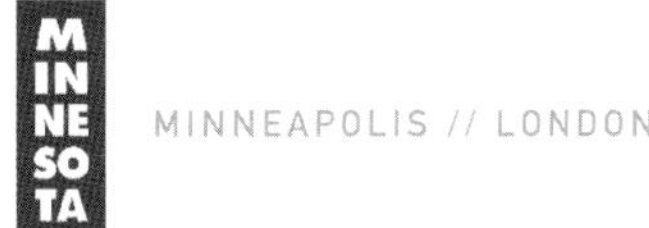

UNIVERSITY OF MINNESOTA PRESS MINNEAPOLIS // LONDON

Frontispiece: Lee Ufan, *From Point*, 1973. Collection of Museum of Contemporary Art, Tokyo. Courtesy The Pace Gallery. Copyright Lee Ufan.

This book was supported by the Academy of Korean Studies Grant funded by the Government of the Republic of Korea (MEST) (AKS-2011-BAA-2102).

The University of Minnesota Press gratefully acknowledges financial assistance provided for the publication of this book by the Department of Art History, University of Michigan.

Portions of the book were previously published as "Contemporaneity as Calculus: The View from Postwar Korea," *Third Text* 25, no. 5 (October 2011): 563–76; reprinted with permission of Taylor & Francis. Parts of chapter 3 were previously published as "Points, Lines, Encounters: The World according to Lee Ufan," *Oxford Art Journal* 31, no. 3 (October 2008): 403–24.

Published by the University of Minnesota Press
111 Third Avenue South, Suite 290
Minneapolis, MN 55401-2520
http://www.upress.umn.edu

A Cataloging-in-Publication record for this book is available from the Library of Congress.

ISBN 978-0-8166-7987-4 (hc)
ISBN 978-0-8166-7988-1 (pb)

Printed in The United States of America on acid-free paper

The University of Minnesota is an equal-opportunity educator and employer.

20 19 18   10 9 8 7 6 5 4 3 2

CONTENTS

Despite the introduction of the revised romanization system by the Korean government in 2000, *Contemporary Korean Art: Tansaekhwa and the Urgency of Method* uses the McCune–Reischauer system, as it remains the system by which Korean-language sources are identified in English-language databases, archives, libraries, and other information centers. I occasionally used a commonly accepted or preferred romanization of a proper name or term, for example, Park Chung-hee, Yushin, Seoul, and tansaekhwa. With the exception of certain artistic movements and groups (such as Mono-ha, Minjung), names of key organizations and institutions have been translated into English. Names not romanized are included in a list of Korean proper names in *han'gŭl* in the Appendix.

This book generally refers to the environment in which tansaekhwa emerged as the "Korean" art world: visual art from the Republic of Korea is usually referred to as "Korean art" without further modification. In those cases where this world is compared to that of North Korea, however, I use "South Korea" to clearly distinguish it from the North.

All translations from Korean are my own, except when otherwise designated and except those quotations from *Korea Journal,* where Korean submissions were translated into English by native Korean speakers.

Every effort was made to secure the highest-quality reproductions available for the illustrations. Unfortunately, due to circumstances beyond the artists' control, many works are lost or known only through documentary photographs; several of these images exist only as low-quality reproductions in magazines and newspapers. In a few instances the image quality is not ideal; I chose to include such images when necessary rather than omit them.

The Urgency of Method

his book is about tansaekhwa, one of the most important
artistic movements in the history of contemporary art in Korea.
Tansaekhwa, often referred to as "Korean monochrome painting"—
the word *tansaekhwa* literally means "monochrome painting"—refers
to a loose constellation of mostly large abstract paintings done in
white, black, brown, and other neutral colors made by Korean artists
from the mid-1960s to the mid-1970s.[1] Its promotion in Korea, Japan,
and France in the 1970s and 1980s became the grounds on which critics, curators, and artists most vigorously discussed the parameters of a
distinct contemporary Korean art field.[2] Although numerous efforts to
represent contemporary Korean art overseas had taken place since the
provisional end of the Korean War in 1953, it was only from the mid-
1970s that artworks began to be intentionally grouped according to
certain formal characteristics said to exude a distinct Korean sensibility,
which initially meant whiteness and, as the name tansaekhwa suggests,
a tendency to use monochromatic supports.[3] By the 1980s, the vigorous
promotion of works increasingly described as tansaekhwa led to the
movement's de facto establishment both as the face of so-called Korean
modernism and as a polarizing force symbolic of deep ideological and
generational divisions in the Korean art world.

The story of tansaekhwa's promotion, reception, and rhetoric might
justify its place in an expanded history of contemporary art, particularly
if we understand this history as a protracted fight for symbolic hegemony
structured around struggles taking place in a world defined by profound
inequities of wealth, power, and access, as well as by various imperialist
histories. Korean critics who identified certain series of paintings as
examples of "Korean monochrome painting" did so against the backdrop
of a South Korean state under Park Chung-hee that sought to rational-
ize its control by cultivating the idea of a distinctly "Korean" culture,

FIGURE I.1 Park Seobo, *Écriture No. 31-77-78*, 1978. Pencil and oil on canvas,
130 × 162 cm. Collection of the artist. Photograph by Lee Man-hong.

or what one commentator early described as "cultural nationalism."[4] Along similar lines were the efforts of critics and institutions in both Korea and Japan to promote tansaekhwa as an iconography through which to envision a distinct field of contemporary Asian art. Weary of an international art world that seemed excessively focused on the artistic developments and choices made in parts of western Europe and the United States, certain Korean and Japanese viewers welcomed works such as those displayed in Tokyo at the 1975 group exhibition *Five Korean Artists, Five Kinds of White*, often regarded as the beginning of the tansaekhwa movement. Soon afterward, other exhibitions of contemporary Korean art, especially those taking place in Japan, heavily emphasized works using neutral, earth-toned colors, colors that were cited as further evidence of the works' "natural" or "earthy" qualities and, later, of their Koreanness, and even Asianness.

But if tansaekhwa and the history of contemporary art in Korea that it reflects deserve recognition beyond what they have to say about the formation of cultural identity in a part of the geopolitical world long regarded as artistically tangential, it is because of the way artists like Kwon Young-woo, Yun Hyongkeun, Ha Chonghyun, Lee Ufan, and Park Seobo saw form as a particular kind of action by stressing certain aesthetic and material fundamentals in order to simultaneously engage with and push against specific distinctions symptomatic of what they understood as the "world." Such distinctions included the segregation of oil from ink painting, a division that was brought into play during Japan's occupation of Korea from 1910 to 1945, the period when most tansaekhwa artists were born. Also crucial was the distinction between legibility and illegibility, a divide with critical implications during the authoritarian rule of Park Chung-hee, the deeply controversial army general who ruled South Korea for almost twenty years, from 1961 to 1979. These distinctions opened further onto broader issues raised by Korea's history as a Japanese colony; by the growing numbers of Korean artists showing overseas in what, during the 1960s, was the first great wave of international biennales and triennales; and by the emergence of a dictatorial South Korean state through the declaration of martial law in 1972.

That viewers sensed the engagement of tansaekhwa works was reflected by the frequency with which they were called "methods" (*pangbŏp*) rather than "paintings" or even "artworks."[5] "Method" initially reads as "process," as suggested in works like Park Seobo's *Écriture No. 31-77-78* (Figure I.1), which prompted critics like the venerable Yi Kyungsung to describe tansaekhwa works as "methods of drawing," "methods of spreading," "methods of bleeding," "methods of spilling," and "methods of pushing" as well as "methods of painting."[6] In Korean, "method" can also refer to technique, and in *Écriture No. 31-77-78*, part of a series that was originally titled *Myobŏp*, or "technique of depiction," Park pushes a pencil up and down in repeating wavy patterns on a freshly painted support. As the name *Écriture* suggests, both Park's gestures and the traces he leaves behind strongly allude to the act of writing. His marks, however, impart no demonstration of skill, a central aspect of technique, nor do they communicate anything other than the artist's physical presence and, perhaps, his investment of labor. At the same time, the organization of the work into successive horizontal rows imparts a distinctly systematic affect.

Yet this affect never resulted in a coherent work, a reflection of tansaekhwa artists' view of painting as an inverted teleology: one invests time and labor to produce a work that viewers see as unfinished. This approach was not simply about making transparent the process through which works were made, however. If the goal was to make works that looked deliberately incomplete, it was so that a work could be read as something other than the unique product of a singular author, or even as something outside the bounds of style, the parameters according to which painting tended to be gauged in Korea and elsewhere. In the same overview of Korean art of the 1970s in which he liberally used the word "method" in reference to tansaekhwa works, Yi Kyungsung observed:

Art history as usually discussed is conceived as a history of styles. . . . [Art] exists in preestablished formulas like national style, group style, international style, individual style, and the like. But in a contemporary art [field] that is subdivided and localized in the extreme, it has the effect of conflating each artist's individual artistic worlds to past group styles. In this situation . . . it is of utmost necessity that we focus on the newness of how each artist individually attempts to produce work. The question is not what is depicted or made, as it has been for art of the past, but *how* to depict. [My emphasis][7]

Lee Yil, one of tansaekhwa's most faithful advocates, suggested that the agency of artworks stemmed from explorations of "method." This to him meant explorations of what he regarded as basic to painting, as could be seen in works like *Écriture No. 31-77-78*, in which literal components collaborated with the imagination of the viewer to open up a space that allowed for profound uncertainty.[8] Tansaekhwa was not about the mastery of technique, the transmission of meaning, or even the manipulation of materials. Its makers were primarily concerned with bringing together certain materials and material properties so as to break the painting down. Potentially this opened up room for the reconstruction of a different narrative of painting, one less indebted to reified sets of distinctions founded on particular systems of order and belief repeated over a given period. Thus, in calling tansaekhwa works "methods," critics like Lee and Yi inadvertently called for viewers to recognize the degree to which these works were themselves methods of being present outside those systems of order whose seeming dominance relied on their dual claims to historicity and perpetuity.

REBUILDING ABSTRACTION IN POSTWAR KOREA

That tansaekhwa was abstract painting was no surprise, as abstraction was, in Korea, the least reified mode of depiction at the time the movement first emerged. Histories of abstraction in Korea had yet to be written, and artists vigorously debated its parameters. Those involved in the debates included the presumptive first generation of abstract painters—nearly all of whom were male and affluent—who had studied art in Tokyo in the 1930s. There they took part in the numerous artists' groups, ateliers, and schools bent on investigating abstraction's various manifestations, such as the Second Section Society (Nika-kai), the first antiestablishment group of Western-style oil painters, and the Free Artists' Association (Jiyū bijutsuka kyōkai).[9] Art historian Kim Youngna, in her discussion of the exhibitions hosted by groups such as the Free Artists' Association, notes that artists like Kim Whanki and Yoo Youngkuk enjoyed some modicum of success during their Tokyo years.[10] At the association's second exhibition, in 1939, Kim exhibited *Rondo* (Figure I.2), which reworks the form of the still life as a cartographic problem, breaking the image down into discrete parts identified by color, then putting the image back together as if it were a jigsaw puzzle.[11] Yoo Youngkuk proposed that painting be treated as a function of edges and planes. His relief *Work 1 (L24-39.5)* (Figure I.3), shown in the third exhibition of the Free Artists' Association in Tokyo, emphasized as central the spaces formed by overlapping planes and those created by their edges.

The outbreak of the Korean War in 1950 curbed private artistic production, although the respective governments of North and South

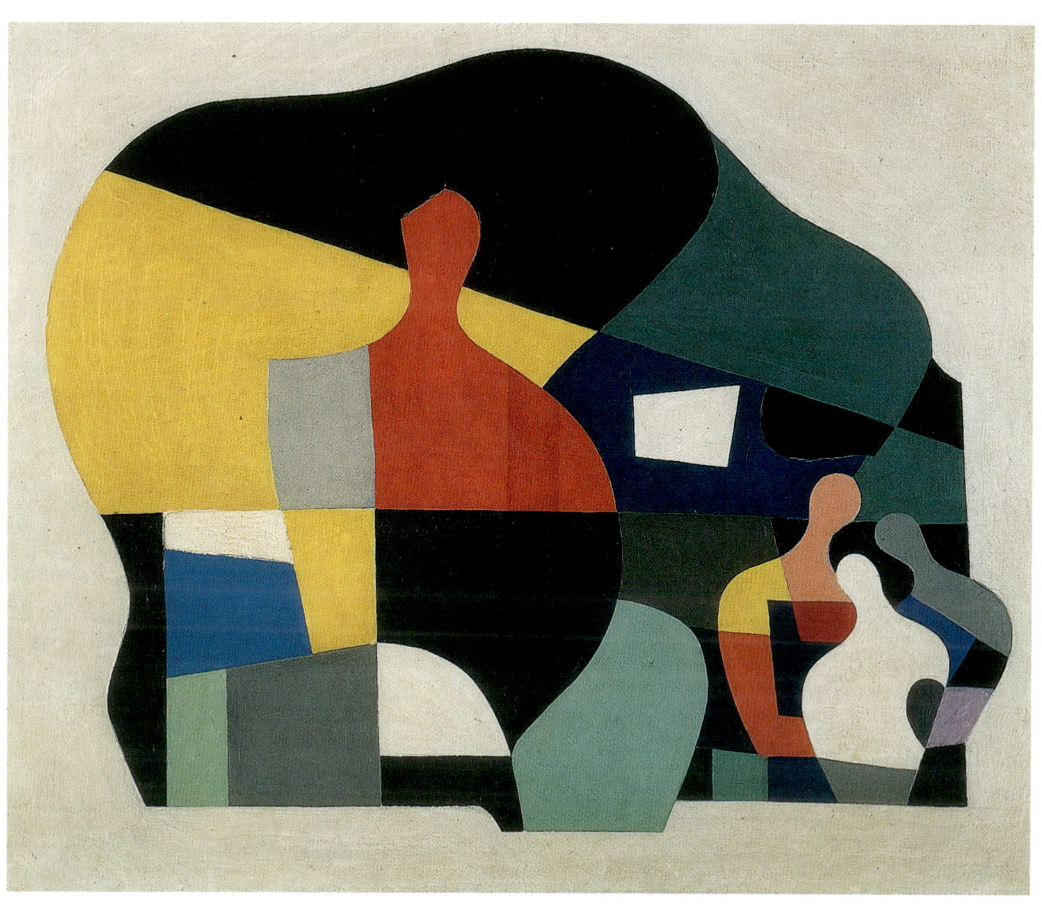

FIGURE I.2 Kim Whanki, *Rondo*, 1938. Oil on canvas, 60 × 72 cm. Collection of National Museum of Contemporary Art, Korea.

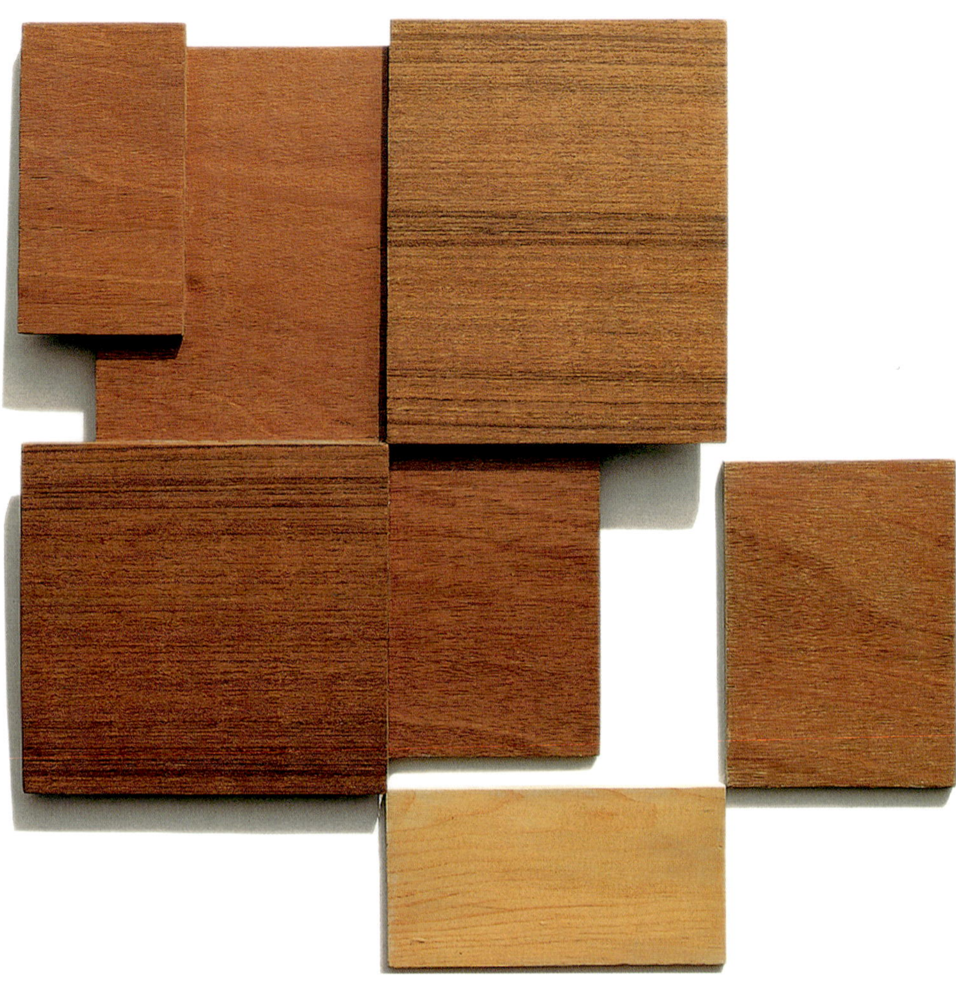

Korea recruited large numbers of artists, sometimes by force, to paint portraits of military leaders, posters, and propaganda scenes.[12] In South Korea these artists were known as *chonggun hwaga* and were officially attached to various branches of the armed forces; tansaekhwa artist Kwon Young-woo, for instance, was affiliated with the air force.[13] Artists able to create works outside an official capacity during this time of severe material deprivation tended toward mimetic depiction that could immediately and specifically convey experiences of physical devastation, desperation, and material hardship. The stress on the distinction between figurative and abstract painting would continue to linger for decades to come.

After the Korean War provisionally ended in 1953 with a cease-fire agreement between North and South Korea, there was a national push for reconstruction (*chaegŏn*). University art departments were soon reestablished, for example, at Seoul National University and Hongik University, the two schools whose students would dominate the South Korean art world for decades and from which most tansaekhwa artists graduated. Building on the infrastructure left behind by the Japanese colonial government, the South Korean government reinstated the juried annual art salon (*Taehan min'guk misul chŏllamhoe*) that had been initially established in 1948 and that was closely patterned after the salon instituted in 1922 by the Japanese during their occupation of Korea. Known by its abbreviated name, the Kukchŏn, the newly reinstated salon would be the leading venue for contemporary art until around 1957, when a critical mass of exhibitions and groups formed in response to Kukchŏn conservatism. Artists also congregated under organizations like the Taehan Art Association (Taehan misul hyŏp'oe), the main umbrella organization for visual artists from 1945 until 1961. On the discursive front, some critics pushed for a closer examination of *hyŏndae misul*, the term used to refer to modern and contemporary art. Kim Yŏng-ju, whose career as an artist and critic began during the transitional period from the end of Japanese colonial rule to the beginning of the Korean War, stated that the task of "current" Korean art lay in confronting "the crossroads formed by the '*hyŏndae*' as an epochal backdrop and '*hyŏndae*' as an ideological condition."[14]

For some artists, including many tansaekhwa artists who attended art school in the 1950s, the process of reconstruction meant embracing abstraction more vigorously than ever before. A large proportion treated abstraction as a language in which they needed to gain fluency in order to communicate with their overseas counterparts. The painter

Nam Kwan, who had just returned from having shown his works at the
1953 Tokyo International Art Exhibition, later known as the Tokyo Biennale,
wrote, "Although there was abstraction before the war [World War II],
it seemed to be more active postwar. I felt this particularly after having
seen the Tokyo International Art Exhibition [at the Tokyo Metropolitan
Art Museum]. Every country has abstraction."[15] In February 1957 Kim
Whanki's friend Yi Pong-sang, a self-taught oil painter and professor at
Hongik University, established a popular studio, or "painting institute"
(*hoehwa yŏn'guso*), that soon became a central "meeting place for young
artists" interested in gestural abstraction.[16]

Gaining fluency in the language of abstraction, however, did not
mean replicating what was taking place in the perceived capitals of the
art world, as was richly indicated by the number of works that simultaneously resembled and diverged from abstraction made elsewhere.
There were practical reasons for this: government restrictions and a
dire lack of funds effectively prevented all but the most affluent and
connected Korean artists from traveling overseas, a situation that
was only fully relieved during the transition from authoritarianism to
democracy in South Korea during the late 1980s. Nam Kwan, for example, recollected knowing of only about ten Korean art students in Paris
while he was there around 1955.[17] Mimicking the works of others was
rejected for other reasons too. As Yi Pong-sang warned in 1953, "What is
deplorable is that in the art schools entrusted with the future of our art
world, it seems that abstraction is being imposed in the same way that
academicism was previously."[18]

More importantly, Korean artists had to contend with both multiple
sources of information and multiple modes of information delivery,
including low-resolution black-and-white photographs reproduced
in Japanese magazines, high-quality color reproductions provided by
U.S. cultural agencies, verbal reports from the handful of artists able to
travel overseas, and casual hearsay. They thus worked under conditions
akin to what scholars of creole languages describe as "chaotic input," a
term borrowed from Noam Chomsky's theory of early language acquisi-
tion and subsequently used to refer to situations in which hearers of
multiple languages are inundated with numerous and irregular stimuli
from which they construct new sets of rules and structures.[19] In order
to devise a sustainable form of communication, speakers must craft a
set of regular rules and structures from these stimuli. Similarly, Korean
artists looking to produce abstraction during the immediate postwar era attempted to restructure painting, a task complicated by the

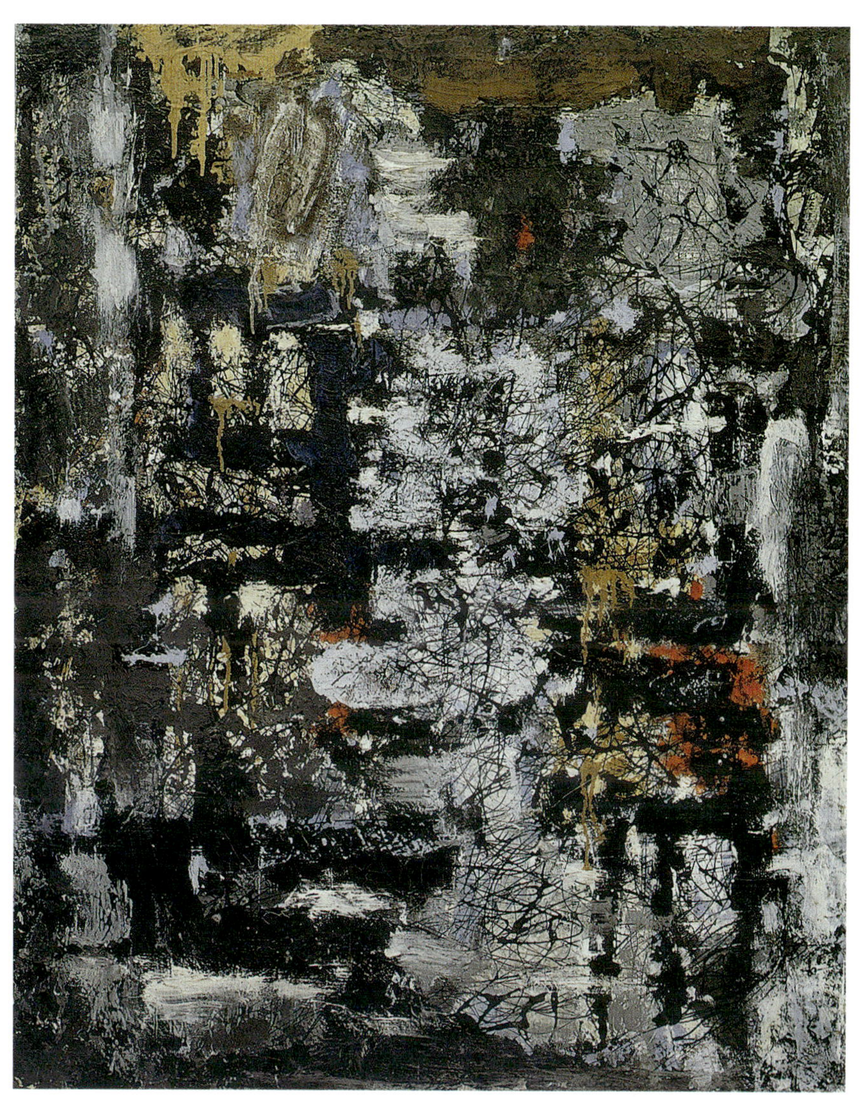

FIGURE I.4 Park Seobo,
No. 1, 1957–58. Oil on canvas,
95 × 82 cm. Collection of
Yoo Seung-pil, Seoul.

availability of materials. Both oil paint and canvas, for example, were expensive, and many Korean artists compensated by painting on tenting canvas and newsprint or by mixing oil with unconventional binders, including sand and concrete. A sizable number of abstract works made from the mid-1950s to the mid-1960s were remarkable for their plasticity and for their embodiments of slowness. Paint was applied as if it were more solid than liquid, even to the point of being laboriously pushed or hauled across pictorial space.

Between 1957 and 1958, Park Seobo painted *No. 1* (Figure I.4), a vertically oriented rectangle of modest size upon which paint of various colors was roughly applied in thick, vaguely perpendicular strokes. Moments at which the brush lost its grip on the surface were duly recorded, as were those at which paint spilled over the support, pulled downward by gravity on the upright canvas. Named in seeming homage to Jackson Pollock's similarly titled works, *No. 1* demonstrates an attention to tactility and gestural vigor that calls to mind gestural abstraction, about which Park and other Korean artists gleaned information from various channels, including French and Japanese art magazines. Many of these works were described as "informel," a word first introduced into Korean art criticism in 1956 by the critic Kim Yŏng-ju.[20] *No. 1* was first exhibited in May 1958 as part of the third exhibition of works by the Modern Artists' Association (Hyŏndae misulga hyŏp'oe) and was initially grouped as part of what another critic, Syngboc Chon, called "the new '*peinture informelle*,'" in which "young" painters would "paint amid extreme privation and discomfiture."[21]

U.S. agencies and institutions played a role in the new abstraction, and Park himself recalled that American "action painting" was a "strong stimulant" for artmaking between 1957 and 1960.[22] Critic Yi Ku-yŏl, who began his career as a journalist in 1959, recalled seeing color plates of Pollock's work, as well as plates of Willem de Kooning's and Robert Motherwell's works, in artist studios in the years before and after 1960. These plates, Yi stated, were taken from *Life* and *Time*, both pro-America magazines that were available in Korea through the U.S. Information Agency, the agency established by the U.S. government in 1953 to promote the image of the United States overseas.[23] Likewise, the U.S. government facilitated shows like *Eight American Artists*, which took place at the Tŏksu Palace in downtown Seoul in April 1957. Organized by the Seattle Art Museum, the show included works such as Mark Tobey's tempera painting *Gothic* from 1943, which was later reproduced for the cover of the October 1958 issue of what was then the

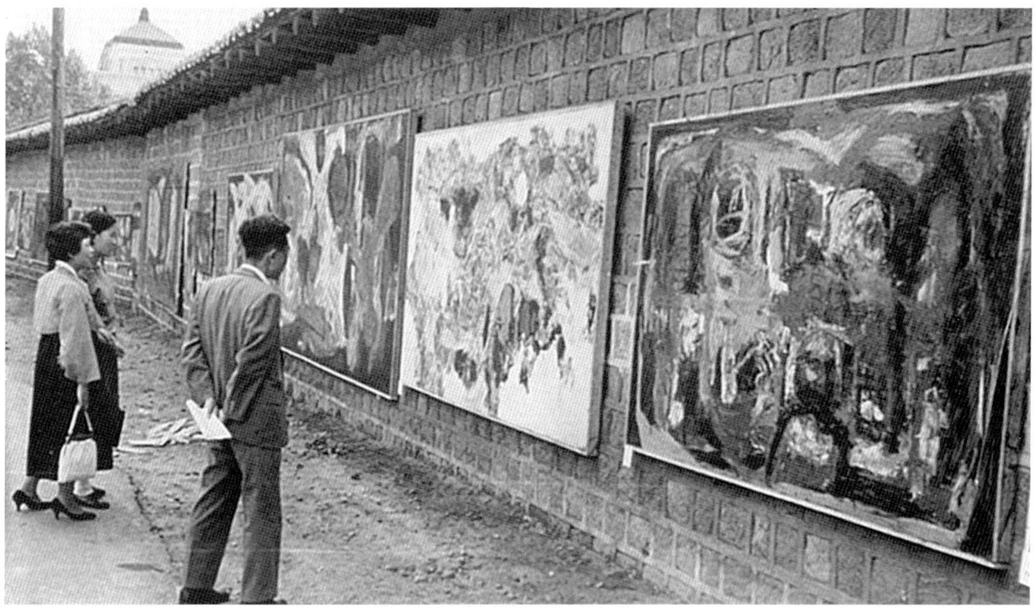

country's only art magazine, *Sin misul*. North Korean critics, who, at least until the early 1960s, were arguably better informed about artistic developments outside their country than were their counterparts in the South, quickly discerned the connection between the promotion of abstraction and U.S. political interests; art historian and critic Han Sang-jin, who had once taught oil painting in Seoul prior to joining the North Korean army during the Korean War, argued, "Having neither the spirit of self-reliance [*chuch'e*] nor a national conscience, the abstractionists of the South receive the active support of Americans and copy them diligently."[24]

In the mid- to late 1950s, a number of artists began to collectively explore various modes of abstraction in earnest. Some, like Kwon Youngwoo and Yun Hyongkeun, worked mostly on their own. Others, like Park Seobo, worked in small groups like the Modern Artists' Association (Hyŏndae misulga hyŏp'oe), the Ink Forest Society (Mungnimhoe), and the 1960 Artists' Group (1960 nyŏn misulga hyŏp'oe). Perhaps most memorable was the Wall Group, formed in protest against the conservative selections of the Kukchŏn jury whose inaugural show, the *Wall Exhibition* (*Pyŏkjŏn*), took place on the rough-hewn stone walls of Tŏksu Palace in downtown Seoul (Figure I.5), at the same time that the national salon was taking place in the museum situated on the palace grounds. Widely circulated in the mass media, photographs of the *Wall Exhibition* lingered in the popular imagination well after the show ended.

No. 1 drew praise from the critic Yi Kyungsung for its "adventurous spirit," even if it and similar works had "precedents in Euroamerica."[25] Influenced, perhaps, by certain descriptions of informel and abstract expressionism, Park would later cite the Korean War as a powerful motivating force: his brushstrokes were no mere applications of paint but, rather, "the shrieks of a single cry of death issuing forth."[26] The mark, or the moment of contact between discrete materials, was exclusively read as traces of the body or artistic will, an interpretation that recalled multiple engagements with Pollock, whom Park described in 1960 as one who "vigorously attacks the four sides of the canvas," adding, "By doing this, he is able to express his life force onto the canvas."[27]

Yet even as Korean artists tacitly shaped their works around what they knew of gestural abstraction associated with abstract expressionism and informel, which to them seemed to represent the international standard of artmaking, gestural abstraction in Korea diverged considerably from its Euro-American counterparts in its aims and effects. Translation was a major factor for this divergence; as Chung Moo-jeong has discussed, articles originally published in one language often underwent several rounds of translation before reaching artists living in Korea. Korean artists who read Michel Tapié's discussion of informel based on his 1952 book *Un Art autre* in the December 1956 issue of *Mizue* were actually reading a double translation; the original French was first translated in English, which was then translated into Japanese, which many Korean artists at this time understood, having attended primary school during the Japanese occupation.[28]

In *No. 1* Park is less interested in exemplifying the full body gesture than he is in generating a surface from various forms pressed together. Their bond is tenuous and viewers can easily identify the points at which this surface might be teased apart. That Park uses a striking range of colors, including yellow ochre, a hint of orange red, stark white, periwinkle, and forest green, indicates a will to make this tenuousness known and, in turn, to recognize the surface as something both constructed and on the brink of dissolution. Pictorial space, in turn, is regarded as a blank physical site upon which to build an edifice of paint. Thick black, blue, and whitish strokes serve as a scaffold upon which the artist then suspended dollops of paint. Throughout the image is the motif of the right angle, produced by two straight, perpendicular lines. Park's brushwork is not that of a liberated brush unencumbered by precedent, convention, or duty; instead, it exhibits a greater degree of control than the athletic tug-of-war with paint that so often character-ized the works of his counterparts using the French informel style or of the Gutai group in Japan, even as the paintings were alternately hailed and criticized as Korean reenactments of overseas developments. The repetition of the right-angle motif, the snug interlocking of shapes, and the overall centripetal flow of energy that brings the eye from the center to the edges and then back, all suggest a strong resonance with the act, if not the image, of construction.

One might compare *No. 1* with Lee Ungno's *Exultation* (Figure I.6), exhibited two months before the former in March 1958. As a profes-sional ink painter, Lee took a somewhat different path to abstraction. Born in 1904, Lee was trained in the literati tradition, which in 1920s Korea took its cue from Chinese paintings made in the twelfth and thirteenth centuries and classified as Southern Song painting. But like many of his colleagues working in the cosmopolitan environment of colonial Seoul, Lee took a flexible approach to ink painting that drew as much from photography and newspaper cartoons as it did from the kinds of literati painting most admired at the time. Lee hinted at these earlier interests through his approach to space, which took form through staged oscillations between flatness and depth.

Like Park Seobo, Lee was interested in making and showing work to an overseas audience, especially after having been encouraged in 1957 by the French critic Jacques Lassaigne to show his work in Paris the following year. But Lee was not interested in being understood as part of the Korean response to informel and action painting, as were some other artists working with oil and canvas. Instead, Lee emphasized the way the mark relayed a sense of energy throughout pictorial space. In the mid-1950s, Lee's interests extended to gestural abstraction, and in *Exultation* he may have borrowed from Pollock a sense of how to work the space equally from all four sides of the support. This was not a matter of simple appropriation but, rather, a considerable technical challenge, for it was no easy matter to work with ink and light color on paper. Even a mild slip of the brush could upset pictorial balance, for it required a dexterous hand to manage the various kinds of lines without overcrowding the support. On this count, Lee drew from his extensive knowledge of ink painting, particularly of other explorations of line's capacity to energize an unmarked support into living space, such as those of Qi Baishi, who, while in Beijing in the 1930s, attracted several Korean students, including Kim Young Ki, the son of Lee's teacher Kim

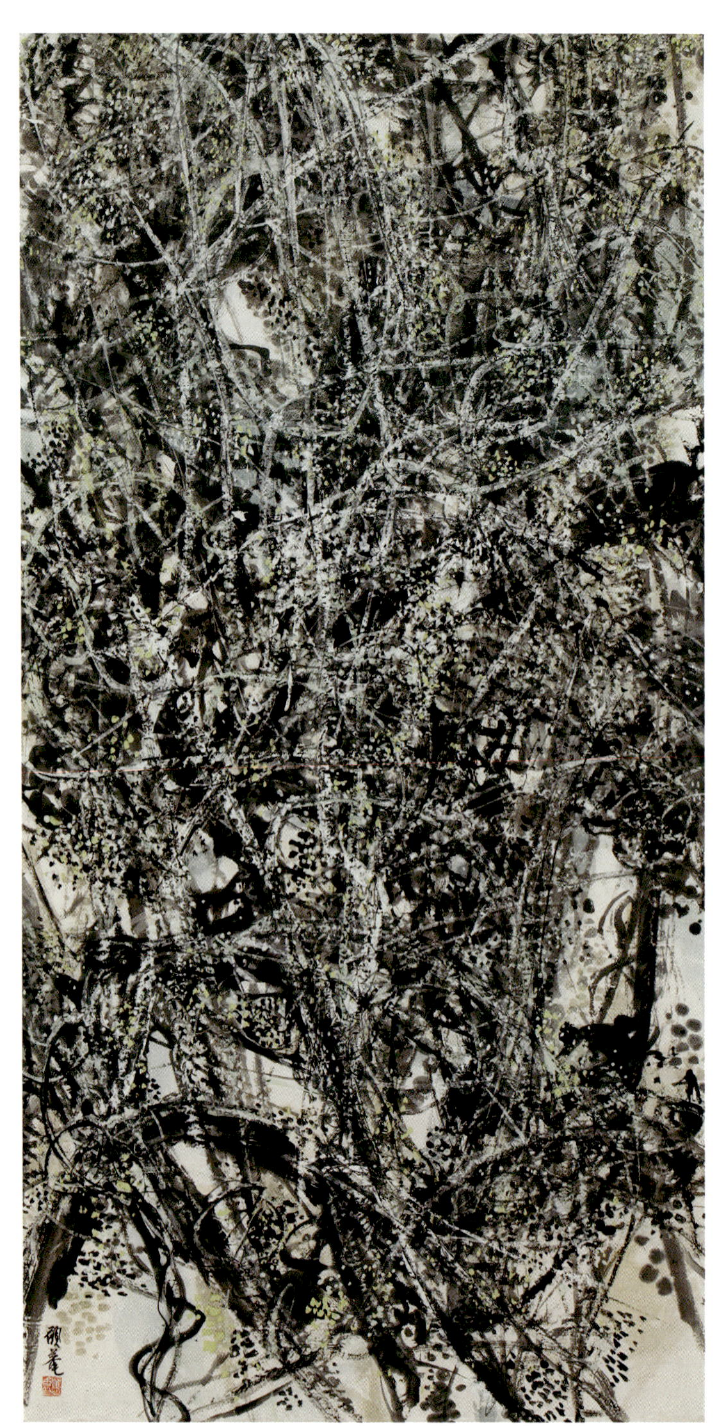

FIGURE I.6 Lee Ungno, *Exultation*, 1958. Ink and light color on paper, 134 × 67.5 cm. Collection of Ungno Lee Museum of Art, Daejeon.

Kyu-jin.[29] Lee's use of line leads the viewer's eye throughout and beyond
the edges of the support so that pictorial space appears to be opened up,
therefore making the painting feel more expansive than otherwise suggested by the canvas's actual physical dimensions.

Abstraction assumed a more official capacity after 1961, when the
army general Park Chung-hee seized control of the South Korean government on May 16. At least one art historian contends that Park's new
government attempted to consolidate its authority by introducing gestural abstraction into the 1962 and 1963 exhibitions of the Kukchŏn.[30]
Certainly artworks that looked gestural were duly rewarded, as evidenced by the kinds of ink paintings awarded special citations in the
Kukchŏn from 1961 to 1963.[31] The recognition of abstraction's importance in the reconstruction of a national image that could speak to
audiences abroad was further emphasized by the increasing numbers of
abstract works representing South Korea in overseas exhibitions. In the
minds of some artists and critics, especially those holding positions of
power in the Korean Fine Arts Association (Han'guk misul hyŏp'oe)—
an organization formed by the newly established South Korean state
in 1961 that forced previously independent artists' groups into one
umbrella organization—there was no question as to what should represent the country in exhibitions like the São Paulo Bienal or the Paris
Biennale. In 1963 Kim Byung-ki marveled at the large percentage of
group shows dedicated to abstraction.[32] Writing in the same year, Bang
Keun-taek declared, "About the question of what is contemporary
art . . . it is unquestionably abstraction."[33] But the preferential treatment of abstraction incensed figurative artists, who in 1967 voted
to ensure that one of their own, Kim In-kyŏm, would head the oil-
painting (Western painting) section of the association rather than
Yoo Youngkuk, the abstract painters' choice.[34]

DOWN TO FORM; OR, THE RISE OF EVERYDAY MATERIALS

Despite such controversies, the creative potential of chaotic input nevertheless persisted, especially as artists began to grapple with a society
that was increasingly being shaped by the state's drive for industrialization. In 1964 Kim Ku-lim made *Corpse of the Sun II* (Figure I.7). Kim
first painted a rectangular wooden panel a rich black that appears to
shine under overhead or direct illumination. To this panel, he attached
an expanse of thin black vinyl, upon which he then bonded small plastic

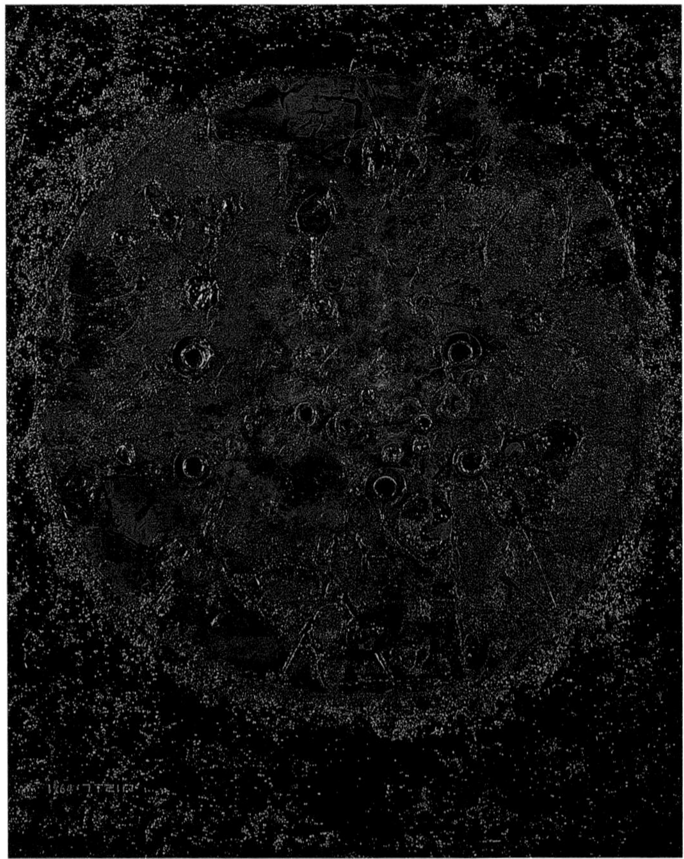

FIGURE I.7 Kim Ku-lim, *Corpse of the Sun II,* 1964. Oil, vinyl, canvas, and other materials on wood, 91 × 75.3 cm. Collection of National Museum of Contemporary Art, Korea.

washers, thin plates with holes in the middle often used to prevent leaks or corrosion. He set fire to the washers, which caused them to partially melt and permanently fuse to the surface of the vinyl and the panel. He drew a large circle on the panel with gasoline, which he also set on fire. The result was a surface of variegated textures.

Initially conceived as one of a pair, *Corpse of the Sun II* is among the first artworks in postwar Korea to recognize the nature of the art object as primarily that of a commodity. This is not to say that Kim was the first to recognize that the artwork could or, as was all too well known by abstract painters in 1960s South Korea, *could not* be exchanged for other instruments of value, but, rather, that he was among the first to make central the relationship between the realm of the artwork and the realm of the production and consumption of material goods. The best-known example of this relationship is arguably U.S. pop art, about which

Thomas Crow has written that the "scandalous" juxtaposition of high and low calls into question the "'normal' hierarchy of cultural legitimacy."[35] *Corpse of the Sun II* evokes this in at least two ways: through Kim's decisions to foreground the washers by placing them at the very heart of the pictorial space, and to allow them to remain recognizable as such.

When *Corpse of the Sun II* was first shown in 1967 at the Public Information Center in the southern port of Pusan, South Korea's second-largest city, Kim held a managerial position at a textile factory. While there, he made several works that incorporated parts gleaned from the factory floor, including threaders and needles.[36] It was still some five years before South Korea would experience what one commentator would dub the "golden age of Korean cotton spinning," but spinning, weaving, and other businesses related to the textile industry were among the most important pillars upon which the South Korean state based its hopes of industrialization and economic development in the 1960s.[37] Even some forms of geometric abstraction paid homage to industrialization. Stacked on top of one another or arranged in a series, the bars characteristic of Lee Seung-jio's *Nucleus* works (such as Figure I.8) impart an overall image of insistent linearity, reinforced by the extreme gradation of each bar, which is in keeping with the Francophilia of the Korean art world as well as with an almost pragmatic fascination with everyday materials, particularly those associated with the world of industrial production. Lee's bars, for example, were said to be modeled after both the pipes of Fernand Léger and the shiny handles of the metal boxes used to deliver food, and in the mid-1960s Kwon Young-woo used the thick brown paper used for wrapping packages.[38]

But *Corpse of the Sun II* was far from being a celebratory representation of South Korean industrial success. In 1964 South Korean textile and spinning factories faced many difficulties, including old, even obsolete, equipment. The washers Kim used were discarded remnants that could no longer fulfill their original purpose. Also notable was the way in which *Corpse of the Sun II* projects forward an image of defacement. Such defacement intimated destruction of the kind that resonated throughout South Korean abstraction, particularly during the Korean War and the years immediately thereafter. While the symbolism of these images as a reflection of wartime destruction and postwar social instability has been frequently iterated, the event of defacement had a much different inflection in 1964. Three years had already passed since Park Chung-hee had taken advantage of a highly unstable political climate to seize the presidency. Under his regime, economic development, national security, and the formation of a national entity took priority. *Corpse of the Sun II* is destruction without apparent cause, an impression supported by the response of one viewer who, on seeing the work, "violently recoiled from it, [and] angrily demanded to know who in hell would consider this art."[39] The violence of this reaction suggests that the work too openly defied expectations of what an artwork should be, a question that within the Korean art world was defined in terms of what art could do: what it could represent, or what it could give back to the viewer in the way of pleasurable sensation.

Most striking of all was the juxtaposition of black vinyl, a material that could be cheaply procured in early 1960s South Korea, with oil paint, an expensive substance by then inextricably associated with notions of fine art, or *yesul*. The divide between fine art and the quotidian was further made palpable by the addition of a wooden frame to the work some years later.[40] Relatively wide, the frame clearly distinguishes the events taking place within its borders from the realm outside. The wooden panel is set apart as a unique object, but the use of the washers and vinyl, along with the very unmarketable nature of abstraction in South Korea, brings it back to the realm of the everyday. Moreover, the use of materials such as vinyl and washers highlights the tendency among Korean artists to experiment with materials not commonly associated with fine art: cotton normally used to make tents, coarsely woven hemp, barbed wire, coiled wire springs, sandpaper, newspapers, and discarded cigarette butts were but a few of the materials used to create abstract work in the 1970s.

Such materials were often used out of necessity rather than studied deliberation, as artists found it difficult to secure a regular supply of canvas and oil paint, both of which had to be imported at great cost from Japan.[41] The flow of imports tightened in the wake of the recession of 1973, when the members of the Organization of Petroleum Exporting Countries (OPEC) halted shipments of petroleum to countries supporting Israel during the Arab–Israeli War, thus precipitating the OPEC oil shock beginning in October of that year. The resulting inflation drove the price of oil paints and good-quality canvas to unprecedented heights.[42] The difficulties of securing painting materials was compounded by the financial hardship of living in South Korea, which ranked among the world's poorest twenty-five countries until the mid-1960s, poorer on a per capita basis than North Korea and most countries in sub-Saharan Africa.[43] Living in a country with an average per capita gross domestic product of US$82, very few artists had the

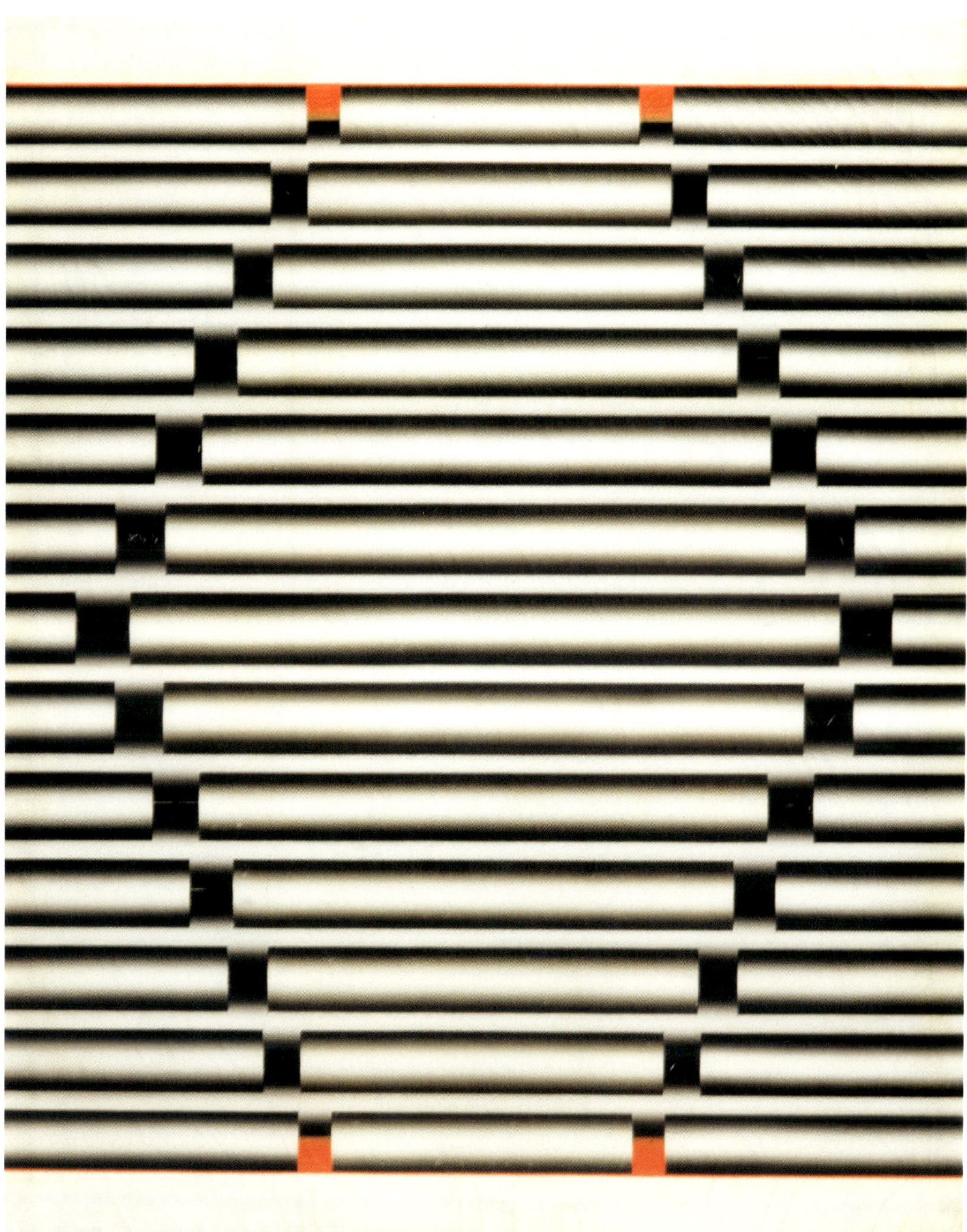

luxury of making artworks full-time, and even those who graduated from Korea's most prestigious art schools found it difficult to make a living in the field in which they were trained. As Bang Keun-taek observed in 1963:

In this whole year, how many artists living in this country sold even just one work? Looking around at the exhibitions organized by our poverty-stricken artists in the dog days of summer, we find that they are in a miserable state. From the copperplate print exhibition of Kim Sang-yu [the first artist to specialize in copperplate prints in South Korea], who showed his works for the first time after teaching school for a decade, to . . . Kim Chong-hak's solo show, which came about due to sheer youthful vigor . . . to the graduating students in a sculpture department who barely scraped together an exhibition by emptying out their pockets. . . . Everyone is in the same situation.[44]

While a lucky few managed to secure coveted positions as university professors, most taught at the secondary school level.[45] Those who failed to secure teaching jobs often resorted to dressing windows of clothing and tailoring shops, especially in the Myongdong shopping district in central downtown Seoul.[46]

Showing work was equally difficult, especially for abstract artists, who generally had three options: enter works in the Kukchŏn, join an artists' group that organized group exhibitions, or rent a gallery themselves. The last choice tended to be something of a risk. Venues in desirable locations like the downtown Seoul Press Center or the Sinsegye Gallery located on the fourth floor of the Sinsegye department store were priced beyond the reach of most artists; the former cost about 10,000 won a day to rent, while the latter's daily rent was 20,000 won, the equivalent of a middle-class white-collar worker's monthly salary.[47]

The lone exception was the Myongdong Gallery, which became one of the primary venues for tansaekhwa. Originally located in the downtown shopping district of Myongdong, from whence the gallery took its name, it was founded in 1968 by Kim Mun-ho, heir to a gasoline-station fortune.[48] Regarded by the critic Park Yong-sook as a "patron of recent avant-garde artists," Kim often loaned his gallery free of charge to young artists, in stark contrast to other gallery owners looking to capitalize on the immense demand by artists for exhibition venues.[49] As recollected by Kim Ku-lim and Chŏng Ch'an-sŭng, artists known for their performance-based works and installations, the Myongdong Gallery was "the one place" that would let nontraditional artists show their works without charging exorbitant gallery rental fees.[50] The gallery hosted a number of exchange shows with foreign galleries; curated exhibitions, including *Abstraction = Situation* (*Ch'usang = sanghwang*) in 1973, the first attempt to historicize postwar abstraction in South Korea; and solo exhibitions of nearly all the artists associated with tansaekhwa.

Despite the exigencies of the period, artists like Kim Ku-lim used materials like newspaper, cigarette butts, roofing tiles, barbed wire, and other effluvia to call attention to objects otherwise regarded as routine, common, and consequently invisible. By treating such objects as if they were oil and canvas or ink and paper without treating them as makeshift substitutes for the latter, Kim and other artists emphasized the importance of recognizing what might be described as everyday objects in terms of their forms rather than of the uses to which they were ordinarily put. The emphasis on such objects intensified in the late 1960s and early 1970s as more Korean artists saw abstraction as a threshold between the internal, imagined world of the artwork and the broader social milieu of which the work was physically a part and, at the same time, from which it was separate.

Lack of oil and canvas did not, however, undermine artists' engagement with abstraction, and in fact it compelled artists to improvise with more readily available materials, from scrap metal to old tires, which resulted in the production of a highly distinctive and productively idiosyncratic body of abstract work. Kim Ku-lim and many other artists active in the 1960s nevertheless wanted their works to be seen outside the domain of the everyday. This is evidenced by their tenacious adherence to the terminology of "high art": in contrast to the small but lively cadre of performance artists wanting to bridge the gap between art and life or to several ink painters who regarded their works as belonging to a greater literati tradition, abstract painters insisted that they be known as artists (*chakka*), and their works as art (*misul*). Yet it was not unusual to see effluvia culled from the so-called everyday treated with the same consideration as painting's more traditional materials. Throughout Korean abstraction was an earnestness that diverged sharply from the appropriations of the *nouveau réalistes* seeking to bring art and life closer together, or the symbiosis of "high" and "low" propagated within pop art. This earnestness was not naïveté but, instead, a reflection of the degree to which abstraction itself was already imbued with social purpose by means of the materials with which artists had to work.

In Ha Chonghyun's *Work 73-15B* (Figure I.9) a square black mono-chrome is neatly divided into smaller squares by intersecting vertical and horizontal lines. These lines, however, are made of barbed wire attached to the fabric support, and the combined tactility of these materials disrupts efforts to see the work as an optical phenomenon. Paramount is a raw, even crude, collision of tropes intended to rational-ize the viewing experience (gridding, serialization, monochromy) with materials presented in their rawest form (bleeding paint, torn paper, soaked canvas). Seen one way, the collision appears to respond to the studied caution and stillness that seemed to characterize minimalism and postminimalism, movements that the Avant-Garde (A.G., a short-lived but influential group of artists and critics) casually followed in its eponymous journal through reports gleaned from Japanese art magazines and occasionally through firsthand reports sent by Korean viewers overseas. Depicted in grainy black-and-white reproductions based on photographed copies of images printed on the low-quality newsprint used in magazines like *Bijutsu techō*, the aluminum boxes and steel plates of artists like Donald Judd and Carl Andre looked almost like readymades. They appeared unspecific, save for their ordered arrangements into rows or grids in a contained rectilinear space. In making his grid from barbed wire—and not from a set of hand- or machine-drawn lines or even from materials like yarn or string that could be worked in ways emphasizing only their capacity to lie straight and flat upon a planar surface—Ha tried to subvert what to him would have read as minimalism's will to nonrepresentation.

The choice of barbed wire was particularly apt given the material's imperviousness to discussion as anything other than barbed wire, and given its ubiquity in South Korea where the draft was, and is, mandatory; where the United States had permanent military bases; and where the state had just declared martial law, citing recent provocations from North Korea as partial justification. The barbed wire irrevocably thwarts the grid's ability to render the work autonomous from the world it physically inhabits. The grid encloses the soft body of the fabric canvas, holding it back from the space of the viewer. Taut and sharp, the wire grasps the black monochromatic cloth, which in turn reveals its own suppliant inertness. During the course of this encounter, the lines of the grid turn brutish as the wire bites into the cloth, thus compromising the aura of authority presumed of the black monochrome, so closely asso-ciated with a particular strain of modernism whose roots were firmly embedded in Euro-American definitions of a teleological modernity

FIGURE I.9 Ha Chonghyun, *Work 73-15B*, 1973. Barbed wire on cloth, 115 × 115 cm. Collection of the artist.

that affirmed linear forms of movement as denoted through such concepts as progress, innovation, and the endgame.

THE WORLD AS PRACTICE

How artists like Ha responded to various modernist tropes reflected
the uneven circulation of information, a critical subject in the late
1960s and early 1970s in Korea, where import restrictions and the
rapidly improving but still relatively impoverished state of the country
made it difficult for artists to obtain information about developments
elsewhere. There was considerable lag time in the dissemination
of information; one artist recalls that during the mid-1960s it took
about three months for an issue of *Bijutsu techō* to come from Tokyo
to Seoul.[51] At the same time, Korean artists recognized how they were
perceived by audiences in western Europe and the United States. These
art worlds were accessible to Korean artists only when they could offer
something deemed novel or innovative according to the standards of
those worlds. Nam June Paik perhaps best summarized this state of
affairs in his 1975 description of himself, only half in jest, to New York–
based critic Calvin Tompkins: "I am a poor man from a poor country
so I have to entertain people every second."[52] Yet the "world" was also
understood by Korean artists and critics as a process necessarily in
formation, rather than as a circumstance over which artists, critics, and
artworks had no control.

Among the artists most sensitive to the idea of the world as practice were those belonging to A.G., based in Seoul, from whose ranks
emerged some of tansaekhwa's most important adherents. Founded
in December 1968 by a group of artists and critics who either graduated from or taught at Hongik University in Seoul, the seminal group
was originally made up of ten artists who committed themselves to
"the investigation and creation of a new plastic order" that would
"contribute to the development of Korean artistic culture."[53] Its ranks
included well-known critics such as Kim In-hwan, Oh Kwangsu, and
Lee Yil, the French literature–aficionado-turned-art-critic whose star
was fast rising in the Korean art world, as well as artists such as Lee
Seung-taek, Kim Ku-lim, Suh Seung-won, and Ha Chonghyun, the last
two of whom became tansaekhwa artists.[54] Although there were numerous small artists' groups in the 1960s, A.G. distinguished itself through
its acknowledgment of both the globalization of the avant-garde (as

manifested through the spread of certain formal principles like the grid, monochromy, and seriality) and the nonlinear, highly specific circuits through which these principles were received. A.G. members were interested in the potential of communication, influenced, possibly, by Marshall McLuhan's theories of communication, which had intrigued some intellectuals in Korea, including a few art critics.[55]

In the second issue of *A.G.,* Ha Chonghyun published "Korean Art, on Entering the 1970s," an essay in which he argued that linear patterns of precedent and antecedent now yielded to simultaneous emergences: "The extreme development of communication technology . . . compresses the time and distance needed to find out about artistic movements in the world's major cities, so that artists live in [a state of] simultaneity [*tongsisŏng*]."[56] A discrepancy between different geographical locations might persist, but it lessened in proportion to the rise in both quantity and access to a presumably shared pool of information. The deferred appearance of a particular formal language was simply evidence of the interconnectedness of things:

Already in Euro-America, there was pop art or op art after informel.
It is impossible to think that we are somehow exempted from
this trend. For because the world has already become practically
one environment, it is a time where each influences the other,
and *I think it is actually natural that such [art] would affect us.*
[My emphasis][57]

In these descriptions, Ha was not arguing that Korean art was now just like Euro-American art, or even that Korean artists worked from the same kind of information as did their peers overseas. Rather, he suggested that contemporary art be identified through the rates at which its components appeared to be moving. His language implied as much with its use of works like "simultaneity" and its emphasis on notions of convergence and parallels.

Ha's approach to the world differed significantly from previous approaches that stressed the relationships among nations. He was not alone, however, in wanting to think differently about the world. Some of his A.G. colleagues, for example, participated in the vigorous debates over the direction of contemporary art in Korea that took place in the first and only issue of *Hyŏndae misul,* the Myongdong Gallery's in-house magazine published in 1974. In a lively roundtable discussion, several artists later associated with tansaekhwa debated how best to approach the international world in which contemporary Korean art now circulated, a prime task being how to address the role of Japan without rehearsing old antagonisms of the colonizer against the colonized. Concerned by the desire of his younger colleagues to "overtake" their Japanese peers, Suh Seung-won rhetorically asked whether the "Korea of today [was] the same as the Korea of the past."[58] Lee Ufan, the Japan-based Korean artist who helped Korean artists find Japanese audiences and whose discussions with Tokyo Gallery director Yamamoto Takashi helped lay the groundwork for *Five Korean Artists, Five Kinds of White*, observed in the same issue, "Almost all [the Korean works] failed to distinctly present a 'motif' or 'theme' that could overcome the lively and intense experimentalism, adventurousness, and originality demonstrated by Western artists, or a number of Japanese artists."[59] To Lee it was inevitable that contemporary Korean art would be relegated to the margins of the international artistic establishment. Artworks might have agency, but they were still agents bound to the teleology that underwrote the international art world.

For others, the goal was to push back against these kinds of worldviews that too readily assented to the notion of a center versus a periphery. Shim Moon-seup, for example, was less concerned with a desire to negate the present, as he termed it, than were some of his older colleagues.[60] Park Seobo urged his colleagues to act as if the center-versus-periphery model had already imploded. The "world," which to him meant an international network of art worlds held together by various geopolitical agendas, was no longer centered on America. Alluding to U.S. economic and political troubles created in large part by the OPEC oil shock and the Vietnam War, Park argued that the diminution of American power created a vacuum that could potentially allow for the rise of Asia as a symptom of what he described as polycentricization (*tagŭkhwa*).[61]

It was notable that these arguments took place in a magazine called *Hyŏndae misul*, the Korean term used to refer to either modern or contemporary art. First used in the 1920s to describe "new" art and sometimes used interchangeably with *sidae ŭi yesul*, or "art of the times," the term *hyŏndae misul* came under renewed examination after the state established the National Museum of Modern Art (Kungnip hyŏndae misulgwan) in Seoul in October 1969.[62] Critics took issue with the state's definition of *hyŏndae misul* as "modern art." Yi Ku-yŏl wrote, "The word *hyŏndae* is vague. The *hyŏndae* museum is referred to not as a contemporary museum but as a modern one."[63] In the same roundtable where Yi made his remarks, Lee added, "There was no clear temporal divider separating *hyŏndae* from *kŭndae*" (another term then used to refer to the "modern" and used generally to refer to the late nineteenth and early twentieth centuries, when tensions between Korea and various foreign powers reached a critical level). For him there "was no distinction between the modern and the contemporary."[64] What was clear was the extent to which *hyŏndae misul* was then calibrated according to extra-artistic events, namely, Japanese colonial occupation and the Korean War, or to overseas artistic movements such as abstract expressionism and op art. Some of this calibration could be dated to the mid-1950s, when art historians like Ch'oe Su-nu began to historicize *hyŏndae misul* by dividing the period into two sections, with the events of 1945 as the line of demarcation. Ch'oe identified the "international" as the new benchmark against which to measure the emergence of *hyŏndae misul*:

It is my contention that the significance of ideas like the world known as the Oriental past, or of the margins of the West, have almost completely vanished in today's contemporary art. Instead, the idea [now relevant] is of Korea as having international connections.[65]

Ch'oe's optimism anticipates Ha's emphasis on simultaneity as well as Kim Mun-ho's reasoning in declaring 1957 the beginning of contemporary Korean art. In *Abstraction = Situation*, the 1973 exhibition of postwar Korean abstraction he helped organize, Kim regarded 1957 as the year that Korean artists began to consciously and reflexively engage with the rest of the world.[66]

But as the influential critic Lee Yil noted in his own summary of the history of contemporary art in Korea published in the August 1975 issue of *Simunhak*, it was not enough to simply engage: "How are we to parse the reality in which we live?"[67] It was a question he later rephrased as, "How do we respond to the question of what it is that our reality wants from us?"[68] According to him, the most viable option was to assert the cultural uniqueness of certain works, even if it meant thinking about the world as yet again a site defined by the existence of a center and a periphery. As "poor artists from a poor country," to adopt Nam June Paik's self-description, Korean artists were sensitive to the expectations of international audiences that demanded uniqueness, whether expressed as formal and conceptual innovation or through proofs of novelty vis-à-vis appeals to cultural specificity.

For Lee Yil, the best solution was to emphasize the Koreanness
of a particular group of works, which he identified in the mid-1970s
as tansaekhwa, or Korean monochrome painting. Although Lee was
well aware of the psychological and discursive costs of promoting
work based on its alleged capacity to offer viewers direct access to an
unfiltered Korean sensibility, it was a price he felt he could not afford
not to pay, given the circumstances. Tansaekhwa artists seemed to share
Lee's sentiments, for although some, like Lee Dong Youb, one of the
participants of *Five Korean Artists, Five Kinds of White*, later confessed
to feeling irked by a term that too readily invited viewers to consider
tansaekhwa a localized version of monochrome painting, no artist
classified under the tansaekhwa rubric ever publicly objected
to the term or to the idea of "Korean monochrome painting" when it
first appeared in the mid-1970s.[69]

POINTS, LINES, ENCOUNTERS: BRIEF NOTES ON NARRATIVE STRUCTURE

The promotion of tansaekhwa discourse by critics like Lee Yil and by
Japanese institutions eager to establish a non-Western approach to
contemporary art helped frame tansaekhwa works in a way that made
it difficult to consider them as anything other than symptoms of cultural and national identity. But Kwon Young-woo, Yun Hyongkeun,
Ha Chonghyun, Lee Ufan, and Park Seobo painted in ways intended to
ensure that viewers would regard painting as an open-ended question.
That they partly succeeded was indicated by the number of commentators who felt compelled to develop a semantics that could more
adequately describe what they saw. Frequently invoked was the phrase
kŭrimi anin kŭrim, or "pictures that were not pictures." Although this
phrase was mostly used in reference to describe the apparent blankness
of tansaekhwa, it also referred to what tansaekhwa works wanted from
their viewers, which was to be seen as something more than the bearers
of a depicted image. The great ambition of many tansaekhwa artists was
to make work that could function as an integral, and not symptomatic,
means through which viewers could more readily discern the physical
and social connections upon which their worlds were based.

For these reasons, this book relies more heavily on close formal
reading than is usually found in analyses of non-Western modern and
contemporary art, which generally privilege ethnographic mediations

of cultural difference as the primary index through which to understand such art. Granted, the dearth of basic empirical information about postwar Korean art before 1990, particularly in English, makes extended description of various exhibitions, personalities, and institutions necessary. Yet the book's main focus lies in discussing the specificity of tansaekhwa by focusing on particular sets of work made in response to equally particular, and frequently conflicting, streams of thinking. These streams often require the use of different methods, therefore rendering the story of tansaekhwa a particular challenge.

Another challenge is narrative structure. Articulating the elasticity and interconnectedness of tansaekhwa's emergence requires a particular narrative form, one devised not in terms of an internal logic but for the sake of what the literary scholar Franco Moretti sees as the need to widen the epistemological domain of the commentator and reader.[70] The structure of this book takes its cue from the paintings and writings of tansaekhwa artists such as Lee Ufan, who emphasized points and lines as the epistemological units through which the artwork's seemingly contradictory capacity to be at once cohesive and open may be effectively articulated. As Lee observed, a presence, like a point, exists doubly, both as an autonomous presence (its "discontinuity") and as a component imminently part of a continuous trajectory.[71] Lines are made up of points, which themselves are the moments at which two ontologically discrete agents meet, intersect, or otherwise come into contact.

One might apply this thinking to narrative structure by treating the point and line as metaphors; a point refers to the viewer's encounter with an artwork, a meeting between artists, or an event whose significance elevates it to the status of a discrete entity, and the line, for its part, can denote lines of thinking, embedded lineages, or trajectories of behavior. Points denote the contacts, or in Lee's phraseology, the encounters, that help define an artwork. These encounters may be explicit, as in the viewer's experience of the installed artwork. Or they may be implicit, realized as a probable or possible encounter between the artwork and certain social, political, or economic phenomena. Acting as a centripetal source, the point recalls lines, or lineages situated in different places or spanning different periods of time. Eventually, the point functions as a node, revealing how certain lines, trajectories, and lineages intersect while others meet only asymptotically, with only the suggestion of actual convergence. In some cases, the nodal point might call forth another, similarly situated point, but one bound to a line moving in a completely different direction. The aim of this model is to more systematically rephrase art's recensional impulse, that is, its tendency to move forward by doubling back on previously explored lines of inquiry. It is also useful in emphasizing the historicity of the subject without having to preemptively align the discussion to one particular starting point, event, person, or work. It allows inquiry to begin at any number of points that directly refuse models of influence in which subjects are identified by a concurrent identification of possible precedents, as well as to avoid more dyadic narrative models that rely too unilaterally on artificial distinctions pitting a center against a periphery, tradition against modernity, form against content, and perhaps the most commonly invoked of all, the local against the global.

Accordingly, the first chapter takes up some of the lines of investigation outlined in this introduction in order to show how certain tansaekhwa artists took up abstraction as a means to work through broader questions of medium, materiality, the viewing encounter, and the place of the viewer. The "point" from which chapter 1 begins is an extended discussion of the 1966 solo show of Kwon Young-woo, an ink painter who made some of the earliest works later classified as tansaekhwa. The only major tansaekhwa artist not to use oil and canvas, Kwon exclusively used paper to address the segregation of ink painting from oil painting, a core assumption that was both upheld and challenged with the emergence of what was increasingly known as "abstract ink painting" in the 1960s. Kwon's line of inquiry ran parallel to that of Yun Hyongkeun, whose *Umber Blue* series challenged prevailing notions of medium by exploring the tension arising from the viewer's simultaneous awareness of painting as both a pictorial composition and an object cohabiting the same physical space as the viewer through the device of the interval.

Chapter 2 builds on this discussion of medium through an extended analysis of Ha Chonghyun's *Conjunction* series, whose debut almost coincided with that of *Umber Blue*. Ha was, among tansaekhwa artists, the least concerned with the internal arrangement of elements on a canvas; in *Conjunction* he explored the relationship between two- and three-dimensionality as a function of raw materiality. Much of this exploration was facilitated by what Ha understood of Mono-ha, the seminal Japanese group whose primary theoretician, Lee Ufan, deeply affected many Korean artists in the early 1970s. *Conjunction* is situated as a response to perceptions of the international art world, which, as Ha's notion of simultaneity implied, was less about the circulation and reception of overseas artistic developments than about recognizing different rates of change. These rates concerned the accelerated pace at which the horizons of the Korean art world expanded as well as an emerging sense of delay vis-à-vis increasing encounters with Japan, following the restoration of diplomatic relations in 1965.

Described by some Korean art historians as "a formidable mountain over which the history of contemporary Korean art must climb," Lee Ufan himself is another point of heuristic departure.[72] Born in Korea but based in Japan since 1956, Lee and his career epitomized in many ways the ambivalences of the postwar Korean art world that sought international recognition yet remained acutely conscious of a world order that had yet to fully address the legacies of empire, nationalism, and colonization. Chapter 3 discusses how Lee tried to work through these circumstances in two series of paintings titled *From Line* and *From Point*. Begun in 1973, both series sought to affirm the place of the viewer as a first step in overcoming the authoritarianism of a world that put too high a premium on authorship and the act of creation.

Chapter 4 picks upon this line of approach with the *Écriture* works, which also made their debut in 1973. Painted in Korea by Park Seobo, Lee's close friend who also commanded a preeminent place among contemporary artists in Korea during the 1960s and 1970s, the series was described by critic Lee Yil as the one of the three most important works of Korean art made since Korea gained its independence from Japan.[73] They exude a certain presence that took as its subject the viewer's relationship to the artwork, a move possessing a special charge in light of Park Chung-hee's declaration of martial law in 1972. Rather than embodying a specific form of resistance, the *Écriture* works throw into relief the position and presence of the viewer as questions of social and political urgency.

In accord with the considerable professional ambitions of their maker, the *Écriture* works were also exhibited overseas, particularly in Japan, where they were folded into a larger effort on the part of Japanese institutions and individuals to promote the idea of a distinctly Asian approach to contemporary art. Chapter 5 thus suggests an initial origin point from which to track a history of what would later be called contemporary Asian art by surveying the initial emergence of tan-saekhwa rhetoric in Japan, France, and Korea in the second half of the 1970s. Here, "method" takes on new relevance as various works, especially those of Kwon Young-woo, Yun Hyongkeun, Ha Chonghyun, and Park Seobo, were used to promote a distinctly Korean cultural, ethnic, and national sensibility. In chronicling the history of this rhetoric and the promotion of tansaekhwa works outside Korea, this chapter also illustrates how some Koreans and Japanese in the late 1970s struggled to establish another stream of identification that avoided both national and cultural differences and utopian idealizations from which such differences were excluded.

Recalling these efforts, the epilogue takes a retrospective look back at the heuristic assumptions underwriting the idea of a global art world as seen through the subsequent reception of tansaekhwa in the 1980s and after. Central among these assumptions is the question of context, which reemerged with special intensity after the ascent of Minjung art, widely known as tansaekhwa's main antagonist. Particularly active during the turbulent 1980s, which saw numerous protests against the authoritarian rule of Chun Doo-hwan, another military strongman, Minjung artists and critics considered it their moral duty to explicitly reflect the sociopolitical context in which they and their subjects lived, partly in response to what they saw as tansaekhwa's indifference to the world outside the physical boundaries of the artwork. In the 1990s the emphasis on context took a different turn as two lines of action converged: the relaxation of restrictions formerly imposed on overseas travel by South Korean citizens and the sequence of moves that eventually accumulated into what is now referred to as contemporary art's "global turn." Often treated discursively as a palliative measure intended to compensate for previous worldviews based on the exclusion of works, the global turn seeks to include as many previously marginalized, namely, non-Western, works as possible. Yet the global turn has also inadvertently yielded to a kind of contextualism in which the discursive value of an artwork is measured according to how well it meets expectations implicitly set by major institutions in wealthy Western, and to a limited extent East Asian, metropolises as to what cultural difference should look like. For artists like Kimsooja—herself a student of various tansaekhwa artists in the late 1970s—and Yang Haegue, contextualism has inadvertently evoked other kinds of distinctions that are as problematic as those the global turn purports to displace.

Reflecting upon the history of tansaekhwa, Oh Kwangsu, one of the most observant critics in late 1960s and early 1970s Korea, recently speculated as to whether "contemporary Korean art was an art that could not be anything but otherly. . . . It was evaluated by others who acknowledged it because those others saw it as other in turn."[74] Implicit in his remark is the question of whether other interpretations are possible and whether those tasked with the responsibility of this interpretation can adequately struggle with one of the great paradoxes of contemporary art: even as the boundaries of contemporary art expand to include artists previously excluded or marginalized from an implicit mainstream, those artists remain bound to a system of thinking that could only be described as profoundly undemocratic, one that acknowledges the existence of an artwork (and artist) when it is found to have successfully acted as evidence validating—or invalidating—larger social and historical phenomena. As in Jean-Luc Nancy's formulation of the image, the task at hand lies in conceptualizing a world art history that can say something about the sociopolitical world without being tethered to its systems of order.[75]

This argument is especially worth making at a time when contemporary art history seems torn between restatements of postmodern disjunction and long-entrenched heuristic models premised on received ideas of nationality, ethnicity, and culture. Non-Euro-American art is especially vulnerable to such conditions, as many examples tend to be validated mostly on account of the geographical mobility of their makers, on their records of exhibition in Western Europe and the United States, or on their relationship to a specific historical event around which extra-artistic histories tend to be written. Ushering into view lineages of thought and impulse that continue to reverberate in an ever-expanding present, the study of tansaekhwa is thus as much an effort at encouraging other methods of interpretation now as it is a reflection on tansaekhwa's attempt to rescue itself from necessarily responding to the imperatives of a particular historical past. The urgency of this effort is especially apparent if we accept, as many tansaekhwa artists did, the idea of the world as not a site but a practice expressed through various categorical distinctions. Is it possible, then, for the study of tansaekhwa to help us rethink some of the distinctions on which we practice the world at present? Such is the point from which this book begins.

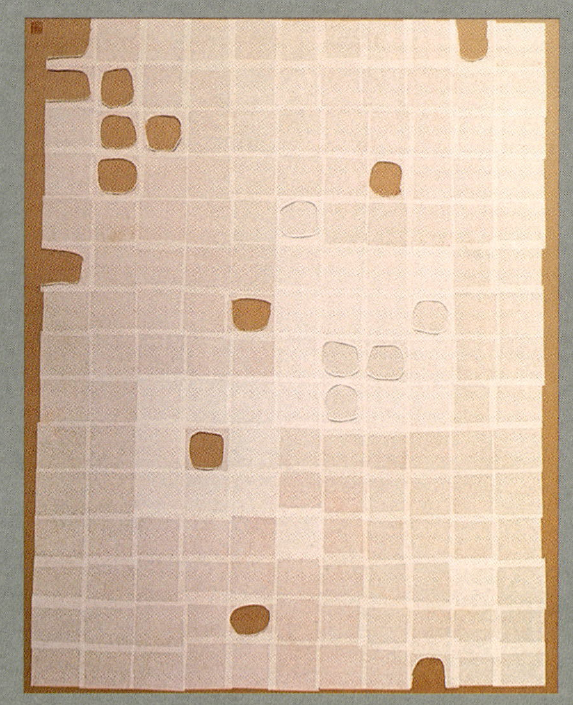

ONE

Kwon Young-woo and Yun Hyongkeun Rethink Painting

In June 1966, the ink painter Kwon Young-woo "stirred a quiet controversy" in the Korean art world by exhibiting works in which he abandoned the brush in favor of direct contact between the paper support and the hand.[1] Taking place at what was one of Seoul's best-known rental venues, the Sinsegye Gallery located in the Sinsegye department store in central downtown Seoul, the show consisted of thirty works ranging in size from 73 × 60 centimeters to an enormous 180 × 300 centimeters. Works such as *65-9* (Figure 1.1), titled to indicate both the year in which they were produced (1965) and their place in the sequence of works made during that year (ninth), were created using rectangular bands or sheets of thin, semitransparent white paper made from the inner bark of the paper mulberry tree. Known as *hanji*, or literally "Korean paper," the more fine-grained versions of this paper were used as bases for calligraphy and traditional ink painting. Using glue made of flour, Kwon attached this paper to veneered plywood panels covered with thick brown kraft paper—a major product in Korea—of the type used for office envelopes and for wrapping packages.[2]

In some works, Kwon even attached objects (for example, corks in *66-7,* shown in Figure 1.2) to the surfaces of the panels, which he then covered with sheets of white paper so that the works resembled monochromes that verged on sculpture. In others, such as *65-9,* a detail of which was published alongside the June 28, 1966, review that appeared in the newspaper *Chungang ilbo,* the artist took advantage of the properties of *hanji,* cutting certain parts of the paper with a pair of scissors.[3] The friction generated by the artist's nails unfurled the compressed fibers that then coiled into narrow ridges that protruded from the panel's surface. Grouped near the center of *65-9* are four such instances where the artist has scratched the top layer of paper to reveal another white layer below, an effect described by Yi Ku-yŏl,

FIGURE 1.1 Kwon Young-woo, *65-9,* 1965. Korean paper on plywood, 130 × 110 cm. Location unknown.

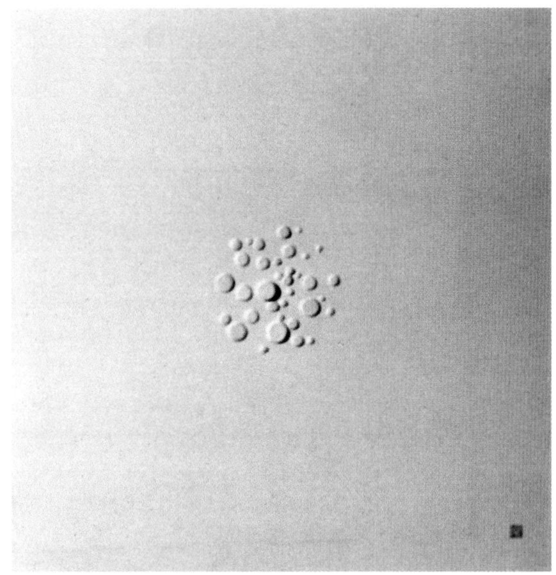

whose review of Kwon's 1966 exhibition centered on the "drama of paper" produced by the moment at which white emerges from a white surface, or *paeksangpaekch'ul*.[4] The viewer discerns the fruits of Kwon's labors in the form of four rounded, and vaguely squarish, openings that show a layer of *hanji* closer to the underlying brown kraft support. But the labor itself is best indicated by the tightly coiled edges fringing these openings.

Kwon had previously introduced a few of these works in the 1962 Kukchŏn, as well as in 1965 at the Ninth Invitational Exhibition of Contemporary Artists. The annual Invitational Exhibition of Contemporary Artists (Hyŏndae chakka ch'odaejŏn) was begun in 1957 by one of the country's largest newspapers, the *Chosun ilbo*, as an alternative to the conservative Kukchŏn. It was the most significant venue for recently produced art until it ceased operation in 1969. Yet the 1966 Sinsegye exhibition marked the first time that Kwon showed several of his paper-based works together, a decision whose impact was immediately evident in the number of viewers who registered puzzlement, even suspicion, at what seemed to be Kwon's defection from ink painting, or from being, in the language of the Korean art world, an "Oriental (Asian)" painter (*tongyanghwaga*). In the eyes of the anonymous reviewer writing for the *Chosun ilbo*, the works appeared "as if to rebel" against the entire tradition of ink painting, which emphasized the symbiosis between its three fundamental materials: paper, brush, and ink, collectively known as *chip'ilmuk*.[5]

Finger painting, or *chiduhwa*, a mode of depiction that involved using all parts of the hand to produce images on a planar support, had long been part of the Korean ink painting tradition, though it had become less important by the early twentieth century, and Kwon was certainly aware of its constituent techniques.[6] He was not interested, however, in resuscitating what at the time would have been regarded as tradition. Nor was he interested, as were some of his viewers, in proving the modernity of ink painting by linking it to established strategies of modernist painting. In his review, Yi Ku-yŏl tried to slot Kwon's new works within a history of the monochrome calibrated according to Euro-American works, including Kasimir Malevich's *White on White* and Robert Rauschenberg's paintings.[7] A critic who belonged to that cohort of viewers especially interested in exploring possible linkages between contemporary art in Korea and other parts of the world, Yi would probably have known of the prominent article on monochromy published in the February 1, 1961, issue of the *Chosun ilbo*. The unsigned article focused on paintings "that were white canvas, with nothing else." It mentioned the works of Yves Klein and Piero Manzoni, and it also included a large, if somewhat unclear, reproduction of *Superficie bianca* by Enrico Castellani. Manzoni's close friend, Castellani had penned the introduction to the 1960 exhibition that signaled the return of monochromy, *Monochrome Malerie*, at the Städtisches Museum in Leverkusen, Germany. *Superficie bianca* was composed of white fabric stretched over a relief background of nails embedded by a nail gun. Castellani's inclusion of nails throughout his *Superficie bianca* series (Figure 1.3) paralleled Kwon's occasional tendency to attach objects to the support before covering both with white paper. Kwon, however, leaves uncovered a thin border that frames the work so as to make what he has done with *hanji* seem like a subject intended for scrutiny. It is as if he was still pondering this new direction, in which the materiality of *hanji* played a main rather than a supporting role.

But even as Yi did his best to relate Kwon's works to a particular history of the monochrome, he seemed to have doubted himself. The gridded surface of *65-9* may have shared with Castellani's similarly configured works an affinity for systematic organization, but Kwon also compromised his commitment with his imperfect handmade marks, whose asymmetry and rounded edges call attention to the similar imperfections of his grid. Yi sensed the difference between these works

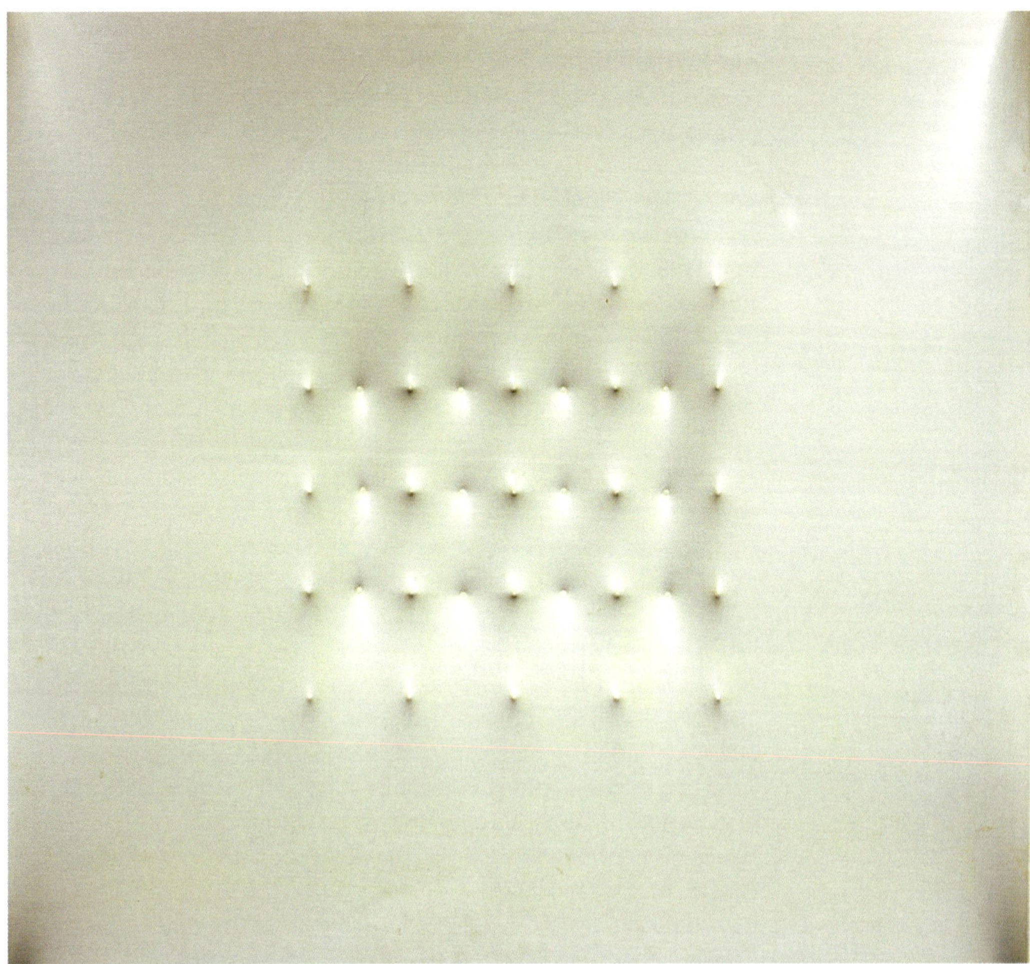

FIGURE 1.3 Enrico Castellani, *Superficie Bianca*, 1962. Acrylic on canvas embedded and lifted, 79 × 84 cm. Photograph courtesy of Tornabuoni Art, Paris; copyright 2012 Artists Rights Society (ARS), New York / SIAE, Rome.

and those acknowledged to belong to a particular modernist genealogy of monochromism, even if he seemed unable to express this difference in any other way save for an essentialist view of cultural difference: "The belief in the expression of space known as white stems less from contemporary Euro-American aesthetics than from an important and deep spirituality long affiliated with Asian aesthetics."[8] He saw Kwon as trying to negotiate among multiple ways of thinking about form seemingly comparable to the condition of chaotic input that characterized Korean abstraction in the decade immediately after the Korean War.

Kwon's 1966 exhibition signaled a critical moment in an emerging discourse about the concept of medium, a discussion that was perhaps most vigorously catalyzed by the deliberate exploration of abstraction by artists who self-identified as ink painters, including Lee Ungno and Suh Se-ok. For them, this exploration turned on the question of what it meant to create abstract ink painting, a point with which Kwon grappled at length in the works he created prior to the Sinsegye Gallery show. But where his contemporaries often regarded abstract ink painting as a utopian project undertaken in hopes of reaching a dialectical synthesis of ink and oil, of East and West, Kwon saw it as a materialist challenge in which medium might be understood as the mediation of the distinctions on which it was based.

THE MEANING OF ABSTRACT INK PAINTING

The techniques, history, and basic compositional principles of ink painting were familiar to most artists active during the 1950s and early 1960s, including the artists associated with tansaekhwa. Yet ink painting was understood primarily as a medium defined in contrast to oil painting, an opposition expressed in the terms used for both: *tongyanghwa*, or "Oriental painting," and *sŏyanghwa*, or "Western painting." Although this distinction has largely been regarded as a distinctly twentieth-century phenomenon, it actually reflected a shift in priorities taking place over a much longer span of time. Art historian Hong Sun-pyo contends that the rise of the *silhak*, or "practical learning" school of philosophy, in the late eighteenth century triggered a surge of interest in different modes of depiction, particularly among those involved with cartography and Western-style oil painting.[9] As its name suggests, *silhak* was a philosophical movement that emphasized the practical applications of ideas as a means through which to initiate social reform. Many *silhak* followers were of the literati class and were thus obligated to uphold a certain tradition of painting. Yet some also approached painting in almost instrumental terms that directed focus away from a painting's capacity to reveal the moral character of its maker and toward the techniques used in its production. By the advent of the Enlightenment period (*kaehwagi*) in the late nineteenth century, when significant intellectual experimentation was well under way, artistic production had altogether been reconfigured so that it no longer revolved around the social rank of the maker, or specifically, around the idealized figure of the literati painter seeking self-cultivation rather than for economic gain. In its place was a concerted emphasis on materials, and especially techniques, a shift in priorities that signaled a radical exchange of authority that imparted new value to the act of labor and the physicality of actually bringing different materials together.[10] It was this exchange of authority that helped make possible the formation of another art world, one centered entirely on the issue of medium.

This history was all but forgotten in the 1950s, when visual art in Korea was subdivided into categories like "Western painting," first introduced into general use during the Enlightenment period, and "Oriental painting," a definition first used in Korea in 1920 to push back against the popularity of Western painting.[11] Such terms coincided with the formation of an artistic infrastructure by the Japanese during the colonial era as part of a larger attempt to consolidate Japan's authority on cultural and racial grounds. Of special note was the distinction between oil painting, known as *yōga*, or Western painting, and *nihonga*, a mode of painting that was largely distinguished by the use of "traditional" materials—such as mineral pigment, ink, and silk supports—and techniques culled from multiple schools of ink painting and from Western-style oil painting, lithography, and photography. Literally meaning "Japanese painting," *nihonga* was first developed in late nineteenth-century Japan by artists and critics troubled by oil painting's growing popularity. *Nihonga* was vigorously promoted throughout the Japanese Empire in government-sponsored salons such as the *Chosŏn Art Exhibition* in Korea, abbreviated as "the *Sŏnjŏn*."[12] Indeed, so closely associated was *nihonga* with the Japanese state that it continued to be associated with Japanese colonial rule well after Japanese control ended in 1945.[13]

After Korea's liberation, a number of ink painters reflected on the colonial legacy, pondering what it meant to work within an artistic infrastructure still based on the segregation of media and their associated

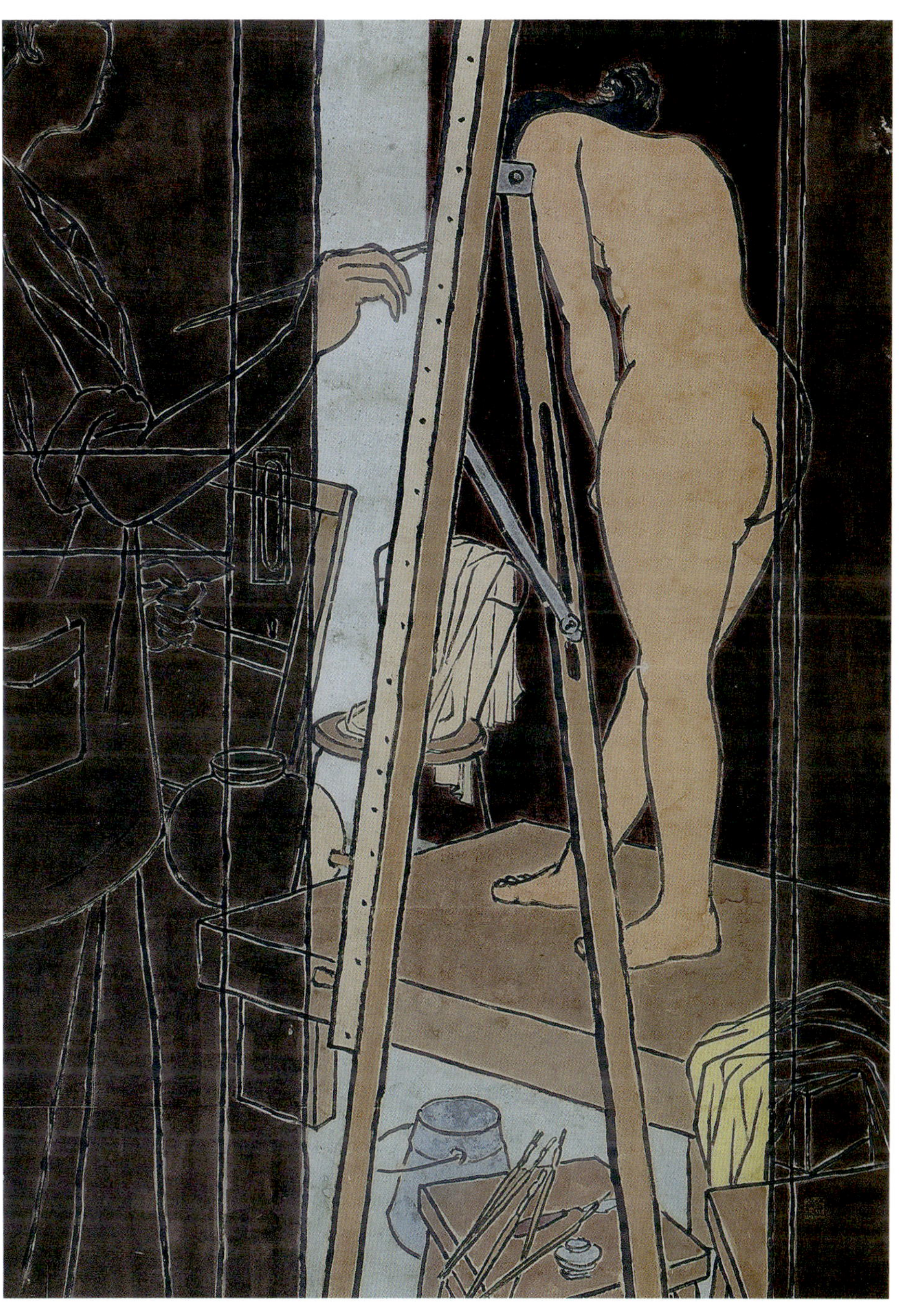

materials. In 1956, five years after he graduated with a degree in ink painting from Seoul National University's art school and a year before he earned a master's degree in the same field from the same school, Kwon painted *A Glimpse into the Studio* (Figure 1.4). This work shows a faceless artist painting a nude female model bending slightly over, so that we see none of her head and shoulders except a part of her chignon and the undulating curve of shoulder blades. According to Kwon, the painting is based on what the artist recalled of his student days, when he would surreptitiously visit the oil-painting classes where students concentrated on drawing and painting from nude models.[14] The range of colors immediately signals his encounter with the world of oil painting. Two brown bands, the color of wooden doors, flank the painting's middle section, allowing the viewer a titular glimpse into the classroom. A nude female model poses on a raised light-brown dais set at an angle, and our sense of the classroom's interiority is mediated through the figure of the nude who bends forward into recessional space. Her right leg steps forward, and she seems to rest her hands on her thighs. The platform on which she stands is obliquely angled to the left, and two of its corners are covered by dark green vertical bands that flank either side of the painting. Rendered in a color so carefully chosen that it cannot help but be called "flesh," the nude is all ample voluptuousness, brought to life through the manipulation of a thin black contour line suggesting the presence of mass.

But the nude was not what interested Kwon most, nor was it the question of access, despite the numerous points at which the brown doors visibly overlap with the objects inside the classroom. Toward the top of the painting, a hand protrudes from behind the left-side door into the space of the classroom. It holds a pen or brush that makes direct contact with a canvas propped upright on an easel whose scale seems disproportionately large compared to that suggested by the nude. The canvas nearly traverses the height of the work, and the upright, open easel is almost as wide as the open door through which we look into the space of the studio. Set at a lateral angle, the easel and canvas further divide the painting so that one's glimpse into the classroom is governed by the shape of the canvas. Moreover, the sizes of the easel and canvas throw off the sense of scale so that the viewer's attention is redirected to the strongly linear composition, an aspect Kwon would pursue in greater depth a few years later. The hand belongs to an anonymous student whom Kwon draws in great detail, a speculation in line over what the artist imagines must go on beyond the doors that otherwise shut him out. At the very foot of the painting, the threshold over which the eye must cross to virtually enter into the space of the classroom, is a worktable heaped with brushes and what looks like a small inkwell.

The subject of the painting, in fact, is the practice of artmaking as mediated through the conventions of Western oil painting. But Kwon was not interested in forsaking ink for oil, neither at the time he made his semiclandestine visits to the oil-painting classrooms nor afterward.[15] Nor did he seem to think, as did some of his peers, that abstraction was separate from ink painting. In Kwon's paintings from about 1950 to 1961, he structures his images around the black ink line so critical to ink painting rather than around the volumetric forms or marks meant to suggest the three-dimensional presence of those forms. That he outlines almost every image, even down to surface details, registers as an attempt both to secure each image within the picture and to emphasize its discreteness. One example is *On the Way to an Island*, a work from 1959 based on the artist's trip to Tŏkjŏk Island, not far from the Inch'ŏn shoreline on Korea's western coast (Figure 1.5). Composed of a matrix of straight, occasionally broken, lines from which the image of a sailboat emerges, it is a monochrome ink painting of considerable size. At over two meters tall, the painting's height emphasizes the way the vertical lines appear to pull the painting in a north–south direction. Kwon counters these verticals with two sets of horizontal lines, the sketchy ink wisps punctuating the painting's upper half and the more concrete outlines holding the painting down at the bottom. That the painting was awarded the Minister of Culture and Education Prize at the Kukchŏn in 1959 indicates what other ink painters regarded as a priority during this time. The work's singular organization into straight lines that run parallel or perpendicular to each other demonstrates what might be described as an intentional engagement with forms of abstraction.

In 1960 Kwon returned to one of his favorite subjects in *The Sea* (Figure 1.6). To convey the impression of the presence of a boat and rippling water and hazy clouds, Kwon uses different kinds of brushwork. He also takes into account the format of the picture to emphasize each line's capacity to embody the idea of what he attempts to represent. Horizontal lines depicting ripples of water echo the painting's bottom edge, for example, and two vertical lines that parallel the height of the work emphasize the boat's stationary position. These two lines, which terminate in the short, thick, horizontal line depicting the prow, commit the boat to a particular set of coordinates in an otherwise indeterminate space. The boat is imbued with solidity and concreteness,

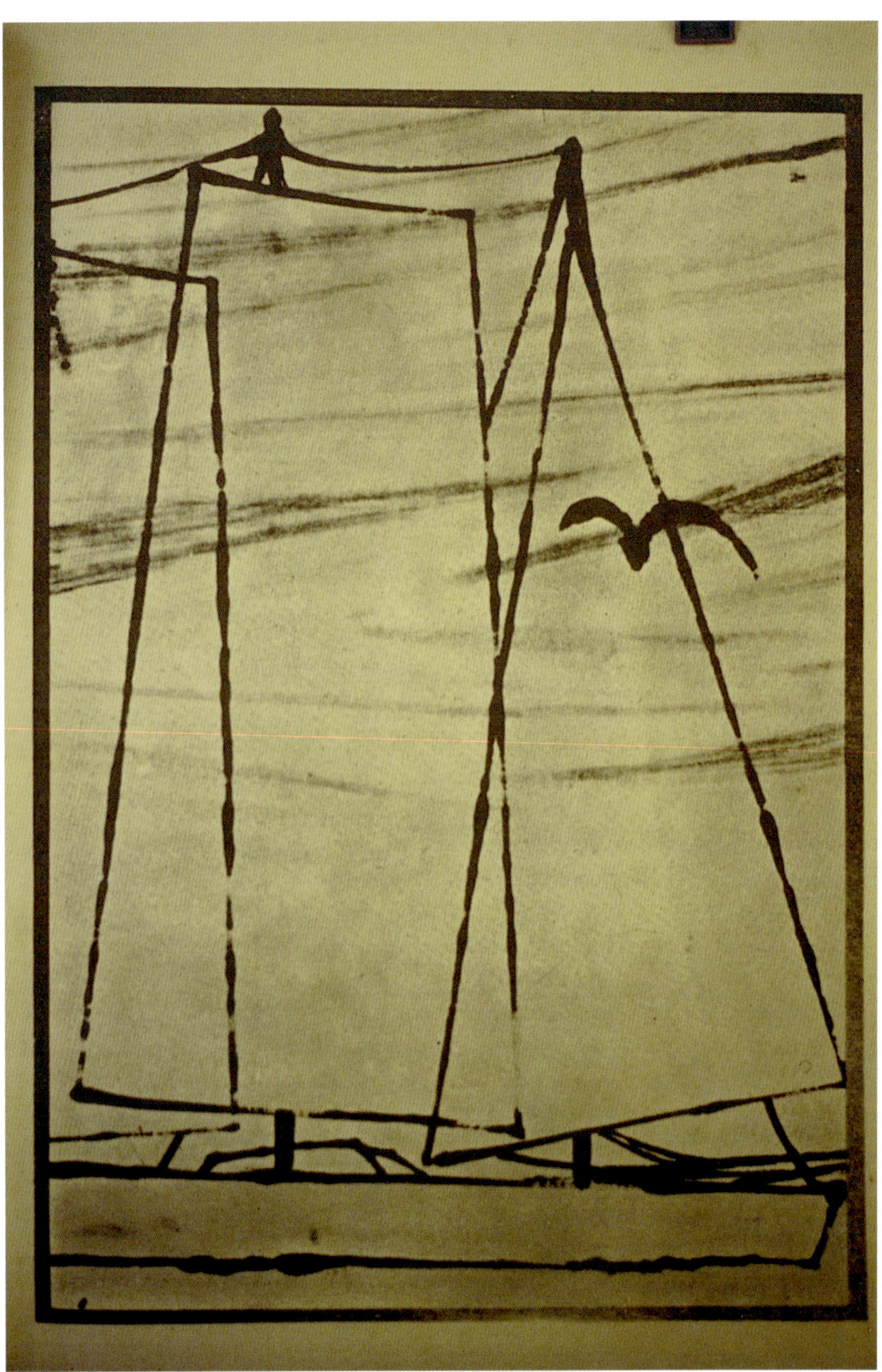

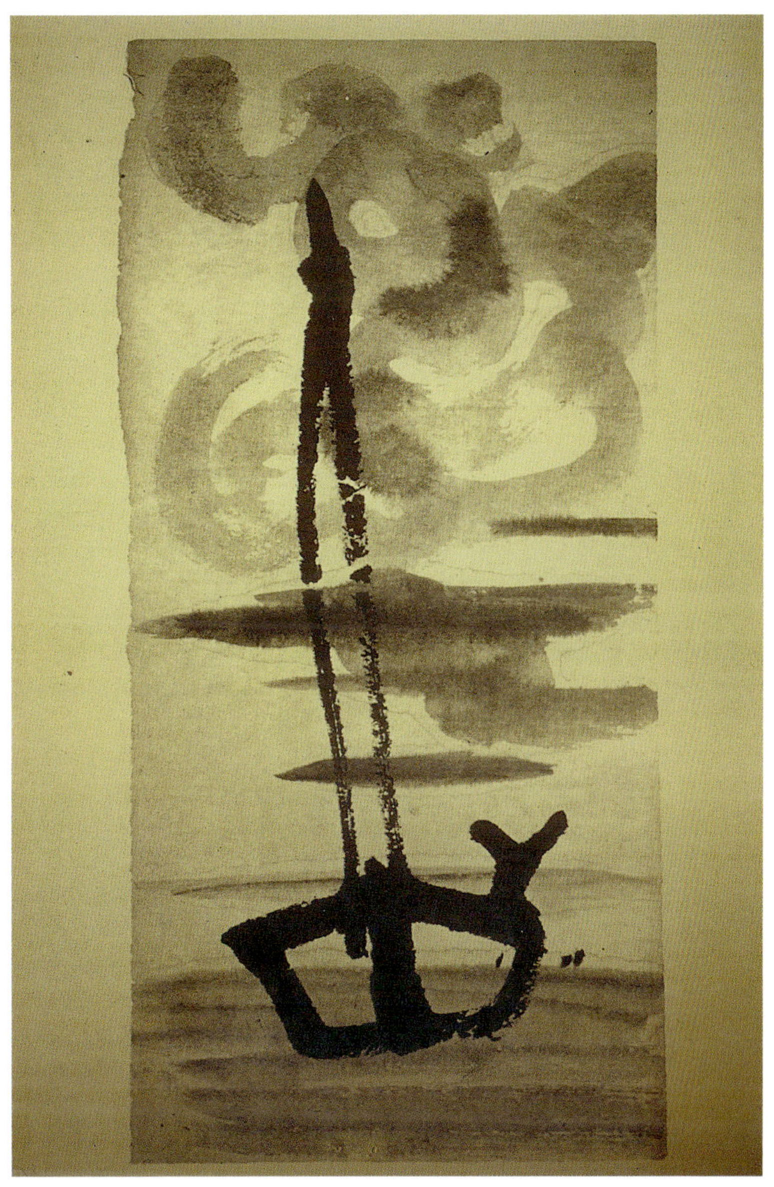

FIGURE 1.5 Kwon Young-woo, *On the Way to an Island*, 1959. Ink on Korean paper, 224 × 170 cm. Location unknown.

FIGURE 1.6 Kwon Young-woo, *The Sea*, 1960. Ink on Korean paper, 43 × 20.5 cm. Collection of the artist.

setting it apart from other images in the work, such as the loose constellation of curves toward the middle of the painting, an efficient depiction of the kinds of cumulus clouds that are a portent of fair weather and are much desired among fishermen. In these works, Kwon broke down forms or coaxed new ones from an economy of means. As he later remarked of his works from 1958 to 1960, he was interested in "simplifying the subject" and in "using the brush as little as possible."[16] The question of what to paint was far less interesting than the question of how to paint, and subject matter became largely incidental to the ways it was made to take material form.

In structuring his works around the line, Kwon indicated his awareness of what was, in the second half of the 1950s, a more general turn to abstraction in the Korean art world. For many of Kwon's peers, abstraction was a material point of contact between what was taking place at home and artistic developments abroad. As art historian Bert Winther-Tamaki has noted, Euro-American artists regarded ink painting as a novel means through which to prove the universality of certain kinds of artmaking but not as itself a bona fide medium of modern art.[17] By contrast, Nam Kwan and his Korean associates, for example, initially saw ink painting as itself constitutive of a kind of abstraction that could hold its own with abstract painting circulated in Paris and New York. As Nam declared in 1953, "Ink painting is, at heart, abstract."[18] In the November 1956 issue of *Sin misul*, artists, architects, and critics tried to make a case for ink painting's modernity by citing artists whose works appeared to nullify the separation between Western and Oriental painting, including Mark Tobey, whose works especially interested Korean artists because of his openly acknowledged debt to calligraphy and ink painting, and Paris-based Chinese expatriate painter Zao Wou-ki, who used oil to express concepts he first encountered while receiving instruction in ink painting.[19] Kwon considered his own works, even those that were clearly figurative, to be nonmimetic.[20]

But the meteoric rise of gestural abstraction as represented by works like Park Seobo's *No. 1*, and their subsequent designation as representatives of contemporary Korean art in overseas exhibitions, cast serious doubt on Nam's preemptive claims. In response, several younger ink painters turned to abstraction to prevent what was fast being referred to as "Korean informel" from monopolizing the conversations on what might constitute abstraction.[21] That their determination was not primarily motivated by professional jealousy, or even by the desire to push back against the presence of foreign influence, was suggested by the considerable authority ink painting still retained within the commercial and critical worlds; records of the Bando Gallery, Korea's main commercial gallery from the late 1950s to the early 1960s, show that from 1958 to 1963 ink painting and calligraphy generally outsold oil painting.[22] If many ink painters of the generation that received their university degrees after 1945 turned away from figuration, their defection was spurred in large part by abstraction's increasing importance in what since the end of the Korean War had become a newly revitalized quest to define contemporary art in Korea.

THE INK FOREST SOCIETY ON MATERIAL SPECIFICITY

In 1959 Suh Se-ok, then a thirty-year-old professor of ink painting at Seoul National University and a former classmate of Kwon's, had already started to rethink the fundamentals of ink painting in a number of small studies. In *Point Variation* (Figure 1.7), Suh impressed his brush in consecutive horizontal lines at brief, regularly occurring intervals on a vertically oriented support; likewise, in *Line Variation* (Figure 1.8), he showed a series of successively drawn lines made with a brush dipped in black Chinese ink. In both works Suh examined what he identified as the primary formal characteristic of inkbrush painting, "that it came forth from one 'point,' and from that point's continuation, the 'line.' Restated, inkbrush painting consists exclusively of the 'point' and the 'line.'"[23] Both works dispense with literati brush painting's preoccupation with encoding in the mark the moral character of its maker, or with the supposed urgency of the initial moment at which the brush came into contact with the mark. The initial contact is of commanding importance, for it determines the fate of the picture: the durable *hanji* used for brush painting renders permanent even the slightest contact, thus disallowing the possibility of redoing or effacing a mark once it has been made. Properly situated, however, the point can extend into a line that initiates the eye's journey across pictorial space. In *Point Variation* the marks are made without a parallel consciousness of how they might activate unmarked space. Suh presses the brush against the support in various ways; some marks are tilted, some are rounded, and others look as if they could be incipient lines. Similarly, what is most pronounced in *Line Variation* is not the line as an element deliberately and specifically located so as to enable the production of a more complex image but, rather, the line as that which refers the viewer back to the properties

FIGURE 1.7 Suh Se-ok, *Point Variation*, 1959. Ink on Korean paper, 95 × 74 cm. Collection of the artist.

FIGURE 1.8 Suh Se-ok, *Line Variation*, 1959. Ink on Korean paper, 74 × 95 cm. Collection of the artist.

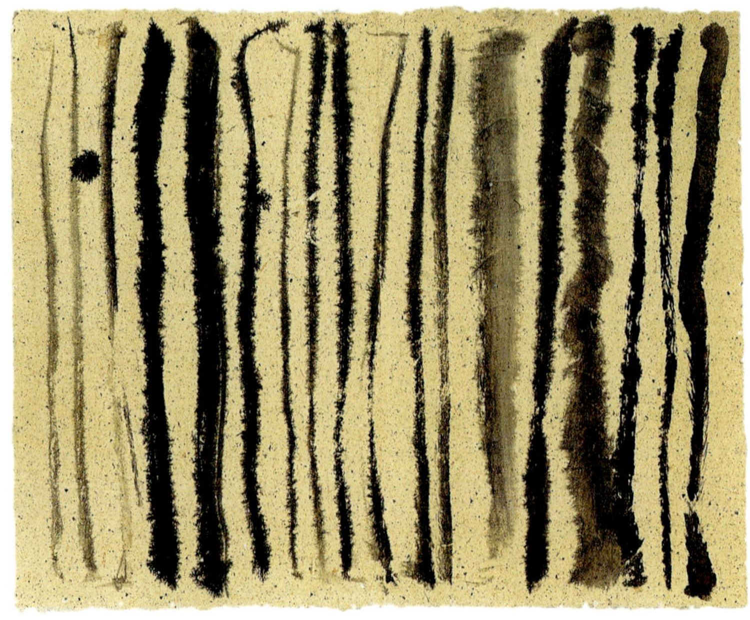

of the materials used and to the labor expended in the mark-making process. Each line is distinctive only to the extent that it differs from its counterparts in value, width, and rate of absorption into the paper, which in this case is markedly coarser than the kind ordinarily used for ink painting and calligraphy and thus allowed ink to diffuse more freely across space. The appearance of the line changes depending on the speed at which the brush moves from one point to another, the magnitude of the force with which the artist, collaborating with gravitational pull, presses the brush down on a supine piece of paper, and the amount of ink the brush absorbs and disperses onto the paper.

Encouraged by these early studies and by casual discussions with his peers about what he described as a desire to "introduce a new experimental spirit," Suh founded the Mungnimhoe, or the Ink Forest Society, with his students at the very end of 1959.[24] Active between 1959 and 1964, the Ink Forest Society was known for producing and exhibiting works that evoked the properties of ink painting's core materials of water, paper, and ink.[25] Like the artist Kim Ch'ŏng-gang, who urged the state to issue a mandate renaming "Oriental painting" as "Korean painting" (*han'guk'wa*), the Ink Forest Society's members wished to reclaim ink painting from what they saw as Japanese influence. In particular, they sought to purge from Korean art all vestiges of *nihonga*, which, in the immediate postwar era, became a byword for Japanese colonial influence.[26] To the society, these vestiges were most apparent in the selection of works for the Kukchŏn.[27] The urgency of the group's mission was reflected by its efforts to recruit new members, including Kwon, who was urged to join by his friends who were already members.[28]

An announcement for the inaugural exhibition of the Ink Forest Society lists Kwon as a participant, yet he seems to have withdrawn from the group.[29] He later explained his refusal as being the result of his unwillingness to feed what he saw as a heated "rivalry" between different artists' groups and his disinclination to work under the direction of a single "boss," by whom he tacitly meant Suh Se-ok.[30] His withdrawal may have also had to do with the group's oedipal nature: those most engaged with *nihonga* and its visual possibilities were also those under whom members of the society and their contemporaries studied. A case in point was Chang Woo-sung, an influential professor at Seoul National University who first gained prominence in the mid-1930s, when the promotion of *nihonga* in Korea was at its height. As a leading practitioner, instructor, and arbiter of ink painting in the immediate postwar era, Chang immersed himself in the process of reconstruction that took place in the wake of the Korean War, painting works like *Young Generation* (Figure 1.9). A large ink-and-color painting executed to commemorate the tenth anniversary of the founding of Seoul National University, it shows a cluster of students, four men and one woman, flanked by another woman and man.

More pronounced was Chang's use of color and line in an attempt to follow through on his own teachings against ever "blindly follow[ing]" *nihonga*.[31] He urged his students at Seoul National University to use the black line as a counterpoint to what he criticized as *nihonga*'s penchant for the "very realistic [and] extreme [sense of] color."[32] Kwon, who later identified Chang as the only teacher to have influenced his thinking during his university studies, took this call to heart by making extensive use of the black line in *A Glimpse into the Studio* and *On the Way to an Island*.[33] Matters were more difficult for Chang. His figures are fuller and fleshier and occupy pictorial space in a markedly different way than do the wispy and almost anticorporeal women for which his own teachers were so recognized during the colonial era. Rendered in a myriad of colors, the scene oscillates between flatness and illusionistic depth in a way that expands on similar negotiations in *nihonga*. Chang outlines the figures with a thin black line that flattens the contoured image against the picture plane. Depth within the central cluster of students is suggested by the overlap of one figure over another. At the same time, he tries to counter the flatness by shading the clothes his figures wear. To draw the eye into the picture, Chang angles the feet of the chattering students in different directions, which has the effects of affirming the unmarked space below as a distinct ground able to bear weight, and of creating a convincing sense of pictorial depth.

To the members of the Ink Forest Society, Chang did not go far enough in relinquishing all that in Korea was considered typical of *nihonga*, including the use of vibrant color and the emphasis on technique. Instead, society members concentrated on making ink paintings expressly based on the physical properties of black ink—for instance, on the way it could be made to lie flat and matte against a paper support, or the way it could appear to float unmoored across pictorial space when combined with water. For the society's inaugural exhibition in March 1960 at the Press Center in downtown Seoul, Suh Se-ok showed *Noon* (Figure 1.10), a large painting depicting a multitude of birds flocking together on a long, narrow support reminiscent of that used for hand scrolls and calligraphy. Massed groups of birds extend in three directions, toward the top, the bottom, and the left, as if forming the spokes

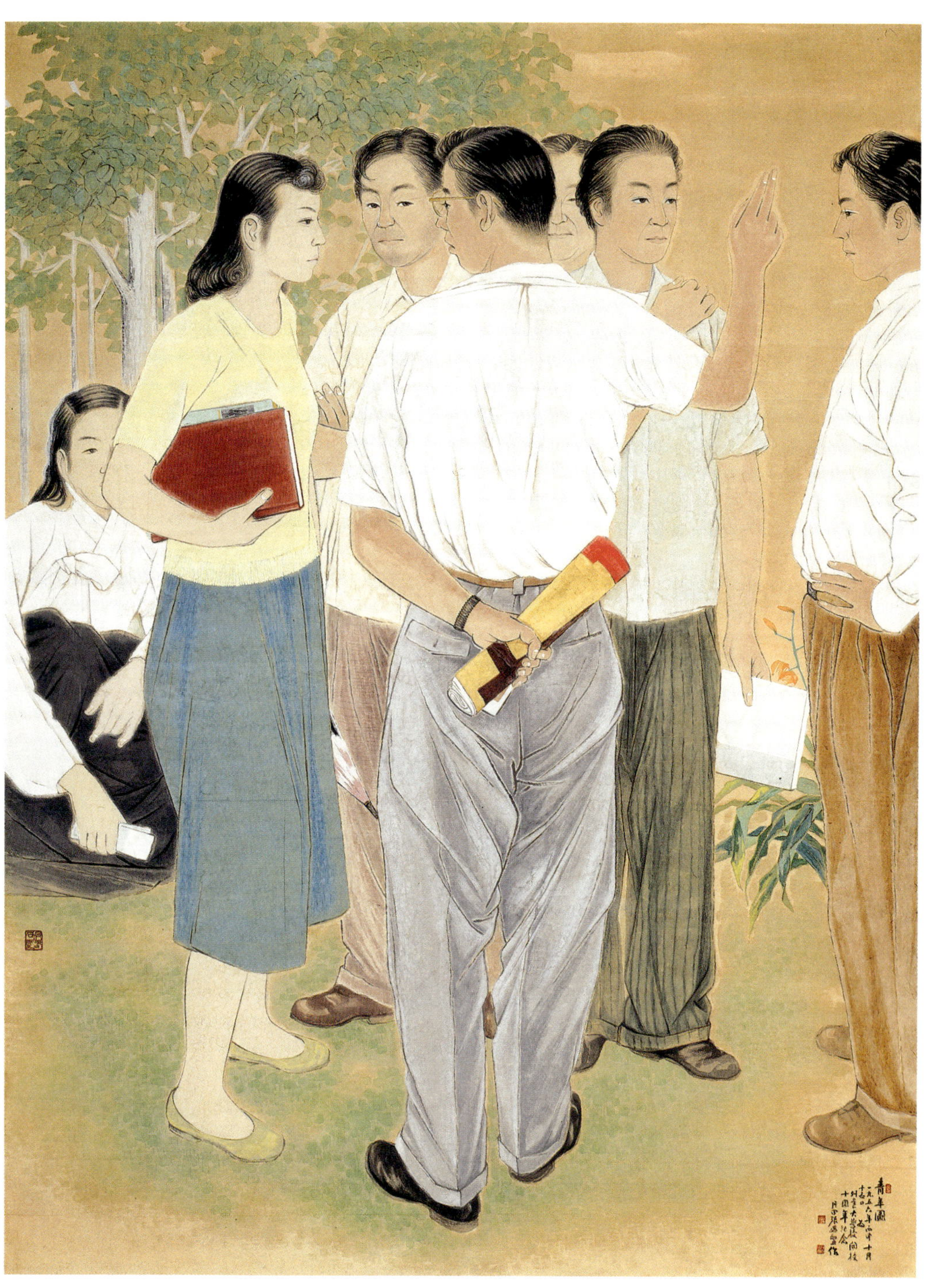

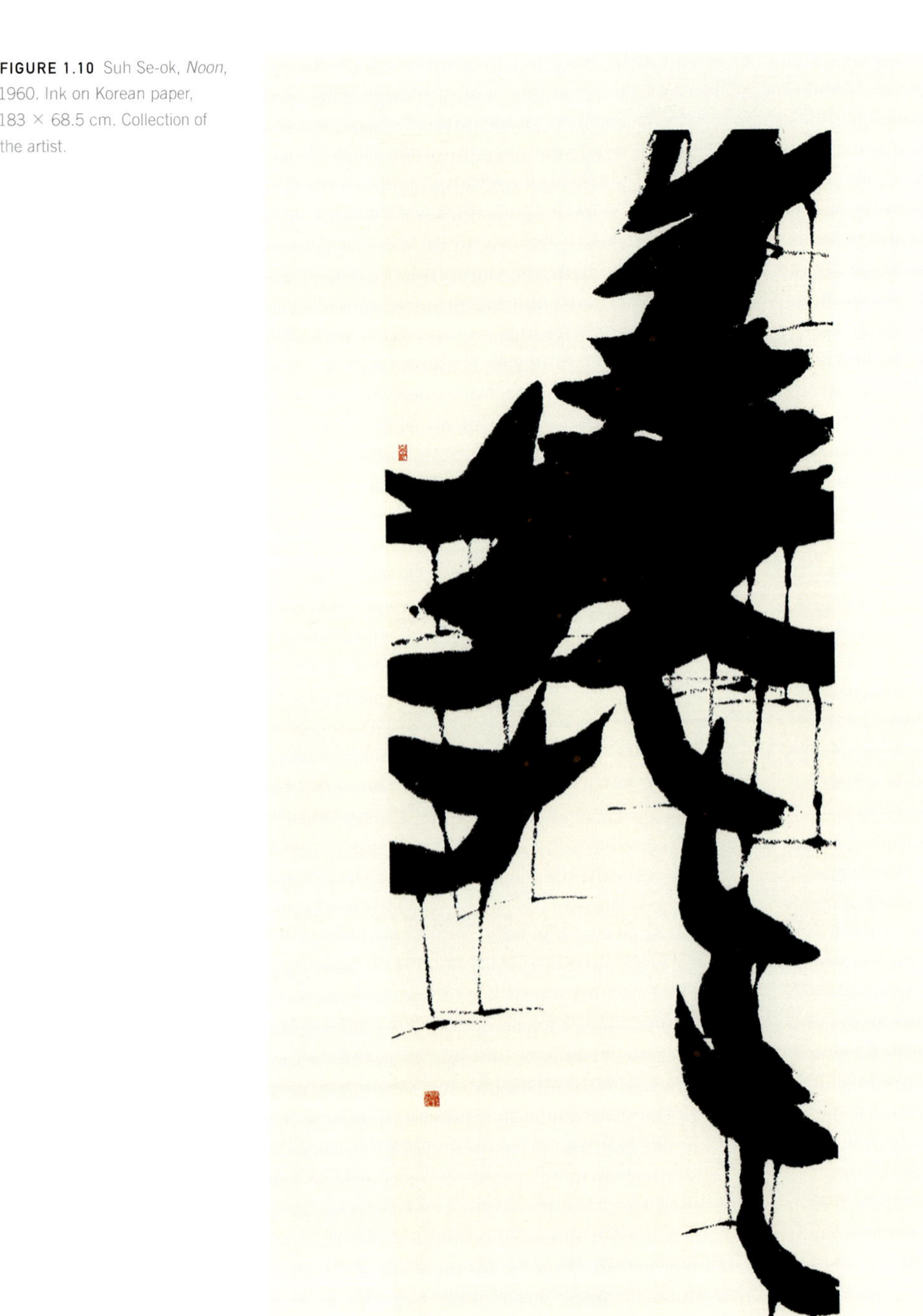

FIGURE 1.10 Suh Se-ok, *Noon*, 1960. Ink on Korean paper, 183 × 68.5 cm. Collection of the artist.

of a very large wheel whose true size can only be imagined. The flatness
of *Noon,* however, appears to underscore the immediacy of the crowd-
ing. The figures of flat, crescent-shaped birds overlap and meld into
a visually indistinct mass in the middle, and the viewer comes away
from the painting with a sense of spread—of ink spilled across a length
of paper, hurtling toward its edges and beyond. *Noon* was praised as
a worthy search for "freedom" by Kim Ki-ch'ang, another ink painter
whose own affinity for the possibilities of black ink led him in the mid-
1950s to make architectonic forms out of brushstrokes more commonly
employed in the service of calligraphy.[34]

The special adherence to ink responded to the ascent of Western
painting, which threatened to scuttle the attempts of ink painters
anxious to preserve what remaining status they had as contemporary
artists. In the mid-1910s ink painting was already beginning to be
regarded in the Korean art world as distinctly premodern, an image that
flourished in subsequent decades.[35] By the early 1960s, as Korean artists
began to participate in an extensive international biennale circuit, most
ink painters were passed over in favor of their oil-painting counterparts. The only exceptions tended to be those whose works resonated
with the kind of gestural abstraction then being promoted as examples
of "Korean informel."[36] Interestingly, those ink painters selected to
represent Korea often attracted more overseas attention than did their
oil-painting counterparts; Suh Se-ok's friend Chung Chang-sup won
a bronze medal at the 1962 International Exhibition of Fine Arts in
Saigon, as did Kim Ki-ch'ang's wife, the artist Park Rae-hyun. At home,
however, ink painters found themselves having to defend their claims to
be contemporary artists, as seen in the declining number of ink painters
chosen to participate in the Invitational Exhibition of Contemporary
Artists, the presumptive index by which contemporary art in Korea
during the 1960s was assessed. In 1966, for example, six ink painters,
including Suh Se-ok and Kwon Young-woo, were chosen to participate
in the Invitational Exhibition of Contemporary Artists, compared to
sixteen oil painters, including Ha Chonghyun and Park Seobo. Acutely
aware of their marginalization within the field of contemporary Korean
art, some ink painters turned to nationalist sentiment in a last attempt
to defend their contemporary status. During a roundtable discussion
hosted by Seoul National University on Korean participation in international exhibitions that same year, Suh admonished his non-ink-painter
peers that if "the Korean avant-garde continued to appropriate from
Western avant-gardes, it would soon lose its understanding of art

altogether," a statement apparently meant to defend the contemporaneity of ink painting.[37]

Although some critics cited the 1963 Invitational Exhibition of Contemporary Artists as a turning point whereby ink painting was "brought into intensive focus," they also bemoaned what they saw as a lack of independent direction.[38] Bang Keun-taek, for example, wrote that looking at such works was like "watching our images reflected in the eyes of strangers."[39] The works were but a "passive reflection" of "the international tendency in the fine arts," by which Bang meant gestural abstraction.[40] He urged artists not to "live in a world of 'non-method'" but instead to take "command of method"; by so doing, they would be less beholden to "international" tendencies.[41]

Although the Ink Forest Society was not exclusively dedicated to abstraction, some of its members explicitly engaged it by exploring the material properties of ink painting. Submitted to the 1965 Kukchŏn rather than the Invitational Exhibition of Contemporary Artists, as if in defiance of the Kukchŏn's conservatism, Suh's *Work* (Figure 1.11) shows how he further denatures his marks into amorphous forms suspended in pictorial space without any adherence to spatial order. This effect and the large size of the work both suggest that Suh may have regarded this piece as an alter ego of the similarly large canvases that typify many examples of so-called Korean informel. But whereas artists associated with this tendency emphasized the mark as a direct trace of the artist's presence, Suh took care to make his marks so indistinct as to give rise to a presumption of handlessness, in which the hand of the artist is deliberately vacated from the space of the painting. Water played a key role in achieving this effect. So many of the works produced by the Ink Forest Society looked as if they were still wet because their attempt to remove all traces of a deliberate hand depended on the interaction between ink and water as recorded on an inert support. The flow of water, rather than the movement of the hand, directed the production of the mark.

PAINTING WITH PAPER

In recognition of the growing number of abstract ink painters, the Kukchŏn established the unwieldy category of "nonfigurative Oriental painting" (*pigusang tongyanghwa*) in 1971. Yet the word "abstraction" was conspicuously omitted from the name given this category, further indicating the extent to which "abstraction itself was regarded in

[1960s] Korea as the exclusive domain of Western painting."[42] Like Bang Keun-taek in 1963, Kwon wondered if this was because ink painters were too caught up in chasing the priorities of Western painting, by which he meant the kind of gestural abstraction produced in close connection with the uneven flow of information about informel and abstract expressionism.[43]

Kwon himself turned to a certain kind of gestural abstraction, most notably in some of the works he exhibited in 1966. Using scissors or, more frequently, his nails, Kwon tore paper to emphasize the primacy of ground: "At that time [when the *hanji* works were first made], I had to make my own supports and when the *hanji* [on the support] ripped I pasted it back together. The changes [in the paper] that took place when this happened intrigued me, and this is how the works began."[44] Yet whereas his counterparts in Korean informel prided themselves on the flamboyant athleticism of their mark making, his rips were tentative, occasionally hesitant, and above all careful to maintain an equilibrium between marked and unmarked space. Of *65-9*, one reviewer commented, "The plane of the paper looks as if it was trying to follow the tracks of a worm."[45] That these works do not replicate the sometimes histrionic brushwork of Korean informel is suggested by the number of reviews that described Kwon's works in his 1966 exhibition as too "simple."[46]

But Kwon was not satisfied with the largely defensive role ascribed to ink painters seeking to participate in the ongoing discussion on abstraction. As he saw it, the real task lay in evoking the materiality of the work without also reinforcing the rapidly crystallizing distinctions between Western painting and Oriental painting. For Kwon, this entailed stressing the physical properties of a particular material with the express purpose of denying that that material was ever the basis for the distinction between Western and Oriental painting. Kwon addressed this challenge by first interrupting the chain of interactions on which the medium of ink painting was generally understood. Like Suh and other ink painters of his generation, whose training was heavily mediated by the popularization of literati painting in the late nineteenth and early twentieth centuries, Kwon initially understood ink painting in relation to the history of literati painting and of the scholar's studio.[47] In turning so resolutely to paper and in eliminating the brush altogether, Kwon tried to move away from what had long been a discourse of exceptionalism surrounding ink painting, which to him only reified the distinctions between oil painting and ink painting without leaving open the possibility of working through them.

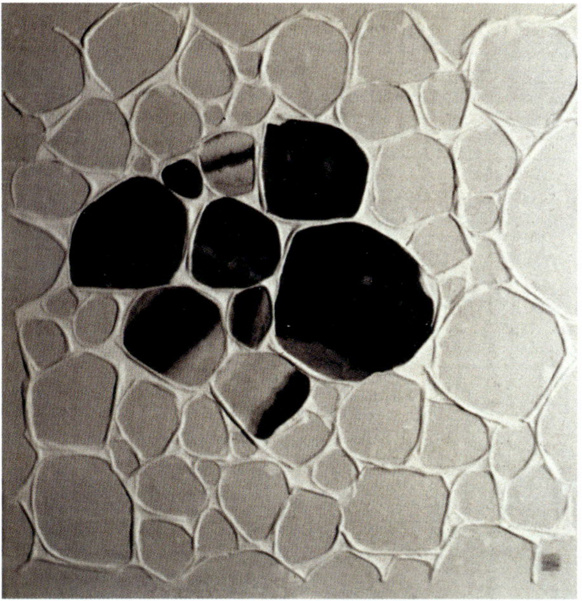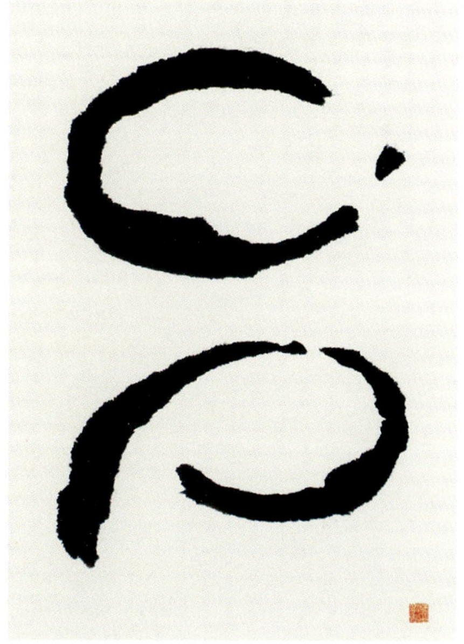

Kwon's interest in paper appeared early. In the mid-1950s he began to experiment with *kaengji*, cheap, grayish newsprint made from wood pulp. Speaking of his 1956 work *Old Moon*, he explained that the roughness of the paper allowed ink to bleed freely into and across the surface so that the work looked "as if it was taken out of the water and in some places still looked as if the picture was underwater."[48] After 1962 he shifted to *hanji*, but with a vested interest in thinking about paper as a substance meant to be handled manually. In *66-12* (Figure 1.12) he glued multiple sheets of delicate *hanji* onto a plywood panel. While still wet, they were carefully torn into a web of egg-shaped areas ringed by coiled ridges of soft, sticky paper. To some of these areas he attached sheets of black photographic paper that was specially cut to fit the contours of each area. Kwon soon discovered, however, that it was not so easy to wean himself from what he had been taught. Of the works he included in his 1966 exhibition and for which comparatively clear reproductions exist, more than half allude to the presence of black ink. From a distance or in reproduction, the blackened areas in *66-12* read, for instance, as patches of ink. In *66-14* (Figure 1.13), Kwon tore the paper support to approximate the trace left behind by a brushstroke dipped in black ink. He later remarked that he had never intended to "abandon" the brush and ink altogether.[49]

But at the time of his Sinsegye Gallery exhibition in 1966, Kwon stated that his new works "are not mountain-and-water landscapes. Nor are they ink works. This [exhibition] is but me gluing paper together. Perhaps this is where my own ink paintings begin right now."[50] Instead of painting by using a brush to energize blank pictorial space with black ink, Kwon took advantage of both the delicacy and the tensile strength of paper to effectively "paint" with it. Paper, like ink or the brush, was only a "tool, [or a] method."[51] In shifting his interests from only working *on* paper to working *with* and even *against* it, he found a means of working outside the categorical bounds imposed by the question of medium on which the Korean art world had so long depended. The focus on paper was intended as a recasting of the notion of ink painting as just one possible approach among many to questions of mark making and pictorial space, rather than as a defensive reaction to gestural abstraction and Western art generally.

In *65-8* (Figure 1.14), also shown in Kwon's 1966 exhibition, the artist cut blocks of *hanji* with a pair of scissors and affixed them on top of one another. Yi Ku-yŏl suggested that these resulted from Kwon's possible familiarity with the collages of Lee Ungno that were exhibited in Seoul in 1962 at the Central Information Center.[52] Begun after Lee's relocation to Paris in 1960, the collages were his interpretation of what he had seen of the Parisian response to ink painting and calligraphy via enthusiasts like Henri Michaux and Georges Mathieu, both of whom had shown with the Galerie Facchetti, where Lee also exhibited his work. Gone from works like Lee's *Composition 10* (Figure 1.15) is the fluidity of line that had characterized Lee's earliest engagements with abstraction; in its stead are short, irregular strips of paper that freed the brushstroke from the kind of mystification to which it was subjected at the hands of Lee's new Parisian colleagues. As Lee discussed in the preface to his solo exhibition at the Galerie Facchetti in 1962, his works were meant to "personally show the West a new technique of ink painting," a mission whose promise he tried to fulfill by establishing an academy of ink painting two years later.[53]

Also evident in *Composition 10* is a renewed appreciation of the possibilities of allover painting and of materiality, the likely effects of Lee's brief dalliance with Jean Dubuffet's *Matériologies* series, which had already made their debut when he again traveled to Paris in 1960. Lee aggressively pushed still-wet strips of paper across the support, sometimes causing the strips to fold back onto one another, sometimes making small holes in the support itself. Yet when *Composition 10* was

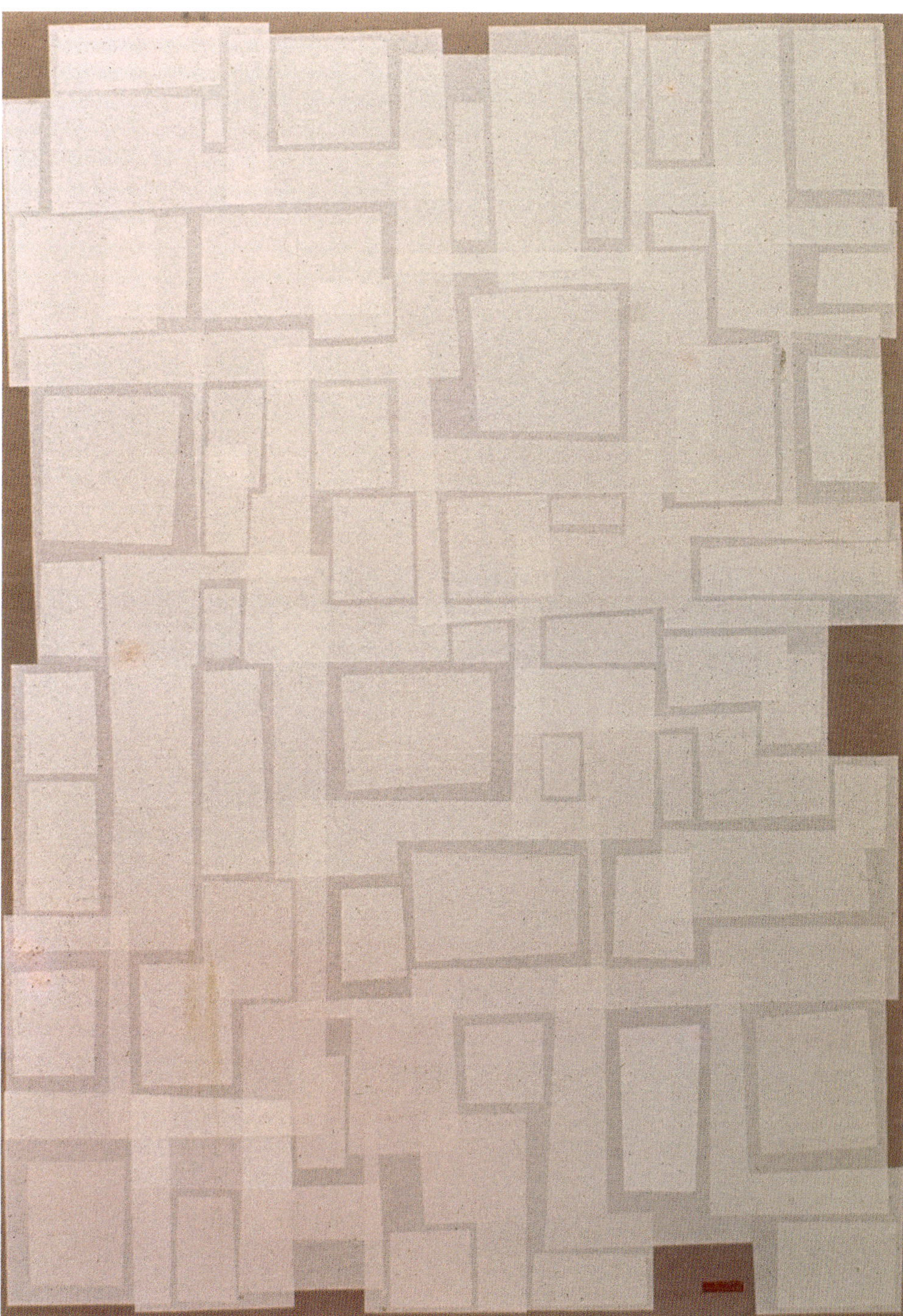

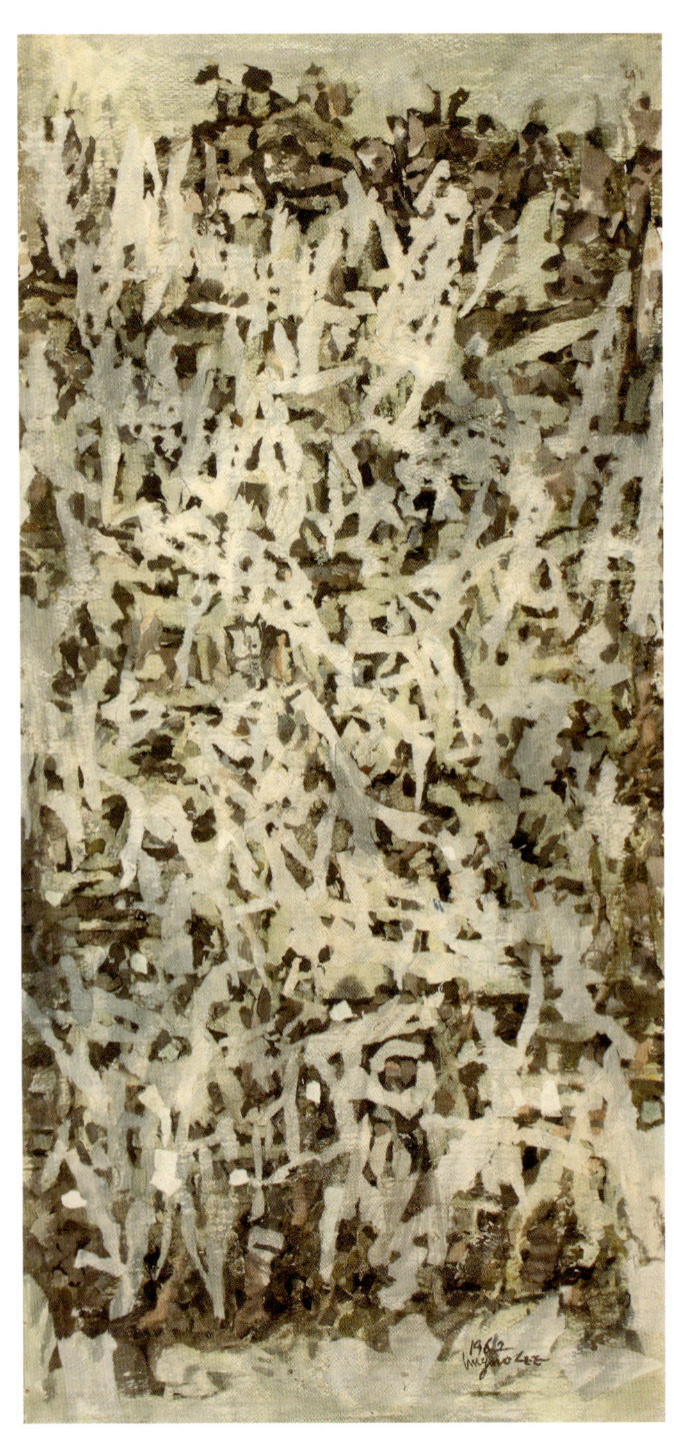

FIGURE 1.15 Lee Ungno, *Composition 10*, 1962. Ink, color, Korean paper, and newspaper, 164 × 78 cm. Collection of National Museum of Contemporary Art, Korea.

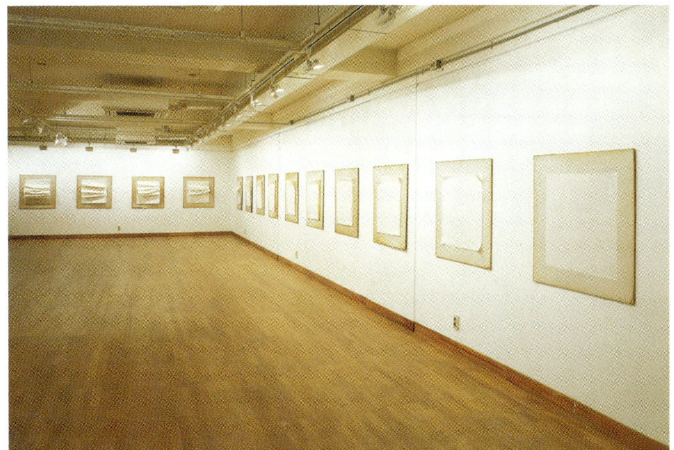

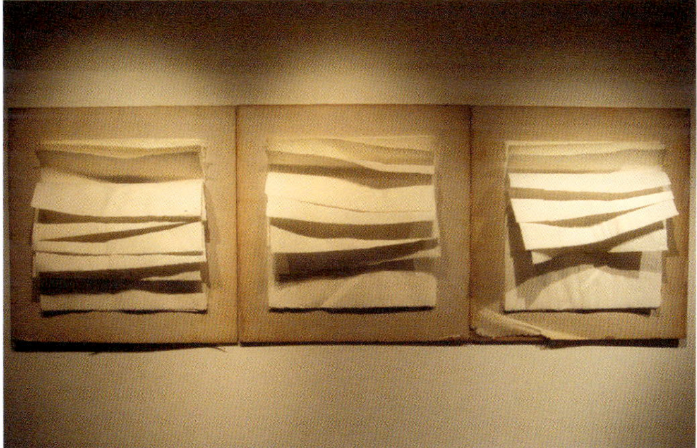

shown in Seoul, the essayist Kim Hyangan, who also happened to be the wife of Lee's colleague Kim Whanki, remarked that the collages "generate the effect of oil paint being applied to canvas."[54]

Kwon, whose Paris debut in 1976 resulted in part from Lee's recommendation, was also interested in evoking the materiality of paper.[55] He sought to emphasize this through work whose creation required only paper, the force of his own hands, and occasionally an awl or a pair of scissors. But Kwon was not interested in materiality in the way that Lee or some of his contemporaries were. Consider Suh Seung-won's *Simultaneity* (Figure 1.16), first exhibited at the Central Information Center in Seoul in 1971 as part of the A.G. group's inaugural exhibition, *The Dynamics of Expansion and Reduction*. The work consists of twelve square panels successively positioned in two straight lines that intersect at a corner. Attached to each panel are several sheets of *ch'anghoji* (*hanji* of a much coarser grain than that ordinarily employed for ink painting, generally used for traditional sliding doors and windows). Suh cut large sheets of this paper into squares, which reflects a certain awareness of extra-artistic materials being repurposed in the name of "art." But unlike Kwon, who was firmly committed to the idea of painting as capable of encompassing its own internal realm distinct from that of its presumed audience, Suh was intent on establishing a contiguity between the work and the viewer by pasting multiple sheets onto each of twelve same-size square panels. On some squares the sheets are pasted flat against the support, securely ensconced within the frame implied by the panel's four distinct edges. So admirably does paper perform its role as an upright support that it begins to resemble a monochrome, the moment at which a painting is both an unmarked support awaiting activation by contact with the brush and an emerging object inhabiting three-dimensional space. In other panels, Suh allows only a few sheets to cling to the panel so that the sheets bend back at an almost ninety-degree angle to the support (Figure 1.17). As the viewer walks from one panel to the next, paper looks less like a support and more like a material defined by its weight and volume.

Suh may have been affected by what he knew of minimalism, in which the A.G. took a passing interest, as indicated in the first issue of *A.G.*, which carried short features on the works of Donald Judd and Robert Morris.[56] Conversely, Kwon, who in 1971 had just been appointed to chair the inaugural committee responsible for selecting abstract ink paintings for the Kukchŏn, continued to insist that his works be read as paintings.[57] A smaller untitled version of *65-9* (Figure 1.18) demonstrates his fascination with paper as a substance. He took care, however, to make sure that his rips make sense compositionally, and he mapped most of his early works in advance through preliminary sketches or drawings.[58] In this untitled work, the holes are evenly spaced so as to make it easy for the viewer to read the work as a coherent picture. Moreover, Kwon tore the paper with the aim of making his rips as perfectly round as possible. The papered surface was then encased within a frame implied by the thin margin of kraft paper that the artist left untouched. The geometry of *65-9* is also striking, and for Kwon the grid proved highly useful in producing balanced compositions. In another work exhibited at the Sinsegye Gallery (Figure 1.19), Kwon took advantage of the dissonance between the softness of the paper and the

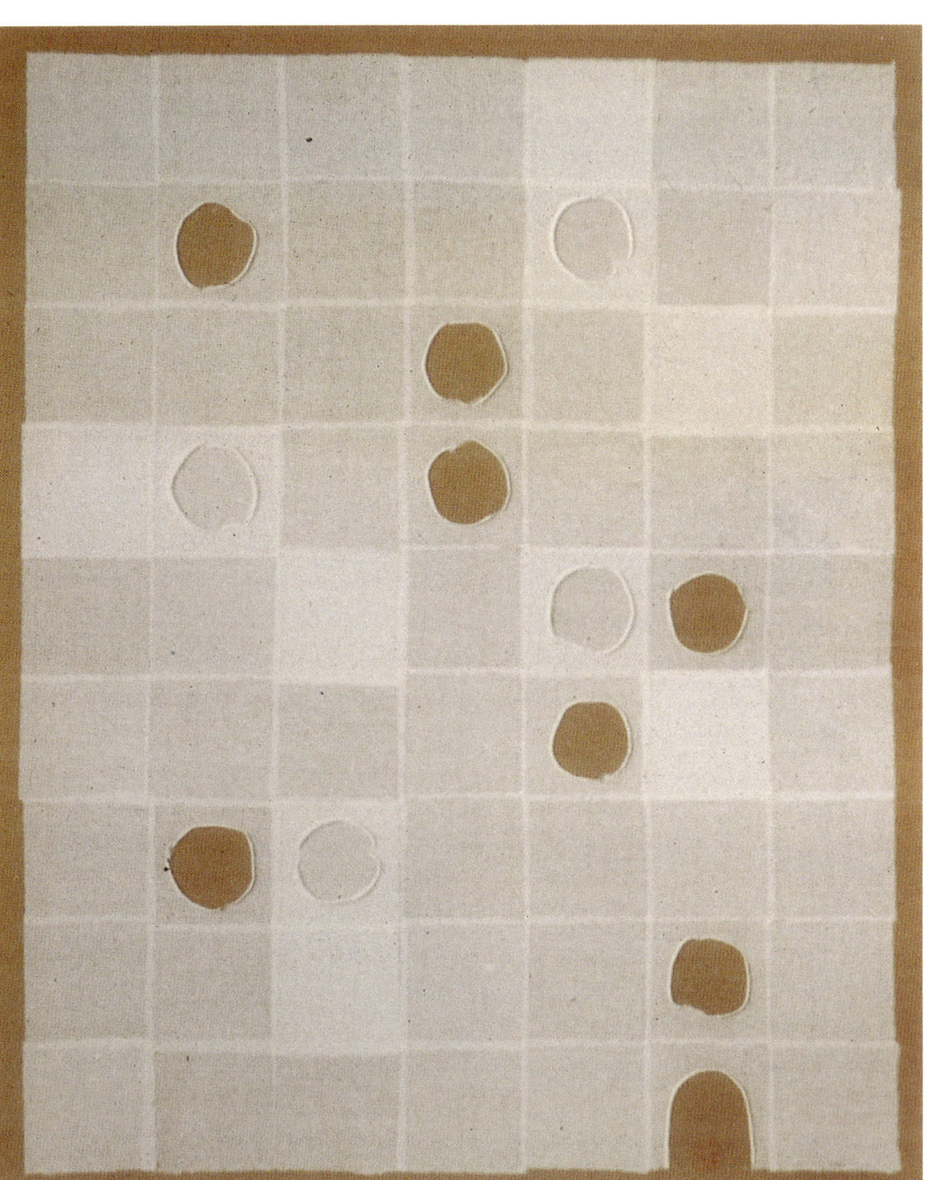

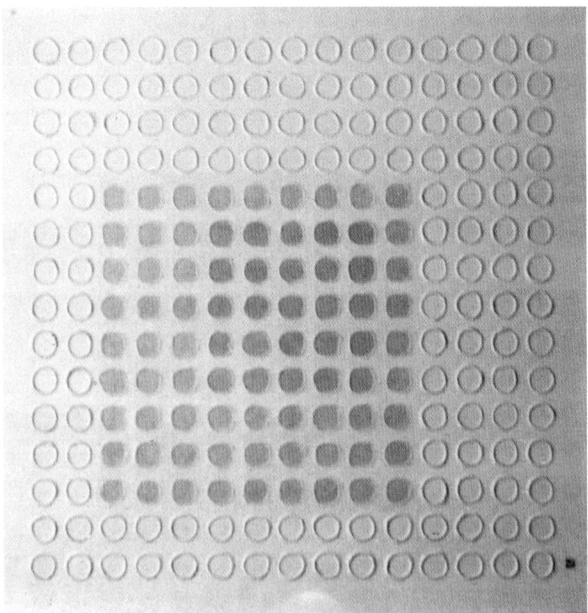

straight edges of the grid. He also observed the modes through which authorship is established in ink painting, impressing upon each work his personal seal, the traditional marker confirming authorship in ink painting and calligraphy. As was also typical in ink painting, the seal is positioned in a way that implies that the painting was organized to make room for it. In *65-9*, for example, the seal hovers in the upper left-hand corner, where a particularly generous portion of the *hanji* layer has been torn away so as to frame its presence.

KWON STANDS HIS GROUND

The question of painting and its relationship to materiality continued to intrigue Kwon, who in the early 1970s began to concentrate more intently on evoking the viscerality of paper. In 1974 he was invited to show his new works at the Myongdong Gallery from April 26 to May 5. Although he had shown a few works since his first exhibition in 1966, this exhibition was the first extensive look at what he had been thinking in the intervening eight years. The exhibition featured twenty-two works of various sizes, all made in 1973 and 1974. Each was made of multiple layers of *hanji* affixed to a veneered plywood panel; Kwon then covered the layers of *hanji* with thin animal glue. This softened the layers closest to the surface so that even brief moments of contact or light applications of pressure would rupture or tear the paper. While not yet dry, the glue-covered panel was mounted on an easel, and Kwon scratched, pushed, and pulled at the paper to reveal the layers underneath.

In *Work 74-1* (Figure 1.20) Kwon groups a multitude of small, fan-shaped marks toward the upper edge of the panel; the marks later unfurl downward onto the white paper support. The marks diminish in size as they appear to fall away from the uppermost cluster, so that they are barely visible toward the panel's bottom edge. Evident throughout is an attempt to strike a balance between the performativity involved in tearing the paper support and the urge to refrain from engaging in such a direct form of address. In other works, an abundance of blank space acts as a stabilizing element. It is significant that Kwon refused to describe the untouched expanses as "empty," "blank," or "void," a move that leads us to consider blank space as that defined by the absence of touch. Indeed, the smoothness of the paper offers itself to the viewer as a challenge: dare we touch the surface?

Certainly the question was present in Kwon's mind. A few weeks after the Myongdong Gallery show in 1974, Kwon was photographed for the weekly general interest magazine *Chugan kyŏnghyang* where he is shown almost gingerly touching the paper support. While some of his presumed trepidation stemmed from his own self-consciousness at being photographed, his deliberation of touch bore itself out in his efforts to strike a balance between the specificity of materials with a countervailing, and no less insistent, need for pictorial composition. Achieving that balance was no easy task, however, for the *hanji* practically demanded that Kwon play the role of an iconoclast (Figure 1.21). Known for its ability to withstand the pressure of a hand as it presses the brush against the surface, *hanji* provoked Kwon into testing its durability. He tears at the paper; the result pleased several viewers, such as Kim In-hwan, who applauded the way Kwon tried to "evoke the transparency and give of *hanji*," which to him read as an attempt to see "just how much he could make this thin *hanji* come alive."[59]

Others sensed Kwon's struggle in establishing a balance between his interest in materiality and composition. A year after the Myongdong Gallery exhibition, Oh Kwangsu stated, "Because of its excessively calculated setup and operation, the contrived nature of artmaking is occasionally exposed."[60] To him, Kwon's new works felt too deliberate. In attending so meticulously to both process and composition, the artist,

FIGURE 1.20 Kwon Young-woo, *Work 74-1*, 1974. Korean paper on plywood, 162 × 122 cm. Collection of Seoul Museum of Art.

FIGURE 1.21 Kwon Young-woo, *Untitled*, 1973. Korean paper on plywood, 162 × 122 cm. Collection of the artist.

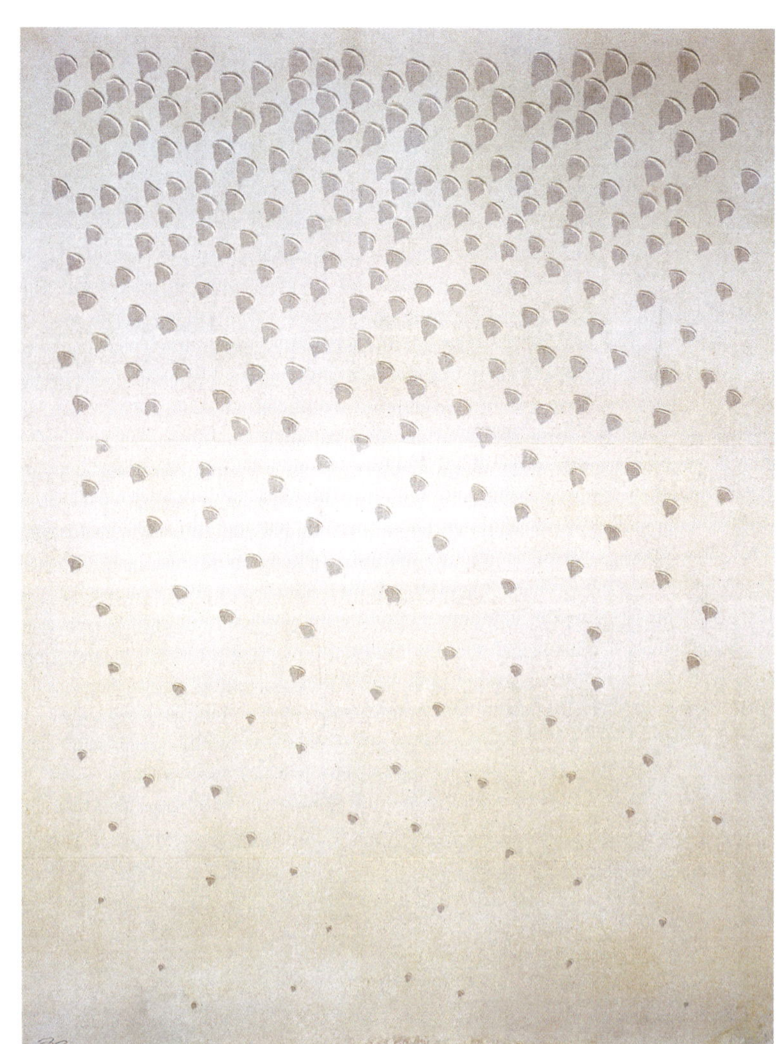

in Oh's view, produced work that felt overly labored, and perhaps even too refined. But this kind of effort was what was especially needed in the early 1970s, when even the staunchest champions of abstract ink painting faltered. Only a few days after Kwon's Myongdong Gallery exhibition ended, Min Kyung-kap publicly returned to figuration, declaring that nonfigurative ink painting had "hit the wall."[61] The emphasis on ink painting's constituent materials, which had seemed so radical in the late 1950s, now felt stale or excessive as subsequent generations of artists took this return literally by almost drowning pictorial space in black ink, or by leaning too heavily on the texture of *hanji* without concurrently raising other questions that would enable their work to be more than a restatement of its physical properties. Yi Kyungsung put matters even more frankly in 1975 when he remarked that ink painters lacked an "experimental spirit" and that thus it was difficult to include any ink painter among the ranks of the most advanced contemporary artists.[62]

Although something of a loner and not one to follow critical reception closely, Kwon nevertheless understood that his status as an abstract ink painter meant that his works would be subject to additional scrutiny. His response was to vigorously push the dichotomy between performativity and restraint. In *S 74-9* (Figure 1.22), also shown in the 1974 Myongdong Gallery exhibition, paper layers are torn in undulating sections that cumulatively generate the effect of paint dripping down a vertical support. Organized into horizontal rows, the rips decrease in size as the eye moves up the work, again suggesting the illusion of pictorial space receding into the distance. This work, a version of which was later exhibited at the Jacques Massol Gallery in Paris in January 1976, prompted one viewer to consider these works as evocations of spatial depth: "The parts of dazzling whiteness overlapping the discrete parts showing the ochre and gray background," wrote Denis Roger, "provide a double sense of light and depth."[63] Whereas the white paper and the brown or black support in Kwon's earlier works read simply as the juxtaposition of two different materials, here the subcutaneous layers of *hanji* read as shaded counterparts of the uppermost white layer. French critic Alain Bosquet, in his review for *Le Figaro*, likened the fourteen works in the exhibition to a "transparent membrane" or an "abstract landscape" and tried to relate Kwon's works to a longer history of the monochrome: "In the remote line of Moholy-Nagy and Malevich, he [Kwon] is an unexpected virtuoso of white on white."[64]

The same works were differently received in Seoul, where they were exhibited at the Sinsegye Gallery in 1977. Seeing works like *S 76-6*

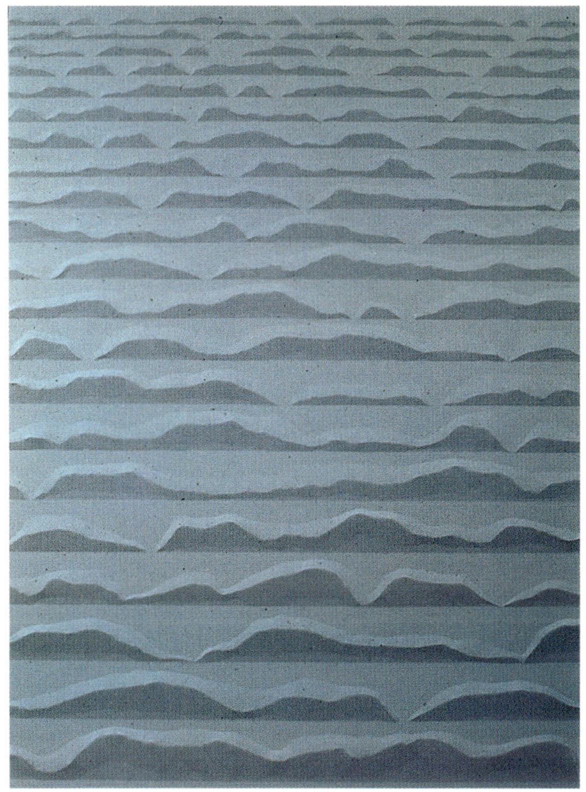

(Figure 1.23), viewers quickly picked up on the tension between his desire to celebrate the "pure and clear light of white" and his penchant for making "pictorial surfaces that made you want to destroy an excessively tidy and still surface."[65] In *S 77-15* (Figure 1.24), Kwon divides the panel into horizontal rows, with each row wider than the one above it. Taking the bottom edge of each row as his point of reference, he then tears the paper to reveal subterranean layers of paper darkened by the seepage of the glue. The contrast between the initial white layer and these underlying darker layers is made especially intense by Kwon's use of unprocessed *hanji,* which absorbs liquid more quickly than regular *hanji.* At the very top of the panel, the rips are miniscule in both height and width, but the rips become increasingly larger as Kwon works his way down the panel's surface. The effect is one of spatial recession, comparable to that suggested in a hanging scroll landscape mounted on vertical supports, where spatial depth is commensurate to the physical distance from the bottom edge of the support.

Around this time, Kwon began to make his marks only after the papered surface had completely dried: "The paper absorbs the glue, making it stronger and especially taut and hard and so induced me to rip and cut the surface [with a knife]."[66] (Figure 1.25) he tears at the surface with his fingers, but instead of cleanly detaching the flaps of torn paper, as he does in his other works, he leaves them to lie flaccidly against the surface. Kwon states his case for seeing through touching by having the work installed so that the central horizontal band of paper flakes is almost at viewers' eye level. Seen in contrast to the undisturbed support, the band encourages in viewers a desire to reach out and touch the flaps, as anticipated by Kwon's own process of creation, in which the support is mounted vertically on an easel. Viewers imagine raising an arm to touch the painting's surface, consequently becoming aware of their own upright posture and of their rootedness. Hoisted from the torso, the arm concurrently reinforces gravitational pull, securely anchoring the body to the ground. The raised arm, moreover, indicates the distance at which viewers stand from the work, in turn reminding them that they occupy real space as a discrete volume. The painting is now defined not by the invisible boundary separating its own contained and internal world from that inhabited by viewers but by the permeability of that boundary. One might extend this argument further by suggesting that the work is an affirmation of viewers' ability to experience real physical space, particularly in those versions where the paper flaking is concentrated toward the middle of the work. Marks are made in such a way that the support appears to expand and merge with surrounding space so that the wall on which the physical work hangs begins to look like an extension of the paper support. In this way, Kwon emphasized painting as that which inhabits real space coterminous with the viewers' own.

Many viewers were intrigued by what they saw of these works, which addressed the distinctions between painting and sculpture. Upon seeing Kwon's works in *Korea: Facet of Contemporary Art* at the Central Museum of Art in Tokyo in 1977, critic Barbara Thoren described them as "integrating painting and sculptural qualities for an environmental, wall-less ambience."[67]

Similarly, the poet and critic Yi Hŭng-u praised what he saw as "the increased chaos of patterns which had previously looked orderly."[68] Lay viewers were also struck by Kwon's efforts to make work that moved beyond the assertion of its own materiality. Having seen Kwon's 1977 Sinsegye Gallery exhibition, journalist O To-gwang was taken by his

ability to think of his supports "not only [as] paper, but as flat canvas planes."[69] Even Oh Kwangsu, who received Kwon's 1974 Myongdong Gallery exhibition with skepticism, praised the works of the 1977 show as "having overcome the old notion of *tongyanghwa* [ink painting]." The works in the Sinsegye Gallery exhibition, he averred, "had an Oriental foundation, but in terms of facture and their understanding of space belong to the context of experimentalism in postwar abstraction."[70] Park Rae-kyung developed Oh's point further by discussing Kwon's success in "making works appropriate to their time by incorporating Western painting techniques," by which she meant his persistence in responding to certain aspects of modernist abstraction with indigenous materials.[71] Kwon reworked the grid by pasting layers of *hanji* in early works like *65-9*, ordered the pictorial space of *S 74-9* in repeating horizontal bands, and brought the allover effect to bear in *S 78-72* (discussed in chapter 5, Figure 5.6). These efforts "were not easy," for Kwon had to face "the heavy burden of tradition" as expressed through the enduring persistence of distinctions that separated ink painting from media more readily accepted as "contemporary."[72] As the ever-critical Oh pointed out in his 1977 review, a number of works exuded a distinct awkwardness.[73]

Yet one wonders whether the awkwardness was the result of Kwon's wanting to ask, what in fact were the conditions allowing viewers to recognize an object as painting? On the one hand, he treated his supports as if they were flat screens on which to project images that resembled shadows rather than marks. On the other, he scratched the surface as if to affirm the materiality of negative space. He also emphasized the interaction between mark and space that was central to the way ink painters understood painting. Yet he did so without the defensiveness that sometimes accompanied the insistence with which his colleagues stressed the properties of ink. To Kwon, the real challenge was to recognize the extent to which the viability of ink painting depended on the artist's willingness to foreground the negotiability of its core assumptions, a willingness particularly vital to a shifting contemporary art field that favored artists who could work in a given medium without pledging undue allegiance to that medium's most recognized aspects.

LIKE OIL FOR INK: KIM WHANKI AND YUN HYONGKEUN

Kwon was not alone in teasing apart the threads that upheld the consensus opinion regarding what an ink painting—or for that matter,

what painting—should be. Sharing his concern with materiality was
Yun Hyongkeun, who in many respects approached oil painting in ways
analogous to those of Kwon. Born in 1928, Yun studied oil painting
at Seoul National University just before the Korean War, then completed his studies at Hongik University, receiving a bachelor's degree in
Western painting in 1957. Like many oil painters, Yun joined one of the
numerous small groups that clustered around the gestural abstraction
boom of the late 1950s and early 1960s. For his first solo exhibition at
the Press Center in Seoul in October 1966, he mined the possibilities
arising from the materiality of oil paint, even if some viewers were not
convinced of the results:

[They were] intensely lyrical color compositions of a bright green
background on which a number of points were impressed at the
top and the bottom. The colors he selected were navy blue, yellow,
pink and others that might be called local colors, and the pictorial
composition showed a strong resemblance to that of his father-in-law,
Kim Whanki. However, the rough *matière* that he used imparted a
sense of crackling and strength, but this did not cohere well with
the bright cheerful colors he used.[74]

Although Yun largely stopped showing work for the next seven years,
he continued to explore his interest in materials. In May 1973 Yun had
his second show at the Myongdong Gallery, where he displayed twenty
oil paintings ranging in size from 53.5 × 45.5 centimeters to 162 × 112
centimeters. Each work was named for a particular color or set of colors, such as "black and white," "blue" (as in Figure 1.26), "dark brown,"
"white in ultramarine," and "umber blue." Some works looked as if they
had been submerged in water; others seemed to altogether drown in a
sea of dark oil paint. Bang Keun-taek described the new works in Yun's
1973 exhibition as arising out of "an eruption of moral high-mindedness,"
a declaration that Lee Yil tried to clarify in later years by explaining
Yun's new works as a response to the Korean War or to his brief imprisonment in 1973 after criticizing the admission policies of the high
school where he worked.[75] But such biographical explanations cannot
account for the lavish, almost indulgent, use of paint that unfurled
across Yun's canvases. Here was a sense of materiality that owed much
to Yun's earlier engagements with the works of his father-in-law, the
noted oil painter Kim Whanki.[76] When Yun attended university in the
late 1950s and early 1960s, Kim was attracting attention for works

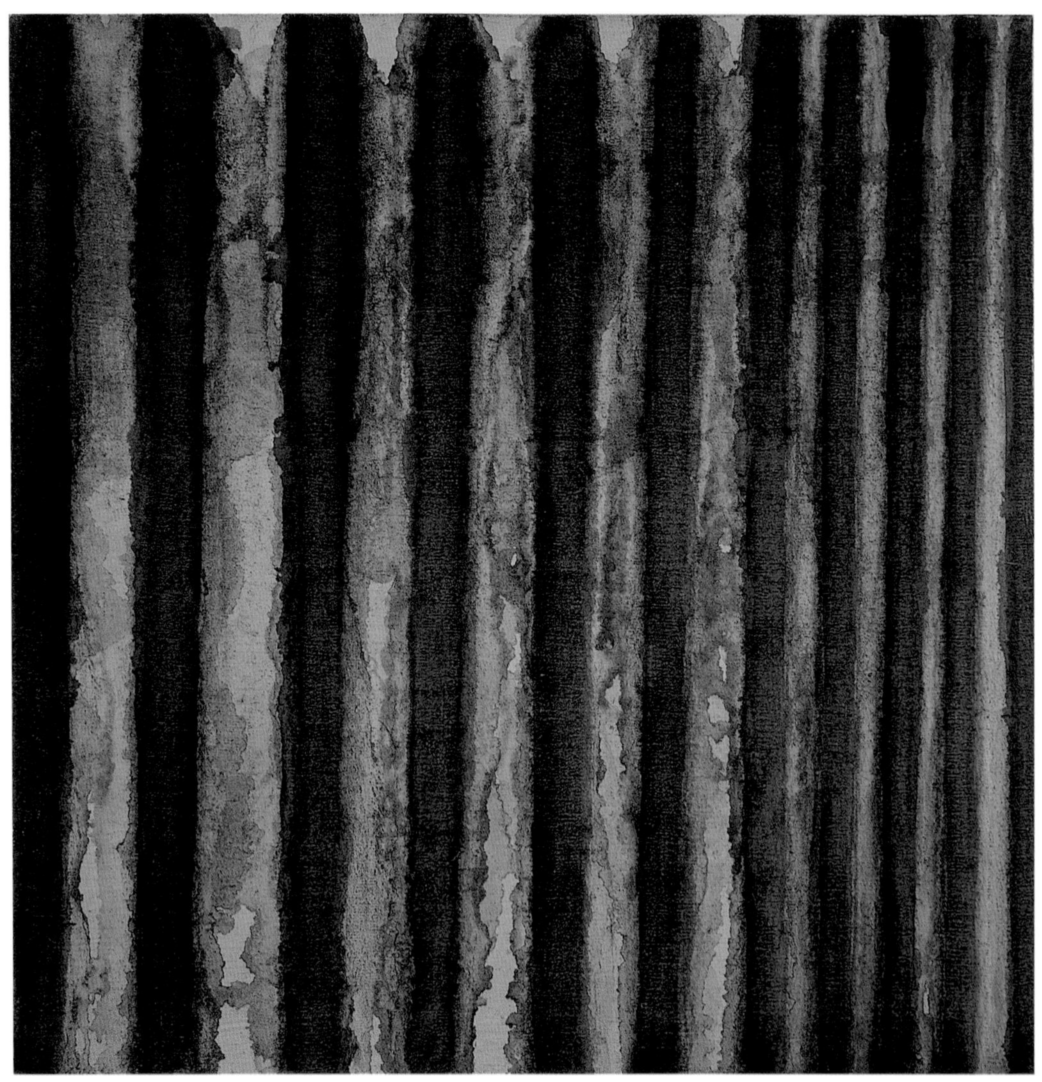

FIGURE 1.26 Yun Hyongkeun, *Blue*, 1971. Oil on canvas, 69.5 × 69.5 cm. Collection of the artist's estate.

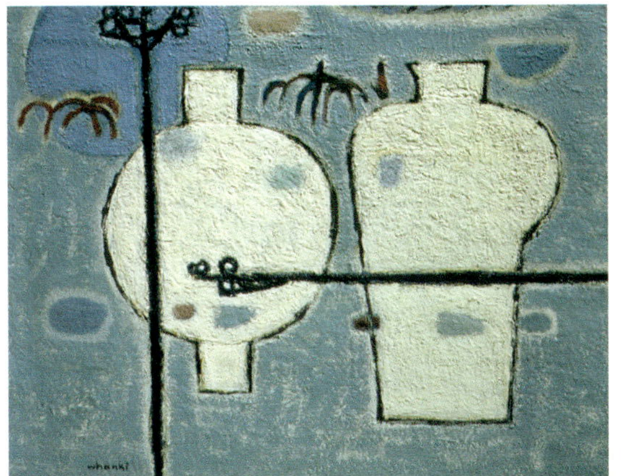

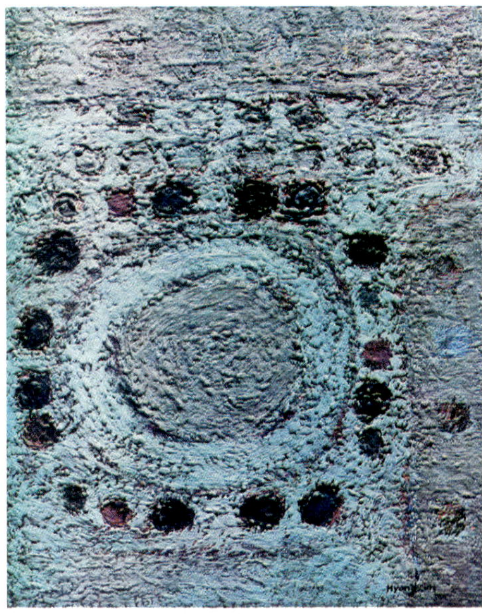

whose most distinctive feature was their thick impasto surfaces. For example, in *Jar* (Figure 1.27), which featured the round white porcelain jar considered a symbol of Korean artistic achievement, Kim applied layer upon layer of oil paint, which eventually coagulated into a thick crust. The thickness of the oil paint fixes the depiction in a certain time and place, an effect enhanced by the use of thick black contour lines that brand each image onto the surface. But when viewed in the flesh, the depiction is less immediately noticeable than the roughness of the surface, which competes with the smoothness of the walls on which *Jar* was intended to be shown. The buildup is such that the surface appears to project itself toward the viewer. This projection inhibits the will of the image to spread across the pictorial field so that it might interact with other images in an internal pictorial world of their own. Each image is instead fixed in time and space, petrified.

Yun spent many hours watching his mentor paint, and Kim Whanki's building-up of material influenced Yun, as seen in *EM-66* (Figure 1.28), the earliest work by Yun for which an image still exists.[77] Made in the same year as Yun's first solo exhibition at the Press Center in Seoul in October 1966, *EM-66* is a rectangular work painted in the kind of bright, almost fluorescent, blue that characterized Kim Whanki's works. The painting is anchored by a globular form in the center of the canvas, around which smaller, squarish marks of navy orbit.

Attempts to make out the image are frustrated by the encrustation of the surface, whose roughness is so pronounced that it prompted the critic Lee Yil to compare the work to a close-up view of Claude Monet's *Water Lilies*.[78]

In *Blue* (Figure 1.26), Yun appears to recall the blue of his earlier work and of those of his works so closely associated with Kim Whanki. Yet whereas Yun emphasized the weight and buildup of oil in *EM-66*, even to the point that Bang Keun-taek dismissed the work as "crude," *Blue* was all about thinning paint so that it behaved more like water, or even ink.[79] The critic Yoo June-sang described *Blue* as a painting of lines, a subject of long-standing interest to Yun since about 1967. Yoo wrote that the vertical stripes of *Blue* were residual traces of the upright viewer: man remained the measure.[80] Yun applied a smooth layer of gesso on a support made of thick, low-grade canvas "originally used for tenting," and he also used a more viscous type of oil paint than for other works in the exhibition.[81] Paint appears to move stochastically across the surface, like soluble particles suspended in a liquid rather than dense oil paint impressed onto a solid support.

Also significant is the application of the paint, which seems guided primarily by chance rather than by an intentional hand. In *Umber Blue* (Figure 1.29) Yun used highly viscous oil paint similar in consistency to that used by his mentor. He first applied a blue, somewhat more muted than that used for *Blue*, and let it run down over the canvas. Over this, he applied umber brown to create four vertical bands. The result was a painting that both looked and felt diaphanous in spite of its large size and the roughness of the canvas used. In emphasizing the rate at which pigment was absorbed into the canvas, as opposed to the deliberate application of pigment, and, more important, its aleatory nature, Yun declared his own independence from the kind of highly metaphysical rhetoric that had characterized discussions of mark making in Korea since the initial promotion of Korean informel from approximately 1957 to 1965. Such rhetoric had lost much of its force by 1973, yet its emphasis on allegory continued to affect the way many Korean artists thought about the encounter of materials. Yun was not interested in materiality for its own sake, but he was committed to stressing its significance, as indicated even in previous works such as *EM-66*.

The movement of paint across canvas strongly recalls ink seeping into absorbent paper, an effect not lost on viewers like Yi Kyungsung, who would describe Yun's works as attempts to "realize in oil the image of the ink mark found in inkbrush painting."[82] Like numerous others

of his generation, Yun acknowledged his debt to ink painting, from which he had "acquired a great deal," both as a child and as a student at Hongik University.[83] His intention, however, was not to make oil perform like ink so much as it was to rebut the suggestion that oil could not. By 1973 the coupling of abstraction and oil painting was far more relaxed than it had been even a decade earlier. Yet despite the case for abstract ink painting made by artists like Lee Ungno, Kwon Young-woo, and Suh Se-ok, abstraction in circa 1973 Korea was still closely associated with geometric abstraction like that produced by Lee Seung-jio in *Nucleus G-99* (Figure I.8), or gestural abstraction such as that perpetuated by Park Seobo in *No. 1* (Figure I.4) and later during his storied career as a teacher at Hongik University, Yun's alma mater. Of special note is the type of paint used and the way it was applied: geometric abstraction tended to feature extremely matte, consistent applications of highly saturated colors, often made to look mass-produced; gestural abstraction featured heavy impasto that looked as if it had been dragged or pushed across the canvas. Yun was no rebel, but his use of heavily diluted paint to stain the canvas suggests his attempt to wrest himself from these associations.

Somewhat ironically, it was Kim Whanki's later works to which Yun attributed his newfound interest in using diluted paints to stain the canvas. In mid-October 1963, Kim moved to New York, encouraged, perhaps, by winning honorable mention at the 1963 São Paulo Bienal for *Moonlit Night in Kijwa Island*, a semi-abstract work of 1959 using the same thick impasto as *Jar*. His wife, Kim Hyangan, recalled that he was "impatient to measure his own work against that of the artists [in New York]."[84] Further evidence of Kim's eagerness to prove himself in New York is found in a diary entry from November 13, 1963: "Let's go to New York [I said to myself], let's go and fight."[85] Still thinking about abstraction as a form of communication, Kim tried to posit a different language, one that took advantage of certain rudiments of ink painting by using diluted paint that mimicked the look of ink, as well as brushes ordinarily used for Chinese calligraphy. Form, he averred, was a "gathering of points," a phrase that strongly resonated with Suh Se-ok's own advocacy of points and lines.[86]

Among the most complete reflections of Kim's approach is *Where, and in What Form, Shall We Meet Again? 16-IV-70 #166* (Figure 1.30), a large, brilliant blue oil painting on unprimed canvas exhibited in Seoul at the National Museum of Modern Art from June 10 to July 9, 1970. Kim regarded pictorial space as a divisible area, in which the point was to play a decisive role, a marked departure from Yayoi Kusama's contemporaneous use of dots as a means of enacting what she would call "self-obliteration." Formally speaking, the fastest resolution would be to simply grid the work, yet Kim chooses the most labor-intensive means of division possible. After painting the surface of a cotton canvas in a deep cerulean, he laid the canvas on the floor or another horizontal surface and impressed his brush onto it. He then encased each point within a small square; the squares are organized into horizontal rows that are slightly askew. The overall effect is akin to looking at a magnified cross-section of stained cells. By organizing pictorial space as an accumulation of very small units, Kim rescales the painting so that it feels intimate, even personal, to the individual viewer. The result is noticeably different, for instance, from Kusama's dotted environments, to which Kim's works were compared by one critic in 1975. Kim was less concerned with a "multiplication to infinity" than with taking the measure of a distinctly finite area.[87]

For this work, Kim was awarded the grand prize at the Han'guk Ilbo Grand Prix, the first privately sponsored art competition in Korea, whose establishment was much-anticipated in the mounting discontent with the Kukchŏn and after the demise, in 1969, of the Invitational Exhibition of Contemporary Artists. Few artworks in Korea were as frequently reproduced or as highly publicized, and Yun would have been well acquainted with *Where, and in What Form, Shall We Meet Again? 16-IV-70 #166*. But Yun, who later acquired the painting, read the work as something other than an appropriation, a translation of different media, or even what the Paul Gauguin–like title (borrowed from a poem written by the artist's close friend Kim Kwang-sŏp) implied about Kim's nostalgia for home. As demonstrated in *Blue*, Yun was interested in the organization of pictorial space, which he expressed by dividing the canvas into poles or bars. Initially, these divisions suggested an interest in serial order, but Yun soon turned his sights to the spaces between each pair of bars or poles, which he often left unmarked. By the time of his third solo exhibition in June 1974, these spaces were sometimes so wide as to take up most of the canvas. Korean audiences of the time described these spaces as *yŏbaek*, a word frequently used to refer to the "void" in traditional ink painting. Yun, however, who never used this word himself in reference to these works, emphasized the materiality of these spaces by leaving them unpainted. For him, the challenge lay in thinking about the role of unmarked spaces without having to appeal to ideas like the void, which, despite its long-standing position in discourses of ink painting, tended to be invoked within the contemporary art context as a metaphor of Asianness. Certainly one might "sense a non-Western Orient in Yun's works," as Yi Kyungsung did.[88] Yet one was also meant to realize that Yun was not interested in replicating ink painting with oil paint and canvas. Instead, he set out to paint for viewers "all over the world," an ambition that would be realized to some extent, although not always in the ways Yun hoped.[89]

UMBER BLUE AND THE INTERVAL

Held at the Myongdong Gallery from June 17 to 23, 1974, not long after Kwon Young-woo's second solo exhibition, Yun's third solo show featured works with a drastically reduced palette in which the artist made consecutive applications of ultramarine and umber pigments on designated sections of the canvases (Figures 1.31 and 1.32). As Yun later recalled this third solo exhibition and his subsequent decision to name all his works *Umber Blue*: "I merged the two [umber and ultramarine] together, and kept putting one on top of the other so that they darkened and became the color [that they are]."[90] After applying an initial topcoat of paint, Yun quickly applied another layer before the first had dried so as to, in his words, "erase" the first layer.[91] Taking advantage of the different times required by different color paints to dry, as well as of the nonsoluble nature of oil paint, Yun successively built up layers of paint to produce an intense, and above all thick, darkness. He then diluted the pigments so that each layer of paint seeped quickly into the canvas fibers, untreated save for a light application of ox-hide glue. This process, he observed, was time-consuming: "There are times when it takes several days, or sometimes several months for a work to be complete."[92] The result was painting that required the viewer to visualize time. Absorbed by the support at a faster rate than the oil substrate, the turpentine solvent moves quickly, leaving behind one, two, and sometimes more penumbras. In one of his *Umber Blue* works (Figure 1.32), the disparate rates of absorption call attention to the narrow strips of unstained canvas separating one dark-brown vertical band from another. These strips break up the canvas area into parts, yet the uneven rates of absorption soften the effect. The bleeding tempts the eye into moving laterally across the canvas, so that the painting is again visible as a holistic unit.

Yun had further opportunity to ponder the implications of these blurred edges after traveling to New York to attend the funeral of Kim

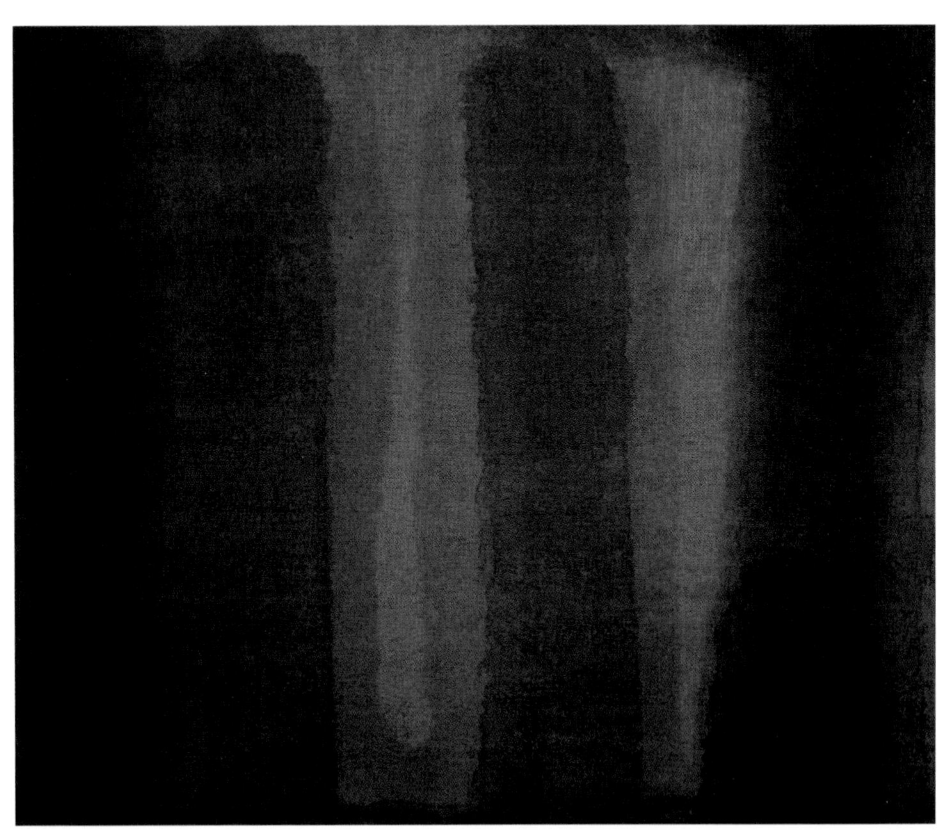

FIGURE 1.31 Yun Hyongkeun,
Umber Blue, 1974. Oil
on hemp, 50 × 60.6 cm.
Collection of the artist's estate.

FIGURE 1.32 Yun Hyongkeun,
Umber Blue, 1973. Oil on
canvas, 54 × 41.5 cm.
Collection of the artist's estate.

Whanki, who died in July 1974. At the Museum of Modern Art, Yun encountered the works of Mark Rothko (for example, Figure 1.33), to which he felt the "most affinity."[93] Like Yun, Rothko experimented intensively with multiple combinations of binders and pigments. Rothko mixed oil paint with alkyd to produce a matte impasto and then applied onto this impasto a "watery" kind of transparent oil paint heavily thinned with turpentine.[94] The extremely viscous nature of this thinned paint allowed Rothko to create a surface that seemed to glow from within and that, like the *Umber Blue* of Figure 1.29, appeared to compromise, or at least make less overt, the largeness of the canvas.

What Yun took away from his encounter with Rothko's work was a belief in the possibility of dividing pictorial space without allowing such organization to become the work's exclusive focus. Rothko's painting is a function of part-to-part relationships, in which parts are separated by circumstantial implication rather than by any overt marker of separation. Even colors as distinctly different in value, chroma, and saturation as the burnt orange and warm marigold, for example, of the work in Figure 1.33 appear to blend together. The blurred edges of each part lead the eye into thinking of the parts as an integrated unit.

Although the blurred edge had been part of Yun's repertoire since the early 1970s, after his return from New York he considered how this conceit might help mediate his interests in contrast. Most *Umber Blue* works made from late 1974 until the mid-1980s consist of a rectangular canvas featuring a large portion of unmarked space flanked by two, occasionally three, columnar dark sections running up and down the entire height of the canvas. In an *Umber Blue* work from 1976 (Figure 1.34), Yun uses enough turpentine to take full advantage of the different rates of absorption. The two stained pillars on either side of the canvas appear to glow; the thin perimeter of colorless turpentine on the pillars' outermost edges softens the transition from dark to light and vice versa. In another *Umber Blue* from 1976 (Figure 1.35), the pictorial space is roughly divided into thirds, with the middle third left untouched. The edges of the darker thirds are fringed by tiny spiked barbs that slowly draw in the eye. One thinks of the painting less as an exercise in obvious contrasts and more as an attempt to emphasize the places where contrast first takes place: the edges, or the cumulative set of terminal points at which paint stops moving across the canvas.

Throughout these versions of *Umber Blue* is a renewed attention to the role played by unmarked space in shaping the nature of the work. In the very middle of an *Umber Blue* from 1975 (Figure 1.36) is

FIGURE 1.34 Yun Hyongkeun, *Umber Blue*, 1976. Oil on canvas, 80 × 100 cm. Collection of the artist's estate.

FIGURE 1.35 Yun Hyongkeun, *Umber Blue*, 1976. Oil on hemp, 53 × 45 cm. Collection of the artist's estate.

a strip whose width compares to that along the work's far-left edge. It does not exactly divide the canvas into parts, for very narrow estuaries of pigment connect the painting's left and right. Yun suggests that his painting be read as a visual continuation of parts, with the central unmarked bar an intentional moment of recess that simultaneously asserts its own presence and anticipates that which is yet to come. Despite being unmarked, the central bar cannot be regarded as an attempt to visualize absence or lack. Nor can it be explained as a dematerialized void; the canvas weave is visible, as is the ductile nature of the support, emphasized by the seepage of pigment and turpentine. In the exhibition catalog for Yun's fourth solo exhibition, at the Munheon

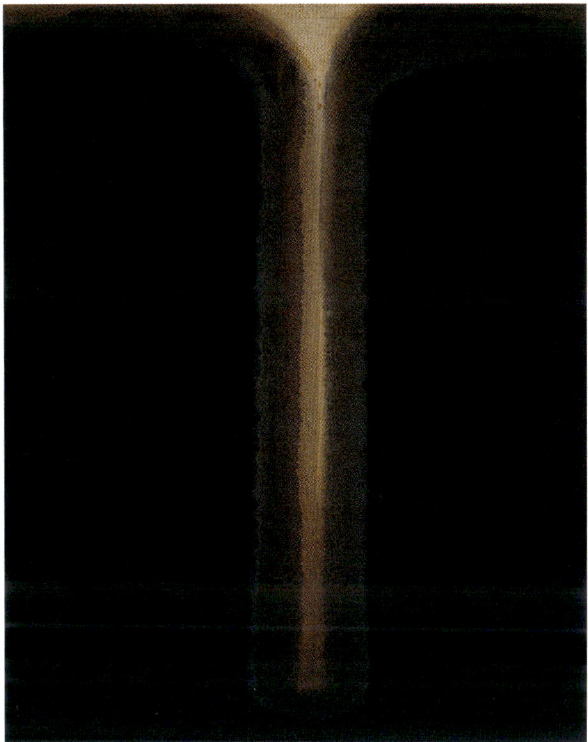

Gallery in December 1975, Lee Yil used the word "void" to describe the *Umber Blue* works, but he also added that they should not be regarded as "intrinsically East Asian." These works, he argued, must be viewed through "the relationship between the unstained and stained spaces."[95] In a work like this *Umber Blue* from 1975, Yun tried to stress the temporality of painting by having the unmarked space play the role of the interval.

Many viewers, however, persisted in describing these spaces as voids. Lee Yil's introduction notwithstanding, reviews of Yun's Munheon Gallery exhibition constantly emphasized the "aesthetics of the void" or of the "Oriental mind-set" inherent in Yun's decision to take the "void as his subject."[96] Other viewers, however, sensed his efforts at investigating the significance of distinctions. Joseph Love, who was allegedly "stopped in his tracks" upon first seeing examples of *Umber Blue* at the Second Seoul Indépendants Exhibition at the National Museum of Modern Art in December 1974, was taken by the materiality of the series.[97] He was especially interested in the rawness

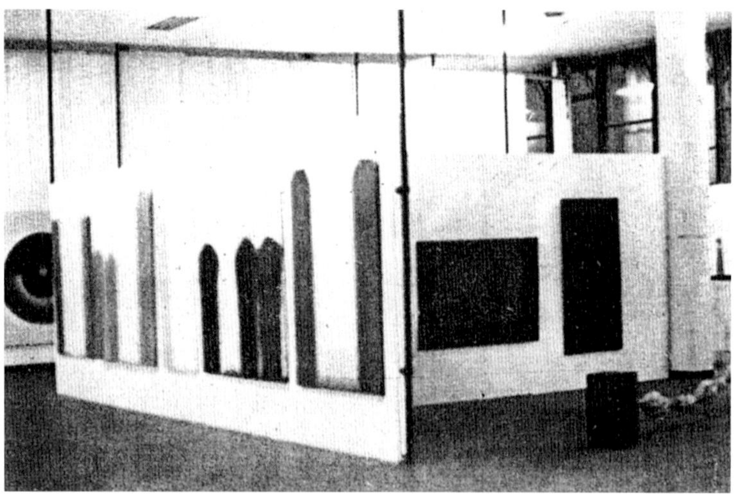

of *Umber Blue,* commenting specifically on what he saw as Yun's refusal of a "clear image" in favor of evoking what he called "texture."[98] His observation indicated Yun's commitment to the tactility of materials, an allegiance borne out in such works as an *Umber Blue* from 1977 (Figure 1.37). The crispness of the edge is often blunted by the paint's bleeding into the support, a seepage that was enhanced by Yun's turn to hemp and linen rather than canvas as the painting support. Overlapping layers of umber and aquamarine look almost black, but this look is more succinctly described as matte, or velvet-like. As with Kwon's paintings in paper, Yun's emphasis on what Love describes as "texture" compromises painting's image-bearing function. Its capacity to host an autonomous domain explicitly separate from that of the viewer is weakened, although not to such a degree that the work is read exclusively through the nature of its constituent materials. Noted in both Korea and Japan for stressing the relationships among various materials, the artist and critic Lee Ufan applauded Yun for not forcing his own intentions onto the work: "Neither the brush nor the umber paint is a slave or tool used for expression."[99]

Perhaps the best indication of Yun's intention was the display of *Umber Blue* for the 1975 São Paulo Bienal (Figure 1.38). Kim Chŏng-su, the commissioner of the South Korean section for this version of the biennale, stated that the installation was arranged for practical reasons, to fit as many works as possible within a small space.[100] Yet the end-to-end placement of works clearly revealed Yun's attitude toward unmarked space. Audiences would have seen the paintings as one continuous frieze divided by phases of dark and light, an effect heightened by Yun's decision to leave the paintings unframed, highly unusual for Korean painting at this time.[101] Absent a frame, the painting seemed coterminous with the wall and the space to which the viewers belonged. Viewers were encouraged to approach the canvas, and in so doing, they eventually reidentified the mark as a function of spreading oil and solvent. The apprehension of this spread compelled viewers to distribute attention differently by catalyzing the surrender of their belief in painting as an integrated and holistic work based on a centripetal structure.

For Kwon Young-woo and Yun Hyongkeun, the initial goal lay in challenging viewers to reconsider how they understood painting via categories like "ink painting" or "Western painting." Structurally, however, both artists recognized the potential of distinctions, as made especially clear by the possibilities and limitations inherent in using certain tools and materials. They saw the distinctions between various media as an invitation to consider more extensively the possibilities of materiality. This did not mean simply unraveling painting into a loose constellation of unworked materials or upholding reductive beliefs in the "purity" of painting. If the works of Kwon and Yun had a subject, it lay in the evocation of particular details that could only be traced back to the moment at which certain materials were brought together—for instance, the moment when oil made contact with raw canvas, or the moment when fingernails were scraped against a pulpy paper surface. These details demanded of the viewer a deeper level of somatic involvement than could otherwise be achieved through essentializing views of medium. The point was to work with distinctions, not for or against them.

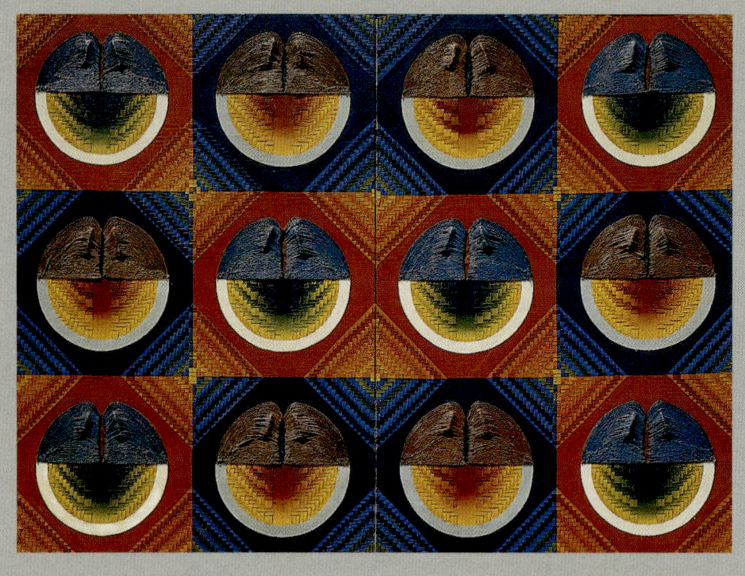

TWO

Rates of Exchange in Ha Chonghyun's *Conjunction*

W

hen Kwon Young-woo and Yun Hyongkeun took up abstraction, they did so against a background in which the idea of abstraction not only was about Western versus Oriental painting but also was grounded in the way Korean artists understood the "international art world" (*kukche misulgye*) as a function of dueling rates of change. In the 1966 roundtable discussion hosted by Seoul National University on the subject of international exhibitions, oil painter Yun Myeong-ro, himself associated with gestural abstraction, questioned the attitude of those who believed that since "contemporary Korean painting" was "only twenty years old," it "must persevere for another 480 years in order to reach the level of the West," whose art history spanned "five hundred years."[1] Already sensitive to their increasing marginalization within a self-consciously contemporary art world that persisted in upholding the boundaries separating Western painting from Oriental painting, ink painters were especially vocal in their disapprobation. In the same roundtable discussion where Yun Myeong-ro voiced his concerns over those anxious about the seeming tardiness of contemporary Korean art, Suh Se-ok tartly asked in reply whether it was then the case that "the West must persevere for thousands of years to reach the level of inkbrush painting in Korea."[2] There was a sense of acceleration generated by the increasing speed at which the Korean art world absorbed information about overseas artistic developments. Supporting this acceleration was a flourishing circuit of biennales, triennales, and other recurring large-scale arts events intended to bring together delegations from all over the world. Many tansaekhwa artists participated in this circuit, including Ha Chonghyun, Suh Seung-won, and Lee Ufan, whose work appeared in the Paris Biennale in 1965, 1969, and 1971. Likewise, Yun Hyongkeun was chosen to show work in the 1969 São Paulo Bienal. After Japan and South Korea restored

FIGURE 2.1 Ha Chonghyun, *Birth-B*, 1965. Oil and yarn on canvas, 144 × 193 cm. Collection of the artist.

diplomatic ties in 1965, the quantity of information and frequency of exchange increased dramatically.

Yet, as suggested by Yun Myeong-ro's remarks at the 1966 discussion at Seoul National University, the accelerated pace at which information was circulated also increased the risk of obsolescence, creating much anxiety for some Korean artists and critics, who already struggled with rebuilding an art world seriously affected by the trauma of the Korean War. Complicating this struggle was a resounding sense of belatedness that intensified after diplomatic relations between Japan and South Korea were restored in 1965. Although this event greatly hastened the speed at which Korean artists became integrated into a presumptive international art world, particularly through improved prospects for showing work overseas, it also renewed memories of Japanese colonial occupation, which had ended only twenty years earlier. Much of the ambivalence over this period was channeled through discussions arising over categories of medium and genre established in tandem with Japanese colonial rule; of special note were the frequent attacks on ink paintings that appeared to borrow too heavily from the materials and techniques associated with *nihonga*.

More evocative still were the efforts of artists like Ha Chonghyun to reconsider the medium of painting. Having attracted early attention for his ability to make work in lockstep with movements identified as current outside Korea, such as informel and op art, Ha also made freestanding three-dimensional work that resonated with the Mono-ha, the Japanese artistic movement that emerged around 1968 that was soon closely followed by many younger Korean artists. Spurred in large part by the writings and works of Korean-born artist and critic Lee Ufan, the Mono-ha advocated seemingly casual arrangements of nonspecific objects in order to escape both the reductive categories of medium through which art in Japan was perceived, as reflected by the circulation of terms like "antiart" and "nonart." For Ha, such art-versus-nonart distinctions were less meaningful than what might be yielded from exploring the distinctions allegedly separating painting from sculpture and vice versa. In *Conjunction*, the series of paintings he began some time in 1972 or 1973, Ha called upon viewers to integrate problems arising from the experience of three-dimensional objects into their understanding of painting. In so doing, he proved himself most invested in producing a type of abstraction that was physically specific in a way that other modes of abstraction were not.

IN ACCELERATION: KOREAN ART AND THE BIENNALE CIRCUIT

From the end of the Korean War in 1953 to the mid-1960s, the pace of the international art world for Korean artists seemed determined by what took place in New York and Paris. Those Korean artists fortunate enough to show in Paris were held in awe by their less peripatetic colleagues. In 1956 *Sin misul* eagerly reported the details of Kim Whanki's solo exhibition at the Galerie Bénézit in Paris.[3] Even though the gallery was only of modest importance in the Parisian art world, the anonymous writer for *Sin misul* made a point of emphasizing that Kim's show was the first time a Korean artist had had a solo show in "Paris, the center of the international art world."[4] Two years later, another anonymous writer shared these sentiments, exclaiming, "Paris! Just hearing the name makes our limbs tremble."[5]

Some Korean critics tried to calibrate artworks according to what they saw as the current trend in New York. In 1965 Ha Chonghyun made *Birth-B* (Figure 2.1) by weaving colorful strips of canvas into a nonrepresentational geometric pattern. Despite its emphasis on decorative patterns and on depicting craft as a function of manual labor, *Birth-B*, which was shown in the 1966 Invitational Exhibition of Contemporary Artists, was heralded by critics in Korea as a Korean instance of op art vis-à-vis shows like *The Responsive Eye*, the large group exhibition held at the Museum of Modern Art that year. Another example was the promotion of Lee Seung-jio, whose painting *Nucleus G-99* (Figure I.8) was cited as a "Special Selection" (*T'ŭksŏn*) by the Kukchŏn jury in 1970.[6] These connections were undone almost as quickly as they were made, and by 1968 op art was being criticized by critics once involved in its promotion.[7]

The speed with which these calibrations were made and unmade was partly a function of the degree to which the Korean art world gleaned its information from the burgeoning circuit of biennales in the 1960s. Hardly a relaxed gathering of like-minded artists, this circuit revolved around what Oh Kwangsu called "searing competition."[8] Recalling the 1964 and 1966 Venice Biennales in the September 1968 issue of the general-interest journal *Sedae*, Oh observed that France and the United States each sought to establish international precedence over the other. He pointed out that 1964 was the year Robert Rauschenberg claimed the international prize for painting at the Venice Biennale, and that 1966 was the year French artists and artists represented by French galleries received their due.[9] It was telling that the first instance of Korean participation in the international biennale circuit was the delegation sent to the Second Paris Biennale, which offered a relatively easy point of entry, given its focus on artists under the age of thirty-five.[10]

For Korean artists, the stakes of this "searing competition" were raised by their sense of affiliation with a broader Third World mandate to push back against Euro-American influence. In explicit or implicit response to the established biennales and triennales was the staging of comparable events intended as alternatives, or even correctives, to those held in major European capitals and in São Paulo, such as the stunningly ambitious World Festival of Negro Arts initiated by Senegal's president Léopold Senghor. Held in 1966, this massive event sought to consolidate a global black identity based on ideas that Senghor tried to advance through the négritude movement, developed as an ideological response to French sociopolitical domination, exploitation, and racism.[11] In Asia, a number of biennales emerged in the 1960s, including the International Exhibition of Fine Arts, which took place in Saigon in 1962 and was meant to follow "the examples of Venice, São Paulo, and Paris."[12] Twenty-one countries were invited to send artists to participate in what was basically a communion of anti-Communist countries "friendly" to the Vietnamese government then under duress from insurgent Communist forces, a mission that cohered well with the anti-Communist government of newly installed South Korean president Park Chung-hee.[13] The foreword to the exhibition catalog cited a visit from a Korean delegation that had gone to Vietnam in hopes of establishing a recurring international exhibition that would travel between New Delhi, Bangkok, Manila, Taipei, Saigon, and Seoul.[14]

The exhibition promised to be among the leading visual arts events in Asia, a hope that was unfortunately extinguished with the escalation of the Vietnam War. As an alternative, some artists and critics in Korea considered remaking the annual Invitational Exhibition of Contemporary Artists into a future "Biennale de Seoul." In a letter to Austrian artist Adolf Frohner, Park Seobo referred to the Invitational Exhibition of Contemporary Artists as the "mother" of a future biennale in Seoul.[15] Park had returned not long before from participating in the Second Paris Biennale, also known as the *Young Painters of the World* (*Jeunes Peintres du monde*) exhibition, where he had established a rapport with Otto Muehl, later the cofounder of Viennese actionism. Muehl, who would perform his first "*aktion*" not long after this meeting, had seen in the works of the bald-headed young man from Korea the glimmers of a kindred spirit: "He is a very good painter" and "works in a similar manner to us [Muehl and fellow actionist Frohner], using all kinds of material."[16] Described by Bang Keun-taek not long afterward as a man of "fiery ambition," Park was likewise taken with the works of Muehl and Frohner and invited them to show in Korea, in the Sixth Invitational Exhibition of Contemporary Artists.[17] The invitation was enthusiastically received by Muehl, who told his collaborator, artist Erika Stocker, that "Korea offers a singular opportunity. We can achieve an international breakthrough [there]."[18] The invitation to show in Seoul and Muehl's reception suggested a different view of the world. Seoul may have been a novel stopover on an itinerary that began and ended in Western Europe, able to confer international status by the mere fact of its remoteness from New York or Paris. Moreover, the reciprocity of appreciation expressed by Park and Muehl for each other's work suggested an art world in the round. In this world, artists from two widely separated places could be allowed to arrive at similar artistic conclusions without being accused of being derivative or of lacking creativity.

The persistence with which some artists and critics took New York and Paris as the measure by which to evaluate the pace of contemporary Korean art troubled other commentators, including those who encouraged certain modes of depiction initially practiced in these cities. Bang Keun-taek, whose first exposure to non-Korean art had allegedly taken place during his tenure as a translation officer in the Korean army during the Korean War, established his reputation as a critic in the late 1950s by enthusiastically promoting what he and certain other colleagues designated Korean informel.[19] Yet by 1963 he was urging readers to remember that "the West is not the center of the world."[20] Speaking of the enthusiastic reception of informel-like abstraction among younger Korean artists, Bang stressed the need to find what is "ours," or at the very least, the need to refrain from blindly accepting both the modes of expression, and in turn, the standards of Euro-America.[21] Park Seobo, the former doyen of gestural abstraction, turned more overtly to a particular arrangement of colors reminiscent of that associated with *tanch'ŏng*, a traditional technique of architectural decoration whose most visually distinctive characteristic is its reliance on five colors—blue green, white, a vermillion-like red, black, and golden yellow—signifying the directions east, west, south, north, and center (Figure 2.2). In shifting toward this kind of color scheme, Park ascribed to his geometric abstractions an intention to convey a distinct sense of cultural identity that could separate his work from its presumed counterparts.

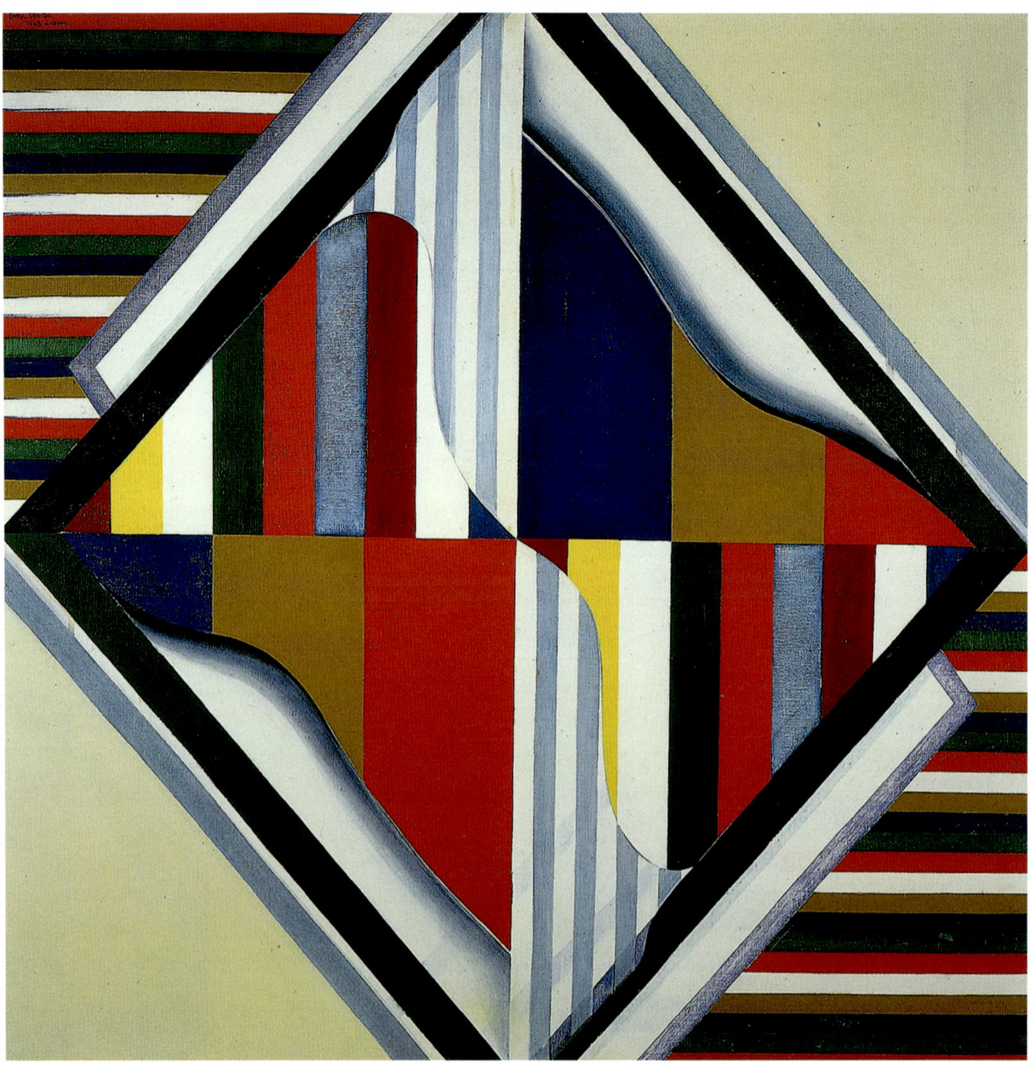

FIGURE 2.2 Park Seobo, *Yujonjil 4-68*, 1968. Oil on canvas, 131 × 131 cm. Collection of National Museum of Contemporary Art, Korea. Photograph by Lee Man-hong.

VIA JAPAN: ARTISTIC EXCHANGE AFTER 1965

The general sense of acceleration that accompanied Korean artists'
entry into the international biennale circuit greatly intensified after
South Korea and Japan reestablished diplomatic relations in 1965.
Anxious to develop capitalism in the East Asian region in order to
contain the threat of communism posed by China and the Soviet Union,
the United States was instrumental in brokering the normalization
of relations between the two former antagonists, especially because
of their respective geographic proximities to North Korea, the Soviet
Union, and China.[22]

For Japan, normalized relations with South Korea meant the continuation of an asymmetrical economic relationship in which South
Korea was both a steady source of cheap labor and a ready market for
Japanese goods. Conversely, it also meant the introduction of a new
artistic frontier to Japanese collectors being increasingly priced out of
a rapidly expanding domestic art market.[23] Prices for Korean art rose in
the early 1970s, but the work of an established Korean artist with a solid
record of exhibitions and critical attention could nevertheless expect
to fetch less than half of what was paid for works by Japanese artists
at comparable points in their careers.[24] In Japan, the work of a midcareer artist could expect to fetch up to 100,000 yen per *ho* (about
22.7 × 15.8 centimeters, roughly the size of two postcards) in the
Japanese art market, whereas a midcareer Korean artist commanded
at best only 50,000 yen per *ho*.[25] Oh Kwangsu claimed that the disparity
was far more pronounced than reported, asserting that while emerging artists in both countries sold work for about 5,000 won per *ho*, an
established Japanese ink painter's works could cost as much as 800,000
won per *ho*, whereas the works of established-to-midlevel artists in
Korea brought 20,000–30,000 won per *ho*.[26] Tempted by the promise of acquiring high-quality work for much less than what they were
accustomed to paying at home, Japanese buyers entered the Korean art
market between 1970 and 1973, just before the OPEC oil shock.[27]

For Korean artists, the restoration of diplomatic ties between
South Korea and Japan meant greater access to more and more varied
kinds of information. Although some cultural exchange between South
Korea and Japan had taken place prior to 1965, it was only beginning
in the late 1960s that Korean artists really began to show their work
in Japan.[28] In January 1966 the progovernment daily *Sŏul sinmun* ran
a large feature on the emergence of Korean artists in Japan.[29] Also

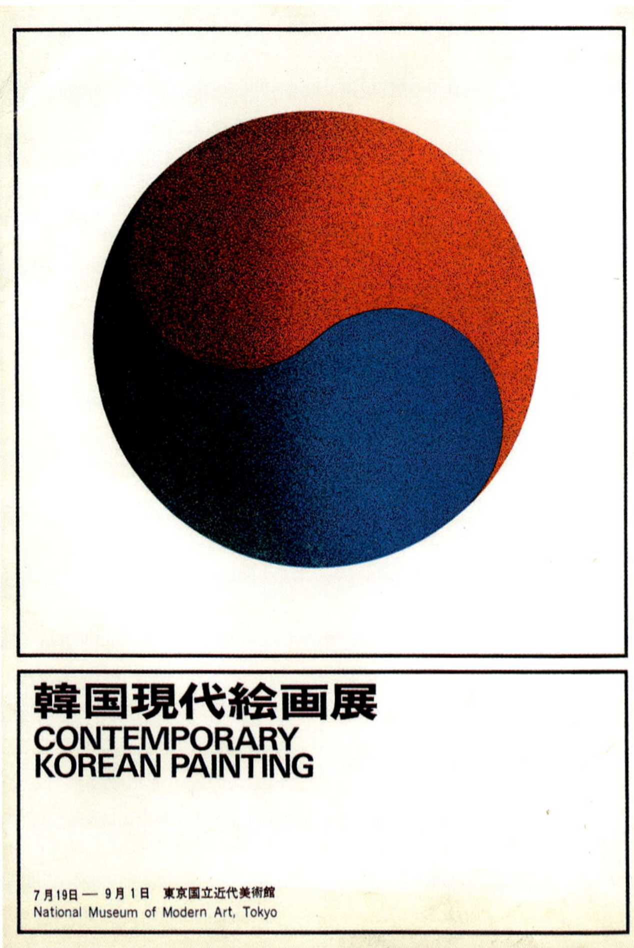

in that year, the Japanese National Committee for UNESCO hosted
the International Symposium on the Fine Arts in the East and the
West. Held in Tokyo, the symposium explored the impact of Asian and
Western art on contemporary art.[30] South Korean artists who went to
Japan tended to be well established and well connected, prerequisites
at a time when the South Korean state heavily restricted overseas travel
by its citizens. It came as no surprise, for example, that painter Kwon
Ok-yeon, one of the first Korean artists to show his works in Tokyo
after the reestablishment of diplomatic relations, was a judge for the
Kukchŏn, the state-run salon. For viewers in Japan, national concerns
were never very far away, as Thomas Ichinose suggested in his review

of Kwon's 1965 show: "In a time of some tension between the two countries, it is heartening to see a fine Korean artist in one of the best galleries in Tokyo. One only hopes hostility doesn't extend into art."[31]

The most outstanding instance of artistic exchange was the 1968 exhibition *Contemporary Korean Painting* (*Kankoku gendai kaiga ten*), cosponsored by three organizations: the newly established South Korean embassy in Japan, the Korea Information Service (Kongbogwan, an agency set up by the South Korean government to promote Korea and especially Korean culture abroad), and the National Museum of Modern Art in Tokyo. The nature of the exhibition was succinctly defined by the choice of cover for the exhibition cover, a shaded version of the *t'aegŭk*, the symbol on the South Korean national flag (Figure 2.3). As Yoo June-sang noted, the show had implications that reverberated well beyond the domain of art or even culture.[32] Held July 19–September 1, *Contemporary Korean Painting* featured seventy-eight works by twenty artists from all career stages. The idea for the show was first proposed to the museum by artist Lee Se-duk, a frequent art adviser to the state and one of the most enthusiastic supporters of internationalizing Korean art through exhibitions.[33] Together with Honma Masayoshi, the National Museum of Modern Art curator who in Japan ranked among the most active investigators of the meaning of contemporary Japanese art, Lee sought to present the "face of today's Korean art" in Japan, "the country that was at once so near, yet so far."[34] A letter from the exhibition's organizing committee addressed to the culture desk of the *Kyŏnghyang sinmun* described their hopes that the show might culti-vate "a proper awareness of Korea–Japan artistic and cultural exchange as well as grounds of pride for Korean residents living in Japan."[35]

Save for the Tokyo-based artists Quac Insik and Lee Ufan, who were selected by the Tokyo branch of the Korea Information Service, all the artists were chosen by a five-member jury consisting of historian Choi Su-nu (the National Museum's curatorial head) and critics Yi Kyungsung, Lim Young-bang, Yoo June-sang, and Lee Yil. Each judge was asked to nominate a pool of artists from which the final exhibition participants would be chosen after another round of anonymous voting.[36] Selected works ran the gamut from giant pink fluorescent monochromes to gestural abstraction. Especially preva-lent, though, were works regarded as Korean versions of op art (such as Figure 2.4), geometric abstractions similar to those Ha Chonghyun had shown a year earlier in the 1967 Invitational Exhibition of Contemporary Artists.

As the largest show of contemporary art from Korea held outside the country, *Contemporary Korean Painting* was the first major introduction to contemporary Korean art for many Japanese artists, critics, and curators, even for one as well versed in contemporary art as Honma Masayoshi, who exclaimed, "We [in Japan] don't know anything about the Korean art world."[37] The exhibition attracted wide media coverage in both Japan and Korea and many reviews published in Japan were translated into Korean and republished in the December 1968 issue of *Space*.[38] Founded in 1966 and funded in part by the South Korean government, *Space* was the only outlet for art criticism in Korea readily available at bookstores from 1966 until the mid-1970s.[39] But while some critics, such as Arima Hiroaki, praised the show for demonstrating "a unique Korean sensibility," others bemoaned its lack of curatorial depth.[40] Writing in the Japanese design magazine *SD* (on which *Space* was allegedly modeled),[41] the critic Ishiko Junzō insinuated that many of the works shown had failed to convince the viewer of the exhibition's significance because of an impossibly naive view of contemporary art on the part of its organizers and even its participants. He contended that instead of focusing on "how to express the imagined world," too many works seemed to imply that contemporary art was simply about work of recent provenance, or worse, about trends popular in the West.[42]

If Ishiko was unimpressed with what he saw at the National Museum of Modern Art, it might have been a reflection of his own disenchantment with optical illusionism. His own exhibition, *Tricks and Vision: Stolen Eyes*, coorganized with Nakahara Yusuke, featured "tricky" works that investigated the effects of representation intended to deceive the eye and had just closed on May 18, only two months before the opening of *Contemporary Korean Painting*. Still more explicit was Haryū Ichirō's review published in the popular weekly *Asahi Journal*, which saw *Contemporary Korean Painting* as evidence that Korean art, like that of Japan, was far too invested in the trends of New York and Paris; Haryū suggested that the task lay in defining an "Asian conception" of art, modernity, and internationalism.[43]

The harshest evaluations came from the artists and critics who had actually participated in the show. Exhibition juror Lee Yil felt that the artists selected were not very different from those chosen to represent Korea in the international biennales. Though he advocated the inclusion of younger, more "experimental" artists, those who were chosen were almost all established artists, a reflection of jurors' preference for artists who had already shown abroad.[44] Lee expressed his disappointment

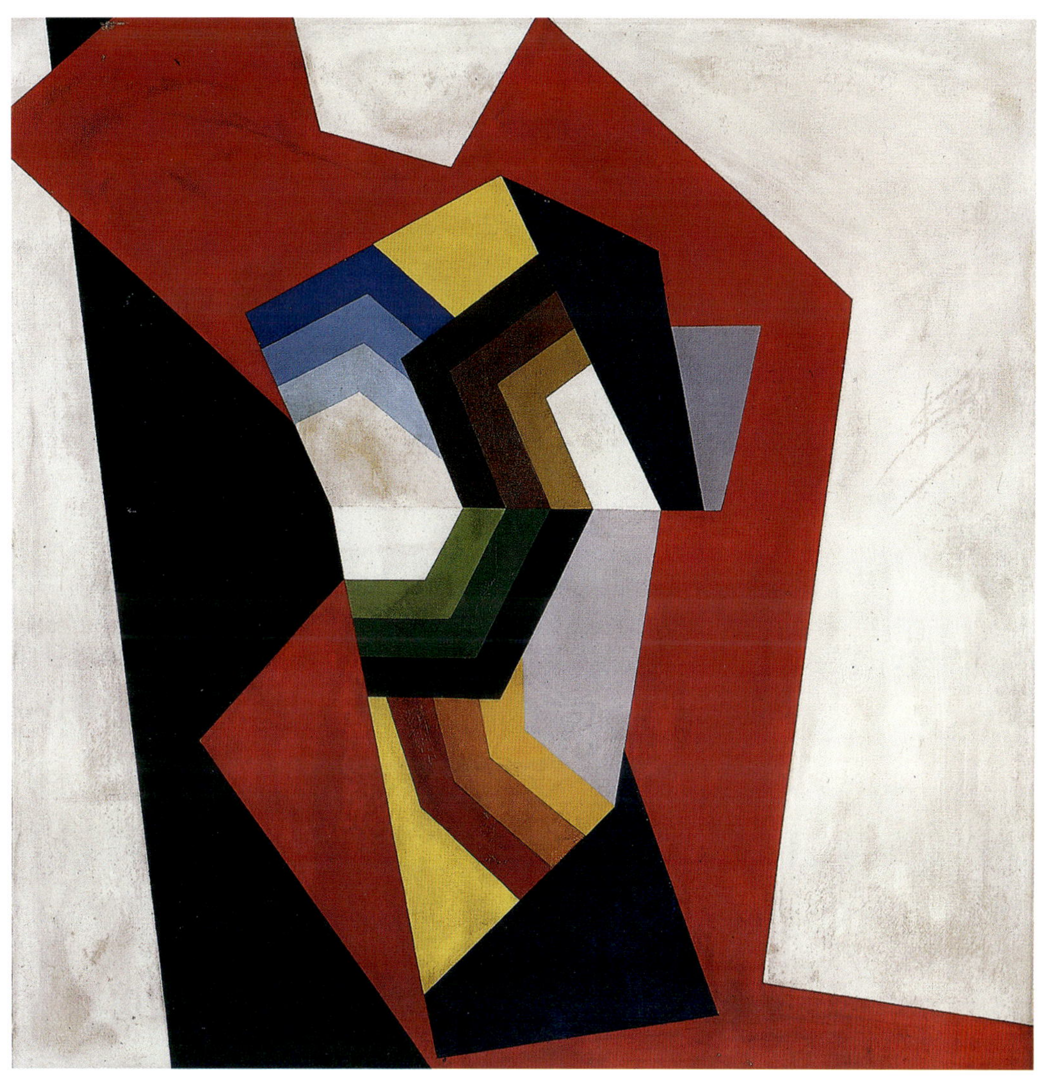

FIGURE 2.4 Ha Chonghyun, *White Paper on Urban Planning*, 1968. Oil on canvas, 80 × 80 cm. Collection of the artist.

over what he saw as a failed "avant-garde" project, even if the show did successfully introduce contemporary Korean art to a Japanese audience.[45] More indicative was the irate exchange between Yoo Youngkuk, then regarded as one of the stalwarts of modern Korean art, and Lee Ufan, who played the role of upstart in the roundtable discussion accompanying *Contemporary Korean Painting*. Despite his situation as an emerging artist struggling for recognition in the competitive Japanese art world of the late 1960s, Lee brashly suggested that cultural difference was insufficient for survival in the international art world; what was needed instead was rigorous interpretation and theory.[46]

Tall, imperious, and possessed of a stylishness so imposing that it made at least one of his peers feel like a "country hick," the fifty-four-year-old Yoo never dreamed that Lee would be so bold in expressing his opinions.[47] He countered Lee's arguments as best he could by asserting that no amount of interpretation or theory, however sophisticated or logical, could ever compensate for fundamentally weak work.[48] Adding further insult was Lee's characterization of Korean culture as problematic. Acknowledging the chilling effect that blind faith in past convention, now rationalized as an expression of nationalism, had on cultural production, Lee argued that Seoul was a place where cultures or cultural trends brought in from elsewhere could not survive.[49] In later years, Park Seobo, who was well acquainted with Lee, Yoo, and the circumstances of the roundtable discussion, would describe an infuriated Yoo telling him of the "young whippersnapper of unknown nationality" who "needed to be taught a lesson."[50] According to Park, Yoo remarked that the "very idea of a young person directly putting forth his ideas on art" was "extremely insolent," a telling indication of the deep generational fault lines beneath the Korean art world.[51]

ON DELAY: THE COLONIAL PAST NOW PRESENT

In less than a decade, the relationship between the Japanese and Korean art worlds grew from near nonexistence to real engagement. In 1971 the Japanese artist Suzuki Yoshinori reported that "almost nothing was known of contemporary Korean art"; in 1973 Park Seobo's solo show at the Muramatsu Gallery was attended by some of the brightest stars of the Japanese art world's firmament. Attendees included the critics Nakahara Yusuke, Minemura Toshiaki, and Ishiko Junzō, as well as leading artists Takamatsu Jirō, Maeda Josaku, and Tanaka Shintarō,

the recent Japanese representative to the 1972 Venice Biennale.[52] A
similar turnout celebrated the opening of *Five Korean Artists, Five
Kinds of White,* the alleged origin of tansaekhwa, which took place at
the Tokyo Gallery in 1975.[53] In 1973 the Myongdong Gallery organized
Abstraction = Situation (*Ch'usang = sanghwang*) and *Plasticity and Anti-
Plasticity* (*Chohyŏng kwa panjohyŏng*), the first attempts in Korea to
mount a historical survey of postwar Korean art. Printed on the invita-
tions to both shows was a short legend stating that the opening would
be "specially visited" by Tokyo Gallery director Yamamoto Takashi,
as well as Nakahara Yusuke and artists Maeda Josaku and Takamatsu
Jirō.[54] Yun Hyongkeun was specifically promoted by Joseph Love, who
urged his colleagues Yamamoto Takashi and Nakahara Yusuke to meet
the artist, which they did at the end of 1975.[55] Yamamoto and Nakahara
later arranged for some examples of *Umber Blue* to be shown at the
Muramatsu Gallery in 1976 and then at the Tokyo Gallery in 1978.[56]
Other exhibitions involving both Korean and Japanese art would take
place throughout the 1970s, including exchanges between universities
as well as commercial galleries.[57]

But the still-recent memory of colonial occupation meant that
Japan was as much a source of anxiety as it was an opportunity for
access. The majority of artists and critics active in the 1960s had been
educated in Japanese schools in Korea or even in Japan. Yi Kyungsung,
a graduate of Waseda University in Tokyo, recalled, "[When I was young],
I thought in Japanese and translated those thoughts into Korean."[58]
Japanese influence persisted; in 1965 the journal *Sedae* devoted the first
part of its October issue to photographs showing alleged instances of
Japanese influence in Korea, from Japanese-language signs on Korean
restaurants to market stalls selling Japanese-language publications.
The captions accompanying those images asked, "Since when did a
Korean become so Japanized?"[59] Korean artists and critics welcomed
the speed at which their world seemed to expand, yet they also worried
about what some regarded as their belatedness in relation to the West.
These concerns intensified as they realized that the expansion of the
Korean art world depended on the growing closeness between Korea
and Japan generally. Just before the debut of *Contemporary Korean
Painting,* the critic Yoo June-sang, in no uncertain terms, cautioned
Korean readers to check their enthusiasm:

Accordingly, the erosion of such regionalism and national
boundaries and the stronger sense of globalism is the current state

of affairs, so that it feels very belated that we are only just beginning
to stand on the [world] stage now. We cannot help but feel awkward,
just like an aging spinster who appears at a formal introduction
only because she is still unmarried.[60]

Yoo further predicted that the show would attract lots of viewers but
that they would come primarily out of "curiosity" rather than out of
any real interest. Indeed, he even went so far as to suggest that some
viewers might look at the show as being "nothing much," or even a pale
imitation of Japanese works, not because the works were inherently
bad but because of the context in which they were framed.[61]

Yoo's pessimism seemed to be confirmed in part by reviewers like
Kim Chong-hak, who realized the hard truth of Korean art's peripheral
status within the contemporary art world by pointing out that Japan's art-
critical establishment paid little real attention to the show except for the
architecture-centric *SD* and the visual arts magazine *Sansai*.[62] In his review
of the 1968 show *Contemporary Korean Painting*, one of the show's participants, Kim Chong-hak, scoffed at the Japanese art world, disdainfully
remarking it was "nothing to write home about, as of yet." However, in
the same breath he also added, "The reality is that the art worlds of Euro-
America pay no attention to us, nor do we have any ties to them. Faced
with this reality, it is only natural that Korean artists turn their attention
to the Japanese art world, to which they can connect."[63] Yet what consti-
tuted a major international enterprise in the eyes of Korean artists and
critics was hardly esteemed as such by their Japanese colleagues.[64]

Kim's suspicions were supported by the statements of Nambata
Tatsuoki, one of the elder statesmen of abstract painting in Japan who
helped found the Free Artists' Association (Jiyū bijutsuka kyōkai), in
whose exhibitions Kim Whanki and Yoo Youngkuk had participated
in the 1930s. Nambata suggested that what qualified as avant-garde in
Korea was a direct function of what occurred earlier in Japan, citing as
an example the works of Yoo Youngkuk. Yoo, who had moved to Tokyo
in 1935, participated in the exhibitions of the NBG (Neo Beaux-Arts
Group), one of the artists' groups that emerged in 1930s Tokyo to rebel
against established forms of art and concurrently move toward the new.
That Yoo partook of Japan's earlier embrace of abstract art made him
a member of the vanguard. "Postwar abstract art," Nambata observed,
"would be led by the members of these groups. . . . Given this [situation],
Yoo is a pioneer of avant-garde Korean painting and a vanguard for
change in Korean painting."[65]

Many Korean critics and artists, including most tansaekhwa artists, were old enough to remember life in colonial Korea, particularly the difficult final years preceding Japan's defeat in World War II. They struggled openly with what the critic Lee Yil called a "dichotomy between emotion and reason" in which artists and critics tried to come to terms with their perceptions of colonial rule and their present dependence on the Japanese art world.[66] Kim Whanki, himself educated in Tokyo at the height of the colonial era, declared that efforts to establish an independent avant-garde in Korea during the first third of the twentieth century were effectively blocked "by Japan." It was not, he implied, only the lack of political or even psychological sovereignty that disabled the attempt to construct an autonomous avant-garde, but also the lack of alternative conduits through which to have access to information about theories and techniques. The artists who went to study in Tokyo, including himself, learned nothing but "what was second-, or third-hand information from Europe."[67] In like manner, Oh Kwangsu argued to his A.G. peers that although Korea had been independent from Japan for some thirty years, its political liberation did not mean cultural liberation.[68] He stressed the point again that year in the multidisciplinary journal *Yesulgye*. Criticizing what he regarded as "cultural colonization," or the continued dependence of Korean art on Japanese institutions, modes of organization, and infrastructure, Oh demanded to know why "artists in their forties and older, who were trained in the Japanese art educational system, felt absolutely no urge to question this training."[69] Both he and Kim suggested that Korean artists were mired in a state of delay, perpetually behind what was taking place in Japan.

Anxiety over this supposed delay was sharply indicated by the considerable ambivalence expressed over taxonomical approaches to medium as imposed by colonial institutions established during the Japanese colonial era. By the early 1970s, categories like "Western painting" and "Oriental painting" had been sufficiently challenged as to render suspicious any attempt to insist on medium specificity predicated on an emphasis on materials; the disbanding of the Ink Forest Society was a case in point. That such categories persisted nevertheless reflected the extent to which colonial-era distinctions continued to affect artmaking in postcolonial, postwar Korea.

Consider, for example, what in 1974 was touted as the "greatest controversy of the Korean art world."[70] In the June issue of *Space*, a young professor of Buddhist art named Moon Myung-dae severely criticized the works of Suh Se-ok exhibited at the Hyundai Gallery on March

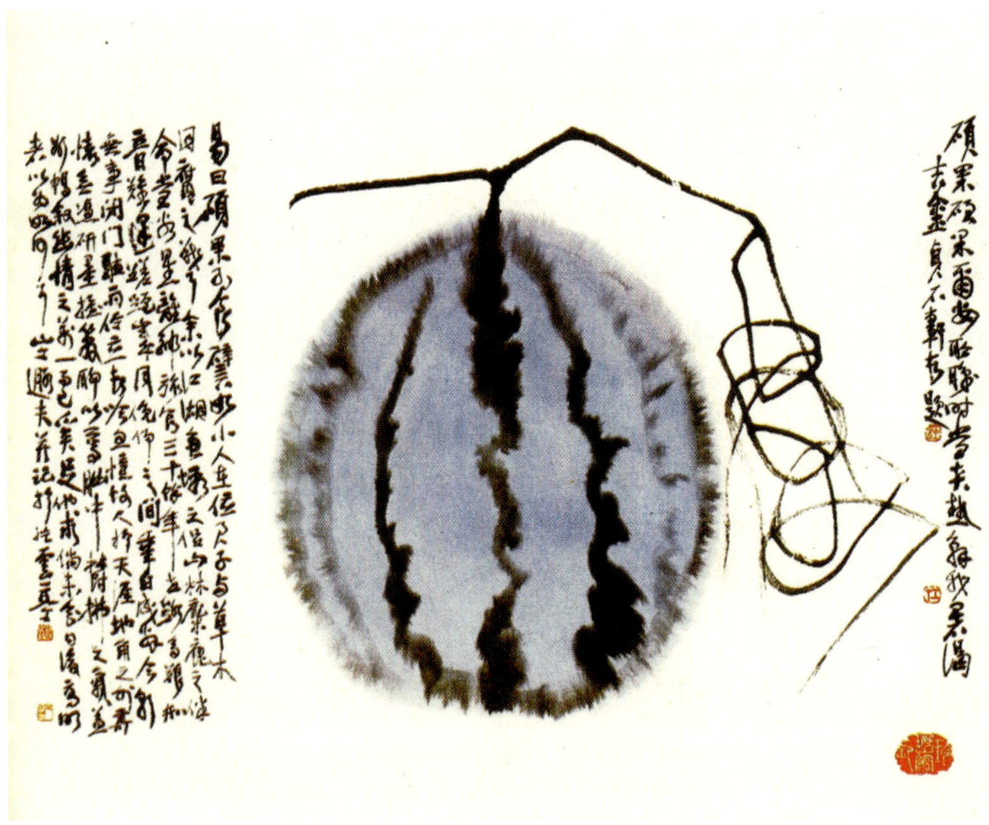

21–30, accusing Suh of copying techniques found in Japanese inkbrush painting and *nihonga*. In works like *Pitted Fruit* (Figure 2.5), as in many of his previous works, Suh investigated how the seepage of heavily diluted color might unintentionally give rise to new ways of visualizing form. This dilution looped back into earlier explorations of the behavior of ink, although this time it took place within the context of figuration. To Moon, however, this seepage all but ignored the line, one of traditional Korean inkbrush painting's most essential components.[71]

What made the critique especially inflammatory was not the charge of derivativeness but what Moon implied by his choice of authority. Citing *Painting and Sagacity* (*Hoehwa wa yeji*), a treatise written by the critic Yun Hi-sun in 1945, Moon cast heavy aspersions on Suh's ideological orientation.[72] Written two years before Yun's death in 1947, *Painting and Sagacity* rehashed ideas he had developed in his 1932 essay "Problems Facing the Chosŏn Art World." Sparing no group of artists or mode of depiction then in active operation, he attacked artists for being essentially apolitical, for being, as he described it, unable to reflect the situation of the people.[73] Moon's article insinuated that because Suh's works copied Japanese painting techniques, they were tantamount to the reification of a colonialist mind-set, one that repositioned Korean art behind the achievements of Japanese art.

The *Chosun ilbo* reported that Suh responded to Moon's accusations by stating, "[Those who] make the extremist claim that my works are '*nihonga* compradors' because they employ 'techniques of diffusion' [are expressing] the narrow-minded opinion of someone who knows nothing of even the basics of inkbrush painting."[74] Although Suh claims that the newspaper misquoted him, Moon's accusations must have been especially provoking, given Suh's activities with the Ink Forest Society, which initially arose out of a desire to purge *nihonga* influence from Korean art.[75] The *Chosun ilbo* reported Suh as defending himself against Moon's criticisms: "The works I have done throughout my life have been [created in order] to drive out vestiges of *nihonga* [from Korean art]."[76]

Park Yong-sook, then the editor of *Space*, recalls the incident as an internal struggle for power within the Korean art world, a struggle whose origins date to the 1950s. By the 1970s Suh was among the most powerful individuals in the Korean art world by virtue of his position in the Korean Fine Arts Association (Han'guk misul hyŏp'oe), the largest artists' organization in South Korea, formed in 1961 by order of Park Chung-hee's new government. Much of the association's power derived from its capacity to form and select the members of delegations to international biennales and triennales. Suh was also a professor at Seoul National University, which had a fierce, and often bitter, rivalry for art world supremacy with Hongik University, a rivalry dating to 1955, when graduates of Seoul National University abandoned the Taehan Art Association.[77] After visual artists were consolidated into the Korean Fine Arts Association in 1961 by order of the state, the two universities' teachers, students, and alumni all battled to gain control over the association. If an inference can be made from the number of artists chosen by the association to represent Korea in the three biennales to which the country was most frequently invited (Paris, São Paulo, and Tokyo), the competition ended mostly in a draw until the early 1970s.[78] By the time of Suh's exhibition at the Hyundai Gallery, however, the power dynamics seemed to have shifted in favor of "the Hongik University clique [*Hongdaep'a*], whose influence threatened to prevail over that of Seoul National University."[79] Although not part of the Seoul National–Hongik duopoly that controlled the fields of art history, aesthetics, and fine arts in South Korea, Moon was still able to secure a position at Korea's leading Buddhist institution, Dongguk University. His critique of Suh's exhibition can be read as a double symptom of the generational and status divides underwriting the Korean art world at that time. Certainly it touched a raw nerve and provoked a furious onslaught of rebuttals from Suh and his Seoul National University protégés, which another critic, Kim Yun-su, deplored a year later as a textbook example of the breakdown of communication between the artist and the critic.[80]

Equally important, however, was the timing of Moon's article. It was published in 1974, when it became relatively common for well-to-do Korean artists to rent gallery space in Japan, partly in response to the comparatively few galleries in Seoul. The October 1973 issue of *Bijutsu techō*, for example, carried exhibition listings from fifty galleries in Tokyo; by contrast, Seoul had only six galleries that were not exclusively for rent.[81] Even more apparent was the tendency among younger artists to closely follow Japanese artistic developments. Moon's article thus reflected the general ambivalence felt by some Korean critics toward a contemporary art world that seemed increasingly dependent on Japan's artistic infrastructure. It was around this time too that a small but vocal legion of Korean critics tried to identify what it was that made certain works distinctively "Korean." That categories of medium and genre introduced during the colonial era should lie at the heart of these debates implicitly reminded artists and viewers to think about, and also through, the distinctions separating one mode of depiction from another.

THE MONO-HA EFFECT

On this count it was not surprising to find many Korean artists drawn to the works of the Mono-ha, the loose constellation of artists that first emerged in Japan at the very end of the 1960s and rose to critical prominence in the early 1970s. Works by artists like Sekine Nobuo, Koshimizu Susumu, Yoshida Katsuro, Narita Katsuhiko, Suga Kishio, and especially Lee Ufan resonated with the efforts of Korean artists to, as Oh Kwangsu remarked of the works of Kwon Young-woo in 1968, work around the "conventional idea that holds a painting as that which must be contained by a canvas [and the similarly conventional tendency to] draw a clear line between painting and sculpture."[82] Literally the "School of Things," the Mono-ha emerged out of a shared commitment among its presumed members to present a world to which access was contingent not on the identity, background, or knowledge level of the viewer but instead on the viewer's capacities to see, touch, and perhaps even hear. Group members intentionally turned to naturally occurring or untreated materials such as unprocessed cotton, metal plates, rope, wooden planks, and glass panes, which they subsequently arranged in ways that felt simultaneously obvious and unexpected.

In *Phase: Mother Earth* (Figure 2.6), the work generally accepted as the first Mono-ha work, Sekine Nobuo dug a giant hole in the ground of Suma Rikyu Park in Kobe near Osaka. Displaced earth was mixed with concrete and then carefully molded into the shape of an enormous cylinder, which was placed next to the hole, a juxtaposition that was at once astonishingly literal and cannily evocative of the relationship between the made and the unmade. The work was reviewed a year later for the June 1969 issue of *Sansai* by Lee Ufan, the young Tokyo-based artist and critic who had made a name for himself with his provocative contribution to the *Contemporary Korean Painting* roundtable. He praised what he regarded as Sekine's ability to enable viewers to more vividly experience the world as a material phenomenon grounded in

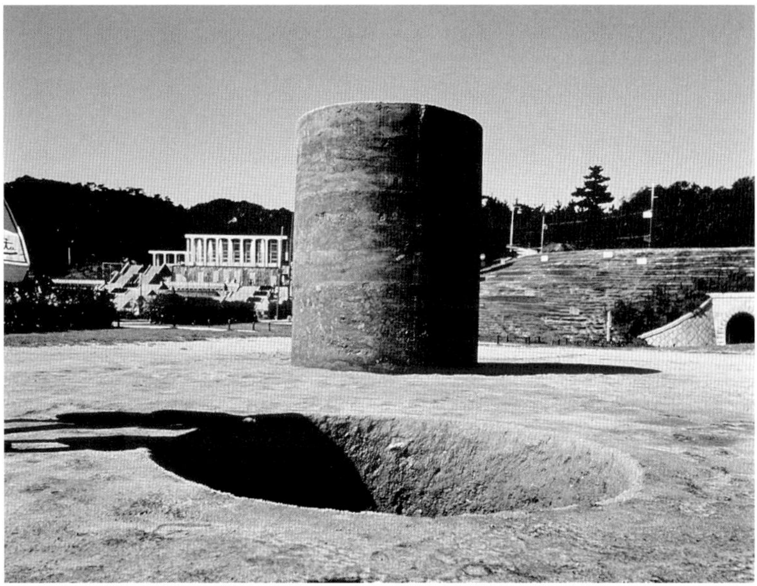

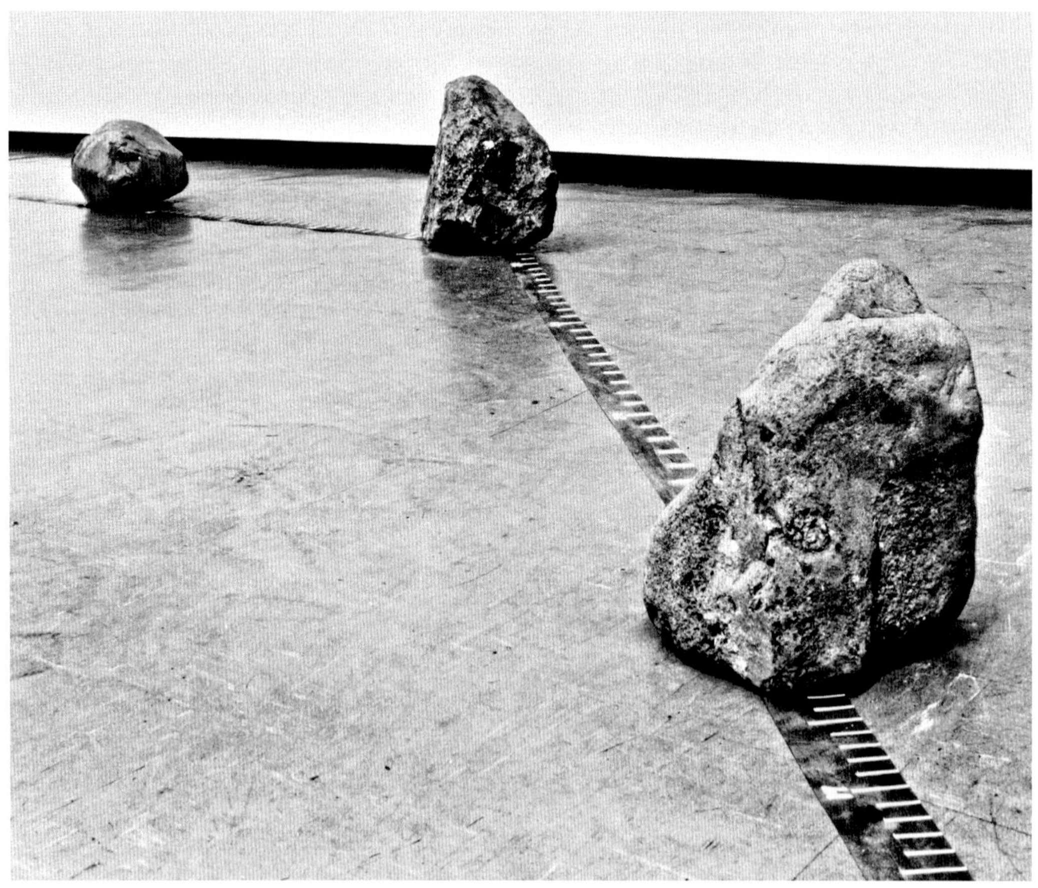

FIGURE 2.7 Lee Ufan, *Cognizance and Mark* (also titled *Phenomena and Perception A* and *Relatum*), 1969. Chalk, rubber, and stones; dimensions variable. Private collection. Courtesy The Pace Gallery. Copyright Lee Ufan.

the balance between the visible and the invisible, as well as between appearance and disappearance.[83]

Lee himself was the primary conduit through which Korean audiences became acquainted with Mono-ha ideas and works. A month after his review of *Phase: Mother Earth* appeared in *Sansai, Space* published Lee's review of the Ninth Contemporary Art Exhibition of Japan. Sponsored by the newspaper company Mainichi Shimbun, these were a series of exhibitions that, during the late 1960s, offered the most comprehensive snapshot of contemporary art in Japan since the dissolution of the Yomiuri Independent exhibitions in 1964. The review of the ninth exhibition, which took place in May 1969, portrayed a contemporary Japanese art scene whose most advanced practitioners were those interested in selecting and placing various objects in ways that would make visible not only the material properties of each object but also the affective tensions that might not ordinarily be discerned without such careful selection and placement. As Lee was quick to point out:

Although not included in this show, there are many young artists
in their teens and twenties whose works are worth considering.
For example, works consisting of a large piece of paper whose four
corners are weighted by stones, or of a rock wrapped with a metal
chain and tied to a post, as if it were a dog.[84]

Lee's discussion attempted to frame contemporary Japanese art to Korean viewers in a very particular light. The review also coincided with Lee's own participation in the Thirteenth Invitational Exhibition of Contemporary Artists in Seoul, where he submitted *Cognizance and Mark* (Figure 2.7), also known as *Phenomena and Perception A* and later as *Relatum*. The work consisted of a few stones placed at various intervals on a giant rubber tape measure. According to the critic Oh Kwangsu, the work only made sense if one first examined the material properties of its parts, such as the "height of the stone, [or] the minimum volume of the string rule." He suggested that it was futile to think of the work in any other way; to him Lee was trying to argue that "a work of art is a mark and [an act of] cognizance before it is an expression."[85]

Oh's comments alluded to what would be a signature concept for Lee, and indeed for certain Mono-ha artists: a refusal of "making" (*tsukuru*), which in turn meant refusing to treat the world and the objects contained therein as simply material for appropriation. In a roundtable discussion published in the February 1970 issue of *Bijutsu techō*, which first applied the term "mono" to the works of six artists later regarded as Mono-ha's core, including Sekine and Lee, another artist, Suga Kishio, identified artistic intention as a necessary component of such making.[86] Yet Suga was not interested in describing his own works as instances of "antiart" (*han geijutsu*), the term introduced by Lee's friend, the critic Tōnō Yoshiaki, to refer to a variety of artistic efforts intended to challenge conventional artmaking in Japan during the early to middle 1960s.[87] Nor did "nonart" (*hi geijutsu*), a term introduced in 1970, seem to adequately describe what Suga or his colleagues were trying to do with these presentations of juxtaposed materials.[88] For Suga, the challenge lay in engaging directly with the assumptions through which objects passed into the domain of art. In *Phase: Mother Earth* Sekine paid close attention to the possibilities of considering the artwork both as free from calculation and as resulting from an intense process. The venue is itself the material, yet both the depth of the hole and the height of the cylinder are scaled to something other than the proportions of the average adult, a fact emphasized by Murai Osamu's well-known photograph in which the cylinder stands like a monument over the hole from which it originally emerged. Here the work revolves less around a consideration of materials used than around artistic choice: At what point did Sekine decide to stop digging? What determined the distance between the hole and the cylinder? More significantly, what of the contrast between the apparent formal, even tautological, simplicity of the work and the considerable amount of physical labor expended in its production?

For Lee, the refusal of making was channeled through what he described as an "encounter":

Fundamentally, I refuse the act of making. Generally, people place the subject in front of them, and try to conform that image to their own selves, in order to make something. But they need to realize that things do not conform to their will. In these cases, I want to liberate the image that is in my head and enable an encounter between myself and the subject. When the subject and I converse on equal grounds, a completely new being appears.[89]

The strong phenomenological current in Lee's thinking is borne out by the titles of his early works, including *Phenomena and Perception A* and *Phenomenology and Perception* in reference to Maurice Merleau-Ponty's most seminal work. At first glance, works like *Relatum* (earlier titled

Phenomenology and Perception) from 1969 (Figure 2.8) recall those of *arte povera*, the term coined by the Italian critic and curator Germano Celant in 1967 to refer to a host of works that shared an affinity for naturally occurring or untreated materials. The materials Lee used were so common as to descend below the level of the everyday and into a state of valuelessness, yet they still remained within the domain of art. On this count, Lee's works differ sharply from minimalism, whose popularity in Japan peaked during the much-discussed Tenth Tokyo Biennale held in 1970 at the Tokyo Metropolitan Art Museum.[90] Curated by Nakahara Yusuke and titled *Between Man and Matter*, it offered a chance for Nakahara, who saw the international art world in terms of what he described as "worldwide competitiveness," to prove to both Japanese and Western viewers that contemporary Japanese art was developing on par with its Western counterparts, particularly those involved with minimalism and postminimalism.[91]

Contrary to the minimalists, who had a penchant for objects that looked neutral and intentionally detached from any specific provenance, Lee and his Mono-ha colleagues, many of whom participated in the Tenth Tokyo Biennale, favored objects that bore the trace of earlier usage. They gravitated toward things that looked worn, rumpled, cut, broken, and, above all, used. Lee, for example, often spoke of his affection for ruins, that state when an object's material existence is primarily mediated by the visibility of its erosion and "before which I feel great humility and emotion."[92] Lee's works thus read in some respects as a rejoinder to the almost puritanical reductionism attributed to certain minimalist works that strove to achieve an ideal form devoid of traces that might link such works back to a particular time or place, or as Lee wrote, to the minimalist attempt to separate the image from the larger, phenomenological site of the "world."[93] In *Relatum* from 1969 (Figure 2.8), for example, the uneven mass, weight, and hardness of rocks are evoked in their placement on top of a glass plate whose transparency and fragility are made evident in turn. Likewise, in a *Relatum* work shown as part of the Korean delegation for the 1971 Paris Biennale (Figure 2.9), a rubber sheet is pulled by two stones placed diagonally across it. The pliable support wrinkles beneath the weight of the stone, so as to underscore the material properties of both the stone and the support. The work illustrates Lee's standing motto of wanting "to see everything as it is, the world as it is" as an engagement with another famous dictum, Frank Stella's celebrated instruction of 1964, "What you see is what you see."[94] The tautological force of the latter hinges upon

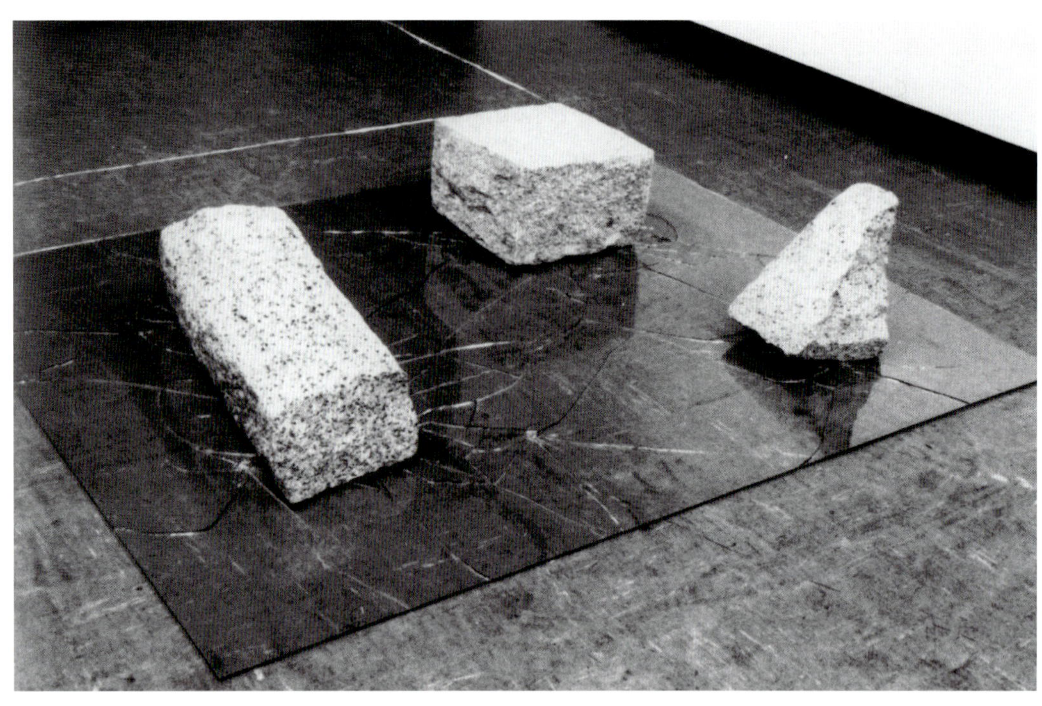

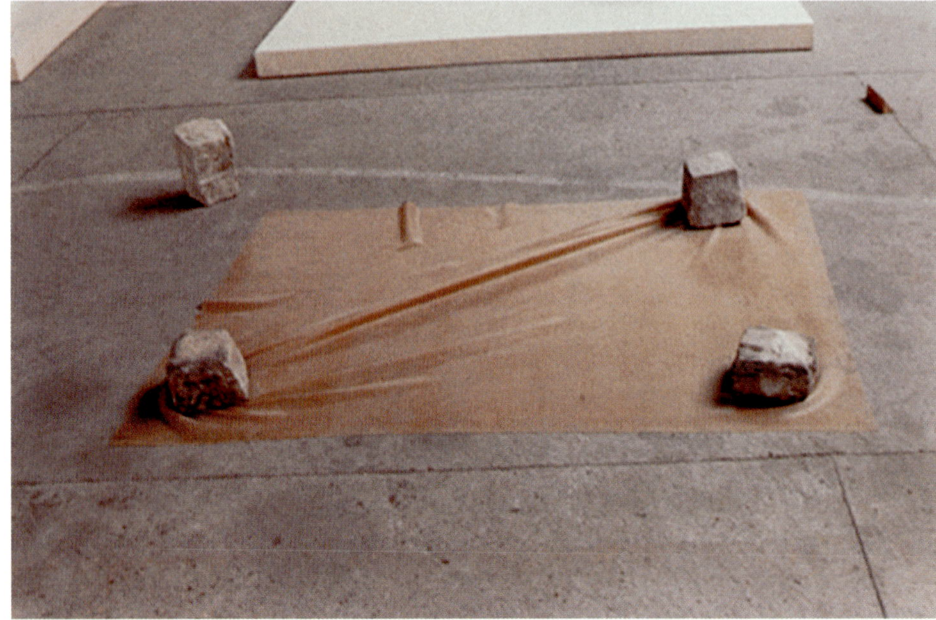

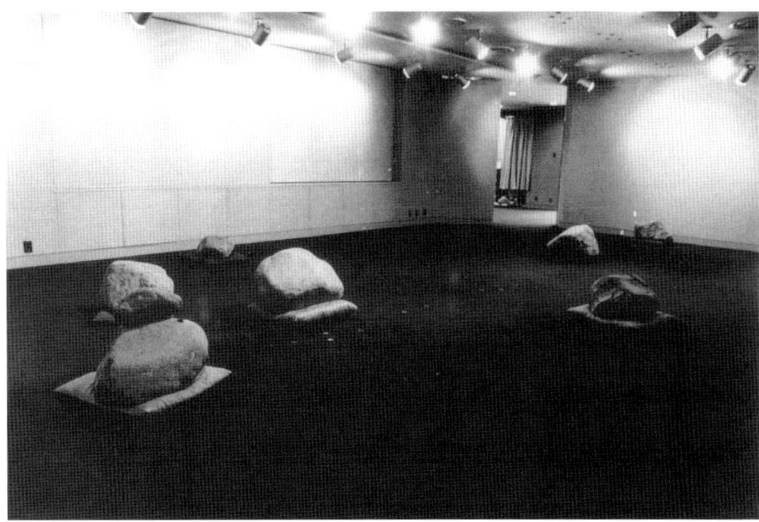

an unsaid addendum so that the statement reads more like "What you see is what you see and nothing else," in line with the negative ontology notably declared by Donald Judd in his essay "Specific Objects": "Half or more of the best new work in the last few years has been neither painting nor sculpture."[95] Foreclosure of this kind was not what Lee had in mind. Like his Mono-ha colleagues, he valued materials insofar as they could invoke the properties of other materials: steel plates precariously leaned against one another, while cushions were placed underneath stones so as to capitalize upon gravity's capacity to dually illustrate the pliancy of one and the weight of the other.

In another *Relatum*, shown at the Pinar Gallery in 1971 (Figure 2.10), objects are arranged so that the interstices separating one object from another appeared just specific enough to remind viewers that this configuration of familiar, unworked objects constitutes its own autonomous realm. Interstices are just wide enough to invite the viewer to walk around and through the configuration of objects. The work avoids a sense of enclosure, the open effect reinforced by the stones, which were precisely small and low enough to enable, rather than impede, access into the space they inhabited. Viewers are free to direct the course of their experience, thus adopting some of the responsibilities of realizing the work. Entirely absent from *Relatum* is any direction for viewing the objects, a goal that Lee diligently worked toward as he tried to strike a compromise between calculation and chance, between control and spontaneity.

For all Lee's emphasis on the "encounter," however, his works did not obligate viewers to actually see them in order to grasp their point. There was no need for a viewer to physically walk among the stones of *Relatum* to experience the tension generated by their spacing; the experience was readily captured through photographs. Similarly, photographs of *Relatum* from 1969 vividly evoke the moment at which the stone made contact with the glass plate, perhaps even more so with high-contrast film capable of emphasizing the weight of the stone by expressly capturing shading and the capillary-like fissures threading through the glass. In such works there is a double awareness of the work as both a three-dimensional entity and a two-dimensional image, an awareness that tacitly appealed to Lee's Korean colleagues interested in the relationship between flatness and plasticity in the late 1960s. The interest was somewhat crudely put as a merger between painting and sculpture; as Oh Kwangsu remarked of the works exhibited in the 1969 Kukchŏn, sculpture was "playing an important role in the vanguard movement . . . [the statement] that 'painting imitates sculpture' or a phrase like 'sculptural painting' are indications [of such]."[96]

HA CHONGHYUN'S MATERIAL QUESTIONS

Lee's ideas proved especially appealing to the members of the A.G., perhaps best known for their receptivity to different approaches to creation, an aspect of what Ha Chonghyun described in 1970 as simultaneity (*tongsisŏng*). In 1971 the group published in its journal a Korean translation of the conclusion to *Search for Encounter: The Provenance of Contemporary Art*, Lee's collection of articles and reviews originally published in Japanese that same year. Titled "Preface to a Phenomenology of Encounter: In Preparation for a New Theory of Art," the essay was an extended argument on behalf of phenomenology and its methodological relevance. It excited several young artists and critics, particularly those interested in confronting what Ha Chonghyun recalled as the "beleaguered status" of painting.[97] Just prior to joining the A.G., Kim In-hwan, a critic originally trained as an oil painter, wrote that the 1967 São Paulo Bienal treated painting as if "the idea of a putting color to canvas with a brush was old hat."[98]

Kim's observation doubled as an implicit call for his fellow painters to think about painting beyond the application of color to canvas. Ha, who had participated in the 1967 São Paulo Bienal as a member of

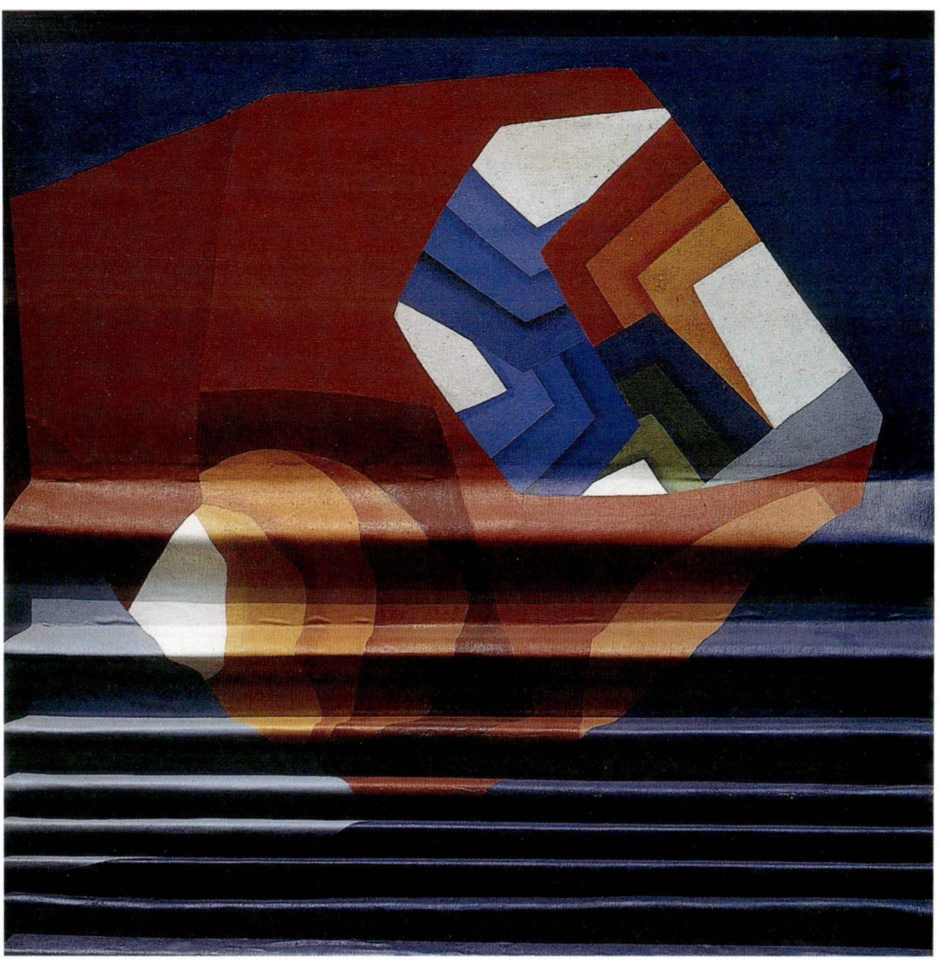

FIGURE 2.11 Ha Chonghyun, *White Paper for Urban Planning*, 1967. Oil on canvas, 105 × 105 cm. Collection of the artist.

the Korean delegation, seemed to have agreed with Kim. Born in 1935, Ha studied oil painting at Hongik University just as "Korean informel" was emerging in the late 1950s with the debut of works such as Park Seobo's *No. 1*. In lockstep with the rise of "Korean informel" during the early 1960s, Ha too made various examples of gestural abstraction, yet he soon relinquished this approach in favor of one that initially held painting to be a distinctly three-dimensional proposition. This meant rejecting flatness at all costs, even if it meant cutting up and reweaving the canvas, as in *Birth-B*, or actually compressing the canvas into accordion folds, as in *White Paper for Urban Planning* (Figure 2.11), on which various polygonal forms painted in bright primary and secondary colors were intended to represent abstracted versions of city plans.[99]

The literalism of this negation may have struck Ha as unproductively blunt, and perhaps as too close to what some of his Japanese counterparts were doing at the time, for he soon abandoned these approaches in favor of juxtaposing materials with radically different physical properties and metaphorical associations, a move strongly informed by the Mono-ha instinct for the possibilities of incongruence as well as by what from the early 1960s in Korea was a renewed awareness of the possibilities derived from incorporating everyday materials into the domain of art.

Using canvas always painted entirely in white or black, and either perfectly square or in the form of long rectangles, Ha arranged strips of barbed wire, tightly coiled metal springs, nails, and other materials more commonly used in industrial production. He also reiterated compositional strategies embedded within a particular history of modernism. In *Work 72-1 (A)* (Figure 2.12), wire barbs press into a yielding fabric support, heightening the viewer's sense of both the sharpness of the wire and the softness of fabric. The barbs are scattered evenly from edge to edge throughout a large white, monochromatic canvas so that the work is equally accessible from all four sides. It acts as a plausible reenactment of the allover painting down to the considerable size of the work except that spiky wire barbs pucker the fabric at regular intervals, thus relieving the work of some of its seriousness.

Ha was no less sincere than his Mono-ha counterparts in exploring the possibilities of juxtaposing different materials in order to recast such materials in an entirely new, or at least unfamiliar, light. He would have regarded as a compliment the bewilderment Oh Kwangsu expressed after seeing the Thirteenth Invitational Exhibition of Contemporary Artists: "Never has any exhibition shown so many

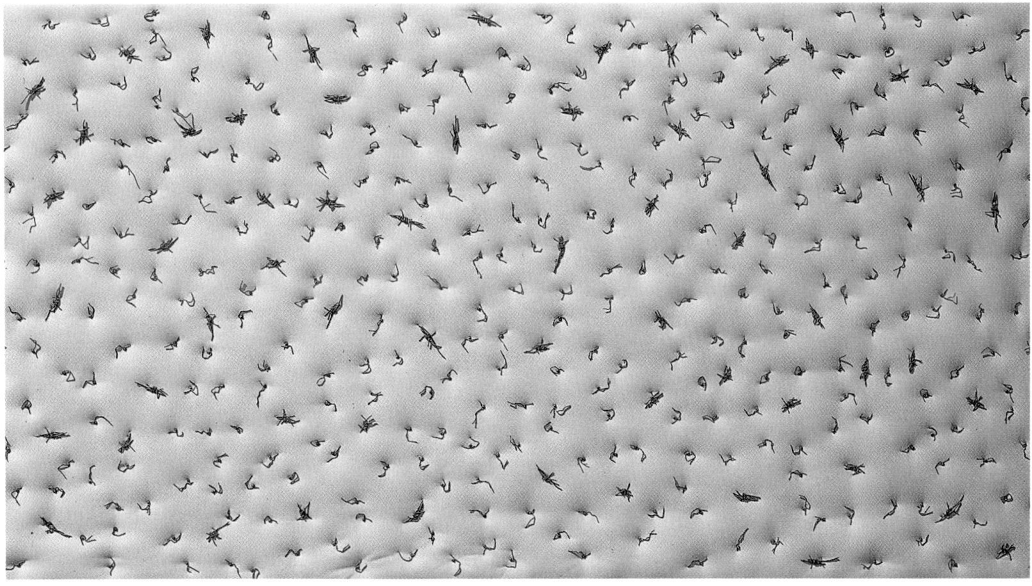

strange and incomprehensible paintings."[100] Certainly he seemed to have regarded the Mono-ha as a critical touchstone of sorts, as indicated by the kinds of works he chose to exhibit in Tokyo at the Gin Gallery in the spring of 1972, including a lumber plinth precariously balanced on a short length of rope that recalled both Lee Ufan's and Yoshida Katsuro's manipulations (Figure 2.13).[101]

But in Ha's work there is an undercurrent of humor, as well as tacit bemusement, at the near-puritanical intensity with which some Mono-ha artists attempted to minimize or vacate any trace of gesture in order to redeem their pledges of noncreation. In *Work 72-1 (A)* and *Work 72-3(B)* (Figure 2.14), Ha put some distance between himself and the polemical obscurantism that frequently characterized much of the writing of Lee Ufan and other Mono-ha artists. In *Work 72-3(B),* shown at the third A.G. exhibition at the National Museum of Modern Art in Seoul in 1972, Ha exaggerates the flatness of a black monochromatic support by stretching black coiled springs from one end of the canvas to another in successive rows. The springs lie flat against the canvas except at the very center, where Ha lets a cluster of coiled spring ends dangle limply against the canvas. His methodical tracking of the length of the canvas with springs pulls the cluster into disarray and frustrates the work's viewing as a highly organized and insistently flat work. The protrusion of spring ends that dangle helplessly in the very center of

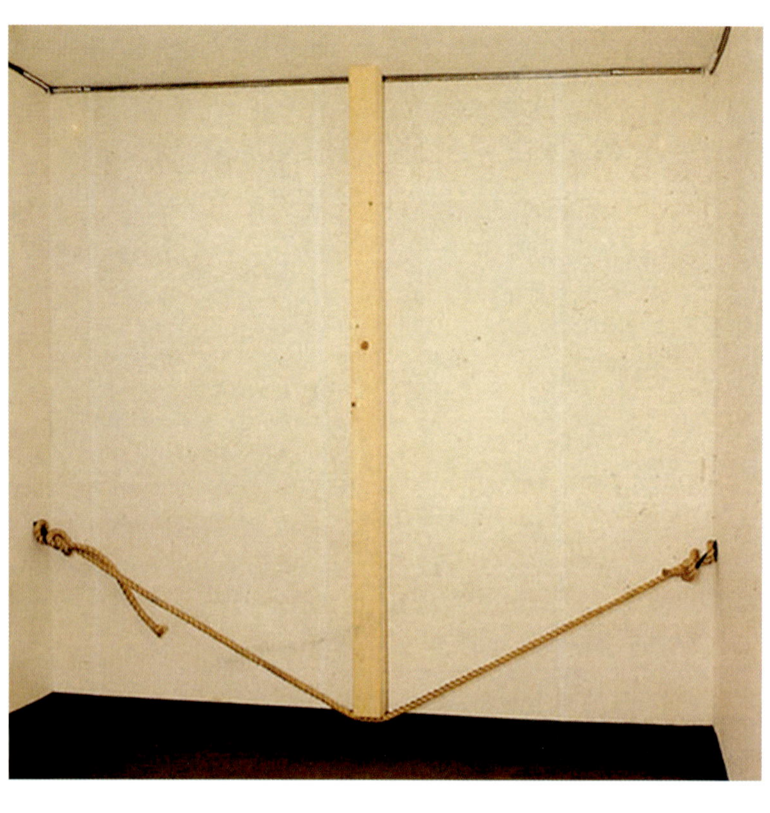

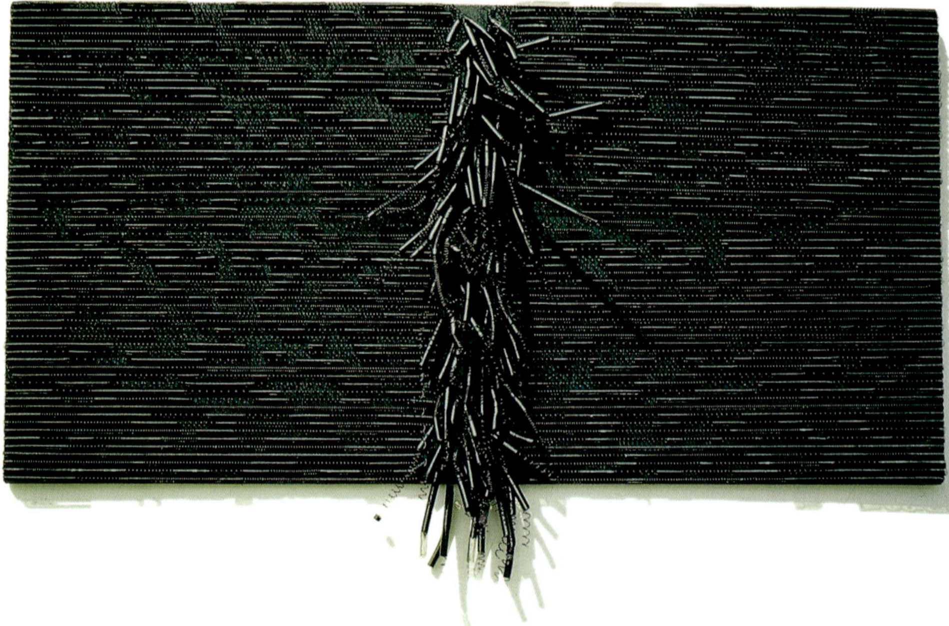

the canvas makes light of the insistence on flatness that so typified approaches to painting as Ha understood them. It also pokes gentle fun at the inclination to think of painting as a carefully orchestrated event in which every aspect must fulfill a purpose. The cluster of spring ends has no apparent purpose in this work, which initially concerns the making of a system—the work reads as if Ha misjudged the length of spring he would need for each row.

Ha still saw much of value in the Mono-ha emphasis on "thingness" and its attendant implications of ontological ambiguity, especially as it offered a means of addressing the remarkable level of energy Korean artists and critics invested in delineating, and then preserving, distinctions among different media as well as among different genres through which a particular medium was frequently construed.[102] He would be reminded anew of this situation in the summer of 1974, when the controversy over Suh Se-ok's alleged indebtedness to *nihonga* erupted. However, it became equally clear to Ha that the Mono-ha emphasis on "thingness" was not enough to productively trouble the lines separating painting from sculpture. In fact, this emphasis came across as sheer escapism, for it all but left the distinctions intact, and even enforced them. "Thingness" was but another category of medium, fated to be no different, and perhaps even as reductive, as the categories its proponents hoped to avoid.

Certainly the idea of the "thing" as envisioned by artists like Lee Ufan was deeply inscribed in a teleological discourse framed by terms like "antiart" and "nonart," both of which insinuated that the very idea of a painting or sculpture was somehow obsolete and therefore not worth considering. Lee argued the point closely in *Things and Words* (Figure 2.15) shown at the Ninth Contemporary Art Exhibition of Japan. Upon initial encounter, the work recalls Takamatsu Jirō's work, at the same exhibition, consisting of a rectangular piece of cotton measuring approximately seven square meters placed on the floor, a work that he described to Lee during the exhibition as an attempt to "leave the world of objects [translated into Korean by Lee as *mulch'e*] and to behold the expression of presence for what it is."[103] For Lee, leaving "the world of objects" meant getting viewers to see what they ordinarily considered as art as itself an object. *Things and Words* consisted of three enormous pieces of white paper similar to that used for ink painting laid flat on the gallery floor, and its size disrupted audience expectations of a one-on-one encounter with each of the paintings displayed on the gallery walls. Viewers entering the gallery would have first looked at the

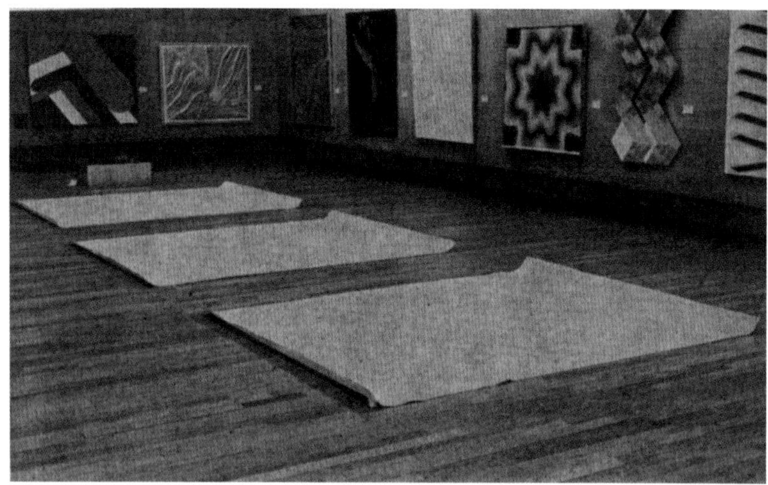

sheets, whose dimensions seemed more convincingly scaled to the proportions of the gallery than to those of the individual viewer. That the sheets were blank and placed on the floor only emphasized Lee's attempt to have viewers pay attention to the space activated by their presence rather than to the paintings, which looked almost decorative by comparison, mere embellishments of the walls on which they were shown.

The ways through which painting was classified in Korea, particularly through its separation into Western painting and Oriental painting, may explain why Ha became so frustrated with painting generally—hence the desire to "destroy" the idea of making a picture. Ha contended that his aim was "not to paint pictures, but to try and destroy, in [his] own way, the structure known as a picture,"[104] and he did diverge considerably from what Korean viewers had come to expect through the promotion of gestural and geometric abstraction. Yet he insisted that his works be called "painting" (*hoehwa*) rather than "things" (*samul*). Even those works that seemed only to adhere to the most rudimentary sense of intentional composition were still recognizable mainly as a framed support hung on a wall, that is, within the conventions of painting. Painting remained vital to Ha precisely because it could be perpetually reconsidered so long as one understood that the distinctions to which it was heuristically subject were initial points of negotiation as opposed to finalized conclusions. Beginning in about 1973, he began to make paintings so that each work contained within it the artist's memory of having worked with freestanding three-dimensional pieces. In this way Ha actively considered the possibilities

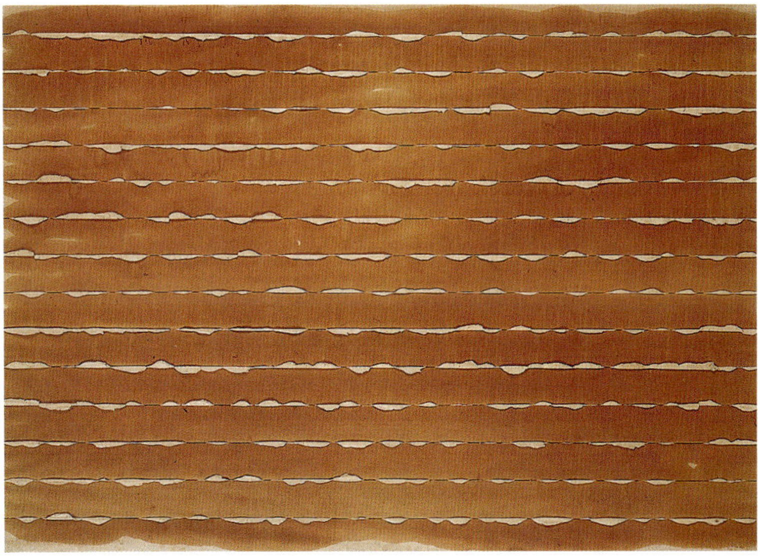

generated through an exploration of the points at which three-dimensional objects became paintings and at which painting ceased to be painting. One might say that Ha explored painting not because he believed in its autonomy, but because he did not.

PAINTING *CONJUNCTION*

Ha laid out his goals rather frankly in *Work 74-A* (Figure 2.16), which he considers the first example of the *Conjunction* series for which he is best known. A flat wooden board was laid horizontally on the floor, then covered with a heavy layer of white oil paint. Wooden slats were subsequently wrapped in thick brown paper acquired from a wallpaper shop and then pressed onto the board with enough force that the still-viscous oil paint was squeezed upward between each slat. Ha then set the entire ensemble upright against a nearby wall so that the paint began to trickle down onto the wrapped surfaces of the slats. Here the main event was not the application of pigment to a receptive support but, rather, the application of objects that might otherwise be used as supports for paint. As soon as the oil from the paint meets the paper wrapping the slats, it leaves behind large dark stains that change the color of the paper from light yellow to deep brown. Left to dry, the white paint hardens into concrete-like dribbles that rise faintly over

FIGURE 2.17 Ha Chonghyun,
Work A, 1974. Oil on hemp,
100 × 80 cm. Collection of
the artist.

FIGURE 2.18 Ha Chonghyun,
Work B, 1974. Oil on hemp,
100 × 80 cm. Collection of
the artist.

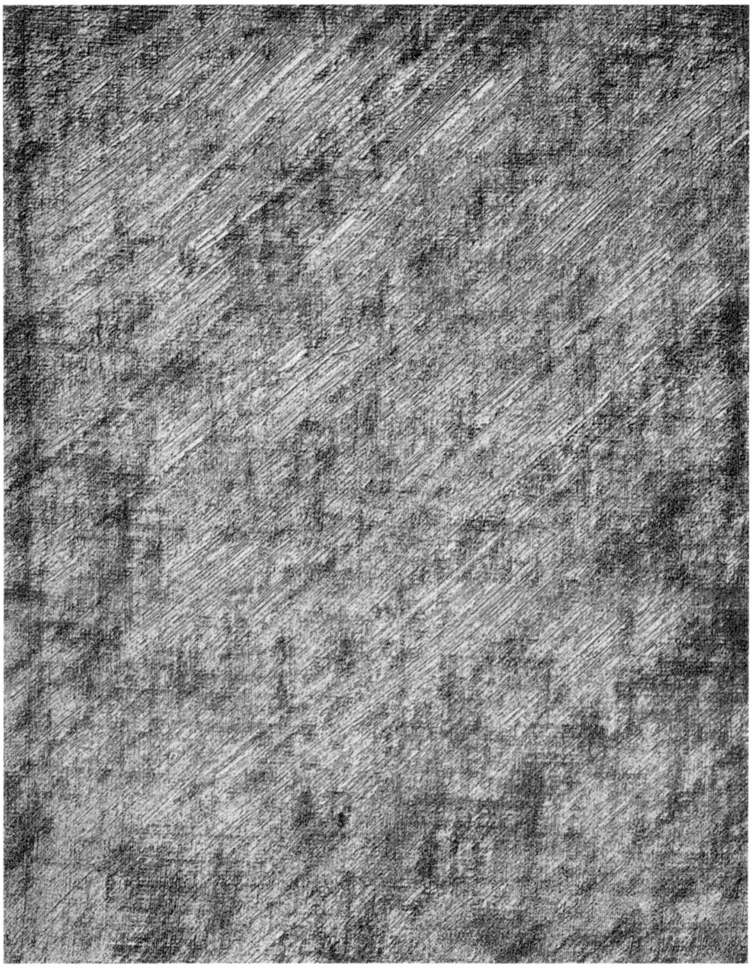

the flatness of the tightly wrapped slats of paper, frequently leaving shadows that intensify the darkness of the stains left behind by the encounter between oil and paper.

Ha recalled of this work that it was "the image of the paint as it appeared to bubble up to the surface" that most quickly captured his interest.[105] For him it was important to think about the possibilities encompassed by each material chosen. Take, for instance, two smaller studies also made in early 1974, *Work A* (Figure 2.17) and *Work B* (Figure 2.18), which shed further light on this interest. Intended to be displayed together, the works are rectangular paintings of equal dimensions and are both medium-brown hempen canvases covered with white paint. *Work A* is distinguished by a roughly rectangular patch of white that covers most of the available pictorial space. The liquidity of paint has settled into a solid puddle that makes part of the dark-brown support look almost like concrete and makes the paint feel curiously heavy, the use of a very bright white notwithstanding. In *Work B* paint has been brushed across the entire surface so that it spreads thinly over the canvas. The once-thick daubs of oil paint have been pushed, brushed, and smeared so that the paint appears to only lightly mist the painting's surface, and the inconvenient messiness of oil has been transformed into something delicate, and even diaphanous. The sensation of ephemerality indicates the range of possibilities available even when using only a limited set of materials.

Both works induced a viewing experience that required viewers to stand directly in front of the work, parallel to the plane of the picture surface. Yet they also emphasize those movements of paint that seemed inadvertent, accidental, and otherwise seemingly incidental in nature. As the series title *Conjunction* suggests, the work was ostensibly about the conjoining of pigment and support without the mediating presence of a brush, hand, or other mark-making implement.[106]

Normally canvas is a means of support that contains the picture surface. But instead of assuming this usual role, I made works that stressed the importance of the weave of the fabric and the materiality of the paint. . . . The act of pushing, or the gesture of pressing has no relation at all to the act of drawing, which takes place on the canvas surface.[107]

The "surface," in Ha's view, went beyond its literal translation as *p'yomyŏn,* or "external face" or "external side," which for him meant treating the surface as that which could induce viewers to move, turn, and rotate. The surface was justified by its ability to make viewers aware of their own capacity to move about in space. As Ha described his *Conjunction* works, "the canvas is that which exists when it is looked at from all around."[108]

For his June 1974 solo exhibition at the Myongdong Gallery, Ha created several works by first affixing the four corners of a fabric support to a four-post metal frame about as tall as a regular desk and then crouching beneath the frame and pushing small, dense lumps of white oil paint through the loose weave of the support from the rear to its front, producing what looked to one viewer like "tiny water droplet–like flecks."[109] He used coarsely woven hemp rather than primed or unprimed cotton canvas, a decision that both facilitated the movement of liquid paint and effectively set off the reflective surface of the oil paint after it dried. The hemp was no more than a very loose frame that reminded Ha of the barbed wire he stretched into grid-like formations in his earlier works (see, for example, Figure I.9).[110] With the canvas tautly stretched on four sides, the already prominent gaps between its warp and weft threads were enlarged, making it relatively easy for the artist to push the paint through. For *Work 74-05* (Figure 2.19), Ha then propped the canvas upright and physically struck the face of the canvas so as to cause paint to dribble slowly down onto the surface, pulled by gravity and its own weight.[111]

In another work, paint was pushed from the back, then swept across the canvas with a broom so that it appeared as if Ha had repainted the canvas front (Figure 2.20). The monochromatic look of the finished product denotes a moment of rest in which the hard labor of pushing paint through the fabric and then across the front of the support has come to an end. Globules of white paint protruding from the support reflect overhead lighting, their sheen further enhanced against the light-absorbing hairs of the support. By pushing paint from the back of the canvas and then smoothing it over, Ha rejected the idea that painting has its own internal world—here the act of painting is but the production of a surface.

Interviewed while the Myongdong Gallery show took place, Ha was quoted as wanting both to "minimize fabrication" and "to eliminate the unnecessary."[112] Later commentators have taken these statements as evidence that tansaekhwa was a "Korean transformation" of minimalism, yet Ha had little interest in channeling minimalism, which failed to attract any significant attention in Korea during this time and which Bang Keun-taek memorably described as "the withered sensibility of

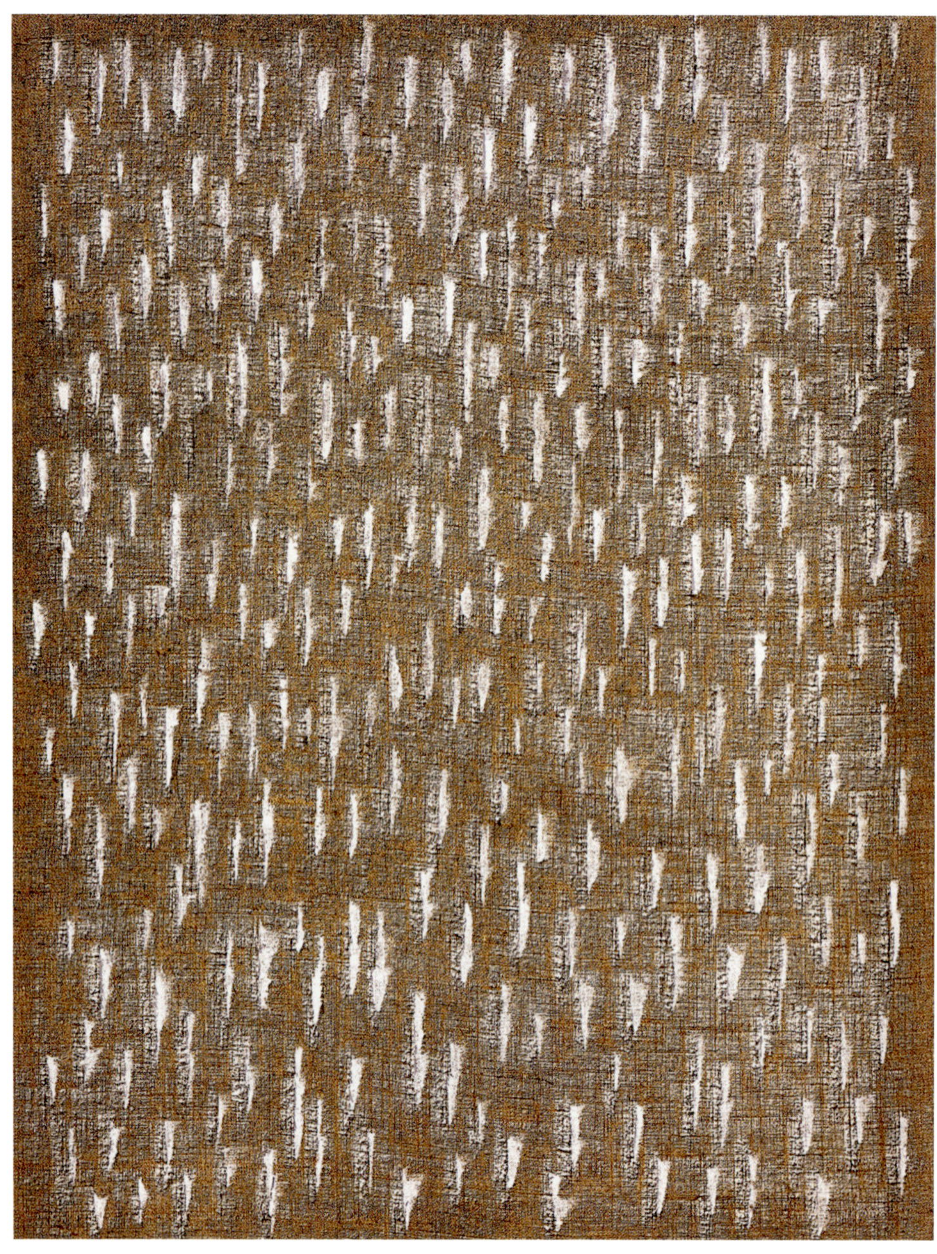

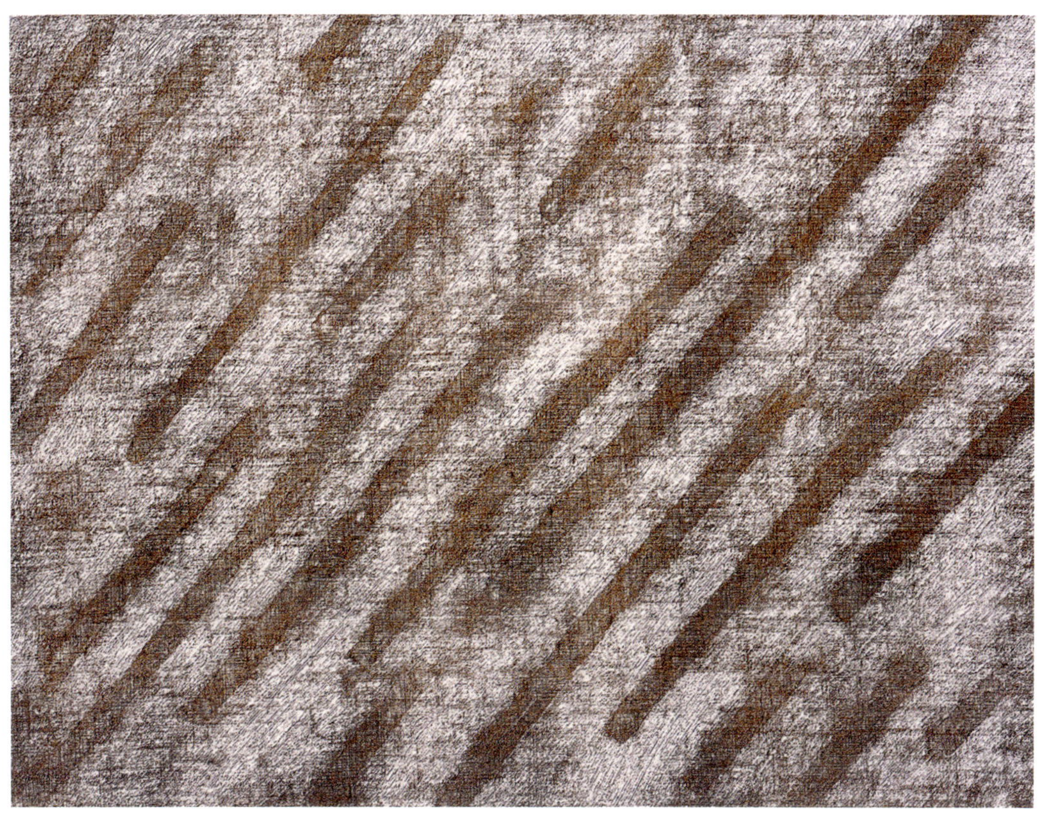

FIGURE 2.19 Ha Chonghyun, *Work 74-05*, 1974. Oil on hemp, 153 × 116 cm. Collection of the artist.

FIGURE 2.20 Ha Chonghyun, *Conjunction 74-11*, 1974. Oil on hemp, 116 × 154 cm. Collection of the artist.

the modern city, which lacks even the faintest trace of the natural."[113] "Minimizing fabrication" referred to the artist's efforts to remove himself from the process of the work's actualization by letting paint slowly drip down onto the surface or petrify into intractably rough and jagged rows. Ha tried to show painting as a world susceptible, and thus open, to forces not exclusively internal to the work. Absent from his works is the prodigious sense of control found in so many of Lee's juxtapositions, which frequently resulted in rarefied, and even precious, configurations that imparted a sense of authorial presence. In works like *Work 74-06* (Figure 2.21), the deposition of paint from the rear eventually freezes into stalactites that dangle precipitously from the loose weave of the canvas. There is a primalness, even a baseness about the formation that inexplicably resonates with the viewer on a visceral level. When Ha spoke of "minimizing fabrication" and "eliminating the unnecessary," he was referring to his attempts to place up front the raw interaction between materials and thus further undermine the assumption that painting was a self-contained world begun and completed by the artist.

Many of the works that would be later known as *Conjunction* were initially titled as *Work* followed by a number that indicated the year of production (*74*), a dash, and then a number indicating the sequential position of the work in the year it was made. Works produced earlier in the year have lower numbers, and those made later bear higher numbers. By his recollection, Ha made, on average, eight works per month. The term "work" called attention to the considerable physical effort involved in pushing paint from beneath a supine surface. At regular intervals Ha pushed paint through the canvas to form abbreviated vertical lines, each of which was subsequently paired with a painted mark of roughly equal shape and size. The painted mark lies flat against the surface, and compels the work to be read vertically.

Competing with this reading is the profusion of textures, from the smoothness of paint applied directly onto the face of the support to the accumulated globules of paint pushed from the rear that draw attention to the support's weft and weave. That the support is of a brown strongly reminiscent of wood adds another dimension to this textural configuration. It is uncertain, for example, whether *Work 74-05* (Figure 2.19) and *Work 74-06* (Figure 2.21) are best approached optically, or whether the viewer's sense of touch is also necessary to fully experience the work. The work supported Ha's belief in the canvas as simply that which must be "looked at from all around."[114] An earlier work in the *Conjunction* series shows Ha having "adjusted the paint [that he had

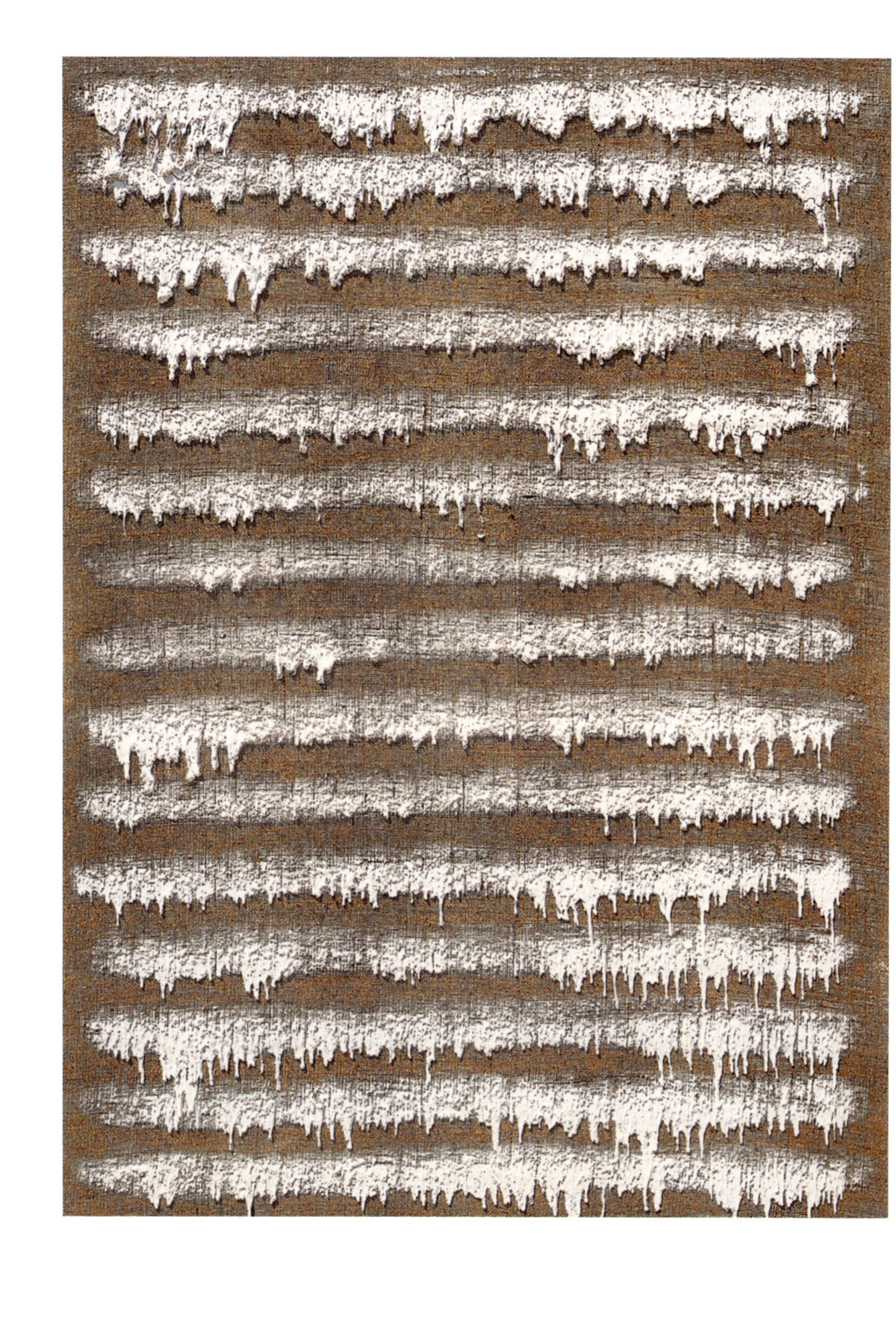

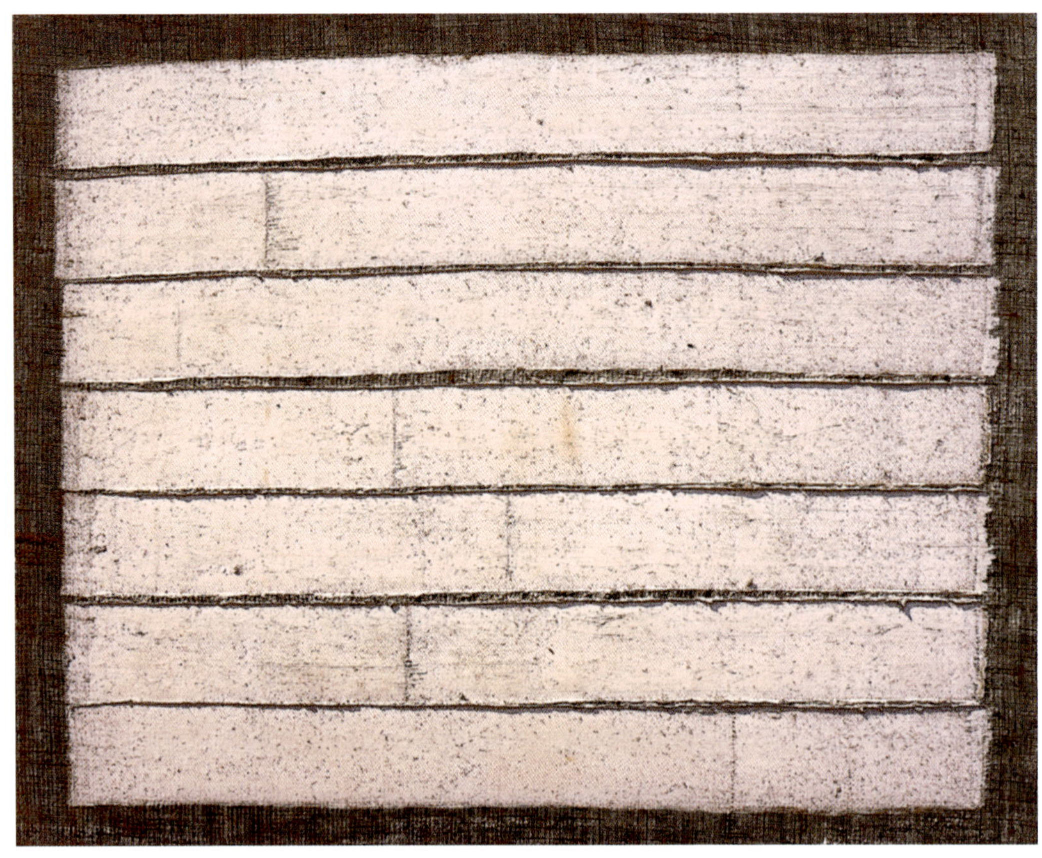

FIGURE 2.22 Ha Chonghyun, *Work 74-15*, 1974. Oil on hemp, 80 × 100 cm. Collection of the artist.

pushed through the weave of the canvas] on the top of the canvas."[115]
As in *Work B* (Figure 2.18), he swept the surface with a short-bristled
broom, thus flattening the bulbous protrusions of paint produced by
pressing pigment through the support but emphasizing the surface
as less a support on which to depict an image than a piece of fabric
covered in paint. In making works that provided a viewing experience
made unstable by competing allegiances to pictorial composition and
materiality, Ha was asking whether it was possible for painting to consist simply of its own materials and the properties intrinsic to those
materials, yet without lapsing into a literal restatement of process. As
Oh Kwangsu remarked in an article on Ha's work in 1978, "In today's
painting, material does not function as a means to an end but is content
to be itself."[116]

In *Work 74-15* (Figure 2.22) Ha pushed paint from the back of the
canvas, but then, using a square-tipped brush, smoothed it into wide
horizontal bands in successive rows. The artist then pressed a spatula
against the canvas with enough pressure that paint bears down on the
hempen surface, compressing and matting its fibers. The sticky buildup
of oil succumbed to the force of the artist's hand, lying rather meekly
against the support in successive wide bands. The only indication that
the paint once possessed its own sense of mass and density are the tiny
spike-like protrusions that represent the paint displaced during the
process of creating the bands. They, however, are made with an eye to
creating a frame for the work. Generous margins are left on all four
sides so that the grouping of bands reads more convincingly as representations in pictorial space rather than as paint spread across the
canvas. The result is the kind of work in which Ha took great satisfac-
tion, one that prompted viewers into wondering whether "it is a work
on hemp or whether it is an oil painting."[117]

As Ha proceeded with the *Conjunction* series, he took up some of the
concerns of then-recent modernist painting, as with *Conjunction 74-98*
(Figure 2.23), which continued the artist's exploration of the grid. In
many respects it is a rethinking of *Conjunction 74-24* (Figure 2.24). Yet
here Ha also stresses the liquidity of paint as he allows some of it to drip
downward onto the canvas in an almost literal restatement of fluidity,
even tapping the canvas to make the paint drip faster. In *Conjunction
74-98*, dabs of paint that resemble somewhat misshapen ovals are organized into rows and columns so as to clearly recall, perhaps even mimic,
the grid. These rows and columns, however, are just off-kilter enough in
alignment that they cast doubt on the ability of the grid to project

FIGURE 2.23 Ha Chonghyun,
Conjunction 74-98, 1974.
Oil on hemp, 225 × 99 cm.
Collection of National Museum
of Contemporary Art, Korea.

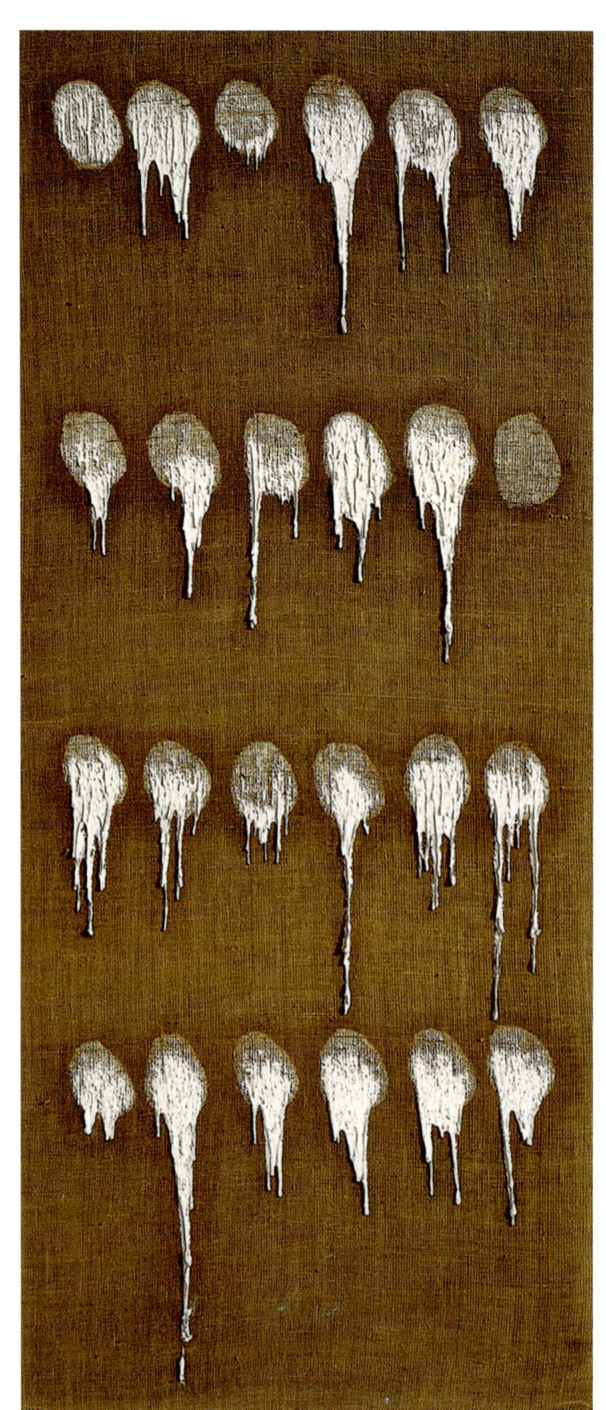

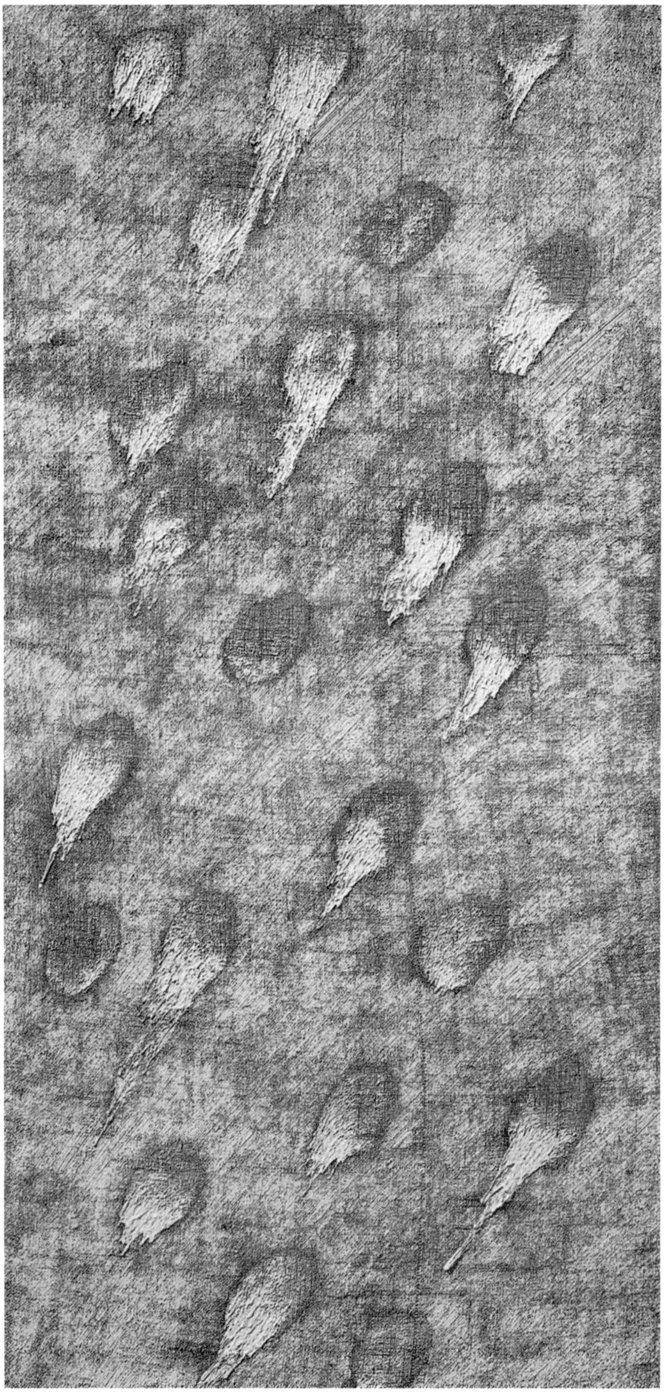

FIGURE 2.24 Ha Chonghyun, *Conjunction 74-24*, 1974. Oil on hemp, 200 × 100 cm. Collection of the artist.

a sense of order and predictability. The geometry of the grid is further compromised by oozing rivulets of paint emanating from each globular mark. The movement reinforces the vertical axis at the expense of the horizontal so that the implied grid is put in permanent danger of implosion. Pulled by gravity, the marks trickle downward so that the entire pictorial surface appears to be melting off the hempen support. The grid is no longer a mechanical means of severing the painting from the world outside its physical borders; rather, it is an image that carries with it a certain flesh-and-blood vulnerability. In *Conjunction 74-98* the grid bleeds, coagulates, and seemingly melts off the canvas and onto the floor.

While much of Ha's interest in pitting pictorial composition against materiality stemmed from a will to accept painting's finitude, it also touched upon another set of issues raised by the decision to use only white paint for the earliest versions of *Conjunction*. He explains that he meant white to act as a foil for hemp, which he bluntly described as "a material whose color is extremely limited, and perhaps could not help but be so monotonous as to reject the imagination."[118] Ha initially considered using colors like red, but he thought such colors might compete with the color of the hemp and undermine his attempts to "incite tension between the essences of hempen support and white [oil paint]."[119] Yet his choice of white relates back to what in the early 1970s had become a distinct stream of anxiety over the effects of Japanese colonial occupation. Ha knew enough of the history of monochromes to understand the transcendental connotations of white, but his understanding was more deeply and immediately affected by the influential writings of Yanagi Muneyoshi, the celebrated Japanese connoisseur who famously described Korean art in 1922 as embodying the "beauty of sorrow," citing in turn how Koreans, regardless of age, gender, or class, wore white, the traditional color of mourning in East Asia.[120] Korean culture, Yanagi suggested, was in a perpetual state of mourning.[121] This emphasis on white was directly linked to his romanticization of Chosŏn dynasty white porcelain, much prized among Japanese collectors and, later, among Korean artists such as Kim Whanki, who made such porcelain something of his personal muse in works like *Jar* (Figure 1.27). The invocation of white as a metaphor of Korean sensibility became so commonly accepted that even critics like Yi Kyungsung would airily remark, "That Koreans prefer white is a fact known by the entire world."[122] In his preface to the catalog for Kwon Young-woo's 1974 show at the Myongdong Gallery, Yoo June-sang wrote of his works as a reflection of "the people in white" (*paek ǔi minjok*), the phrase commonly used during the Japanese colonial era to refer to Koreans.[123]

Yanagi's characterization attracted renewed attention in the wake of a 1974 translation of *Chosen to sono geijutsu* (Chosŏn and her arts) into Korean by Yi Tae-wŏn, an artist, erstwhile curator, and the dean of Hongik University's school of art, of which Ha was an alumnus. The translation included an interpretative afterword by poet and critic Ch'oe Ha-rim, who, like his friend Kim Chi-ha some years earlier, criticized Yanagi's thinking.[124] Ch'oe argued that despite the "love" Yanagi professed for Korea and its art, his unwillingness to explore the identities and circumstances of so-called folk artists betrayed his faith in an essentialist and ultimately imperialist view of the world.[125] While Ha did not set out to challenge these associations, he nevertheless made an effort to stress the materiality of paint in order to undermine the symbolic associations of color. Against the yellowish brown of the hempen support, the white paint in *Work 74-06* appears overly bright and even garish. From a distance, the rows of paint look like rips or tears from which paint appears to bleed. Read in this way, the *Conjunction* works might very well be read as an attempt to escape or even, to use art historian Park Carey's word, "overcome" Yanagi's fraught characterization.[126]

In 1977, three years after he unveiled *Conjunction*, Ha wrote of his initial reasons for embarking on the series in a short but illuminating essay titled "Fusing Materiality and Painting," in which he discussed his desire "to realize the essence of the properties possessed by the materials" used in the making of the work; a straightforward embrace of materiality was not his only aim, however:

I began to make these hempen works since approximately 1973.
These are works where I apply and then push oil paint into the back
of a hempen support. When the white paint seeps into the fabric,
the movement of its force produces a shape—or even no shape—and
the details of this process of organically configuring pictorial space
[*hwamyŏn*] has been of infinite creative pleasure for me.[127]

This quotation shows that Ha moved back into painting from a three-dimensional practice based on the reification of mass, density, and volume. Oil paint, for instance, is considered through its particular degree of viscosity, which enables adhesion to a woven fabric support and resistance against efforts to force paint through this support. Ha's goal, however, was not to just remind the viewer of painting's three-dimensionality, which for him would have been too crude an argument. He is quick to disclaim any interest in representation as defined by the depiction of recognizable shapes (*hyŏngt'ae*), and he was even less interested in repeating paintings that simply took the surface as little more than an intermediate condition suspended between the untreated support and pictorial space.

Yet what piqued Ha's interest was not so much whether painting could double as sculpture, but how it might capitalize upon the tension between its capacities for flatness and plasticity, an interest to which he alluded in his mention of *p'yŏngmyŏn*. As he would remark in an interview in 1975, "unlike works stressing the level surface [*p'yŏngmyŏn*] of the past, I am conscious of the *objet* problems embedded in the surface field."[128] Although generally translated as "picture plane" and invoked as a synonym for flatness, Ha adheres to the literal reading of *p'yŏngmyŏn*, or "level surface," which for him involves much more than an apprehension of flatness. The level surface was a means of actualizing the physicality of the making process and of the viewing experience, for which the discernment of tactility furnished some of the key parameters. He stretched the canvas taut so that paint could be pushed more easily through the canvas and so that viewers could more easily see paint ooze forth. As he stated in "Fusing Materiality and Painting," the pleasure he took in painting the *Conjunction* works lay in what he could do with "pictorial space." In *Work 74-A* (Figure 2.16), for example, the amount of paint pushed forward is both consistent and varied enough in form to exist somewhere between composition and repetition. The placement of drips was not deliberate, but there was care taken in the way the artist applied consistent pressure in laying each wrapped slat onto the panel. The result hovers somewhere between composition and repetition. Similar to the early *Umber Blue* works, whose most outstanding characteristic may be the subtle gradations of color indicative of paint slowly seeping into the canvas, in many *Conjunction* works there is an accumulation of separable details that might have gone unnoticed in a more holistic composition.

Ha's attempts to challenge frontality as a leading condition for painting were even more ambitious. The effects of him pushing paint from behind the canvas is made clear in several examples of *"Conjunction,"* which in turn leads one to imagine oneself retracing Ha's movement. In works like *Conjunction 76-5* (Figure 2.25), he sweeps the surface of the canvas diagonally so that a thick ridge of paint amasses near the

FIGURE 2.25 Ha Chonghyun, *Conjunction 76-5*, 1976. Oil on hemp, 170 × 80 cm. Collection of the artist.

extreme right edge of the work. The ridge anchors the work so that the eye moves from right to left and back. It is a viewing experience markedly different from that offered by *Conjunction 77-12* (Figure 2.26), in which paint is pushed toward the bottom of the canvas. In *Conjunction 76-5* there is a laterality that pulls first the eye, then the head, and eventually the viewer's body from left to right. One thinks of the painting as being approachable from anywhere other than the front.

In requiring viewers to consider a work in relation to its immediate physical surroundings, these were "not [just] pictures"; rather, they depicted something else other than an imagined world defined by their consciousness of existing through the presence (or absence) of a frame. By structuring the viewing experience around the movements of paint, of his body, and of the viewer, Ha contemplated the permeability of painting. As the title *Conjunction* indicates, Ha tried to conjoin various aspects otherwise used to segregate painting from sculpture in order to remind viewers of painting's capacity for perpetual self-renewal, but also, perhaps, to push back against a worldview that so emphatically turned on perceptions of acceleration and delay, which to Ha seemed especially palpable in how painting was regarded.

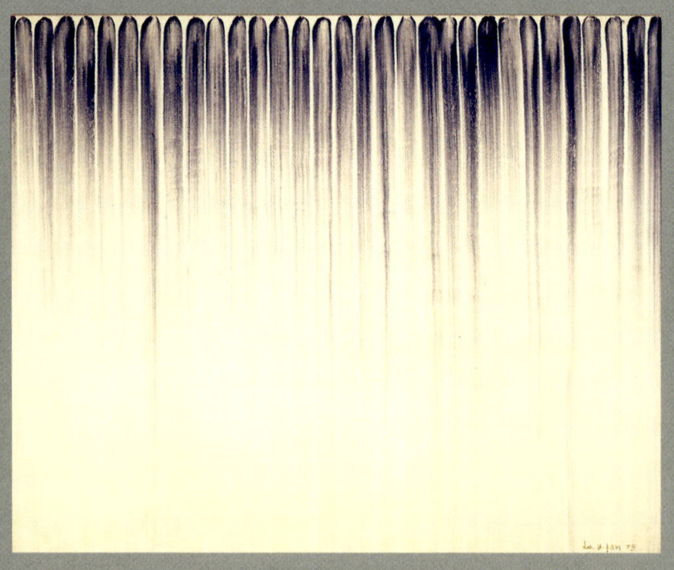

THREE

Encountering Lee Ufan in Korea and Japan

Between September 10 and 22, 1973, the Tokyo Gallery, known for promoting the latest in Japanese, European, and U.S. contemporary art, exhibited seven works from three separate series by Lee Ufan, *From Line, From Point,* and *From Notch.* Most belonged to the *From Line* and *From Point* series and ranged from 60.5 to 182 centimeters in width and from one to two meters in height. Each *From Line* painting (for example, Figure 3.1) relied on the artist's downward pull on the brush from the uppermost edge of the canvas to its bottom. In the *From Point* works (for example, Figure 3.2) Lee repeatedly pressed the tip of the brush against the canvas until the brush exhausted its supply of pigment. To facilitate this process, Lee mixed his own paints and used brushes with artificial hair so as to generate a high level of friction between the hair and pigment particles.[1] The initial point in each set of points was a dense accumulation of pigment, and successive points in the set looked like diminished echoes of the initial point of contact. Due to the pressure applied in creating each point, the pigment in *From Point* disappeared at a faster rate than did that of the lines in *From Line.* Lee could impress the brush only a few times before having to repeat the process from the beginning. To further decelerate the process, Lee used a binder made of animal glue, the mineral-based chalky pigment ordinarily used in *nihonga,* and brushes ordinarily used for ink painting.

Many viewers saw Lee's choice of materials as governed by his stated desire to escape or refute Western ideas of signification.[2] They rightly sensed that this was not abstraction as usual. Two months after the debut of *From Line* and *From Point,* the magazine *Gendai shisō* published Lee's essay in which he distinguished the "art of the Orient" from its Western counterparts, remarking that the latter relied on the "point" and the "line."[3] Certainly the idea and practice of Oriental painting resonated strongly for Lee, who not only was a trained ink painter but

FIGURE 3.2 Lee Ufan, *From Point*, 1973. Glue and mineral pigment on canvas, 182 × 227 cm. Collection of Museum of Contemporary Art, Tokyo. Courtesy The Pace Gallery. Copyright Lee Ufan.

was also an avid collector of Korean folk paintings (*minhwa*). Yet Lee chose his materials primarily in order to take advantage of their physical properties, a decision that was perhaps straightforward enough to deflect accusations of Japanese influence like those that would be directed against Lee's former teacher Suh Se-ok in 1974. True to his Mono-ha roots, Lee remained committed to materiality, as he showed by detaching color from an expressive pictorial language in order to have his viewers interpret the visual movement of the mark through its texture; for this reason, Lee deliberately chose not to use black. Like Yun Hyongkeun, who sensed that using black outright would needlessly simplify the viewing experience, Lee considered black as "too obvious a choice," by which he meant that it would too quickly lead viewers toward considering the mark exclusively within the framework of "traditional" ink painting.[4] Nor was he interested in mixing media solely in the name of challenging sacrosanct ideas of painting and sculpture, à la antiart's followers. Rather, Lee was interested in what might happen when certain materials not usually brought together were forced to interact. The cobalts and cadmiums used by Lee were taken directly from the palette of *nihonga,* but in deploying such large amounts on a canvas support whose texture and absorbency distinctly differed from the silk and paper used for *nihonga* generally, the artist emphasized the mark's tactility. The choice of color bore this out; the intense cobalt and cadmium emphasize the density of the mineral pigment, while the distinctly yellowish supports are hard to see as anything but canvas.

Lee drags his brush against a medium-weight linen canvas upon which a thin layer of yellow paint has been evenly applied. The color of the background paint is just yellow enough to "convey a sense of the natural," and the canvases are about the size of an average adult's arm span.[5] The line is the basic unit from which images are constructed in the medium of ink painting. In Lee's works here it is magnified so that the viewer can apprehend the disparate rates at which the brush expends the pigment and at which it dispels the binder. His use of this kind of pigment ensures that the mark's appearance and disappearance can be gauged in terms of a changing ratio between canvas and pigment, an effect intensified by his decision to use cobalt or cadmium, colors that he felt were "unreal, even unnatural enough to produce a strong impression against canvas supports selected for their 'natural' yellow appearance."[6] Against the yellow support, the brilliant cobalt pigments used in different versions of *From Line* strike viewers, who were accustomed to seeing such bright colors in small accent doses, as ostentatious and perhaps even a touch vulgar.[7] The effect is less jarring in the *From Point* works, in which Lee alternated between using different kinds of cobalt and cadmium so bright as to almost cast a vermillion glow onto the canvas.

Reviewing Lee's 1973 show, the critic Fujieda Teruo described the yellow supports in the *From Line* works as "playing a facilitating role for the artist trying to express a 'line.'"[8] This is not to suggest that Lee supposed the *From Line* and *From Point* works stopped at the level of chance encounter between East and West or, given Lee's interest in challenging Eurocentrism generally, of East refusing West in anticipation of exhibiting the works in the West. Fujieda added that both series were the result of a "system" that brought together both "action and process," a description that tried to reconcile the gestural nature of Lee's mark making with the artist's commitment to facture.[9] Fujieda's word "action" referred back to Lee's ongoing fascination with the works of Jackson Pollock. The artist had been familiar with Pollock's works since seeing photographs of his "drip" paintings in 1958. As they did for many artists, the paintings gave Lee a "shock."[10] At the same time, Lee was interested in the concept of the system, which cohered well with the widespread interest in systems theory in the art circles of Europe and the United States by the mid-1960s. The art historian Chiba Shigeo notes, for example, that Lee's own engagement took its cue in part from an understanding of the writings of Belgian mathematician and philosopher Jean Ladrière, who defined the system as "complex object, formed by distinct components connected to each other by a certain number of relations."[11] Minemura Toshiaki, whose 1977 essay was the most extended commentary on the *From Line* and *From Point* series at that time, argued that the paintings needed to be seen durationally, as a depiction of time, rather than as records of spatial placement.[12] Using the word "flow," Minemura reads the lines and points of Lee's works as a virtual representation of water. Depicted forms are less important than their movement across space, which, according to Minemura, made the passage of time completely transparent.[13]

Both the *From Line* and *From Point* series recalled particular ways of thinking about mark making and pictorial space that indicated Lee's strong awareness of his audience in Japan and of the kinds of information likely to have shaped the views of that audience on painting and on abstraction. Such recalls were not intended only to signal the vastness of Lee's store of artistic knowledge, or even to construct an ad hoc paternity for his works that would make them easier to situate within received histories of painting in Japan and Euro-America. Rather, they were done in order to envision another world based on linkages extrapolated from various formal relationships that work together toward a common set of objectives. But the *From Line* and *From Point* works continued to strike viewers as being different, unfamiliar, or strange mainly because Lee returned to painting, and specifically, abstraction, with the intention of disclaiming the inheritances to which he might otherwise be entitled by way of previous training or exposure. Broadly speaking, the *From Line* and *From Point* series offered a means through which to wrestle with the question of place, an issue of particular significance for Lee.

WORK ON LOCATION

Well before the debut of *From Line* and *From Place*, Lee embarked on his investigation of the notion of place, which he saw in at least three ways: first, as that which results when a previously unspecified space is made specific by the addition or removal of physical bodies and objects; second, as a locality defined by particular events and structures; and third, as a question of belonging mediated through the recognition of his own uncertain position as a Korean national living in Japan. As a student of philosophy, Lee was particularly interested in the concept of *bashō*, introduced in 1926 by the Kyoto school philosopher Nishida Kitarō. Written using the same Chinese characters as the Japanese word for "place," *bashō* was invoked by Nishida as the fundamental unit from which to assess self-consciousness. The self could be in many "places," from which it could see and be seen, or, as Lee wrote in a revised edition of *The Search for Encounter*, "the phenomenon of self-awakening . . . [which] makes possible one's 'seeing' and being 'seen.'"[14] Emboldened by Nishida's writings, Lee embarked on his *Relatum* works, which probed the ability of ordinary objects to transform an otherwise unspecified physical space into a specific yet unenclosed place.

For *Contemporary Korean Painting*, the 1968 exhibition at the National Museum of Modern Art in Tokyo that was Lee's first major show in Japan as well as his first public encounter with the Korean art world, Lee showed three enormous pink rectangular monochromes titled *Landscape I, Landscape II*, and *Landscape III* (Figure 3.3). At first glance, the ensemble reads as a neo-Dadaist provocation along the lines of Yves Klein, whose own pink monochromes were well known in Japan at this time. Far wider than they are tall, *Landscape I, Landscape II*, and *Landscape III* each takes on the format of a panorama, yet

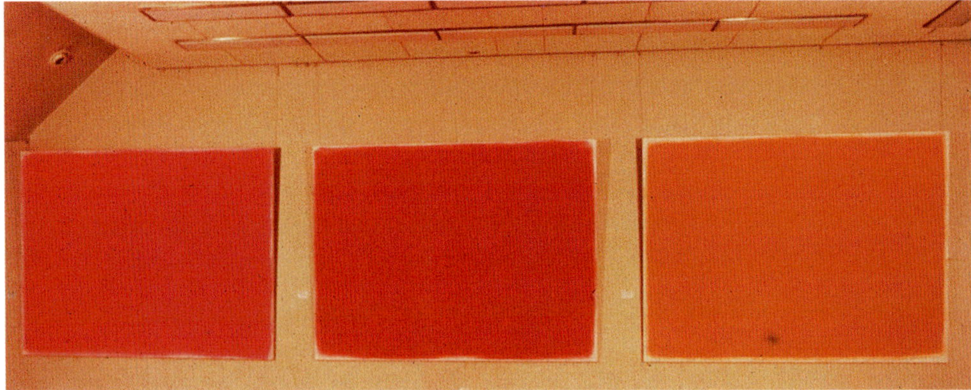

instead of opening onto a coherently organized view of an outdoor setting, each work shows nothing but an expanse of hot orange pink barely contained within the four edges of the canvas. The works divest the landscape of its supposed power to reveal to viewers an illusory world thoroughly internal to the painting. One is left only with the conviction that landscapes are less about seeing a view than about seeing how an object occupies space. It was a strike back at the "illusionism" of which Lee wrote in the September 1969 issue of *Miru* and which he deplored most about painting.[15] Ironically, the works were exhibited not long after Lee had seen *Tricks and Vision: Stolen Eyes,* a group show of artworks engaging in various optical illusions.[16] The show was organized by Ishiko Junzō and Nakahara Yusuke and held jointly at the Tokyo and Muramatsu Galleries in April 1968. Lee later admitted being very much affected by what he saw there, although in a seemingly negative way.[17]

At more than two meters, the length of each *Landscape* work begins to approximate that of the kinds of painting associated with abstract expressionism, which fascinated many younger artists in Japan and Korea in the 1950s. Yet Lee's interest lay not in size for its own sake, or even in the creation of a viewing experience based on sensory overload. In magnifying the painting and then repeating the work three times, Lee was most interested in exploring how size brings forth an awareness of scale and how this leads the viewer to consider the moments at which one kind of space relates to another. The largeness of the three monochromes induces the viewer, for instance, to consider the relationship between the space occupied by the painting and that of the gallery. Eventually, the viewer comes to think of the boundaries between spaces, and in turn, of the formation of place.

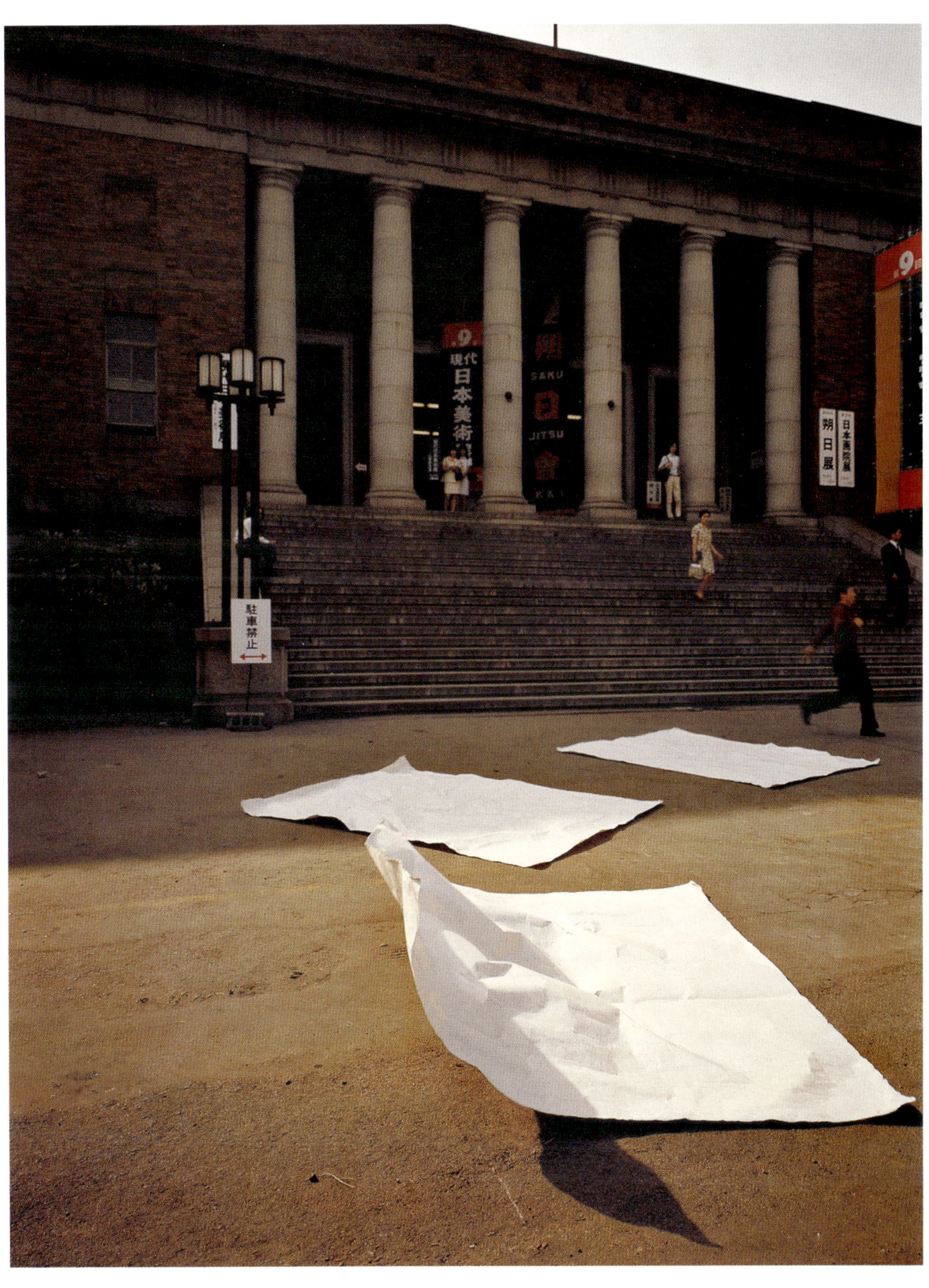

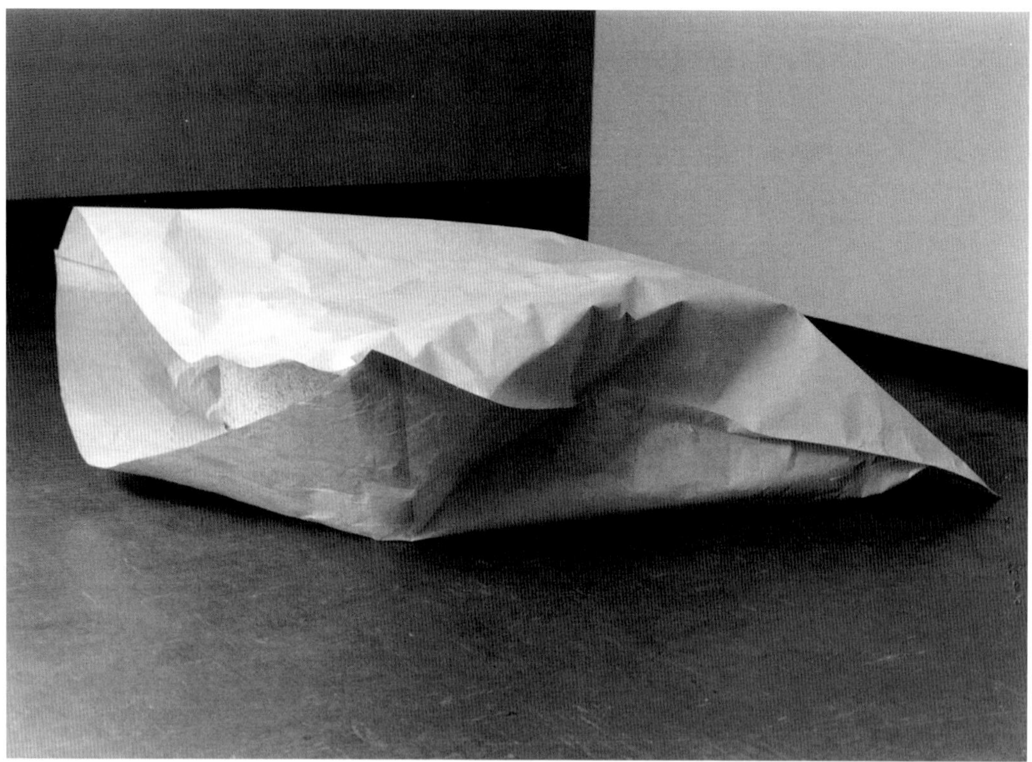

FIGURE 3.5 Koshimizu Susumu, *Paper* (originally titled *Paper 2*), 1969. Paper, stone; dimensions variable. Collection of the artist.

Lee followed *Landscapes I, II*, and *III* with *Things and Words* (Figure 3.4), shown at the Ninth Contemporary Art Exhibition of Japan the next year. In some ways, *Things and Words* was the next step in what by this time was Lee's intention to clear a new place for another approach to medium outside the categories of painting or sculpture. The three sheets of paper symbolize the canvas or support once installed upright on a gallery wall, which has been taken down and placed both on the floor of the gallery and on the ground outside the museum. This in turn alters the viewers' sense of the exhibition space so that it plays a more active role in how they understand the material presence of the work. Citing Michel Foucault's antihumanist view that humans were no longer the "standard" by which all phenomena were measured, and thus no longer the "center of the world," Lee suggested that this work, and particularly the scale implied by its size, was itself an attempt to undermine belief in an autonomous human subject.[18] The Tokyo Metropolitan Art Museum, established in 1926 in response to what its primary donor, Sato Keitaro, described as the need for an "Art Museum" able to reflect upon Japan's status as the premier "Eastern nation of art," is made to look far less imposing than he or the museum's other founders originally intended.[19] The three sheets rescale the serviceable if unexciting example of late Taishō-era red-brick building so that it no longer seems overwhelming or monumental, the building's actual dimensions or its row of classical columns notwithstanding.

Lee's intentions are perhaps clearer when seen in relation to another work in the same exhibition. Made by Koshimizu Susumu, another Mono-ha artist who assisted Sekine Nobuo in the making of *Phase: Mother Earth*, and titled *Paper* (Figure 3.5), the work consists of a large, somewhat crumpled pouch or sleeve made of the same paper as the three sheets of *Things and Words*. Known as *washi*, the paper is made from the bark of the mulberry tree and is similar to *hanji* in color, consistency, and texture. Though anchored by two enormous rough-cut granite blocks placed inside, the sleeve lies on one side but is not exactly on solid footing. It appears to wobble somewhat in a distinctly precarious way. The size of the pocket has the effect of rescaling the viewer's sense of space, which is not calibrated according to the dimensions of either the gallery or the human body. This the artist did as a first step toward getting viewers to stop thinking only about their own uprightness. Placed directly on the ground, *Paper* compels viewers to stoop, crouch, and otherwise reacquaint themselves with gravity and the significance of the ground plane, impulses also excited by *Things and Words*.

The groundedness of *Things and Words* also addressed what in 1969 Tokyo seemed to be a relentless push upward. After 1963 the revision of the Building Standard Law allowed Tokyo buildings to exceed thirty-four meters in height for the first time. Advances in building technology now allowed taller buildings to be erected without compromises to their seismic endurance, a major concern for an earthquake-prone country and particularly for Tokyo, which was devastated in 1923 by the Great Kanto Earthquake. Begun shortly after the revised law took effect, the thirty-six-story Kasumigaseki Building was completed in 1968, using an innovative steel-frame lattice to allow the building to move with, not against, the wind and other natural forces. Lee's three sheets of white paper could not have been more different from the big-box verticality exemplified by the Kasumigaseki Building and, most tellingly, from the gargantuan and expandable structures associated with Metabolism, the iconic architectural movement that emerged in Japan in the wake of a surging urban population boom that saw the number of Tokyo's inhabitants skyrocket from an estimated 11 million in 1960 to 16.5 million by 1970.

Lee, who personally deplored Metabolism as little more than a calculated attempt to conform all natural phenomena to the dictates of a system, a project whose nature he condemned as "colonizing," tried to respond to this push upward by lowering the gaze downward in works such as an early version of *Relatum* from 1968 (Figure 3.6).[20] He surreptitiously placed small, intentionally shaped objects, such as a welded iron plate, near or onto buildings located in some of the busiest parts of Tokyo, such as Shinjuku, where Lee lived at that time. The modest size of the plate urges viewers to readjust their senses of urban scale. The experience anticipates *Things and Words,* which directly fulfilled what Lee described in his 1971 book, *Search for Encounter,* as the need to "let the world express itself by allowing ordinary objects, which are often ignored, to be set free in the vivid and expansive world of incidents."[21] *Things and Words* proposed a different sense of place based on an embrace of horizontality and materials, especially in the version where the three sheets of paper are placed outside the museum, which accordingly draws attention to the scale of the institution. Although the three sheets of paper cover a vast surface area, compared to the museum the work seems manageable to viewers, a phenomenon with its fair share of significance in late 1960s Japan, where individuals were often subject to wills beyond their control.

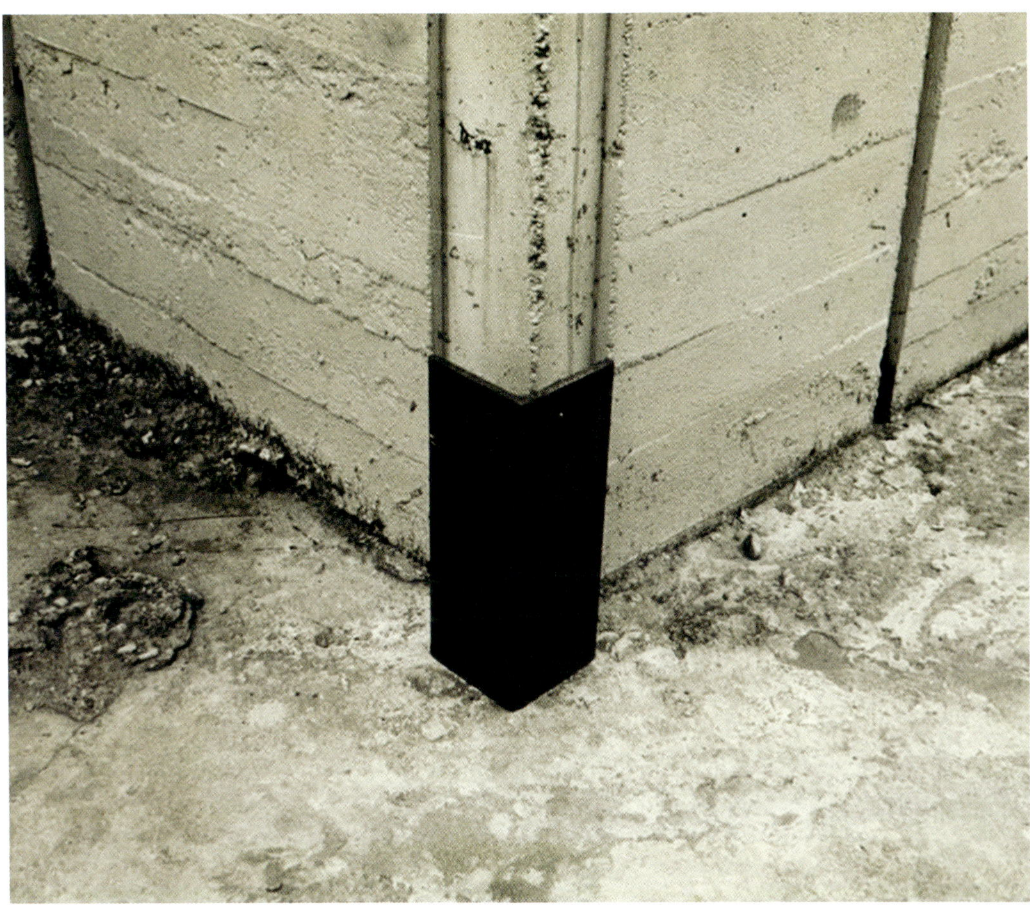

That Lee chose to name his work *Things and Words* after Foucault's *Les Mots et les choses* invokes further questions of authority and power, explorations of which were supplemented by what in late-1960s Japan was a keen interest among many intellectuals in poststructuralist thought. Foucault's works excited particular interest, especially after Foucault delivered his lecture on madness ("La Folie et la société") to a standing-room-only crowd, of which Lee recalled being part, at the University of Tokyo in October 1970.[22] Foucault's arguments, particularly those relating to taxonomy, resonated keenly with Lee's own sense of the instability of his position as a *zainichi*, an ethnic Korean resident in Japan, and with the way this in turn would affect the reception of his works in Korea. The proclivity for categorizing things and people by identifying them as "Korean" or "Japanese" was deeply embedded in both Korea and Japan, hence bringing to mind Foucault's description of taxonomization as a "nominal" strategy for preserving current knowledges.[23] Although Lee's sense of his own identity cannot explain why Lee worked in the ways he did, it certainly gave him a reason *not* to make work that might reinforce the deeply embedded tendencies within both Korean and Japanese societies to make distinctions based on national, ethnic, and racial origin.

Anti-Korean discrimination had long been woven into the fabric of Japanese society, and *zainichi* often found their career prospects, and even their mobility, limited. Film director Moon Yeo-song, who had lived in Japan since he was three years old, wrote poignantly of the "unimaginable struggles that marked the life of Koreans living in Japan."[24] Their predicament was exacerbated by what was widely perceived in Japanese society as the criminal tendencies of Koreans, a prejudice sensitively explored by Ōshima Nagisa in his immensely successful 1968 feature film, *Death by Hanging*. Based on the Komatsugawa incident of 1958, in which an ethnic Korean named Ri Chin'u murdered two schoolgirls, the film treats the body of a Korean as a site upon which the Japanese state unleashes its violence. The most striking aspect of the character is his seeming isolation from any semblance of a community. He is identified only as "R," a Roman-alphabet letter that distances him further from other Koreans in Japan, a trope that recalls how the larger *zainichi* community quickly abandoned Ri in the wake of his crime.[25] Yet as the last scene implies, the detachment has its own promise: the body of the condemned Korean has disappeared from view, evading for good the grasp of the state as literally denoted by the tautness of the hangman's noose in the central frame.

The figure of the trapped Korean was vividly evoked by the seminal comic artist Tsuge Yoshiharu in the July 1967 issue of *Garō*, the influential *manga* journal. Titled *Ri san ikka* (Mr. Lee's family), the comic depicts a Korean family living on the second floor of a deserted house. Several of its members look as if they are contained or trapped; in one scene, the daughters of the titular character are unable to look over the window ledge. In another panel, the entire family is contained within repeating square frames, a trope that Tsuge repeats as the comic's parting shot. Although Lee denied that the strip was based on him, his own life was marked by numerous professional and personal difficulties.[26] As his friend Park Seobo would later recall, "[Lee] had a really hard time of it."[27] That Lee nevertheless remained in Tokyo was an indication of the wider range of professional opportunities available. Bang Keun-taek was lamenting Korea's lack of a viable art market in 1963; by contrast, Yamamoto Takashi, the owner and director of the Tokyo Gallery, boasted in 1962, "Even if a foreigner were to come and ask me for [leading abstractionist] Saito Yoshishige's work, I could not show him twenty pieces. [I have] only two."[28] Even into the 1970s, Korean critics would bemoan the lack of high-quality art galleries.[29]

Still, it was difficult for Lee to negotiate the choppy waters of a Japanese art world that remained relatively closed to outsiders, and especially to non-Japanese. In the March 1967 issue of the Satō Gallery newsletter, Lee wrote of the psychological difficulties of having to negotiate between his Korean nationality and his professional identity as an artist and critic ("a Korean versus an artist"). In his view, the main challenge lay in the task of "unifying" the "consciousness borne out of the historical collective known as being Korean with the free, nihilistic world of the artist." According to Lee, he felt compelled to rise above his Koreanness in order to successfully "engage in creation that possessed an individual character."[30]

The precariousness of Lee's position was underscored by what to him seemed an irreconcilable divide between two models of social organization, the notion of the community and that of the public. On the one hand, Lee owed much of his psychological stability to the larger Korean community in Japan. With little money and few connections, by 1961 Lee was working part-time at the Korean Scholarship Association (Chosŏn Changak'hoe or Chosen Shōgakkai), established in 1900 as

a means for the Chosŏn government, and later the Japanese colonial
government, to keep track of its Korean subjects studying in Japan. Its
role was to disburse scholarships for ethnic Korean students resident
in Japan and to discuss peaceful ways of unifying the Korean peninsula.
Association president Shin Hong-sik encouraged Lee's interest in art,
and in 1965 Lee helped found the association's own exhibition space,
the Gallery Shinjuku in downtown Tokyo, where both North and South
Koreans could show their work.[31]

The Gallery Shinjuku became the catalyst that brought Lee together
with a number of artists and critics in Tokyo, including fellow Korean
artist Quac Insik, whose affiliation with the Mindan (Korean Residents
Union in Japan), the pro–South Korean *zainichi* organization, made
him an ideal consultant for the new gallery. Eventually the gallery
was visited by mainstream Tokyo art critics such as Yoshida Yoshie,
Ishiko Junzō, Nakahara Yusuke, and Tōnō Yoshiaki.[32] In the course of
gathering materials for the gallery, Lee visited numerous exhibitions
of contemporary art, whose audience was not limited to any particular
nationality or culture. For Lee, the viewer was a nonspecific being distinguished only by his or her capacity to stand, walk, see, and touch.

It was to such a viewer that Lee directed his voluminous criticism,
which both won him the award for new critics sponsored by the
publishing house Bijutsu Shuppansha and served as the theoretical underpinnings of the Mono-ha, the loose constellation of artists
joined by their efforts to refuse what they described as artistic creation, a group that dramatically shifted the landscape of contemporary
Japanese art in the late 1960s. Three of Lee's works were also chosen
to be displayed at *Aspects of New Japanese Art,* the influential 1970
exhibition at the National Museum of Modern Art in Tokyo organized
by Tōnō Yoshiaki, one of the few Japanese critics able to regularly
introduce Japanese artistic developments to the art worlds of North
America and Europe.[33] Moreover, although a growing number of
Korean artists showed works in Japan at this time, in large part
thanks to Lee's efforts, only Lee would be afforded the kind of
reception anywhere comparable to that reserved for Japan's most
elite contemporary artists.[34]

Despite these successes, Lee was constantly reminded of the
limitations that came with being Korean in Japan. In the summer
of 1970 he was informed that his works would no longer be among those
shown in the Fifth Japan Art Festival. The exclusion was more than a
professional slight; it was a considerable setback in Lee's foray into the

international art world, given that the festival was to open at
the Guggenheim Museum in New York in 1970. The terms of the agreement for the festival stated that artists were to be selected through
a public competition, with Guggenheim associate curator Edward
Fry retaining veto rights over any of the selections.[35] One artist that
especially caught Fry's attention was Lee's close colleague Sekine
Nobuo, who was reportedly unable to participate in the show.[36] Fry's
selection of Lee, however, was apparently rejected by the Japanese
coorganizers of the festival, the Japan Art Festival Association (Nihon
Geijutsu Mihon Ichi Kyokai), because he was Korean.[37] In this example,
contemporary Japanese art revealed itself to be a mode of comprehension tightly bound to nation-based typologies. These experiences
coincided with Lee's own view of the oft-repeated mantra of "overcoming the modern," which he clarified in 1971: "The words 'overcoming
the modern' have been sullied in Japan. There are various reasons for
this, but this greatest one is the historical role played by these words in
justifying the colonization of Asia."[38]

But national distinctions were also evident in Lee's reception in
Korea. The activities of overseas Korean artists—such as Kim Tschang-yeul and Lee Ungno in Paris and Kim Whanki in New York—were
frequently reported in the press, thus emphasizing the idea of a Korean
art not necessarily restricted to activities taking place within Korea. Lee
Ufan certainly fit this criterion as the theoretical crux of the Mono-ha,
which, though not named as such, had rocketed into prominence in
the wake of the exhibition *Aspects of New Japanese Art* in 1970. And
by the time *From Line* and *From Point* made their debut, Lee had transitioned from showing in rental galleries, such as Satō, Tamura, and
Muramatsu, to appearing in the blue-chip Tokyo Gallery.[39] Due in large
part to the efforts of Park Seobo, with whom he became friends after the
1968 exhibition *Contemporary Korean Painting*, Lee was quickly lionized by the Korean artistic establishment after his review of the Ninth
Contemporary Art Exhibition of Japan appeared in the June 1969 issue
of *Space*. Even those, such as Choi Man-rin, wary of overseas influence
brought Lee into the spotlight, choosing him as one of Korea's representatives to the 1971 Paris Biennale.[40]

By the mid-1970s Lee had come to play what A.G. member Shim
Moon-seup described as a "critical role in the South Korean art
world."[41] Asked to nominate delegates to the 1973 Paris Biennale by
its organizing committee as an in-country "correspondent," Lee chose
younger artists whose thinking was similar to his own. A case in point

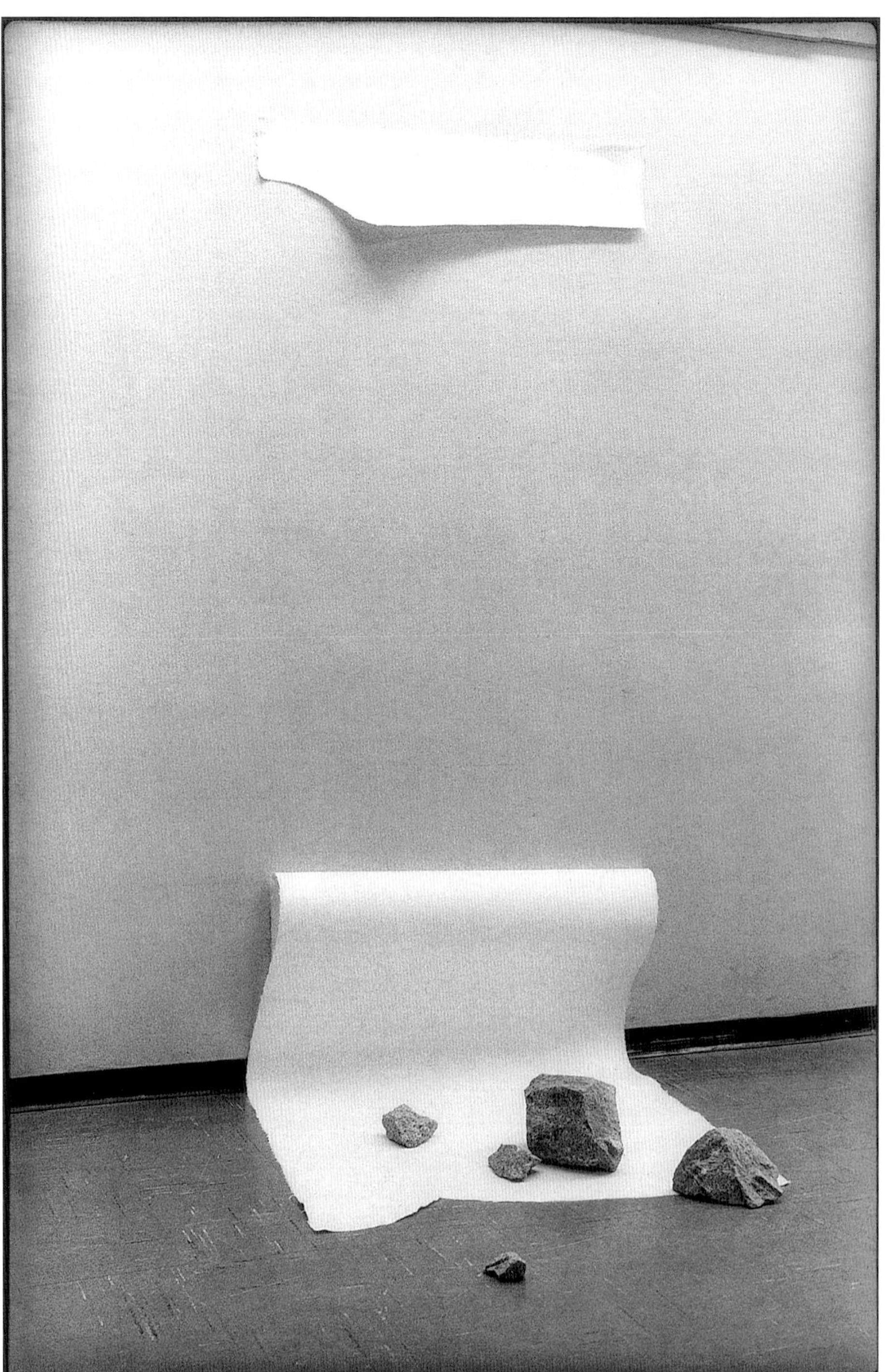

was the thirty-year-old Shim, whose *Relation* (Figure 3.7), first shown
at the First Seoul Indépendants Exhibition at the National Museum
of Modern Art in August 1972, was included among those works designated to represent Korea at the 1973 Paris Biennale.[42] *Space* editor
Park Yong-sook devoted part of the September 1975 issue to Lee, in
recognition of what Park later reminisced was his desire to encourage
younger artists to emulate Lee's achievement of a practice independent of any group or recognizable style.[43] The feature on Lee included
a selection from *Search for Encounter* as well as contributions from
Park Yong-sook, Lee's former Seoul National University classmate Kim
Chong-hak, and Park Seobo.[44] Similarly, when the *From Line* and *From
Point* works made their Korean debut at the Hyundai Gallery in April
1978, the show was easily one of the most publicized exhibitions that
year. Lee Yil, the catalog essayist for the show, described the artist's
influence on the younger generation as "absolute," a description that
was perhaps exaggerated but nonetheless indicative of Lee's popularity
among young Korean artists in the early 1970s.[45]

Yet although much respected by his younger colleagues in what
some commentators termed a "Lee Ufan boom," Lee was nevertheless
regarded with suspicion by his Korean colleagues who were then trying to come to terms with the Japanese colonial past and the Korean
art world's dependence on that of Japan.[46] In 1972 the *Chosun ilbo* published a rumor stating that Lee had refused to surrender his Korean
citizenship, even when prominent critics in Japan told him that doing
so would have helped his chances at winning the grand prize of the
1971 Paris Biennale.[47] Lee saw himself as being neither here nor there,
despite statements made by artists like Nam Kwan, who, in 1971, wrote,
"If it is said that art has no nationality then it should follow that artists also do not have nationality either."[48] And to some extent this was
true; Lee's Korean nationality may have barred him from representing Japan in biennales or in shows like the 1970 Japan Art Festival,
but his prominence in the Japanese art world qualified his inclusion
in shows of Japanese art such as *Japan: Tradition und Gegenwart*, a
1974 group show held at the Stadtische Kunsthalle in Düsseldorf, and,
ironically, *Contemporary Japanese Art*, a large-scale show of contemporary Japanese art sponsored by the Japan Foundation that made its
Korean debut at the state-run Art Center (Misul Hoegwan) in Seoul
in November 1981. Lee, however felt the burden of nationality, as he
recounted some years later: "I do not exist in Japan, and if I go to Korea
I cannot confirm [for myself] a definite reality."[49]

The omissions and slights Lee experienced can be described as symptoms of an escalating tension between different scales of operation. Like their counterparts elsewhere, the Korean and Japanese art worlds tended to be scaled according to the nation-state, meaning that artistic activity took place through national institutions (national museums of modern art), state-funded projects, and rubrics centered on the nation (thematic exhibitions based on promoting Korean or Japanese art, international shows made up of national delegations). Lee participated in many of these projects, yet he could not be comfortably nested within a scalar hierarchy like so many of his colleagues in either Korea or Japan. Active in the Japanese art world to the point that his works could be unmoored from his Korean origins, Lee nevertheless remained firmly conscious of his own cultural identity, even regarding it as something of an obligation as he assisted several of his countrymen to exhibit their works in Tokyo. He did not, however, feel at all obligated to relate this consciousness back to the sign of the national, as he asserted in a 1977 interview provocatively titled "The Problems of Korean Contemporary Art." Recalling the position he took in 1967 in the Satō Gallery newsletter, Lee struck at the idea of the "international," which to him was no more than a concept reifying the difference between the East and the West.[50] Instead, he argued for a centerless world based on a consistent denial of centeredness over one based on the construct of the nation-state, culture, or other predetermined relationships of power. But this kind of argument may explain why so many Korean artists remained suspicious of Lee, even as they envied his success overseas: for them it was clear that he was not interested in promoting the idea of a culturally distinct contemporary Korean art. That he paid dearly for his marked disinterest was early evidenced by Yoo Youngkuk's incensed response following the 1968 roundtable for *Contemporary Korean Painting*. Lee observed decades later that he was seen in Korea as a deserter, even a "traitor."[51]

LEE MAKES HIS MARK

It would be misleading to attribute the production of *From Line* and *From Point* to the discrimination and biases Lee experienced on account of his nationality, ethnicity, and place of residence. These experiences, however, sharpened Lee's awareness of the pejorative nature of certain kinds of distinction. It might explain the force of his avowed refusal of creation as an attempt to eliminate what Lee in 1969 condemned as the "egocentrism" of painting bent on "severing ties with the natural world."[52] Raising the stakes of this refusal was the highly charged political climate of the late 1960s and early 1970s. At a time when eight thousand riot policemen battled with several hundred University of Tokyo student members of the Zenkyōtō (All-Campus Joint Struggle Committee), the dominant student movement on university campuses in 1960s Japan, there were more than a few artists who, as Lee recalled, "considered the making of real works a [political] defeat."[53] Lee, whose own alma mater, Nihon University, had its own share of student rioting after taxation authorities discovered in 1968 that university authorities had embezzled over 34 billion yen, recognized that artists had to do something other than "learn what was taught at school and then make works accordingly."[54]

But the tactics of protest, allegory, and participation did not seem enough, particularly when the confluence of political and economic troubles that beset Japan made it clear that the 1970s would indeed be *fukakujitsusei no jidai*, the "age of uncertainty," a term borrowed from economist John Kenneth Galbraith's book of the same name.[55] What was needed was a redistribution of authority, which Lee and his Mono-ha colleagues had already implied through their shared refusal of creation. To them, this refusal was in fact an attempt to trouble views that regarded as central the identification of the artist as one distinguished by his or her capacity to transform ordinary objects into art.

From Lee's perspective, the only viable means of executing this refusal was to embrace a phenomenological approach that made central viewers' physical capacity to see without requiring that it be contingent on their level of understanding. While many *Relatum* works emphasized this point in rather straightforward terms, Lee challenged himself by returning to painting, the very medium he had earlier condemned for its "egocentrism." His first line of action was to open up the mark so that it could be read variably, through multiple ways of thinking about putting a brush, knife, or other mark-making implement onto a flat support. In a *Relatum* work from 1971 (Figure 3.8), for example, three large stretched canvases are presented as load-bearing supports, each carrying the weight of a single, irregularly shaped stone. Lee not only takes the canvas off the wall, thus causing viewers to rethink the uprightness with which painting has been especially associated, but also emphasizes its three-dimensional aspect as something defined by shape, volume, and elevation.

FIGURE 3.8 Installation view of *Relatum* (formerly *Situation*), at Tenth Contemporary Art Exhibition of Japan: *Man and Nature*, Tokyo Metropolitan Art Museum, May 10–30, 1971. Stretched canvases and stones; three canvases, 10 × 190 × 170 cm; three stones, each approximately 40 cm high. Private collection.

FIGURE 3.9 Lee Ufan, *From Notch*, 1973. Wood, 149 × 127 × 4 cm. Collection of Museum of Contemporary Art, Tokyo. Courtesy The Pace Gallery. Copyright Lee Ufan.

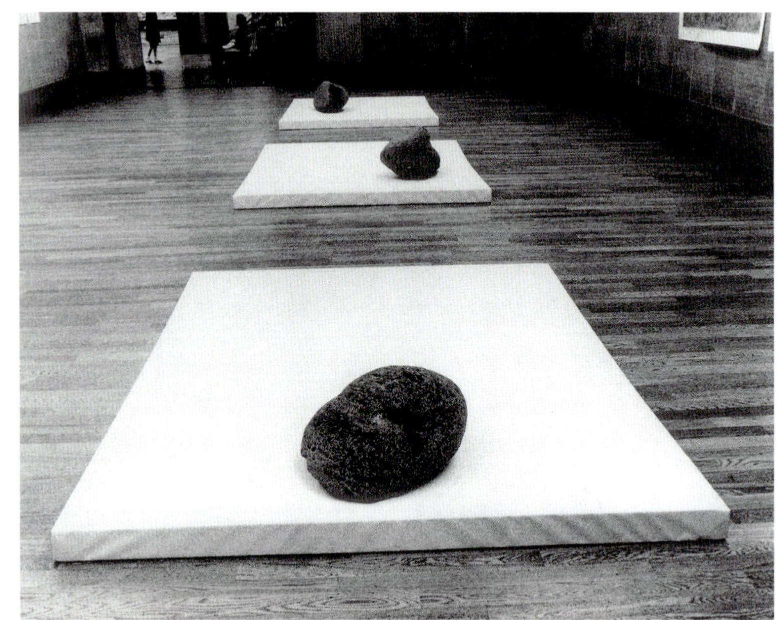

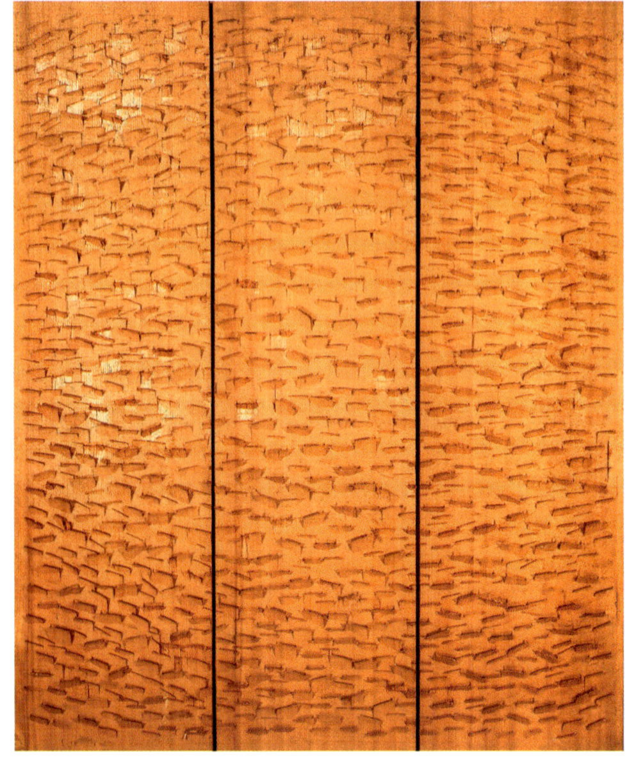

For the 1973 exhibition at the Tokyo Gallery, Lee chose to exhibit *From Line* and *From Point* with a few examples from *From Notch*, the series of works that had previously made its debut at the Shirota Gallery in November 1971 (for example, Figure 3.9). Also known as *Cut Up*, the series consisted of wooden panels of dimensions comparable to those of the paintings grouped under the titles *From Line* and *From Point*. Each panel featured a multitude of closely spaced incisions, made with a chisel, that had all been cut in one direction. Flaps of wood protrude from the panel surface, with some wider and larger than others. The viewer recognizes the flaps as having a presence in the physical, material world. The eye sees the angularity of the flaps and the depth of the cut through the flaps' shadows cast upon the background. At the same time, the plasticity of the flap gives way to a second-order representation of a two-dimensional mark.

No paint was used in making *From Notch*, but in producing the series Lee still had in mind earlier investigations of paint. *From Cuts* (Figure 3.10), painted in 1965, shows a progressive buildup of oil paint toward the center of the canvas that nods to the thick encrustations of informel, particularly given the way the grayish-white paint resembles concrete. The paint looks much thicker and harder than it actually is and is applied without any sense of the feral abandon that characterized informel as it was practiced in France or Japan. The visible disturbances to the flatness of the painted surface establish the work as a material reality, yet without relying on dramatic flourishes, which by 1965 seemed more than a little stale to audiences in both Japan and Korea. By this time, it was very evident to Lee that mark making could no longer be patterned after the grand gesture that had served many artists so faithfully in the late 1950s and early 1960s. Informel had long ceased to be a persuasive countermodel with which to oppose the didactic literalism of reportage painting that had once dominated the Japanese artistic establishment. This was vividly evoked by the Neo-Dada Organizers in 1960 who, while marching in one of the many protests against the first Treaty of Mutual Cooperation and Security between Japan and the United States, abbreviated as *Anpo*, alternated their cries of "Down with *Anpo*" with "Down with *Anfo*," *Anfo* being an abbreviation of *Anforumeru*, the Japanese pronunciation of "informel."[56] By reworking thick oil paint into abbreviated rectangular layers that could hardly be called brushstrokes or even marks, Lee tried to stamp out anything that could be used to resuscitate the existentialism of informel's rhetoric. *From Cuts*, therefore, was a way for Lee to work through the effects of informel without having to pay fealty to its legacy.

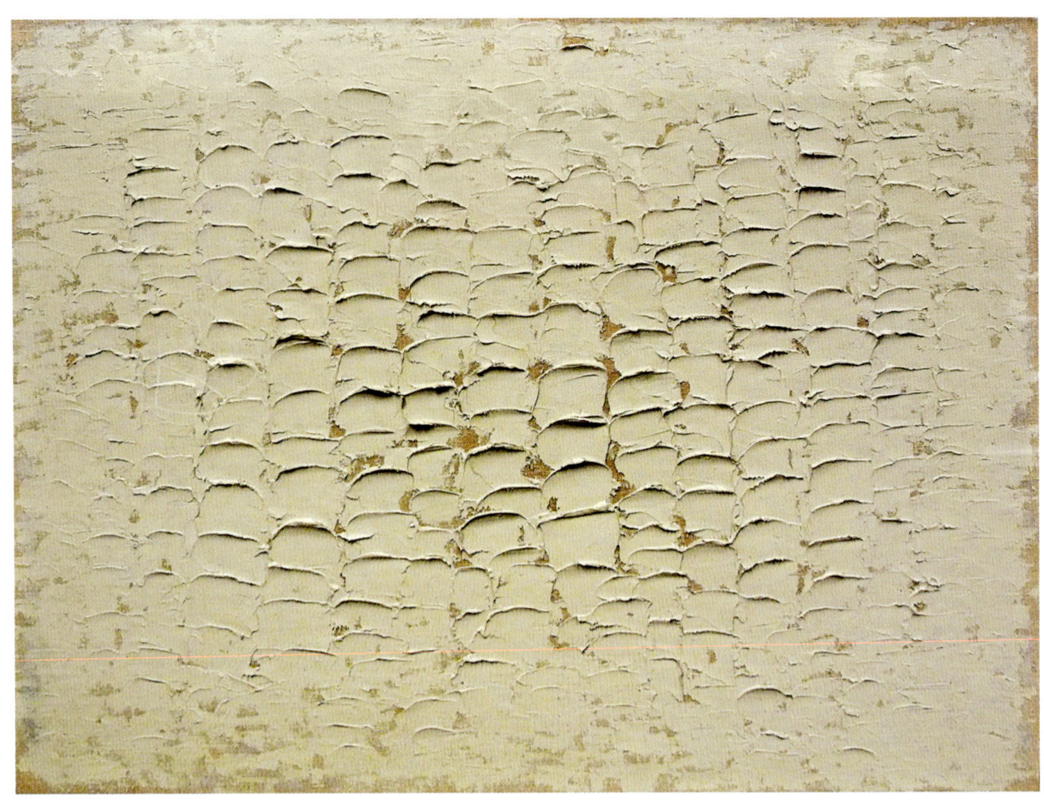

FIGURE 3.10 Lee Ufan, *From Cuts*, 1965. Oil on canvas, 71.5 × 98 cm. Private collection, London. Courtesy The Pace Gallery. Copyright Lee Ufan.

Although careful to avoid the excesses of informel and its various strains, Lee was simultaneously open about his interest in abstract expressionism, especially in the works of Jackson Pollock.[57] A few months after the initial debut of *From Line* and *From Point*, Lee would add that "the many kinds of drippings are, perhaps, not indications of creating or making, but seem to indicate a destruction that thought creating or making to be all wrong."[58] From Pollock, Lee became especially aware of the mark as that which arises from a dialectical interaction between figure and ground, space and mass, and buoyancy and weight. The line in the *From Line* works (such as Figure 3.11) appears to both lie flat on the canvas and fade into pictorial space as represented by the canvas. Likewise, the density of mineral pigment at the very beginning of each line steadily dissolves so that much of the painting appears to open up into blank space. The heaviness of the pigment yields to an ephemeral, thin coat of binder that is almost ghostly in affect. The point, as it were, was to demystify the brushstroke by emphasizing its material properties. But here Lee slows down the painting process, so that the viewer accompanies, rather than chases, the mark.

One is reminded of *Line Variation* (Figure 1.8) by Suh Se-ok, who was teaching at Seoul National University High School while Lee attended the school from 1953 to 1956 and with whom Lee became close.[59] *Line Variation* destabilizes the viewer's gaze by simultaneously imposing two demands upon the eye. The work calls for the eye to view the marks—separated at ample intervals—along an imagined vertical axis affirmed by the upright stance of the viewer. The eye is also urged to read the marks as part of a lateral movement across the canvas. The painting's lateral orientation and the scrupulous preservation of intervals between each line induce the gaze into reading the lines sequentially. Lee too defined the mark in *From Line* as a function of both velocity and vectorial movement. The mark is the result of the speed at which the brush moved from one point to another, and of the magnitude of the force with which the artist, collaborating with gravity, pressed the brush down upon a supine expanse of canvas. The marks stop just short of looking as if they could actually belong to a semiotic context in which all marks are intended to bear meaning. Lee made one mark after another so that repetition vacates each mark of its presumptive capacity to mean something other than what appears on the canvas.

Lee's approach to mark making was also refracted through his sensitivity to the potential of abstraction that, in his words, "could not be interpreted through perspective, image, or color used to discuss

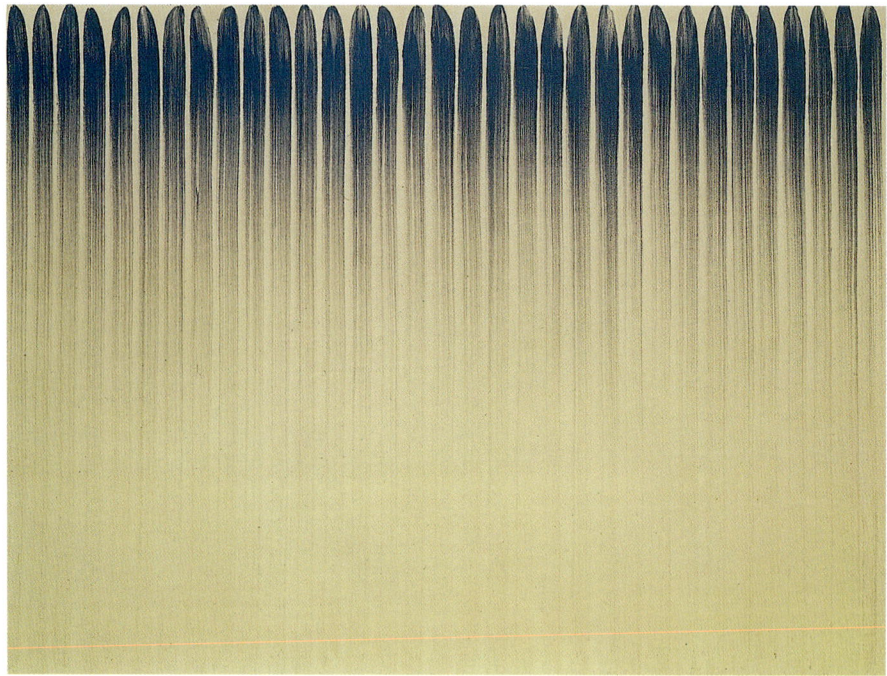

Western-style painting."[60] The marks in *From Line* echo those made in the course of calligraphic writing, a resemblance that would not be lost on Lee, whose initial university training was in brush painting at Seoul National University in 1956 and who joined the Nihongafu, a professional artists' association for the study of *nihonga* from 1962 to 1965. During the course of his involvement with the Nihongafu, Lee created a number of works that expanded upon the notion proposed in works such as Suh Se-ok's *Point Variation* (Figure 1.7), which defined the support as a physical space that was realized only when it was materially filled with marks. In *Pushed-Up Ink* (Figure 3.12), also exhibited in Lee's 1973 Tokyo Gallery show, the artist takes a vertical support made of *washi* of the kind ordinarily used for calligraphy and brush painting and fills it almost completely with round marks made with the tip of a brush loaded with black ink.[61] Made of soot, animal glue, and water, the highly viscous ink seeps through the paper wherever the brush has made contact with the support. In many instances, the marks blend together to form small clumps, so that what should read as evidence of the artist's touch dissolves into an awareness of chance and incidence. The mark was less the result of artistic deliberation than an incidental effect

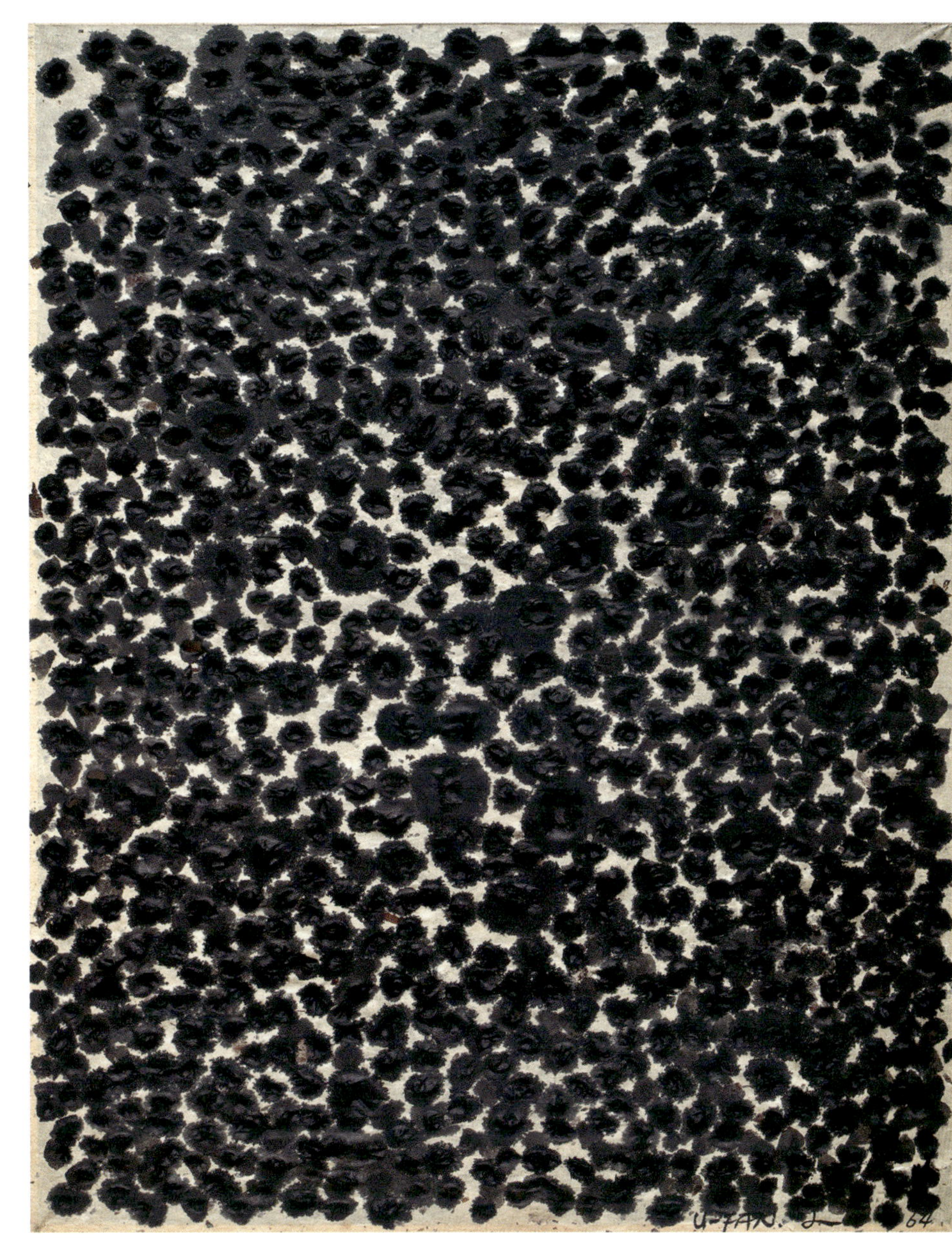

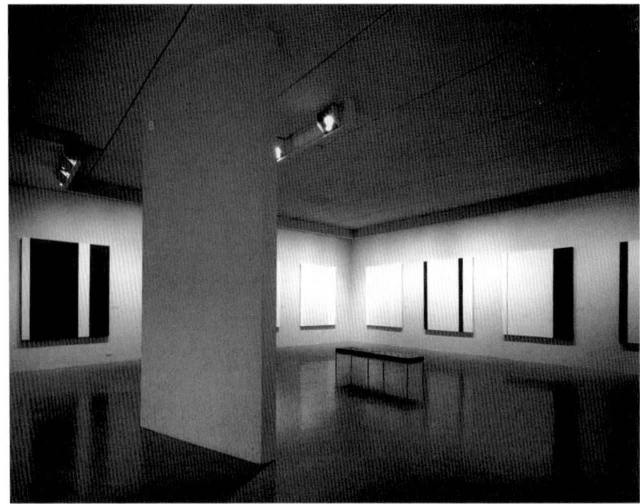

produced in the wake of the encounter between materials. Lee visited Seoul in 1960 and 1962, when the Ink Forest Society was at its most active, but whether Lee actually saw their works, or those of Suh Se-ok in particular, is uncertain.[62] Lee remarked that the notion of both the point and the line was "already part of the metaphysics of ink painting," which he had learned when very young: "The old painter who taught me would frequently declare that all painting came out of the point and the line."[63] Yet Lee pushed the question of ink painting's relationship to abstraction in a way that would have immediately resonated with his Korean colleagues, including Suh, and certainly Kwon Young-woo, whose paper-based works hung in close proximity to those from Lee's *From Notch* series at the 1973 São Paulo Bienal.

Giving Lee further motivation was his maiden visit to New York, which took place in the fall of 1971, just after he installed his work for the Paris Biennale and right before his November exhibition at the Shirota Gallery in Tokyo. Though denied a chance to show his works at the *Japan Art Exhibition* held at the Guggenheim the year before, Lee was still deeply curious about the New York art world. His visit was not a happy one; most of the galleries he visited treated him with indifference.[64] Lee, however, was deeply intrigued by what he saw of Barnett Newman's retrospective at the Museum of Modern Art.[65] Newman opened up for Lee the possibility of painting without having to regard the canvas as itself the grounds of an internal world wholly separate from the viewer or as a literal restatement of painting's constituent

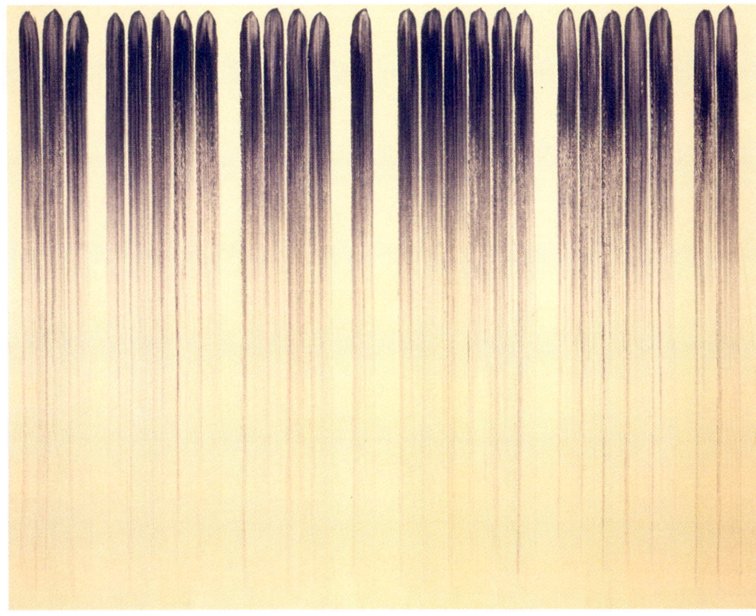

materials. Painting reemerged as a spatial expansion where Newman's trademark "zip" disrupted the presumed left–right symmetry of the work by splitting the canvas into two, three, or more sections in a meiotic manner. As denoted by an installation view of Newman's *Stations of the Cross* (Figure 3.13), a series of particular interest to Lee, the unmarked canvas as well as the physical space between each painting in the series invited viewers to think of themselves inhabiting the same physical world as that of the series.[66]

Newman's effective use of the gap encouraged Lee to expand further on its possibilities. In a number of *From Line* works made between 1978 and 1979 (such as Figure 3.14), a single row of cascading lines is sporadically interrupted by gaps in which a single line might ordinarily fit. The intermittent gaps direct attention toward the left- and right-hand edges of the canvas so that the canvas no longer reads exclusively as its own contained world. At the same time, the gaps emphasize the painterly quality of each line by making it easier for viewers to read each line as a distinct brushstroke rather than as a modular component of a unified system. The gaps thus avert the danger that viewers might read the work as simply a painted version of *Relatum*, or even worse, as an ordinary object completely divested of its artwork status. Like his Mono-ha colleagues, Lee was all too familiar with the banality that often accompanied the debates pitting artworks against their nonart or antiart counterparts. For him it was crucial that his works not invite such discussion, lest it obscure more important questions of authorship and their larger implications for the artwork's place in society.

THE DENIAL OF THE AUTHOR

Lee elaborated upon the broader implications of his turn to painting in May 1978, one month after the Korean debut of *From Line* and *From Point* at the Hyundai Gallery:

For a while, one of the biggest factors as to why I was
misunderstood in Japan was because I wrote [criticism]. Among the
many comments about *Search for Encounter*, words like
"candid," "as it is," and "very natural" were used. But if you read
closely the context [in which these terms were written], these
[terms] are but one kind of desire or hope, and humans are all,
to some extent, creatures of consciousness. I wish instead to add
a proviso that I want to look at the other side of consciousness.
Phrases like "transcending consciousness" [and] "natural" are often
used in Korea but we cannot take them at face value. Rather, one
has to repeat the task of struggling with one's self by thoroughly
denying oneself, [through] self-denial.[67]

Although his remarks were directed to a Korean audience, they also illuminate how Lee might have responded to the criticisms of one of his most vocal critics, the artist Hikosaka Naoyoshi, who had earlier accused Lee and his works of complicity with that which they purported to resist. A cofounder of the Artists' Joint Struggle Council (Bijutsuka Kyōtō Kaigi, abbreviated as Bikyōtō), the art school auxiliary of Zenkyōtō, Hikosaka refused to believe that Lee's ideas could amount to anything more than a pernicious sign of complicity with what he believed were the efforts of an antihumanist society to deprive individuals of their volitional capacities.[68] To Hikosaka, effacing the question of identity undermined what he regarded as an urgent need to act in a time of crisis.

But Lee's emphasis on "denying oneself" can be taken as an expression of his concerns over whether viewers might depend too much on written interpretation rather than on their own faculties of perception. It might also be read as the challenge of making work without also making

the viewer unduly conscious of its having been made, a challenge Lee
took away from his encounter with Newman's retrospective. As Lee
would later state, Newman's works filled him with "doubt" about the
"excessively strong sense of field" and about the distinctions brought
forth by the zips, which Lee referred to as "poles."[69] The idea of "denial"
suggests Lee's intention to yield to viewers so that they can more fully
experience the materiality of the work. Hence Lee chooses bright reds
and blues that vividly stand out against the yellow canvas supports, and
he stresses the tactility of the brushstroke by using large, thick brushes.
He emphasizes the perceptual capabilities of the viewer by taking care
to show the fade of pigment as the brush moves across the canvas and by
indicating how canvas size can affect the scale at which the mark operates.

How this denial actually played out on canvas might be usefully
diagrammed by the propositions set forth by Roland Barthes in his
1968 essay "The Death of the Author." While Lee did not intentionally
make work according to prescriptions set forth in this or any other text,
Barthes attracted substantial attention upon his initial visit to Japan
in 1966, including from artists like Lee.[70] Three propositions direct the
reader to Barthes's conclusion. First is the refusal of the idea that an
artist possesses mastery over the subject: Barthes cites the example of
"ethnographic societies" that value an individual's ability to interpret
a "narrative code" rather than the ability to lay claim to "genius."[71] The
second proposition imparts a double negative: Barthes refuses the claim
of the author to refuse the viewer. He invokes Stéphane Mallarmé's
poetics, reading them as an attempt to suppress the author in favor of
"restoring" the place of the reader.[72] The third, and final, proposition
concerns the denial of the artist's imprimatur to determine the parameters of a work: Barthes contends that assigning an author to a text would
be "to furnish it with a final signified, to close the writing."[73] Among
the essay's core premises is a double negative, the denial of the artist's
denial of the viewer, which acknowledges that any act undertaken by
the artist would be seen as a sign of his or her presence.

When the viewer moves closer to a work like *From Line*, its absolute
size is magnified so that its relative scale exceeds the viewer's. At this
moment, the viewer sees only the marks (the lines and the points) and
the "blank" spaces (the white or ivory-hued canvas). At this moment,
the gesture is implicated as the predominant aspect of the work, thus
running counter to Lee's intention to critique the claims for the artist's capacity for unique creation. Yet while the gaze follows a distinct
trajectory, the notion that it mimics the artist's gesture is challenged by

the presence of the lingering mark. Here "lingering" is used to describe the fade-out of the brushstroke or brush imprint, as opposed to calling it a "trace," for the former more clearly evokes a particular kineticism recurring throughout the series. Lingering connotes a sense of progressive duration, measurable in temporal units as the eye travels from the "point" to its implied disappearance. Moreover, the notion of lingering is appropriate for a mark that inhabits multiple times—the moment the brush applies the pigment onto the ground, when the applied mark begins to elongate into a tail-like form, and finally, during its fade-out. Formed from a finely ground mineral-based paint, the line shows itself against the rounded grain of the canvas at the point when disappearance begins. The viewer is able to see the line or the point as a pixilated mark composed of thousands of microscopic, granular dots against the rounded grain on the canvas. They appear more in sync with the horizontal, flat planes of Lee's floor-bound works than with the upright canvas support integral to painting.

At this point, the viewer begins to reconstruct the line or the point as a process of accumulation occurring over a finite span of time, but the slow process of dissolution also triggers incipient skepticism concerning the *inevitability* of a hierarchy between the ground and the mark. The mark is not there to reveal the empirical surface of the canvas. Both lines and points are loath to release their store of mineral particles. Gradually depleted of its load, the pigment-carrying brush appears to produce marks that disappear into the canvas. Painting refuses to be seen at a glance, but must instead be seen durationally.

After a time, the viewer becomes aware of the minimal presence of pictorial depth within the presumed boundaries of the work. Marked and unmarked spaces reside on a common plane, a coexistence facilitated by the consistent use of a single color, usually cobalt or vermilion, in a mineral-based pigment lacking the high viscosity of most oil or acrylic paints. Certainly the gradual disappearance of color in *From Line* suggests a shallow recession or protrusion of the point into the canvas field. But these delineations are repeated in insistently linear rows that move across a uniform plane rather than into a uniform space. The transfer of physical and psychic energy embodied in the cyclical disappearance and recuperation of pigment occurs over a series of moments. The brevity of each moment subverts the eye's attempt to longitudinally slice the surface into successive planes of illusionistic depth.

Sufficiently distinct in value and hue, the marks appear to protrude from the ground, as in *From Line* of 1975 (Figure 3.15). One can argue

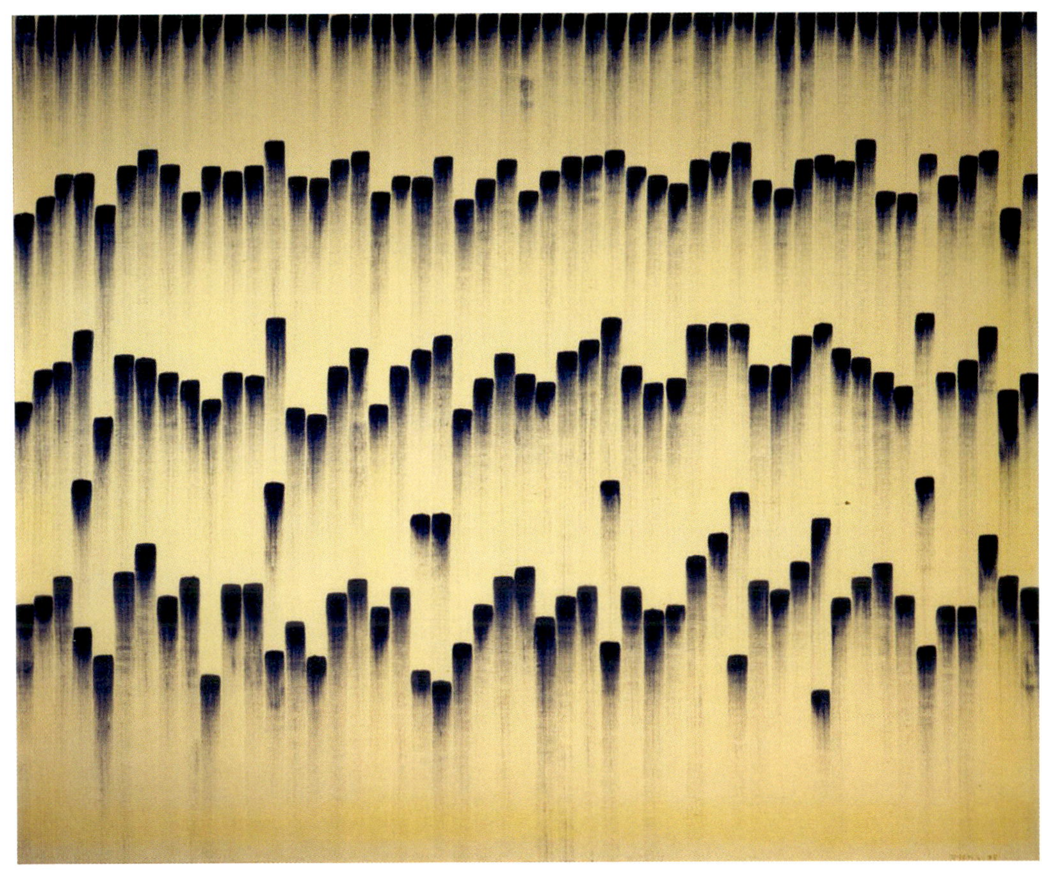

FIGURE 3.15 Lee Ufan,
From Line, 1975. Glue and
mineral pigment on canvas,
162 × 291 cm. Private
collection, Seoul. Courtesy
The Pace Gallery. Copyright
Lee Ufan.

FIGURE 3.16 Lee Ufan, *From Point*, 1976. Glue and mineral pigment on canvas, 117 × 117 cm. Collection of National Museum of Contemporary Art, Korea. Courtesy The Pace Gallery. Copyright Lee Ufan.

FIGURE 3.17 Lee Ufan, *From Point*, 1976. Glue and mineral pigment on canvas, 117 × 117 cm. Collection of National Museum of Contemporary Art, Korea. Courtesy The Pace Gallery. Copyright Lee Ufan.

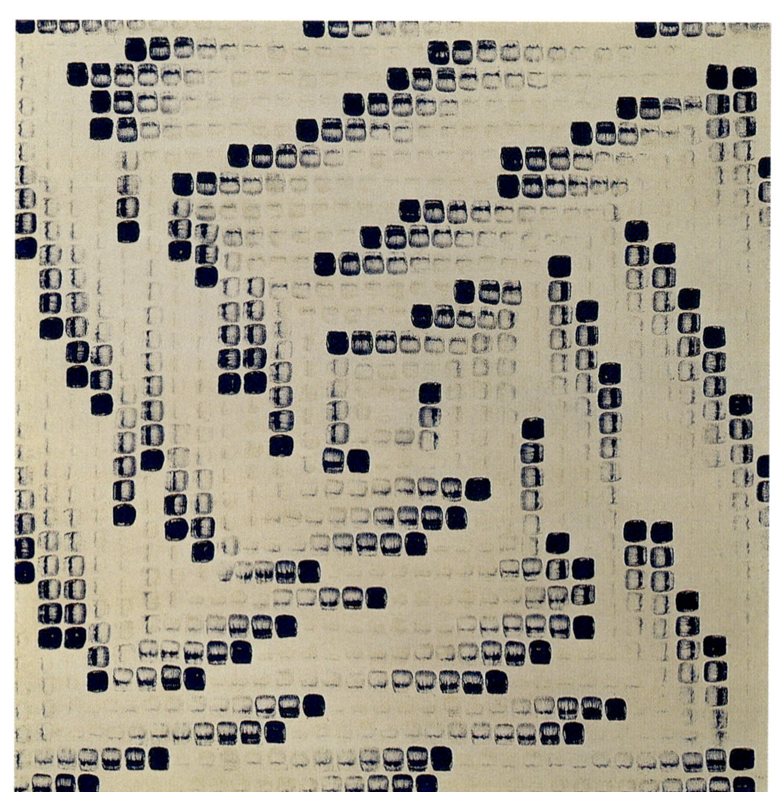

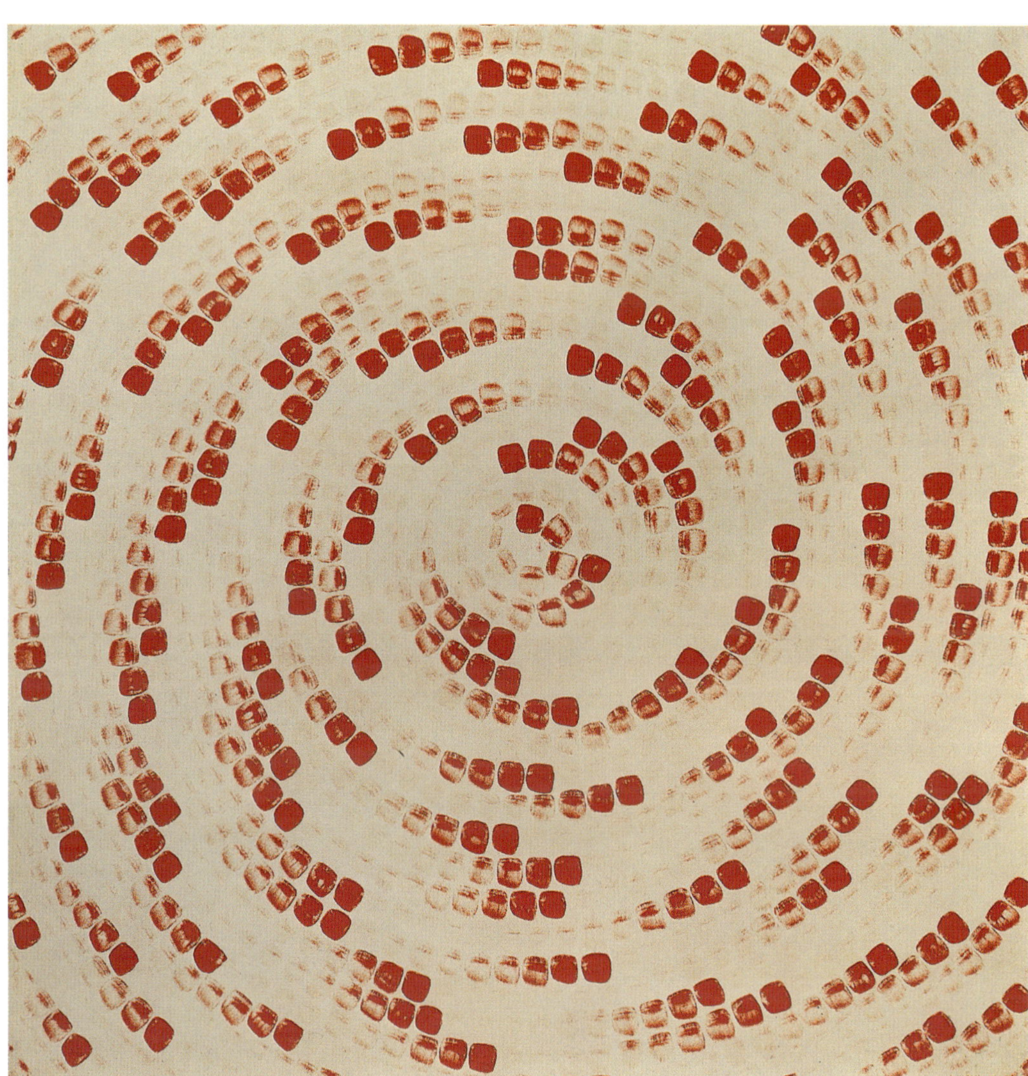

that the implied protrusion, and consequently the insinuation of the presence of illusionistic depth, resituates the work within the paradigm of the artist as creator. Further examination recasts the marks as a pattern, which exists due to recursion and contrast; the unmarked, white, "in-between" spaces make this apparent. The marked and unmarked spaces also maintain a dynamic state of equilibrium in which the initial suggestion of spatial depth enacted by the assumption of the figure–ground distinction yields to the eye's recognition of the supporting surface. As the eye registers this process, the pattern transforms itself into a self-sustaining zone of image and image field.

But the eye continues to follow the marks, whose outflow cannot be contained by the painting's edges. The effect is particularly striking in those instances where Lee chose to work with a square canvas. The square, with its associations to picture-window painting, became a foil for Lee's seeking to overcome the supposition that "a painting must be framed" in such a way that "everything is contained within four edges."[74] In one version of *From Point* (Figure 3.16), from 1976, points are arranged in staggered rows that emanate from the center and progress toward the edges of the work. A few rows appear truncated at the very edges of the work, so that the points collectively appear to put pressure against these edges. In another version of *From Point* (Figure 3.17), also painted in 1976, Lee actively tries to neutralize the square format by organizing points in a whirlpool-like configuration. Arranged in ever-expanding circles, the points train the eye to move well past the four corners of the work. The painting comes to exist as a fragment of a larger physical world, subsequently compelling the viewer to increase the physical distance between them.

Central to *From Point* (as in Figure 3.18) is the visibility of the mark's gradual disappearance. Moreover, each instance at which the fade is enacted differs, reflecting the variable rates at which the brush disburses its load of pigment. By way of elucidating the implications of the fade, consider the work of Swiss painter Niele Toroni, which bears more than a passing resemblance to certain versions of *From Point*. Along with Daniel Buren (whom Lee would meet in the fall of 1971), Michel Parmentier, and Olivier Mosset, with whom Toroni founded the group BPMT, Toroni similarly rejected the notion of painting as a condition defined by its capacity for representation and illusionistic depiction. Art historian Kang Tae-hi suggests that Lee may have seen *Imprints of a No. 50 Brush Repeated at Regular Intervals of 30 cm* (Figure 3.19) when he traveled in Europe during the summer

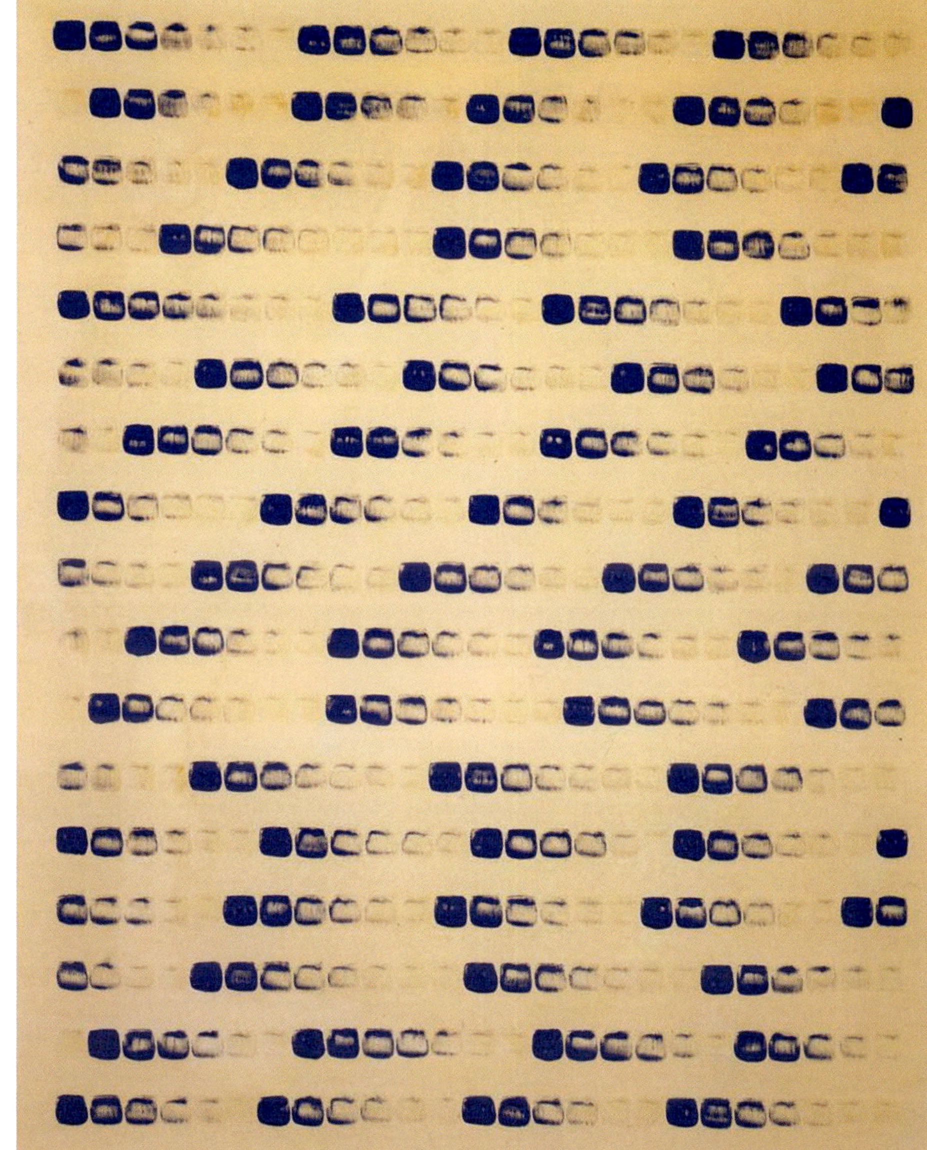

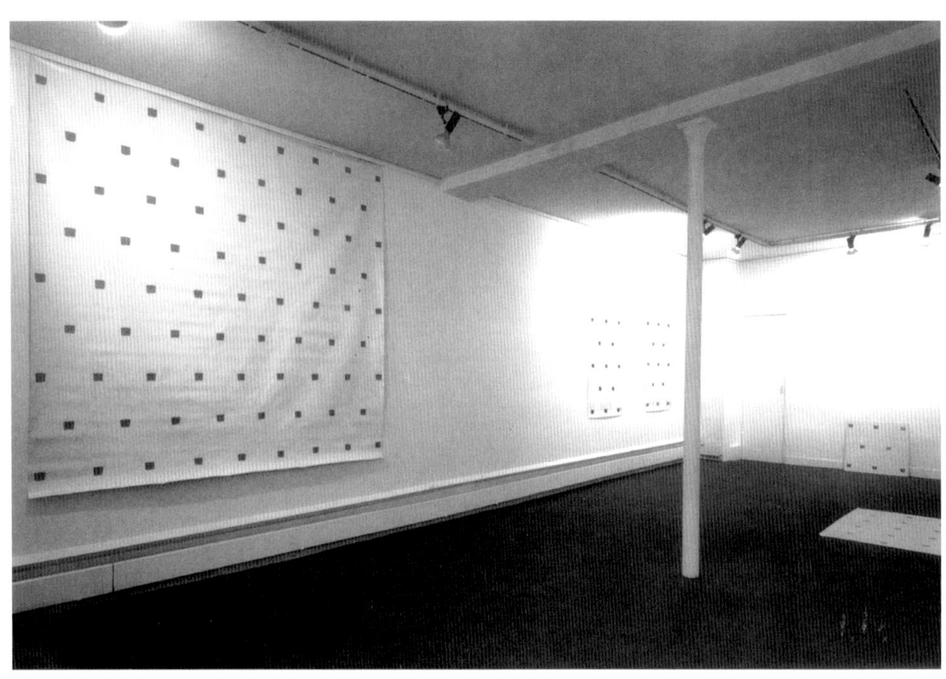

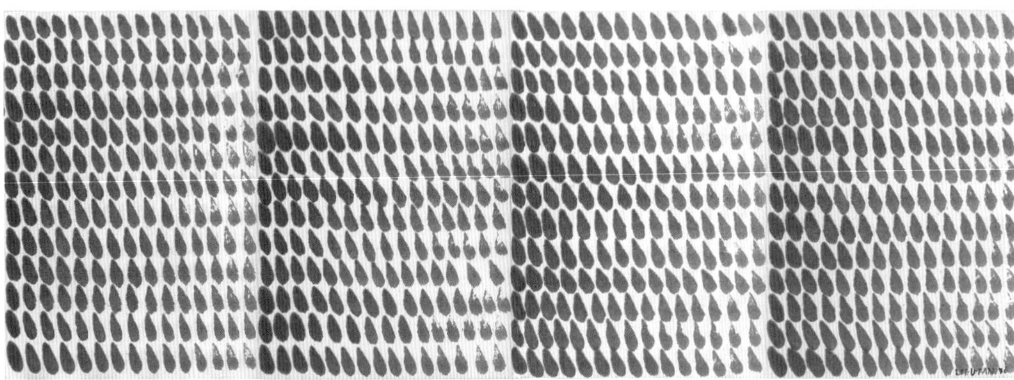

of 1971, just prior to his participation in the Paris Biennale.[75] Though Lee had probably missed Toroni's solo exhibitions at the Galerie Yvon Lambert, *Imprints,* along with the other paintings of the BPMT, had already exerted considerable impact well before then.[76] Lee himself perceived a similarity between his works and those of Toroni in their respective emphasis on repetition.[77]

But where Toroni has done his utmost to standardize the marks, Lee treats variability as central. Even in details of works like *From Point (#76075)* (Figure 3.20), a forty-eight-page album of paintings, where the image of the faded mark is far less apparent than in most versions of *From Point*, no two teardrop-shaped marks are alike. Toroni, in contrast, tries to sever painting from its provenance as a medium defined by efforts to make visible the movement of an artist's hand. The imprints appear as if produced by a machine, as if conforming to the image of a square. Toroni's intent is further implied by the title of his work, which itself specifies the exact distance between the marks impressed. The artist ensures that the liquid acrylic paint—of lesser viscosity than the mineral-based paint used by Lee—does not drip or smear onto the painting surface. The opticality of a depicted image never cedes to its haptic quality, regardless of the viewer's physical distance from the painting.

Yet part of what gives *From Point* its energy is the way Lee exploits the tension between the marks' handmade quality and their arrangement. On first glance, *From Point* is all about somatic inscription that could push back against the kind of programmatic mark making that seemed to be increasingly popular in various parts of the world. But its demonstration of touch hovered between being the result of deliberate intent and of incidental chance. Here Lee appears to have violated his own admonishments against the idea of making, yet his refusal to finalize his divorce from the hand is perhaps unavoidable. Letting the viewer be aware of the hand's presence is possibly the only thing that keeps the work from dissolving into what Lee described as "a 'rhetoric of production' [*saengsannon*], or the expansion of the self in order to produce and satisfy desire."[78] Yet the points are ordered in rows so straight and adamantly horizontal as to suggest the look of mechanical production, a configuration also applied to most versions of *From Line* where lines are not allowed to move freely in pictorial space. Despite being able to recognize each line as the trace of an individual hand moving from the top edge of the canvas to the bottom, the viewer must also recognize the way each is made to line up across the width of the canvas.

Even as one apprehends each line as its own distinct presence, one concurrently discerns that, compositionally speaking, the lines are modular elements with no particular line taking precedence over another. In this way, *From Line* has much in common with Toroni's work, in which the small square marks are deployed so regularly and consistently throughout pictorial space that they give rise to the image of a routine. The painting depicts a conception of time as something ordered and measurable, especially as the marks are shaped and configured in a way that imparts respect for the straight-line geometry of the pictorial space. The affective distinction between the presence of individual touch and the quasi-mechanistic arrangement of marks is pushed even further in *From Point* of 1975 (Figure 3.21), where rows of points are staggered so as to resemble digital signals pulsing across a flickering projection screen.

The prominence of this affective distinction throughout the *From Line* and *From Point* series implies another dimension to Lee's celebrated refusal of "making" and "creation." In refusing "creation," he was refusing approaches to artistic production that took the act of fabrication for granted. By conjoining individual touch and programmatic, non-hands-on compositional arrangements, Lee sought to generate a profound sense of disjunction that would compel viewers to directly confront the ambivalence inherent in any attempt to fashion materials into a specific entity. Refusing the idea of "making" meant accepting fabrication as a necessarily conflicted situation for which a dialectical outcome is the best-case scenario.

Lee was certainly not alone in his will to make known the conflicted nature of fabrication, especially in 1960s and '70s Korea and Japan, where artists were acutely aware of the way culture was made to rest on distinctions between the artisanal and the industrial. Ha Chonghyun brought craft into the domain of abstraction when he created *Birth-B* (Figure 2.1) by cutting canvas into long, wide strips and then weaving them into a grid composed of squares, each of which contained a circular form whose upper half consisted of thickly braided rope. He makes clear both the amount of labor invested into the work and the nature of this labor as handicraft. As discussed in chapter 2, some viewers interpreted the work as a Korean version of op art, probably because of the strong gradations of color and repeating geometric forms present throughout. For his palette, Ha took his cues from a rainbow that could only be imagined through the demands of commercial display. The colors were calculated to attract attention. Yellows were abnormally cheerful, blues

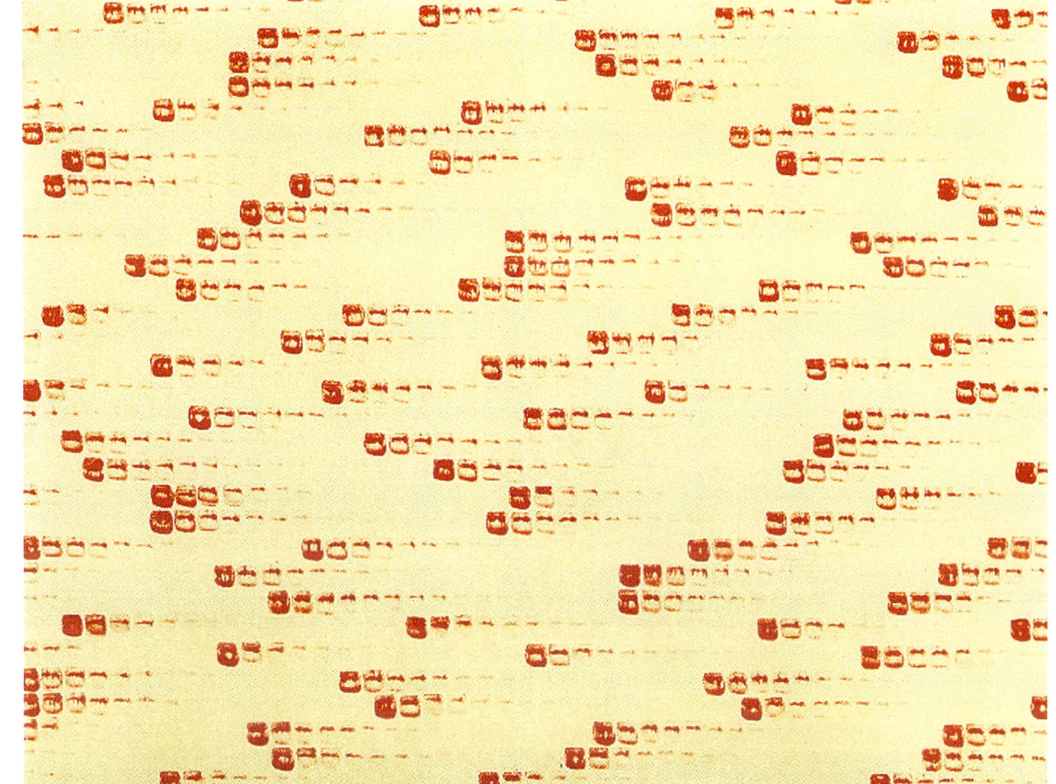

FIGURE 3.21 Lee Ufan, *From Point*, 1975. Glue and mineral pigment on canvas, 130 × 162 cm. Collection of Seoul Museum of Art. Courtesy The Pace Gallery. Copyright Lee Ufan.

excessively intense, and reds too obviously meant as a foil for the white contour lines outlining the bottom half of each circular motif.

Birth-B, however, was not as probing in its exploration of the nature of making as the *From Line* and *From Point* works, partly because Ha leaned too heavily on color. Lee, in contrast, mobilized several aspects of painting that offered a more sustained, if less immediately visceral, sense of fabrication's compromised nature. Going back to the comparison with Toroni's *Imprints of a No. 50 Brush Repeated at Regular Intervals of 30 cm,* one observes that depiction is contingent on the spaces between marks and on the way those intervals relate to the viewer looking directly at the work. Toroni spaces his marks in thirty-centimeter increments, a distance that encourages viewers to imagine how their own bodies might figure in Toroni's depiction of space. The distance between the work and the artist compels some consideration of scale, which for Lee means also a consideration of the mark. In those versions of *From Line* and *From Point* involving the staggered arrangement of marks, Lee treats the mark as units of measurement. The lines of *From Line* that stretch from one edge to the other, and in apparent sequence, confirm the dimensions of the canvas, which then brings to viewers' attention the proportions of the physical space in which the canvas is located. In the *From Point* works, the repeated imprints of the rounded brush size the canvas, thus emphasizing it as an object defined by its proportions.

Through scale, Lee invites his viewer to consider the relationship between the exhibition wall and the physical work. The margins of the canvas are specifically defined to reconfirm the viewers' perception of the work as an object in the material world. Characterizing the *From Line* works is a continuity of touch that induces the eye to commit to the lines as they traverse the length of the canvas. Coupled with the similarity of color between the wall and canvas, the trajectory of the eye that travels the length of each vertical stroke prevents the viewer from seeing an end to the painting. Reviewing Lee's show at the Hyundai Gallery in 1978, critic Kim Yun-su saw the *From Line* and *From Point* works as troubling examples of what he saw as an instance of theory coming before painting, an objection similar to that raised by Yoo Youngkuk during the roundtable discussion for *Contemporary Korean Painting* in 1968.[79] Yet Kim only saw part of the picture, as Lee was careful to defuse this impression by small but visible adjustments that aggregated into an image of incompleteness. The faltering ends of the lines in *From Line* compromised the seeming modularity of images, as did the fluctuating ratio of pigment to nonpigment in *From Point*.

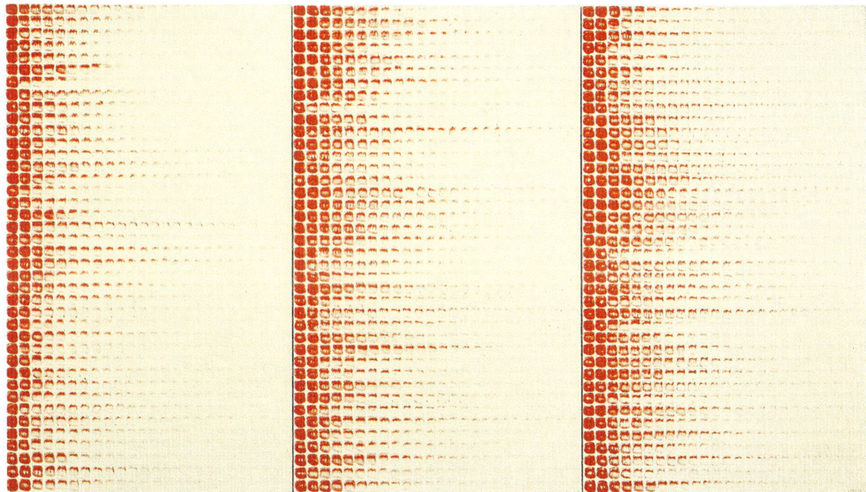

That this process also involves the body of the viewer is under-scored in a 1975 version of *From Point* (Figure 3.22), which neatly plays the literal articulation of the work's physical format against paint-ing's capacity for metaphor. Recalling traditional folding screens in the greater East Asian tradition, in which multiple panels are joined together to form a continuous plane, three canvas panels are joined together. On each panel the artist has painted successive horizontal rows of points, each starting from the left-hand edge of that panel. Because each row appears to end at the edge demarcating one panel from another, the work initially resonates more as a freestanding object defined by its physical limits and less as a pictorial composition. But in drawing attention to the edges at which the rows begin and end, Lee reinforces their verticality as that which paradoxically results from the repetition of horizontal rows.

In *From Point* pictorial space is divided not by painted vertical lines but by an emphasis on the significance of the physical edge. Similar to many examples of folding screens, in which the depicted image awaits activation upon its placement in a room or building, *From Point* shows an image depicted in such a way that its main purpose is to wait for a viewer willing to follow the direction of the points from left to right. It is not, however, a frontal work, which exists to affirm the viewer who looks at it, or sits in front of it. This version of *From Point* is *From Line* rotated so that the steady process of dissolution emphasizes the lateral pull of visual energy from one side of the canvas to the other. It positions the

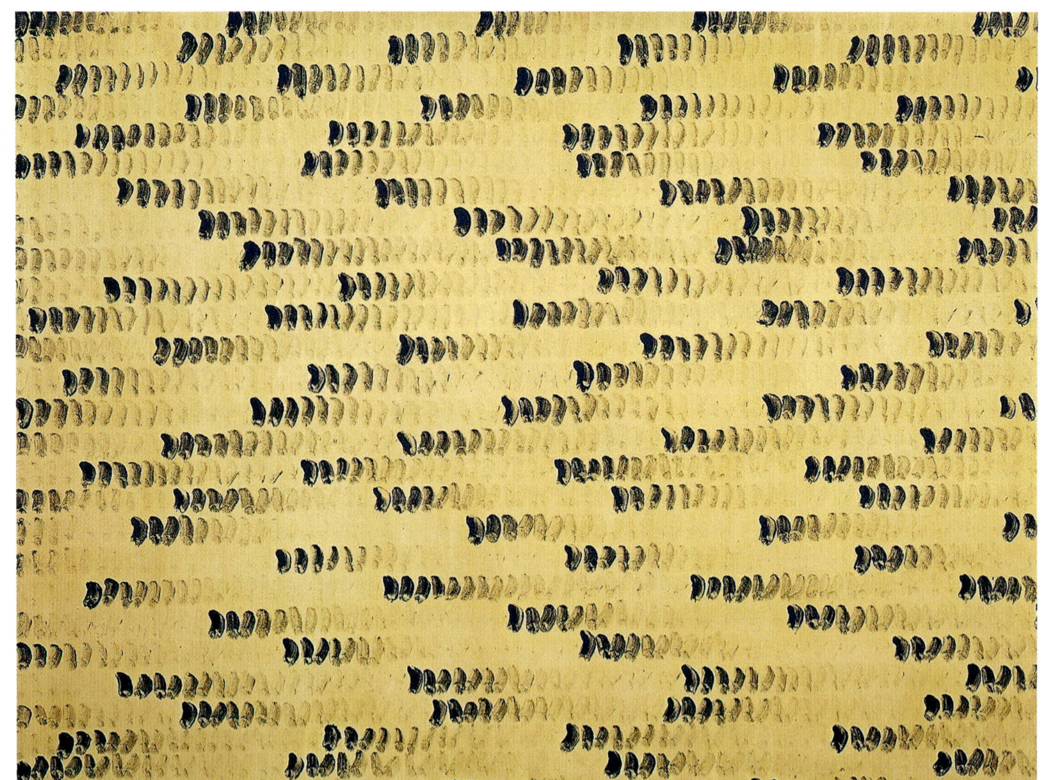

FIGURE 3.23 Lee Ufan, *From Point*, 1973. Glue and mineral pigment on canvas, 194 × 259 cm. Collection of National Museum of Contemporary Art, Korea. Courtesy The Pace Gallery. Copyright Lee Ufan.

viewer as situated within the tension generated from a double awareness of his or her upright body and of the lateral movement of the eye.

As eager as he was to downplay the work as a thing created, Lee was
also aware that any full-fledged denial also risked becoming excessively
programmatic. What saved *From Line* and *From Point* from verging into
dogmatism was Lee's willingness to compromise one goal for the sake
of considering another, which, in this case, was a deeply personal investigation of the self. In works like a *From Point* from 1973 (Figure 3.23),
there is a marked disjunction between the works' affect of control and
the transparent refusal of such.

Then there is the addition of a signature (Figures 3.16, 3.17, 3.21),
usually in the painting's lower right-hand corner. Using a fine-tipped
brush ordinarily used for ink painting, the artist carefully formed block
letters that spell "L. UFAN." From a history of text utterly different from
the kind of writing implied by the long strokes of *From Line*, the Roman
block letters remain distinctly separate from the structure of the composition. Although the decision to abbreviate the first letter of the surname
rather than of the given name may have stemmed from confusion over
Western naming conventions and word order, it nevertheless imparts
an unexpected air of intimacy. It also suggests a desire to have these
works considered in relation to Euro-American abstraction, which may
also explain why Kwon Young-woo chose to sign his works (albeit in
cursive Korean) rather than continue the Asian tradition of affixing his
seal, beginning with his second show at the Myongdong Gallery in 1974.

By putting himself into the work by way of the signature and a palpable affect of control, Lee reminded his viewers that *From Line* and
From Point are ultimately concerned with the artist's negotiations with
place and of being placed. Lee harbored no illusions about what art
could realistically achieve as a political apparatus, yet the *From Line*
and *From Point* series responded to the taxonomic systems by which
artworks and artists were classified. Regardless of the grounds on which
they were based, these systems struck Lee as identical in their rigid-
ity. Well-rehearsed notions of cultural identity persisted, for example,
in grouping artists and artworks under categories of nation, while
similarly reified ideas of genre and originality often precluded particular works from being regarded on their own terms. To paint in ways
that might upset the distinctions upon which these taxonomies were
founded might be the most critical step in remaking a world that to
viewers in 1970s Japan and Korea seemed all too premised on the cir-
cumscription of individuals by much larger forces, attitudes, and beliefs.

FOUR

Reading Park Seobo's *Écriture* in Authoritarian Korea

A few months before Lee Ufan unveiled *From Line* and *From Point* at the Tokyo Gallery in the fall of 1973, his good friend Park Seobo unveiled a new series of paintings at the nearby Muramatsu Gallery. All were on pale gray, off-white, or soft yellow supports covered with multiple thin layers of white oil paint that set off delicate fringes of short, straight lines made with a pencil. In *Myobŏp C* (Figure 4.1), the shape of the canvas determined the composition. Park first drew a line as close as possible to the canvas edge and then drew another replicating the shape of the canvas but situated more toward the painting's center. Using this pair of lines as his general baseline, he then drew short, thin lines at an angle to emphasize the painting as a function of its edges.

As Lee did in *From Line* and *From Point,* Park slowed down the process of painting by taking the act of mark making as his subject. But where Lee stressed the individuality of each mark, Park sought to erase it by massing his lines as tightly and densely as possible. The work has all the trappings of painting—a rectangular canvas mounted upright on a wall—but the repeated incision of angular strokes on paint not yet dried results in a surface that compels viewers to regard the work itself as the skin of a freestanding object. It was partly for this reason that Joseph Love, one of *Myobŏp*'s keenest observers, compared the painting to Korean white pottery, or *punch'ŏng,* the glazed whitish ceramics of the fifteenth and sixteenth centuries decorated with patterns incised on white slip.[1] Park added a further twist by choosing to use pencil, so that the work, when seen from a distance or in reproduction, looks far more like writing than painting. That the artist considered this resemblance is reflected by his initial choice of title: *myobŏp* literally means of "method of drawing," but its first half—*myo*—refers to acts of depiction.

Park's approach to the mark arose from a desire to think about painting outside the terms through which it was ordinarily construed. In this

FIGURE 4.1 Park Seobo, *Myobŏp C* (later retitled *Écriture No. 5-73*), 1973. Pencil and oil on canvas, 162 × 130 cm. Collection of Seobo Foundation, Seoul.

way, he shared much in common with Lee, with whom he worked on at least one occasion during the early 1970s. For Park, this interest meant trying to think beyond what in Korea had become a deeply entrenched binary between abstraction and figuration. This he tried to do in his approach to the line, which in the early years of *Myobŏp*, particularly between 1973 and 1980, seemed torn between its capacities for representation and nonrepresentation. When *Myobŏp* made its Korean debut at the Myongdong Gallery in October 1973, Park remarked: "I am specifically trying not to insert meaning [into them]; my works do not possess that which is called an image. Since there is no image, there is no expression."[2] Yet as Lee did with the brush in *From Line* and *From Point*, Park controls the pencil in ways that compel viewers to consider the resulting marks as traces of the artist's physical presence. Three years after unveiling *Myobŏp*, Park claimed that he began the series after watching his grade-school son practice his penmanship on manuscript paper (*wŏngoji*), a type of specially lined graph paper distinctive for its rows of boxes intended to separate one character from another.[3] Unable to make his letters fit into the squares of the penmanship paper, he became frustrated, scribbling furiously over the practice paper. Inspired by this "instinctive" scribbling, Park claimed to have made his first *Myobŏp* works in the late 1960s.[4] Both the title of the series and the works themselves strongly suggest that Park was at least thinking about how the image of the line figured within writing, as well as vice versa. In Korean, the word *myobŏp* is generally invoked in connection with ink painting (*tongyanghwa*); it refers to methods of depiction associated especially with the line. Along similar lines, some *Myobŏp* works feature lines contorted into long, sinuous curves that recall calligraphy, a medium with which Park and other artists of his generation were familiar and which involved thinking of lines as both text and trace.

What explains Park's interest in mark making as an enterprise so decidedly suspended between the literal enactment of physical presence and its potential function as a means of legible communication? One considers the timing of the debut of the series in 1973, only a few months after Park Chung-hee suspended the South Korean constitution and declared martial law on the pretext of defending the country against Communist aggression. In place of the original constitution, which allotted citizens some civil liberties, the new constitution granted the president almost unlimited executive power for life. Known more commonly as "Yushin," or "Revitalization," this constitution would remain in force until Park Chung-hee was assassinated in 1979.

Censorship, surveillance, and overall state scrutiny reached new highs, and the act of communication, especially written communication, was heavily monitored.

Park Seobo himself experienced this renewed authoritarianism firsthand when he was arrested with Lee Ufan upon the latter's visit to Seoul in March 1974.[5] Yet unlike Lee, whose *zainichi* status was itself grounds for government suspicion, Park was quickly released. His association with Lee seemed to have no ill effects; indeed, Park seems to have prospered during the Yushin era. Not only was he able to hold—and perhaps more important, given the state's intense suspicion of intellectuals, keep—a coveted professorship at Hongik University, he was the vice president of the Korean Fine Arts Association whose responsibilities included the all-important selection of Korean delegates for overseas artistic events.

Even more indicative of his status was his participation in the national documentary paintings project (*minjok kirok'wa*), the largest visual arts project ever undertaken by the Korean government in the postwar era. Begun in 1966, the project was the brainchild of Kim Jong-pil, KCIA founder, future prime minister, and Park Chung-hee's all-around right-hand man. It commissioned some of the country's leading artists to paint figurative and highly idealized scenes of Korean history or of industrialization taking place in the present. Most Korean artists in the 1960s and '70s considered an invitation to participate in the project an explicit badge of state approbation. But Park's involvement in the national documentary paintings project gave him a special understanding of the dynamics of the Yushin era as well as of the state's own attempts at overseeing the formation of a collective identity for its citizens. Other tansaekhwa artists, including Yun Hyongkeun and Chung Chang-sup, also participated in the project, yet it was Park who seemed most attuned to the state's hopes for the project.

Although Park's involvement in the national documentary paintings project has been regarded as an admission of his complicity with the Yushin government, the actual paintings suggest a different set of intentions, in relation not only to Park's national documentary paintings but also to *Myobŏp*. These intentions were alluded to through Park's exploration of the relationship between painting and its viewer. Was it possible for a viewer to be concurrently subject to, and separate from, the depictions taking place in a painting? On another level, what could a painting communicate to its viewer outside of its own material presence? Was it enough for a painting to assert nothing but that presence?

For many Korean artists, the declaration of martial law in 1972 was but the culmination of an inexorable slide into dictatorship. From the time Park Chung-hee took control of the state in 1961, he steadily moved toward full-blown authoritarianism, the pace hastened by such events as North Korean commandos' nearly successful attempt to assassinate Park in 1968 and elections that increasingly challenged Park's authority. In the Korean art world, the effects of authoritarian rule often took the guise of anti-Communist crusades, as evidenced by events like the highly publicized 1967 trial of the Paris-based painter Lee Ungno, who, only five years after his triumphant homecoming show in Seoul, was sentenced to life in prison for espionage after traveling to East Berlin to meet his adopted son.[6]

Granted, artworks continued to be made, exhibited, and sold with comparatively minimal intervention from the state, which considered visual art a vital element of its efforts to promote Korea abroad and to enhance its own credibility at home. Among its most significant initiatives was the founding of *Space*, the multidisciplinary journal of culture that paid so much attention to visual art that even art critics complained of the excessive focus.[7] Although a privately owned journal, *Space* was founded by Kim Swoogeun, who was the state's unofficial but de facto architect in the early years of the Park Chung-hee regime.[8] In raising funds for his new venture, Kim the architect appealed to his well-placed connections, including none other than Kim Jong-pil, who, in the summer of 1966, reportedly gave what was then the astonishingly large sum of 2 million won as seed money.[9] It was further reported that the January 1967 issue cost 800,000 won, more than four times what the average South Korean family earned in 1969.[10] *Space* enjoyed considerable freedom in both content and layout, even going so far as to take indirect aim at government policies, including the push for rapid industrialization.[11]

Yet the state also looked askance at visual art, as noted by Kim Chi-ha, the poet who became a veritable symbol of intellectual dissent in Korea after publishing "Five Bandits," a 1970 poem satirizing the elite.[12] Having majored in aesthetics at Seoul National University, Kim was familiar with the state's confiscation and probable destruction in 1969 of O Yun's painting *1960, Ka* (Figure 4.2), intended to be shown as part of the inaugural exhibition of a group of young student-artists called Hyŏnsil Tongin, or Reality Group, for which Kim wrote a manifesto.[13] Known

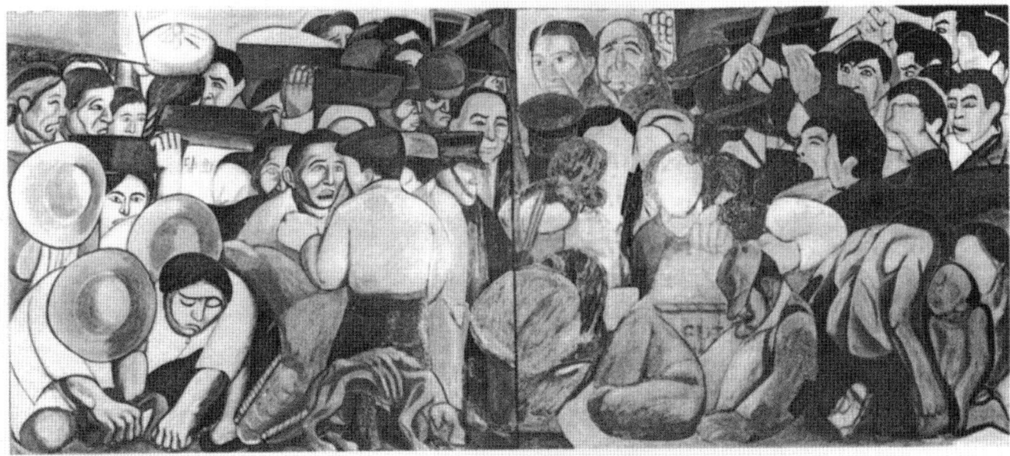

FIGURE 4.2 O Yun, *1960, Ka*, 1969. Unfinished painting published in Reality Group exhibition pamphlet, October 25, 1969.

today only through a black-and-white photocopy of the unfinished painting reproduced for the exhibition pamphlet, the work, which according to O's younger sister "would have probably been painted in very colorful, warm tones," depicted an imagined scene from the April Revolution of 1960 that directly resulted in the overthrow of Rhee Syngman, the first president of South Korea.[14] O's interest in Mexican social realism is evident in *1960, Ka*: in the lower left-hand corner a trio of workers is shown wearing the kind of broad-brimmed white hats often associated with the murals of Diego Rivera.[15] Whether O or his professors at Seoul National University who objected to the work knew of Rivera's Marxist sympathies is uncertain, but according to Kim, the dean's office of Seoul National University's art school accused O of making a work that was "just like those of North Korea or Eastern Europe and thus anti-establishment and anti-artistic."[16] It was more likely, however, that the university, itself a state institution, was alarmed by O's choice of subject and by the parallels that could be drawn between the despotic rule of President Rhee in 1960 and the increasingly unpopular regime of President Park in 1969.

By 1970 civil liberties had eroded to such an extent that it was all but impossible to stage any kind of public assembly without running afoul of the law. Matters worsened the next year when Park Chung-hee barely won the 1971 presidential election over leading opposition politician Kim Dae-jung. Government surveillance intensified to such a point that even casual hearsay became sufficient grounds for condemnation. The December 1971 issue of *Kŏmch'al*, the monthly journal of the chief prosecutor's office, reported, for example, that Bang Keun-taek had praised North Korea in conversation to another person on four occasions.[17] The state also expanded the criteria by which an individual might be found culpable. Those who crossed the political elite or their friends quickly wound up in jail or worse, as Yun Hyongkeun discovered when he protested the admission of a powerful industrialist's daughter to the high school where he taught. Most devastating of all were the Emergency Decrees (*Kin'gŭp choch'i*) initiated shortly after the onset of martial law in early 1973. Intended to muzzle criticism of the Yushin government, they ushered in an era of intense censorship, particularly of the press. Opposition politician and publisher of leading dissident journal *Tari*, Kim Sang-hyun put it best in early 1972 when he described this period as "an age when silence is golden."[18]

The cartoonist and painter Kim Sung-hwan observed that the Park Chung-hee regime of the 1970s "spent a great deal of energy blocking the mouths and ears of the public."[19] The eyes, however, were given some latitude, as the state was curiously literal minded in what it regarded as visual insurrection. Sung Neung-kyung, for example, noted, "The state was liable to take down anything that had the color red in it, simply because of its symbolic associations with communism."[20] But although visual artists generally enjoyed greater freedom than their literary counterparts, this freedom also imposed upon artists a duty to consider carefully what they made visible.

Consider the large number of works addressing censorship of the press and particularly of newspapers, which for most Koreans living in the postwar period were the most vital source of information. Artists with interests as different as Sung Neung-kyung and Choi Tae-shin incorporated the newspaper in ways that visibly drew attention to what was being done to the press in the world outside the space of the exhibition. In the small gallery located in the basement of the National Museum of Modern Art, Sung Neung-kyung performed *Newspaper after the First of June 1974* (Figure 4.3) as part of the exhibition hosted by S.T. (Space and Time), a loose coalition of artists and critics known for their interest in conceptual art, partly in reaction against what Sung recalled was the "overwhelming influence of Mono-ha and their emphasis on the materiality of things."[21] During each day of the exhibition, he used a razor blade to cut out articles from various pages of the *Tonga ilbo*, which for Sung was "the only newspaper at the time with even a hint of critical awareness as to what was happening politically."[22] Leaving untouched the margins between articles and the sections on which

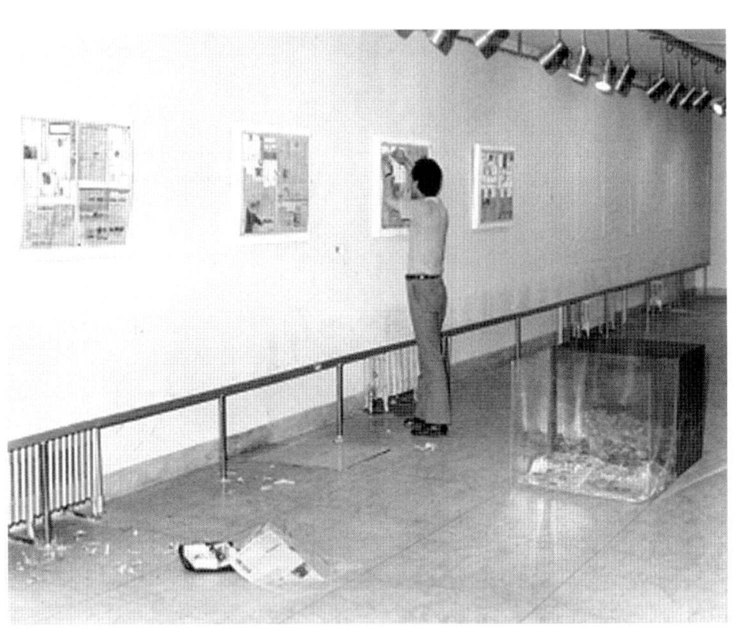

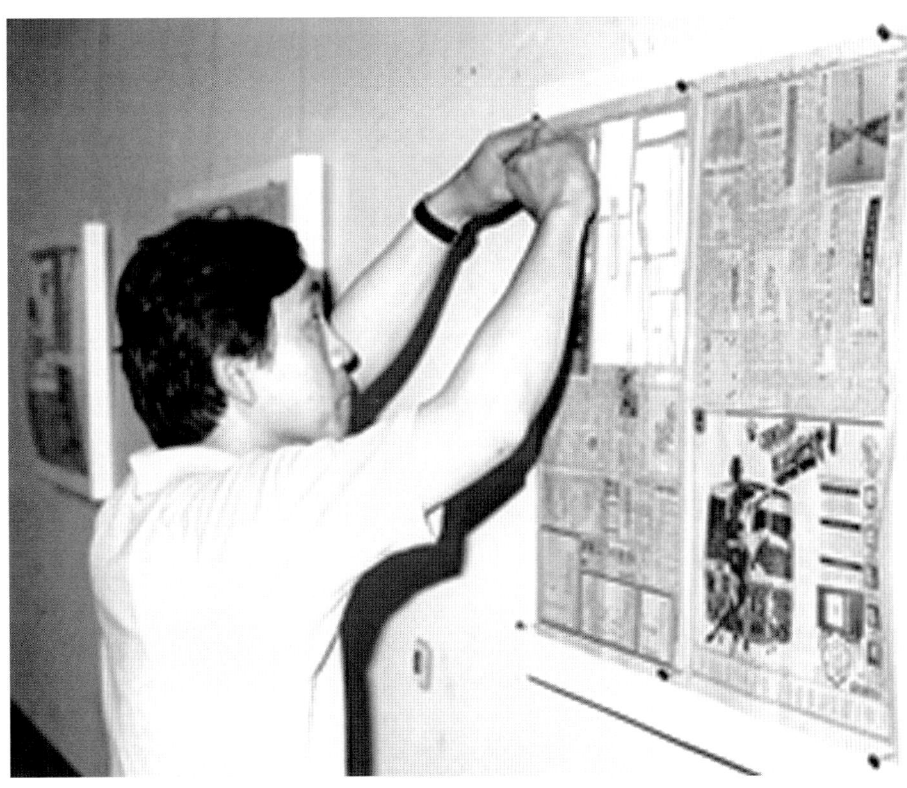

advertisements were printed, each double-sided newspaper sheet was then successively mounted on the wall of the exhibition at intervals "calculated to take account of the dimensions of the exhibition space" but also intended to reproduce the experience of reading proposed by Korean newspaper companies, which often displayed each day's paper in front of their headquarters in a similar manner.[23] Underneath the sheets were two transparent acrylic boxes. One was blue and contained articles clipped from the day's papers. The other was clear, and in this one, at the end of each day, Sung disposed of the newspaper sheets attached to the exhibition wall.

Sung claimed that his intent was to critique the newspaper and its perverting of the truth, an aim he felt was best carried out by using actual newspapers.[24] As he later stated, it was not enough to convey a message; one also had to consider the channel relaying the message: "There was no distinction between method and content," he said. He understood that it would be "far too clear," as well as too dangerous, to simply rip articles out of the newspaper.[25] That Sung took such care in accurately excising articles from each sheet of newspaper suggests an intention to demonstrate a sense of technique that might double as an alibi in case state authorities accused him of insurrectionist tendencies. After he had himself photographed during the performance, Sung recropped some of the photographs so as to bring forth the idea, if not the image, of labor. In one photograph, he is shown in the act of excision, his arms silhouetted dramatically against the wall (Figure 4.4). In excising large blocks of text from the printed page, Sung rewired the viewing process so that viewers expecting to read the paper only discovered that it had been stripped of its legibility as a form of text-based communication. One found that it was only a piece of paper attached to a wall, a discovery emphasized by the intense whiteness of the panels on which each sheet of newspaper was mounted. Sung indicated that censored papers have no more value than the paper on which they are printed. In this way, he reminded viewers that absence too is an image that sometimes speaks more forcefully than the most explicitly present signs.

This train of thought was shared by his contemporary Choi Tae-shin, who "wanted to see what a newspaper looked like if left completely blank."[26] A graduate of Hongik University's oil-painting department, Choi remembers being "fascinated" by Park Seobo's lectures that frequently mentioned what he had seen during his travels abroad.[27] Certainly Choi persisted in thinking about painting as evidenced in his submission to the first of the Seoul Contemporary Arts Festivals (Sŏul

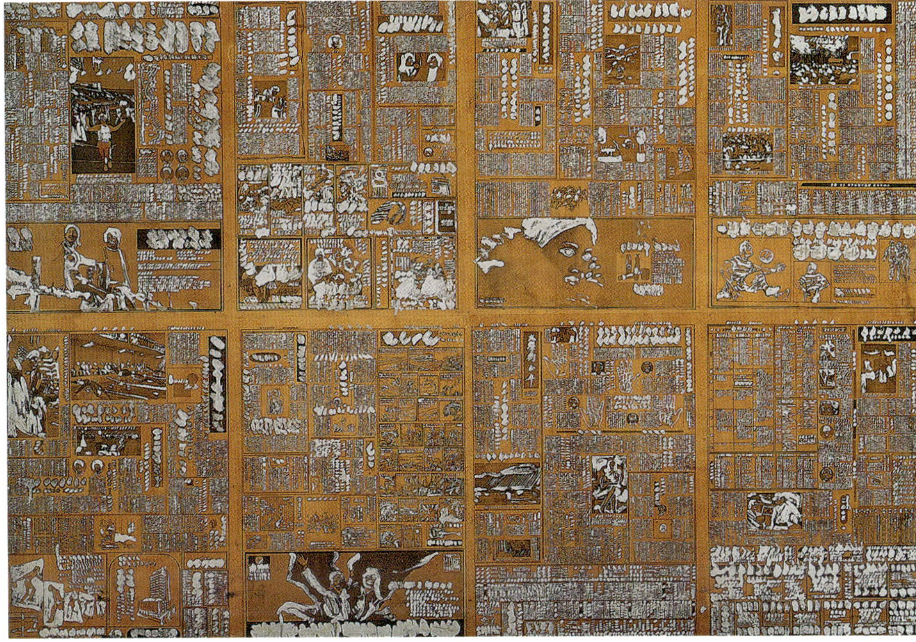

Hyŏndae Misulje), which, like the Seoul Indépendants exhibitions, were a series of large group shows that tried to offer a more inclusive look at contemporary art in Korea than what could be found in the Kukchŏn. In 1975 Choi exhibited *Newspaper 74-3* (Figure 4.5), a work made by gluing two double-page newspaper sheets from the November 24, 1974, issue of the sports and entertainment paper *Ilgan sŭp'ochŭ* on canvas mounted on a wooden panel. Each printed character has been blotted out so that the resulting effect is a Morse code–like string of variably sized dots, mimicking the way readers of the time might have felt about the rhetoric of the state. "Stimulated" by Lee Ufan's writings on phenomenology, Choi played up the interaction between paint and its support so that the dabs, blobs, and expanses of paint appear to merge into a unified surface.[28]

In making central the act of deleting, excising, and concealing the printed word, both Sung Neung-kyung and Choi Tae-shin metonymically reproduced the way the state imposed its presence by subjecting its citizens to the condition of silence. Conversely, Park Seobo and his tansaekhwa colleagues made no specific reference to censorship or to the politics of the era, an omission cast as an ethical failing by revisionist historians and critics troubled by what they saw as the unduly

FIGURE 4.6 Park Seobo, *Écriture No. 8-67*, 1967. Pencil and oil on canvas, 130 × 130 cm. Collection of the artist.

privileged position of tansaekhwa—and to an extent, abstraction—in postwar Korean art history. Tansaekhwa supporters were quick to rush to the movement's defense, including the former S.T. critic Kim Bok-young, who argued that *Myobŏp* was a buried confession regarding the difficulty of life in the oppressive 1970s.[29] He cited Park's "confessional notes" published in *Space* in 1977, where he remarked, "I tried my hardest to survive."[30] Kim argued that the lack of visible imagery in *Myobŏp* is a kind of absence that signaled Park's withdrawal from the oppressiveness of Yushin society.[31] The *Myobŏp* works, he said, showed a "dissolution of subjectivity," by which he appeared to mean the absence of images and actions that invoke the presence of a specific individual.[32]

In attributing to *Myobŏp* a sense of withdrawal, Kim seems to be, and may have been, wishing for the lost modernist dream of an autonomous work, able to escape from the cacophonous fray of ideological combat. Kim may have been exhausted from what he saw of art criticism, which in Korea circa 2006 revolved insistently around assessing a work's presumed ideological sympathies. But the *Myobŏp* works were hardly an art of withdrawal, even if they reflected Park's belief that an "artist needs no words."[33] Instead of withdrawal, the trope that more usefully illustrates what this response entailed was silence. It was not code for resistance; *Myobŏp* was not an art intended to explicitly challenge a known adversary. Park did not think of his works as fulfilling a social purpose in the way that he might have done with *No. 1* during the era of postwar reconstruction in 1957, or in the way that Lee Ufan did in late 1960s and early 1970s Japan. Yet his works turned on a viewing experience that distinctly resonated with the concerns of its viewers living in Yushin Korea, including the increasingly embattled right to assert one's presence, and the relationship between the state and its citizenry as evinced through various forms of representation.

MYOBŎP'S PRESENCE

Despite Park's claims of having first thought of *Myobŏp* after observing his son's initial attempts at manipulating lines into syllables, his grids are overlaid with a fine veil of pencil marks that bear little resemblance to what one might expect of a child's frenzied scribbling. Instead, the faintness of the lines imparts to the grid a sensation of luminescence so that the painting appears to glow from within. The grid of what Park now calls *Écriture No. 8-67* (Figure 4.6) closes off the work to anything

but a restatement of its material parts. It is pictorial space made to heel by its own compositional order.

Écriture No. 8-67 offers a viewing experience fundamentally premised on imminence, as does *Myobŏp C*, which appears to flicker in and out of sight, the humble, even banal nature of the work's materiality notwithstanding. It is just a rectangular canvas on which Park has delineated another, more yellowish rectangle by laboriously repeating the same abbreviated gesture. Yet the result is a work that, seen from a distance, appears tremulous. In *Myobŏp A* (Figure 4.7), exhibited as part of *Myobŏp*'s Tokyo debut, the lightly penciled lines undermine but do not completely destroy the painting's relationship to monochromy. The viewer approaches the work hoping to discover what this means but walks away convinced that the painting need not mean anything at all.

In these early *Myobŏp* works is the belief that painting should not have to commit itself to one visual experience or another. In *Écriture No. 43-73* (Figure 4.8), the same thin, wispy lines used in *Myobŏp C* now take as their cue the top and bottom edges of the canvas. Park arranges the lines into horizontal rows, with each line just long enough to almost touch those in the rows immediately above and below it. This allows

FIGURE 4.9 Park Seobo, *Écriture No. 72-74*, 1974. Pencil and oil on canvas, 45.5 × 53 cm. Private collection, Masan, Korea.

for glimpses of the white oil support to peep through the penciled haze, thus making the painting appear to glow from a distance. That the lines are set at a diagonal running right to left further activates the work, which thus appears to vacillate when seen from a certain distance. Here the rows are far more uncertain than the carefully ruled grid of *Écriture No. 8-67*. They ripple upward and downward, consequently breaking down what would have initially appeared to Park as pictorial space into a quivering surface that resonates to viewers most strongly at a corporeal level. In this work, Park begins to tentatively move away from the security offered by the grid in *Écriture No. 8-67* or even the nested rectangles of *Myobŏp C*, whose subsequent title, *Écriture No. 5-73*, indicates that it was made somewhat earlier than *Écriture No. 43-73*.

There still remains something of the reverence with which Park appeared to have addressed the canvas in *Écriture No. 8-67*. Sensing that this reverence might not be enough to draw attention to the canvas, Park also made works like *Écriture No. 72-74* (Figure 4.9), in which he moved a pencil repeatedly from one side of a canvas to the other. In this Park raises the question of what it is that separates painting from drawing, or perhaps more specifically, what the stakes are in making this distinction in the first place. As he dutifully rehearsed in previous *Myobŏp* works, drawing was about inscribing a line on a surface for the purpose of depicting a figure on a stable ground. But he compromised his own efforts at drawing by choosing to inscribe his lines while the initial layer of paint was still wet. The result is a muddled thicket of furrows and ridges that reads more persuasively as an agglutination of graphite and paint than as a set of lines intended to direct the viewer's attention.

In presenting highly materialist definitions of drawing and painting, Park seemed to have absorbed much of the phenomenological turn initiated by Lee Ufan, one of his closest interlocutors, who encouraged Park to proceed with the *Myobŏp* works when he visited Seoul and stayed in Park's home in November 1971.[34] Lee, however, sought to deny his role as the work's author by vigorously taxing viewers' faculties of perception through unexpected juxtapositions of materials with different cultural associations and physical properties. Conversely, Park was interested in transforming the viewing experience so that the painting appeared to simultaneously present and withhold itself from the viewer. Lee, moreover, emphasizes materials through their most recognizable properties in a way that borders on the literal; Park is more reserved, and even skeptical of the claims presumed of certain materials. In *From Line* and *From Point*, Lee enthusiastically pits the recalcitrant

FIGURE 4.10 Park Seobo,
Écriture No. 21-72, 1972.
Pencil and oil on canvas,
54 × 65 cm. Private collection,
Seoul. Photograph by Lee
Man-hong.

chalkiness of mineral pigment against the stubbly weave of canvas in order to discover what might emerge from the discrepancy. Park, in contrast, chose to make viewers uncertain of how they understand the behaviors of oil paint and pencil. Paint does not always lie flat against the canvas, nor is pencil always a means of actively producing figures upon a passive ground. In *Myobŏp A* lines are massed to form a veil that shrouds the canvas. Very thin gaps of untouched support separate each row; the effect is of a veil being let open to admit light. That the lines seem only faintly incised is the result of a draw between liquid paint and solid lead as a pencil was pushed and pulled through a still-wet surface. Yet the combination of marked and unmarked areas makes the painting appear as if it is in perpetual flux, its contents permanently unsettled.

Works like *Écriture No. 21-72* (Figure 4.10) frustrate the pencil's attempts to triumph over the painted support. The frequently uneven incisions testify to the struggle Park experienced when he pushed the pencil through paint that was still viscous. In *Myobŏp A* and *Myobŏp C*, the pencil traced each line in anticipation of its immediate disappearance into an ever-growing thicket of lines. Incising each line very close to or on top of another resulted in a commingling that made it very difficult to locate individual marks. As the viewer's eyes adjust to the dull reflective glare of the paint under bright overhead lighting, he or she begins to discern faint markings that skitter over the surface, like stray cobwebs or fine skeins of dust. Although faint, the markings are noticeable enough to tempt us into closer proximity with the painting's surface.

This kind of encounter produced in the viewer the sensation of imminence. Despite knowing that the painting is indisputably made of canvas, oil paint, and pencil, the viewer remains uncertain as to whether the work can stand still. Some certainty remains when viewers see a work like *Myobŏp C*, whose material reality is reinforced by the arrangement of marks around the canvas edges. In *Myobŏp A* or *Écriture No. 43-73*, that reality is compromised by the marks' being uniformly distributed throughout pictorial space. Occasionally Park produced works that emphasized the moment at which the pencil made contact with the painted surface. *Écriture No. 6-74* (Figure 4.11) makes clear the moments at which the pencil makes contact with the paint. The painting is organized into rows demarcated by lines of loosely connected dots that, upon closer examination, are discovered to be tiny raised globules of paint that bear witness to the pencil as it made its journey from one end of the canvas to the other. The paint that was once intended as the ground has now accumulated in such a way as

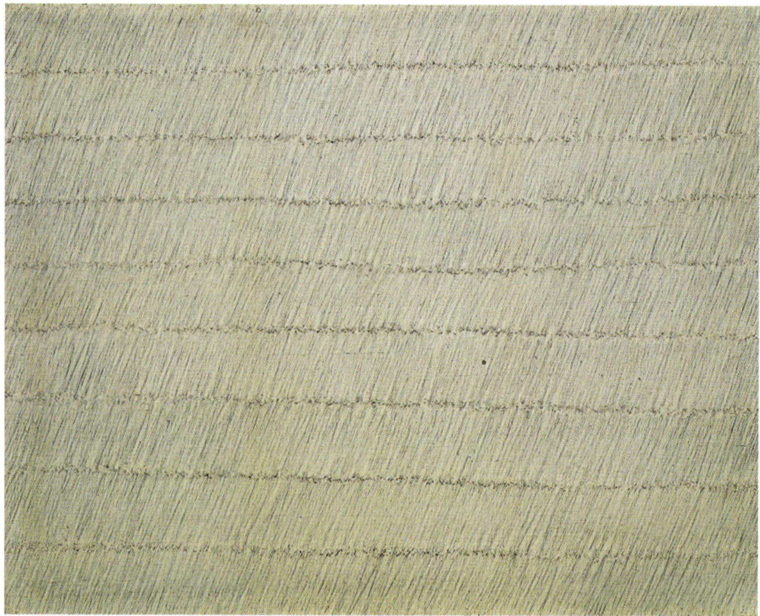

to approximate the look of a figured line. Park summed up his intentions in an interview with the artist Maeda Josaku on the occasion of *Myobŏp*'s debut when he stated his desire to make "paintings that did not resemble paintings."[35]

By way of additional illustration, compare *Myobŏp A* (Figure 4.7) or *Écriture No. 43-73* (Figure 4.8) with the works of Agnes Martin, which engaged paint and pencil in similar ways and received much critical attention. A few years after their debut, Joseph Love, who received a master's degree in art history from Columbia University in 1967, favorably compared the *Myobŏp* works to Martin's.[36] In works like *White Stone* (Figure 4.12), Martin used a pencil to trace delicate vertical and horizontal lines on a pale canvas that in turn formed a net-like grid encasing the entire painting. Spreading over the canvas, these nets pulled the eye in any direction but toward the canvas center. The lines are precisely perpendicular, lending the work a consistent, overall clarity that can be seen only when the viewer is close enough to the painting support. Although there was contrast between the pencil lines and the paleness of the canvas, color was not the issue, as Martin herself stated in 1972: "People think that painting is about color/It's mostly composition/It's composition that's the whole thing."[37] Martin pulled the lines as tautly as the combination of soft graphite and a rigid surface would

FIGURE 4.12 Agnes Martin, *White Stone*, 1965. Oil and graphite on linen, 182.6 × 182.6 cm. Collection of Solomon R. Guggenheim Museum, New York.

FIGURE 4.13 Park Seobo, *Ecriture No. 71-74*, 1974. Pencil and oil on canvas, 193 × 259 cm. Collection of the artist. Photograph by Lee Man-hong.

allow. Lines quiver, and their tremulous movements recorded by the miniscule hills and valleys traced by the pencil navigating the canvas's rough surface.

Size is a foil for Martin and Park, who both tend to work with canvases so large they almost overwhelm the viewer. *White Stone*, for example, is 182.6 × 182.6 centimeters (just over six feet by six feet), and *Écriture No. 71-74* (Figure 4.13) is almost the same height and so long as to make the work appear vast, even monumental. Martin domesticates her space by transposing a grid that parses the expanse to minute squares that bring into the work a sense of the microscopic. The faintness of the pencil lines, especially when seen under bright light or at a distance, blends into the light grayish-white support so that the work appears to vibrate at an intense pitch.

A similar effect takes place in *Écriture No. 71-74*, which takes advantage of the shape of the marks. Their brevity and thinness compel viewers to draw closer to the work, at which point they observe how graphite pencil furrows into the pale creamy surface. In order to take in the entire painting, however, viewers must move away from the surface to a point where the marks again become subsumed into a larger haze that must be seen with the brief moments of respite where pencil has not yet touched canvas, which Park calls "breathing holes."[38] The presence of these holes allows Park to manage the area of the painting and impart to it a double sense of luminosity and weightlessness that again emphasize the painting's imminence. But the lines are also massed in a way that suggests a deliberate obfuscation rather than the clarity often associated with the idea of a system. The marks share little in common with those of Martin, who parses her canvases into straight perpendicular axes that suggest an intention to configure the work into a system even when the unsteadiness of the lines redirect the viewer's attention back to the hand of the artist and to the roughness of the canvas. As Joseph Love pointed out, Park made great use of a delicate "touch" in transforming his paintings into airy expanses of space.[39]

The *Myobŏp* works borrowed a great deal from the kind of temporality associated with viewing works in the round. Although the method of facture suggested to viewers that they look frontally at the work, it was but a suggestion. That there was no one correct way of approach was underscored by the changeability of the work depending on one's physical proximity to the canvas and on the conditions of display, particularly the quantity and direction of illumination. When viewed under overhead illumination in the contained indoor space of

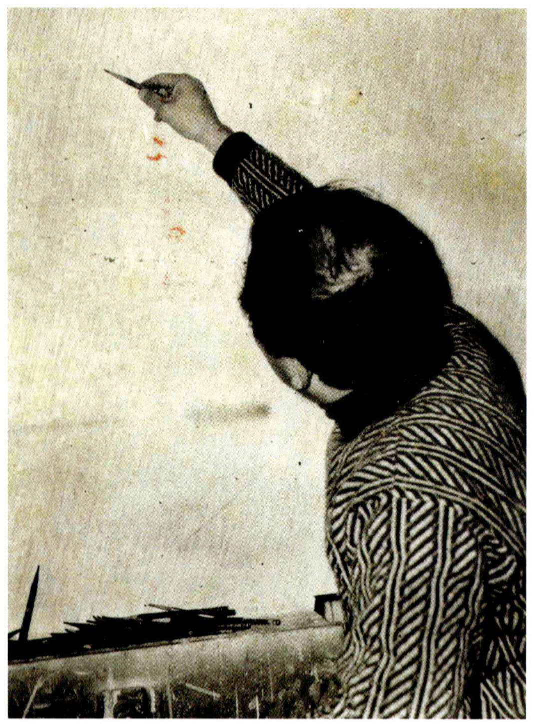

a gallery, the rectangles appear to reflect the light, making the works appear especially bright and monochromatic. The ontological uncertainty of the works is further emphasized in photographs, as Park well understood when he was photographed making a *Myobŏp* work in 1973 (Figure 4.14). His back turned toward the viewer, Park holds his pencil at an angle, as if in the midst of "drawing." But the staged character of this photograph shows what for Park was most important, even more important than the physicality of mark making, to which he was so fervently attached. Park holds the pencil between his thumb and forefinger so as not to put too much pressure on either it or the canvas support. One sees that the work is organized into rows of straight lines, but more important, one sees that the penciled marks are hardly visible. Park, in effect, is painting a void. Shifting between modes of encounter, the mark does not only shed its traceability; it also puts forth the contingency of the mark's existence. It is a dramatically different experience from seeing Lee's controlled arrangement of points and lines, which aggregate into a pattern able to then emphasize the physical support as a uniform plane. The lines in the *Myobŏp* works are less committed to the surface, resulting in works that are more ephemeral and unmoored than those belonging to *From Line* and *From Point*. The photographed image literally appears to slip from underneath his very hand, an evasiveness reflected in Park's own inability to fully describe his works: it was a series "expressed only through pencil lines on top of a whitish base."[40]

The *Myobŏp* works compel viewers to look more closely and intently than might be required from other paintings. In so doing, viewers become more attuned to their own physical bodies working in relation to another physical entity, arriving at a more intense recognition of themselves. One wonders whether Park was attempting to relay back onto viewers a sense of their own presence, a matter of great urgency for Korean audiences living under the conditions of intense state scrutiny undertaken by the Yushin state.

FRAMES OF AUTHORITY: THE NATIONAL DOCUMENTARY PAINTINGS PROJECT AND *EXPORT FRIGATE*

The matter of presence is complicated when the *Myobŏp* works are considered with *Export Frigate* (Figure 4.15), perhaps Park's most important contribution to the national documentary paintings project, the largest initiative for visual art ever supported by the Park Chung-hee government. Under the auspices of the Ministry of Culture and Information, the Office for the Production of National Documentary Paintings (Minjok kirok'hwa chejak samuso) commissioned established artists, mostly oil painters, to paint various idealized scenes of past military glory, industrial progress, and national unification.[41] Organized into five-year plans akin to those designed for the economy, the project was closely monitored by office-appointed committees that both selected the artists and approved preliminary sketches upon which completed paintings were based.[42] Generally, the country's most prominent artists were approached to participate in the national documentary paintings project, including Lee Se-duk, who helped organize the 1968 exhibition *Contemporary Korean Painting* at the National Museum of Modern Art in Tokyo, and Park Seobo, who by 1973 was among the most powerful artists in the Korean art world.[43] Receiving a commission was a highly coveted opportunity, not only for the prestige it conferred on its participants, but also for the financial and material compensations: participants were both paid for their works and given generous quantities of expensive imported oil paints, brushes, and canvas.[44]

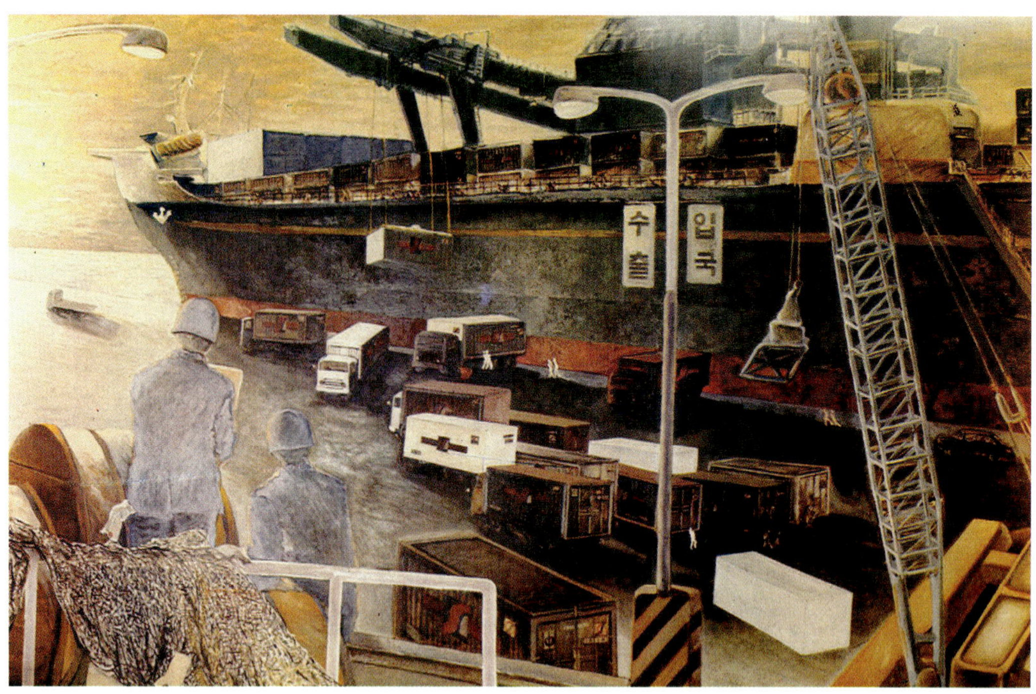

FIGURE 4.15 Park Seobo, *Export Frigate*, 1973. Oil on canvas, 180 × 225 cm. Location unknown.

The artists commissioned to execute works for the 1973 show of national documentary paintings were given in excess of 43 million won.[45] Park himself received 1.5 million won, no mean sum at a time when a salaried worker in South Korea earned around 300,000 won a year.[46] In contrast, nineteen artists' groups who requested funds from the state in 1975 were given less than 10 percent of that sum.[47] Despite the relatively small percentage of artists selected to participate in the project, hundreds of works were created. Most of them were first hung in temporary exhibitions held at such centrally located venues as the National Museum of Modern Art in downtown Seoul and then were permanently installed in key government buildings such as the National Assembly, the intended home of *Export Frigate*. Many national documentary paintings were also used on posters, as illustrations for history textbooks, and even on postage stamps.

The project's strong ideological focus was emphasized in the catalog of the first exhibition of national documentary paintings in 1967. Its preface was written by Park Chung-hee, who reminded viewers of the nation's difficult history and urged that "through such national documentary paintings, the whole race, joined together by one mind and one heart, must strive to avoid repeating the indignities of history and the tragic past by advancing democracy." Park followed up his emphasis on the need for national unity by mentioning, in the same sentence, the imperative to reunify the peninsula with a "victory over Communism."[48] That Park should stress the "tragic past," which readers of the time would have taken to mean both the Korean War and Japan's colonial occupation of Korea, was not unrelated to the signs of popular unrest visible at the time; the show opened on July 12, 1967, only two months after Park had won a hotly contested presidential election. The explicit mention of communism was both a reflection of Park's genuine apprehension of the North Korean threat and a covert reminder of the uncertainty of the present should the public not heed state directives.

That the national documentary paintings were initiated by the government during the most politically repressive years of Park Chung-hee's rule has led to their exclusion from almost all histories of Korean art. Many commentators dismiss them on aesthetic grounds, and others see them as ethically suspect or even as acts of "cultural violence."[49] Even in the late 1960s and early 1970s, national documentary paintings were a source of great controversy. Younger artists who lacked the financial and professional security of their seniors were frustrated by what they saw as yet another example of the stultifying hierarchy of the

Korean art world. Then in his thirties, painter Kim Jeong-heon disapproved of the project, which, he said, "[took] the tax monies of the people to favor, without justification, only a few."[50] Likewise, the performance artist Chŏng Ch'an-sŭng asked why the "*minjok kirok'wa* painters received a few million won per painting," while those in the recent Seoul Indépendants exhibition of 1975 were "made to feel like beggars."[51]

Some national documentary paintings, however, were composed in ways that imparted a certain level of reflexivity concerning the relationship of the viewer to questions of representation. In *Export Frigate*, Park paints his subject in order to generate a representation distinctly different from what the state or even the general public expected from these works. The ship laden with goods for export, a veritable symbol of the South Korean state and its dreams of self-sufficiency, is reworked into a viewing experience that allowed viewers in Yushin Korea to reflect upon the world in which they were made to live, and for whose formation they were perhaps responsible to some degree.

Painted between March and October 1973, *Export Frigate* was part of a new series of national documentary paintings depicting South Korean economic development.[52] A committee composed mostly of specialists in Korean history selected thirty artists to depict various monuments or scenes of economic development, including dams, radio towers, cement factories, and even tangerine farms.[53] Between March 6 and 10, Park was sent to Pusan, South Korea's largest port, to make an initial sketch of his designated subject, ships carrying Korean exports overseas. He first depicted bundles being lifted and loaded onto waiting ships and submitted his initial sketch to the committee of art historians and bureaucrats responsible for administering the national documentary paintings project.

The committee rejected Park's sketch, commenting that "exports were no longer handled in such a manner."[54] The implicit message was that the sketch did not adequately portray an image of a modern, technologically advanced nation, a message Park seems to have heeded by producing another sketch, this time of a large crane hoisting containers from trucks parked just under an enormous freighter. The finished work shows a massive vessel docked in a port being loaded with goods, presumably for export, as indicated by a sign positioned in the middle of the picture. *Export Frigate* was publicly exhibited at the National Museum of Modern Art on March 14–16, 1974, a show whose importance was reflected in Park Chung-hee's widely reported decision to attend the opening.[55] In the preface to the accompanying catalog, the ministry stated that the main emphasis lay in the notion of "Export Korea": "We are proud to present a new image of 'Export Korea' achieved through the export of over three billion U.S. dollars' worth of goods into the world market."[56] The importance of the show was highlighted by the mention of the president in the preface.[57]

Yet for a work supposedly meant to reflect the present, *Export Frigate* seems curiously atemporal. The sky is painted with an alternating series of yellow and gray brushstrokes, suggesting either sunrise or sunset but not committing to either. More troublingly, the viewer is unsure as to his or her position in relation to the presumptive main event of the painting, the loading (or unloading) of the export frigate. The size of the figures depicted in the lower left-hand corner corresponds to that of the viewers, inducing them to extrapolate their own location from that of the figures in the painting. One figure appears to be standing on a wooden ledge, and the other is sitting on it. The eye spies a triangular sliver of ledge occluding part of a large brown truck that is positioned at an almost forty-five degree angle so as to connote recessional depth. This occlusion and the scale of the truck in relation to the two male figures indicate that the ledge is both above the central scene and at a considerable distance away from it. But Park flattens pictorial space so that there is no sense of this distance; the two figures seem contiguous with the picture plane.

Export Frigate alluded to what from 1973 to 1979 was the state's "Big Push" for an economy based on heavy industry and advanced technology rather than one dependent on light manufacturing and cheap labor.[58] Park's subject is the rapidly growing shipbuilding industry, which dramatically increased its output in 1974. From 1973 to 1974, the privately owned Korean Shipbuilding and Engineering Company, then the major shipbuilding company in Korea, increased the number of ships it exported from 12 to 220.[59] Yet instead of a bustling sense of activity, there is but moribund stasis. Though laden with goods for export, the trucks connote little sense of activity. They are inert boxes parked in the center of pictorial space rather than part of a bustling scene. In like manner, the workers on the left appear as if carved from stone, and repeated throughout is the same boxlike shape without much variation. Such pro forma repetition indicates a desire for efficiency on the part of the artist; simply repeating the box allows him to fill the vast canvas as quickly as possible.

Most unusual is the dock, which is strangely bereft of figures, save for three pairs walking along the dock and three figures walking toward the painting's foreground. None appears to engage with the other figure groupings, least of all with the two figures standing in the painting's extreme foreground on the left. By virtue of their attire and position, the two workers on the left should be actively involved in the scene. Both, however, seem paralyzed, even petrified, almost as if Park regarded them as statues rather than as actual people. The upright figure appears to look down at a clipboard, but this is by no means certain, as the head remains fairly erect. The sedentary figure presumably looks out onto the scene, but again, there is no way to tell whether this is actually the case, for there is little sense of volume that would induce the viewer to consider the figures as bodies inhabiting real space. The right side of his back is shaded, but the figure appears to blend into the background. In fact, the seated figure appears to compress what should be a vast distance. Both figures are relatively large, and this also places them within an indeterminate, threshold space that hovers somewhere between the world of the viewer and that of the painting. In this way they appear less as actors involved in the narrative shown than they do as bystanders outside the narrative's immediate purview.

The question of the viewer's relationship to the painting is further complicated by certain details. On the painting's extreme right-hand side is a black hardtop car perched on the edge where the frigate meets the dock. Of the color and make used to shuttle high-level executives and government officials, the car alludes to the state or to the industrialists who benefited tremendously from Park Chung-hee's relentless policies of economic development, no matter the human cost. Compared to the massive ship next to which it is parked, the black car is tiny, yet Park frames the car in a way that directs viewers to it; it is encased within a triangular armature implied by a skeletal metal crane on the left, some cables and a hook on the right, and a yellow structure resembling a dock leveler on the bottom. The implied enclosure functions as a viewfinder, through which viewers observe the car.

Park's enclosure of the car is in some sense a neat rejoinder to what was then a time of massive surveillance by the state and those closest to it. The black hardtop car symbolizes what was, in Yushin Korea, a nearly continuous presence of surveillance. By framing the car in so specific a manner, Park enabled the audience—which in the context of national documentary paintings meant the general public—to look back at those doing most of the watching. The work makes viewers aware that they are being framed, a condition that resonated not only with the culture of surveillance that pervaded Korean society under Yushin rule, but also with the frame as implied by the treatment of the painting's liminal areas. What the artist chose to depict in the areas near the physical edges of the canvas was critical to what the work overall had to say about viewers' relationship to the internal world being depicted. Were viewers part of this world, and if so, what was their position?

Despite the close correspondence in size between the figures and the viewers' own proportions, the figures are not meant to be transposed onto the viewers' own bodies, as the railing in the lower left-hand corner makes clear. Of a bright light gray, the railing stands out from the background and brings other readings to bear. The rail or balcony running diagonally over a lower corner of the painting is slightly tilted so that it marks off the painting as a space separate from that of the viewers. In a scene that almost exclusively depicts hard materials like steel, wood, and concrete, the swath of semitransparent fabric on the railing vies for viewers' attention. Loosely coiled around the rail, it assumes the air of a curtain, screen, or veil, all objects whose main purpose is to hide, protect, or conceal. The viewers' place is somewhere outside the painting. They may look and even project themselves onto the painting through the shadow-like duo in the left-hand corner, but they can never fully enter into its world.

Implied here is a palpable sense of distance between the imagined world of the state and that of the viewer. It is a world imagined not by the artist but by the state, and even, to some extent, by the general public, who actively wanted to be convinced that the society envisioned by the state was actually worth the considerable financial, physical, and psychological sacrifices this public was made to bear in the name of economic progress. At the time Park painted *Export Frigate*, labor disputes between management and nonmanagement employees were on the rise, as was general dissatisfaction over working conditions and wages.[60] But some members of the public nevertheless longed for confirmation that their efforts were justified. Most reviews criticized national documentary paintings for not being convincing; the progovernment daily *Chosun ilbo* reported in December 1976, for example, that those who saw the national documentary paintings shown at the National Museum of Modern Art that year considered the works to be "awkward, unable to handle the picture field" and felt they "[failed] to kindle the emotions." The same issue quotes other viewers who thought the paintings "lacked the ability to explain a situation, thus making the painting no different from a movie theater billboard."[61] The language betrayed a profound sense of disappointment, itself a strong indication of the expectations of those who still believed in the state and its mission.

While there were no published reviews of *Export Frigate*, the divide between national documentary paintings and their intended audiences was already well acknowledged, if purposely expressed euphemistically. *Korea Life*, a magazine whose main purpose was to promote South Korea to the Korean residents of Japan, observed in its August 1967 issue, "There are criticisms which say that the paintings were a bit of a miss resulting from having been made in a short period of time."[62] By the time of the 1974 show, the divide between the state and its citizenry had become inalienable, a gap emphasized by the circumstances of display. Each painting was placed in a deep-set golden frame, and a low unbroken rail kept spectators at a respectful distance.

The divide between the imagined world of the work, itself a metaphor of state ambition, and its audience is made even more pronounced by Park's decision to flatten the pictorial surface. He divides the picture into a foreground and background, most notably through the device of size, as well as through the angling of a dark brown truck in the foreground, yet the effort is compromised by an insistent pictorial flatness emphasized by a consistent level of saturation. The two figures standing at the side centripetally pull the other images, so that they appear to be pressed up against an invisible pane of glass. The surface assumes new prominence as that which is emphasized in order to keep the viewer from entering the imagined world of the state. One looks (and is looked at), but does not belong, much less participate, a sentiment that would have resonated with Korean viewers at the time.

WRITING LESSONS: FROM *MYOBŎP* TO *ÉCRITURE*

There is nothing to indicate that Park consciously thought of *Export Frigate* in relation to the *Myobŏp* works. In keeping with the five-year-plan mentality, he thought of *Export Frigate* as a product meant to fulfill a quota. Perhaps sensitive to the views of those critics who regarded national documentary painters as propagandists for a brutal dictatorship, Park, in a recent interview, sarcastically recalled his participation in the project as little more than a "great part-time job."[63] But his approach to *Export Frigate* shows a commitment to exploring the relationship between the physical work of art and its intended viewer in ways that productively drew forth what he was trying to emphasize in his *Myobŏp* works, particularly those made between 1974 and 1978, the year of his solo show at the Tokyo Gallery and about the time when Park painted more for his overseas audiences than for viewers at home.

One of the most vivid points of engagement was Park's treatment of the frame. In both *Export Frigate* and *Écriture No. 5-78* (Figure 4.16), for instance, this meant considering how depiction enacted on the physical support addressed its viewers. The marginal areas directly abutting the painting's physical edges are given special attention. In *Écriture No. 5-78*, multiple smooth layers of whitish paint yield rather abruptly to the coarseness of a brown canvas support. Flecks of smooth paint appear to evaporate from the canvas surface, evidence, it seems, of the tenuousness with which painting attempts to separate itself from the physical world of the viewer. The dull brown strip of mottled canvas reminds viewers that painting, no matter how vested in securing its own boundaries, remains the synthesis of pigment, binder, and a support. The effect, however, is unlike that of the *Conjunction* works, where the act of pushing paint through the canvas could itself be sufficient to justify calling the works paintings, or where this encounter should be taken as a necessary but not a final step in the process of painting. Park leaves the narrow strip unpainted in order to weaken the usual role of the frame. A painting, he suggests, could potentially be just another physical object.

In *Écriture No. 72-74* (Figure 4.9), the delicate penciling of the painted surface has now turned on an insistent will to dig, scratch, and probe. Whereas Park had formerly approached the canvas from an oblique angle so as to control the force he applied, he now vigorously moved his pencil back and forth on a support laid flat on a desk or the ground. He continued to make some works on upright canvas, but with the same idea of digging into or scratching the paint. But as in *Écriture No. 72-74*, Park emphasized, more than ever, the moment at which pencil made contact with the painted surface. He pushed the pencil doggedly through the layers of oil paint, as if he were trying to confirm for himself the concreteness of the materials. The scratching and digging into paint collapses the surface's presumed function as a boundary separating the "world" of the work and that of the viewer. Park's mark making invites the viewer to touch the canvas, even if actual physical contact only takes place in the viewer's imagination.

Park carried his point further by suggesting that the surface was itself a space on which to be written. He deliberately borrows the look of cursive Roman script, a decision that resonated in this time, at the

FIGURE 4.16 Park Seobo,
Écriture No. 5-78, 1978.
Oil and pencil on canvas,
130 × 162 cm. Private
collection, Taegu, Korea.
Photograph by Kwon Boo-Moon.

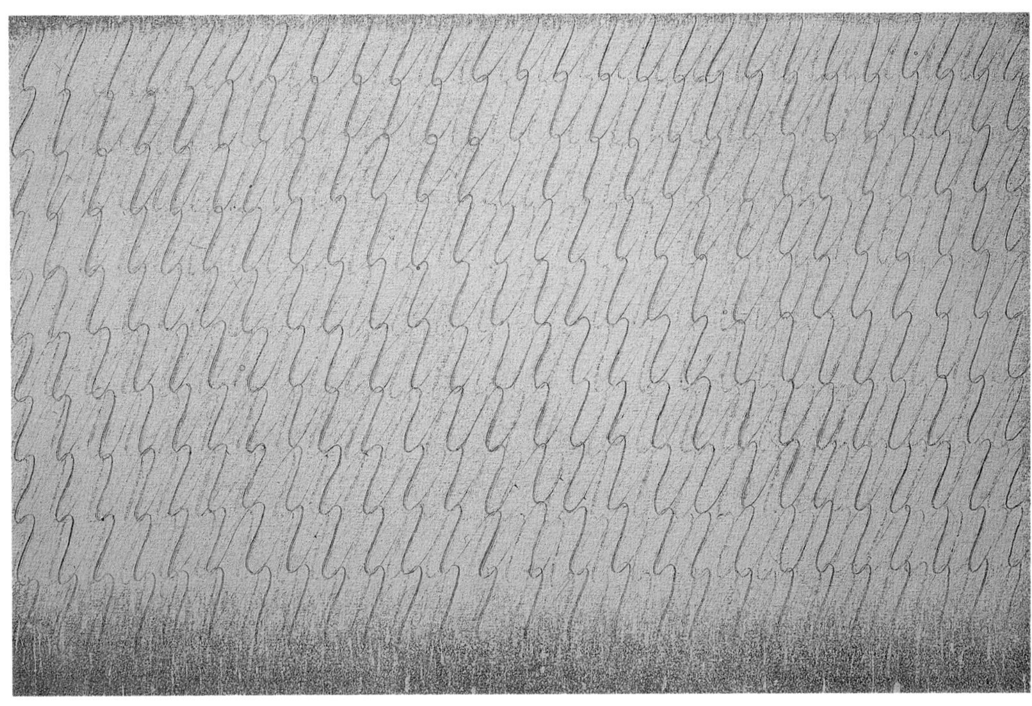

FIGURE 4.17 Park Seobo, *Écriture No. 41-78*, 1978. Oil and pencil on canvas, 194 × 300 cm. Collection of Samsung Art Museum, Leeum Library. Photograph by Lee Man-Hong.

height of censorship. In *Écriture No. 41-78* (Figure 4.17) sinusoidal lines course the length and breadth of the available pictorial space. Their shape and dimensions compel the eye, and later, the hand, to follow its path across the canvas. Viewers eventually find themselves engaging in movements that appear to mimic writing, especially as the sweeping curves of the line call to mind the loops of a signature written in Roman characters, while the horizontal progression of these lines on a whitish surface mimic handwritten text on a blank piece of paper.

In contorting his lines to resemble cursive script, Park recalled the form of the written word, which had particular significance for his viewers living in Yushin Korea. It was over the publication and distribution of written texts through which their relationship with the Yushin state was perhaps most extensively mediated. As demonstrated in the works of Sung Neung-kyung and Choi Tae-shin, censorship of printed media was especially acute, as were the state's efforts to control the distribution of what it regarded as insurrectionist material. In February 1975, the critic Kim Yun-su was stripped of his university teaching job for allegedly distributing copies of Kim Chi-ha's "Declaration of Conscience" ("Yangsim sŏnŏn"), a manifesto protesting the oppressiveness of the Yushin regime.[64]

Park never meant for his lines to represent writing or the act of writing. Yet they were ambiguous enough in form to evoke the question of legibility. Sung and Choi rendered sheets of newspaper unreadable by cutting or by blocking out sections of text. In so doing, they made palpably visible, and thus plainly legible, the effects of state censorship. Park's works turned instead on the distinction between legibility and illegibility, a focus that drew both from his earlier explorations of imminence and from his decision to rename these works "*Écriture*," after Lee Yil brought the word to his attention sometime in 1974. As he knew from his experiences with national documentary painting, the state valued legibility even when the message was already clear to those for whom it was meant.

The decision to retroactively call all past and future *Myobŏp* works *Écriture* deserves consideration, for although it could have been done solely to reflect the shape of the lines, as well as Park's fascination with all things French, it also related to the burgeoning interest in structuralist and poststructuralist theory. The theoretical inflections of *écriture* were becoming increasingly well known in South Korean intellectual circles, particularly after Roland Barthes's 1953 essay "Writing Degree Zero" was translated into Korean and published in the multidisciplinary arts journal *Yesulgye* in the fall of 1970.[65] Although Park never mentioned Barthes in direct connection to his own work, the latter's use of *écriture* in "Writing Degree Zero," where he claims writing as that which refuses the identity of the product as an exclusive function of trace, back to the author's body and past, was taken up by Park's colleague Bang Keun-taek. *Écriture* became a cornerstone of "Fiction and Nonsense," a lengthy essay in which Bang discussed Korean avant-garde art and the *Myobŏp* works in the September 1974 issue of *Space*. Bang seems to deliberately misread Barthes, who maintained that writing was language used for its own sake rather than as a means of transmitting ideas and information.[66] Instead, Bang claimed that *écriture* was "a principle of expression specifically used by a given group."[67]

Bang anticipated what for Park would become a protracted struggle with the issue of authorship. Previously, Park was content to follow Lee Ufan's lead in rejecting the belief that an artwork must have an easily recognizable author in order to exist. One year before the debut of *Myobŏp*, in an article titled "The Crisis of Contemporary Art," Park stated, "When we speak of a 'work' in the plastic arts, we take as our premise the expression of individuality. By this, we mean that there is a single artist, and that there is a unique 'originality' that only he [or she] can make."[68] Yet Park was not quite ready to altogether relinquish the

idea of the author, certainly not when the right to creative expression was being threatened by a military regime that all but declared itself the final arbiter of expression. As if to provide himself with a credible alibi in the face of these conditions, Park continued to insist that *Écriture* was a search for the "noncreative, and nonindividualistic."[69] He did, however, suffuse the work with authorial presence, even if it was of a different kind from the athleticism that had characterized his earlier adventures in gestural abstraction. The line, for example, was deployed in much more controlled strokes than in earlier versions of *Écriture*, where the line appears more as the incidental effects caused by a pencil tapped upon the canvas in short, regular bursts. The looping in *Écriture No. 41-75* (Figure 4.18), for instance, displays a particular level of control that exceeds that required to form letters or characters that could later be arranged into legible words.

An instructive comparison in this regard is that between *Écriture No. 62-78* (Figure 4.19) and an untitled painting from 1968 by Cy Twombly (Figure 4.20). The latter's works exercised a certain fascination for Barthes, who wrote a much-cited essay for the Twombly retrospective at the Whitney Museum in 1979. Seen from a distance, the curlicues of Twombly's untitled work tempts viewers into "reading" them as cursive script in possession of meaning. At a distance, the cursive-like undulations on a smooth ivory support request further examination. The marks' haziness or ambiguity only teases the gaze, prodding it to search the canvas thoroughly. But when seen closely, the loops cannot be viewed as if they really did correspond to a cursive *o* or *e* in the Roman alphabet. In his Whitney Museum catalog essay, Barthes says that Twombly "makes things seen" by permitting substance "to linger," by "withholding the pressure of substance, by letting it come to rest casually."[70] Rosalind Krauss followed up on what Barthes had to say by describing Twombly's mark making as a project of refusal. Again channeling Barthes, this time his *The Responsibility of Forms,* Krauss argues that the mark defies its smooth monochromatic support by appearing as "a mockery, a deflation, as if the humanist turgescence was suddenly pricked."[71]

Compared to the much smaller *Écriture No. 62-78,* Twombly's untitled work from 1968 also asks its viewers to consider scale as a crucial factor in addressing what Twombly was trying to do. Contorted into loops that become progressively taller as the eye moves from the top of the canvas to the bottom, the line rescales the painting according to its dimensions, rather than to the dimensions implied by color, composition, or any other aspect of the work. Twombly's line calls the bluff of

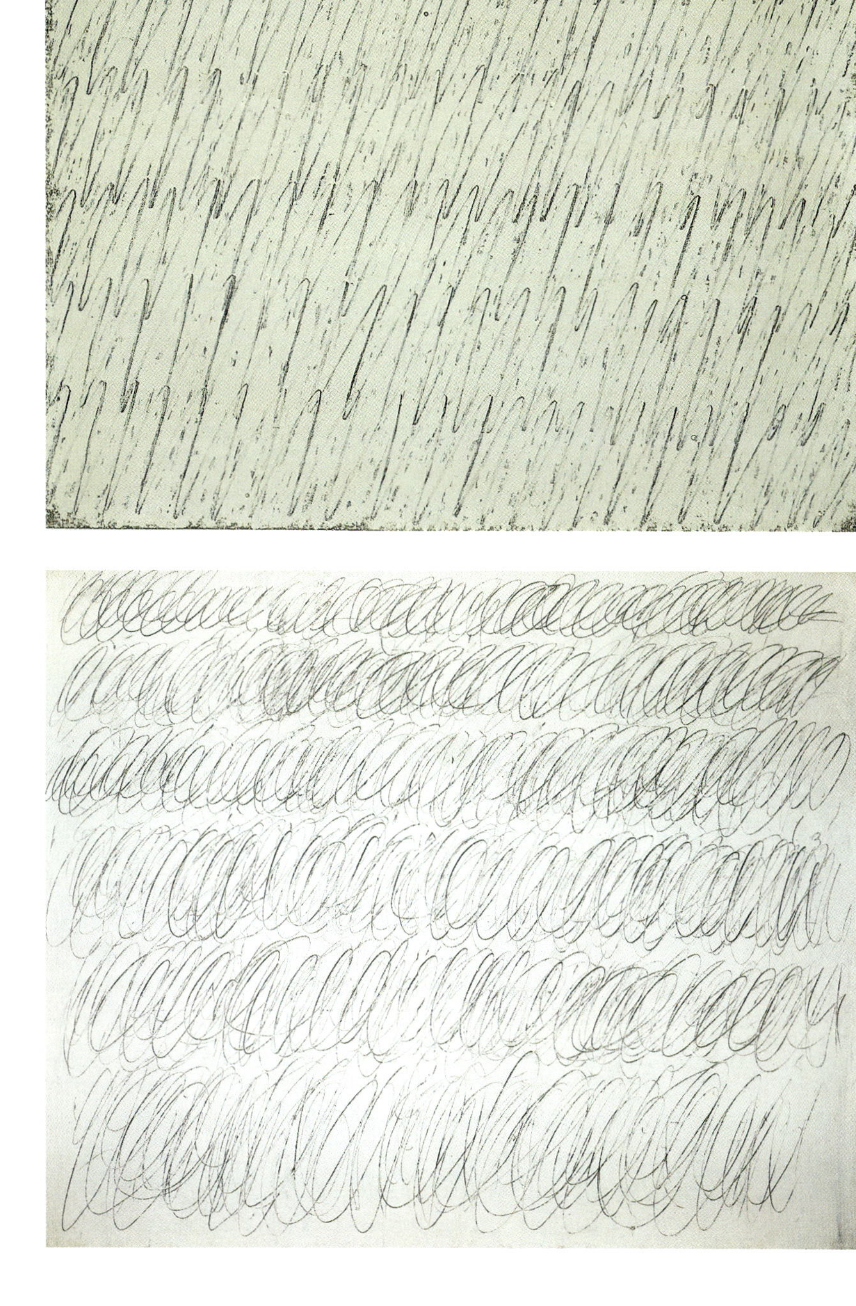

the monochrome and its pretensions to representing infinity. His is a mark that carries, as Krauss suggests, the force of a well-placed jab. It cuts the painting down to size, both metaphorically and literally. In the hands of someone like Agnes Martin or Robert Ryman, a whitish canvas measuring 175 × 218 centimeters might look, if not feel, even larger than it already was. In Twombly's hands, the painting is unmoored from the expectations associated with large-format painting. Indeed, Twombly's curlicues are sufficiently large and rambunctious as to undermine the monumentality often presumed of paintings considerably larger than the proportions of the average adult viewer.

Park's lines were not as unruly as Twombly's, in whose hands the line became unconfined; rather, they were more systematic. In *Écriture No. 62-78*, the lines are there to affirm the size of the canvas, which at 72.7 × 91 centimeters is scaled more to the proportions of what an individual viewer might be able to hold in his or her hands. The sinusoidal line travels from the left edge of the canvas to the right, with each successive line slightly overlapping the one produced before it. Viewers see lines move both vertically and horizontally, but the movements do not cohere into a grid. Worked into peaks and valleys, the line is there to maintain a balance between visual ends and material means. Each peak and valley culminates in a point where viewers can easily discern how graphite displaces oil paint, yet the lines are staggered and dispersed throughout the painting in a way that compels viewers to approach the painting as being more of a field than a physical support. There is neither the whimsy nor the drama that one often discerns in Twombly's works. Lines move up and down at a consistent rate and angle. Yet these lines pay less heed to process than do those of Martin, whose hand is governed by concerns of measurement and accuracy as it directs the pencil along the straight edge of a ruler. *Écriture No. 62-78* looks as if it is being rained upon by a consistent flow of marks, or, as Joseph Love commented about an earlier version from 1975, "dirtied."[72] In thinking of the mark as that without meaning save as a pollutant, one thinks of Twombly's galloping curves that tease the boundary separating artistic gesture from script, yet in *Écriture No. 62-78*, Park is thinking as much about calligraphy, the medium that joins script and gesture, as he is about the physical effects of the imprint his pencil leaves behind.

But as Park commented following the Seoul debut of what was then called *Myobŏp*, "I am specifically trying not to insert meaning [into them], my works do not possess that which is called an image. Since there is no image, there is no expression."[73] What he meant is better

FIGURE 4.21 Park Seobo, *Écriture No. 3-78*, 1978. Oil and pencil on canvas, 130 × 162 cm. Collection of Seobo Foundation, Seoul. Photograph by Kwon Boo-Moon.

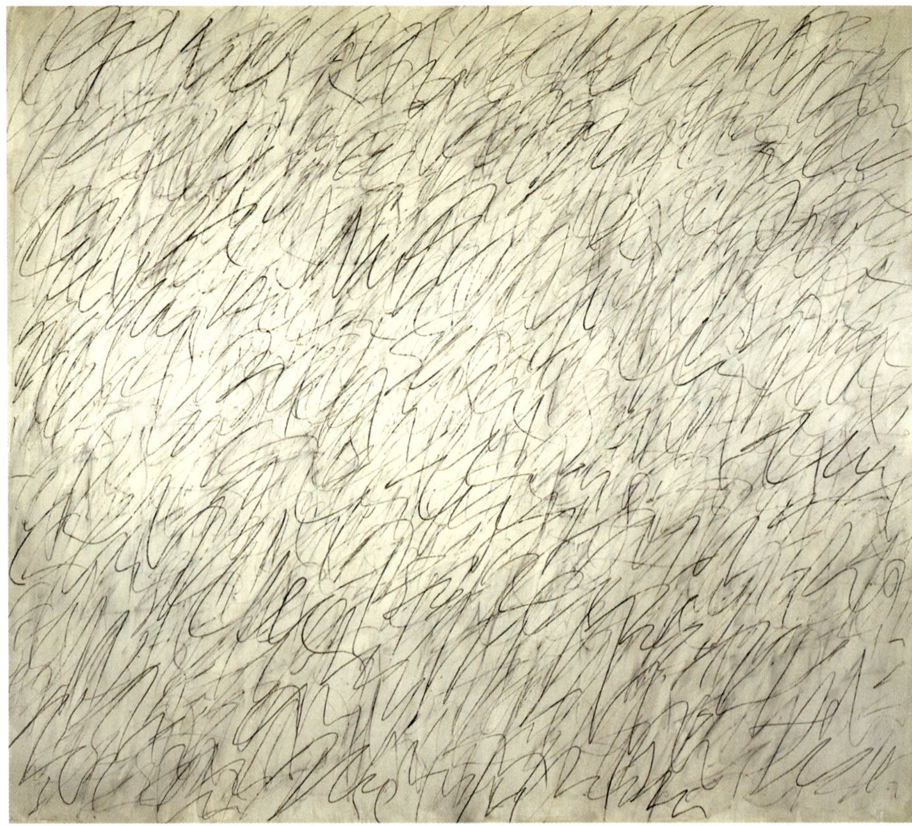

illustrated by a work like *Écriture No. 3-78* (Figure 4.21). Viewers spy a mesh-like overlay of lines, which initially come across as a lawless scrawl unleashed upon an innocent blank surface. Convinced of this initial reading, one stays a little longer with the painting in order to see what lies beneath this penciled jungle. One might even feel compelled to approach the painting, thus bringing the worked surface into view. But what an initial encounter with *Écriture No. 3-78* reveals is how ordered the line actually is. Viewers, such as Nakahara Yusuke, who were interested in assessing Park's place in an expanded history of painting and who implicitly measured his works against recognized works in New York and Paris compared the *Écriture* works with those of Twombly, but Park's line forgoes the willfulness of Twombly's stochastic meanderings (for example, Figure 4.22) in favor of an affect that might best be described as defensive.[74] The viewer becomes more conscious of mark as corporeal trace, or as the result of what happens when the pressure of an arm and hand are brought to bear on a pencil struggling to make its way through putty-colored oil paint. More than most of his peers, and certainly more than any other tansaekhwa artist, except, perhaps, for Kwon Young-woo, Park emphasizes physical exertion to the point of fetish. These carefully incised lines that peak and dip at regular intervals are not the diffident tally marks of certain *Écriture* works made before 1975. Neither are they kin to Twombly's energetic and idiosyncratic flourishes. They hover somewhere between the understated aestheticism of Lee's brushstrokes and Martin's ruled grid, a tribute, it would seem, to skilled labor.

If Park shared with Twombly the ability to make "things seen," it lay in what the *Écriture* works can do to make visible what might otherwise remain invisible. His works emphasize the very modernist tension between considerations of painting as encompassing its own internal structure and as an object itself enveloped by space. Instead of trying to downplay this tension by strategically neglecting it or by redirecting viewers' attention elsewhere, Park made it central to *Écriture* in order to reinstate within his audiences in Yushin Korea an awareness that they too could also see, if not read and write. Park was practical enough to recognize that the act of seeing alone was not enough to cope with a society overwhelmingly determined by the enforcement of norms intended to deliver certainty and stability to its inhabitants. Yet if the *Écriture* works looked permanently unsettled as a direct function of the tension between legibility and illegibility, it was because Park well understood the perverse reassurance that sometimes comes from not knowing exactly what it is one sees.

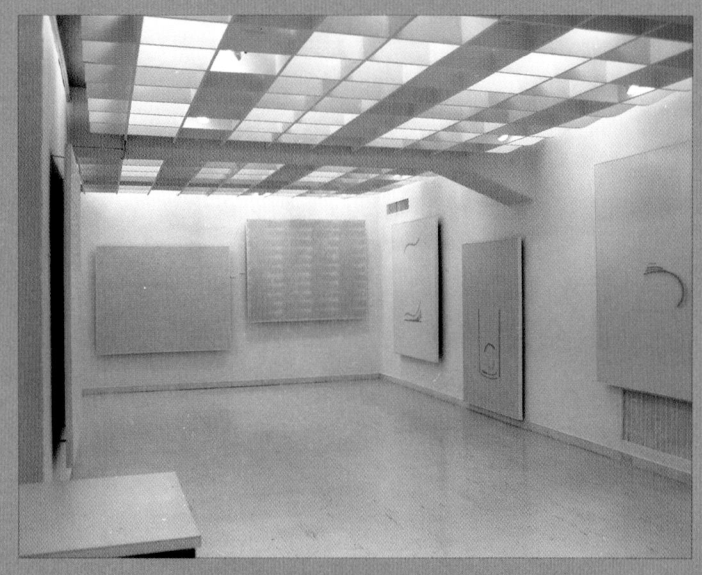

FIVE

Tansaekhwa and the Idealization of Asian Art

The question of what constitutes a viable artwork was not limited
to Park Seobo's having to pick through the political minefield that
was life in Yushin Korea. When Nakahara Yusuke compared works like
Écriture No. 41-75 (Figure 4.18) to those of Cy Twombly, he did so after
having seen the work in Park's solo show at the Tokyo Gallery in 1978.
There the *Écriture* series resonated differently for Japanese viewers, many
of whom looked at art through lenses of comparison and competition
between East and West, or, rather, between an East filtered through the
idea of a singular Asia and the West as defined by artistic developments
in the United States and Western Europe. For viewers such as Nakahara,
whose 1970 Tokyo Biennale was tacitly modeled along those lines, the
Écriture series would help form the grounds on which to construct a
distinct sense of contemporary Asian art. As the history of tansaekhwa's
initial emergence and promotion indicates, the very idea of tansaekhwa
was an attempt on the part of not only Korea-based but also Japan-
based artists, critics, and curators to arrive at a more viable response to
what they perceived as the dynamics of the international art world.

FIVE KOREAN ARTISTS, FIVE KINDS OF WHITE AT THE TOKYO GALLERY

On a warm May afternoon in 1975 no one in the Korean art world was
more excited than the critic Lee Yil. Or more anxious:

The exhibition opening was from four to six in the afternoon of May
6. Given that passport processing [at Kimpo Airport] always took a
long time, and together with the airline strike, I hoped to

FIGURE 5.1 Installation view, *Five Kinds of White*, Tokyo Gallery, 1975. On the back wall:
Park Seobo, *Écriture No. 8-74* and *Écriture No. 9-74*, both 1974. Both oil and pencil
on canvas. On the right wall (from back to front): Lee Dong Youb, *Situation C*, *Situation B*,
and *Situation A*, all 1974. All oil on canvas.

move my departure date up by a few days but the planes were full.
I didn't want to be late for the opening so I was indeed in a helter-
skelter state.[1]

The exhibition in question was *Five Korean Artists, Five Kinds of White*,
a group show at the Tokyo Gallery, which at this time was one of Japan's
leading venues for contemporary art. From May 6 to 24, the prestigious
gallery hosted a show of five Korean artists chosen by the gallery's
owner and director, Yamamoto Takashi, who sought to promote a traditional Korean aesthetic as a deliberate counterpart to that of the West.[2]
Also involved was Yamamoto's longtime associate, the critic and curator
Nakahara Yusuke, one of Japan's "big three" art critics, as well as Lee
Ufan, who translated the show's catalog from Korean to Japanese.[3]
Both Yamamoto and Nakahara had visited Seoul a few years earlier,
where they chose paintings by five artists: Kwon Young-woo, Lee Dong
Youb, Heu Hwang, Suh Seung-won, and Park Seobo.

Lee eagerly recounted his trip to Tokyo not long after the opening of
Five Korean Artists, Five Kinds of White:

I landed at Haneda [airport near Tokyo] at four. Processing took
thirty minutes. I called the Tokyo Gallery from the airport and
went straight away to the gallery. With my trunk in one hand and a
bookbag in the other, I drew near to the gallery at five [p.m.].[4]

Finally making his way to the fifth floor of the nondescript office building in which the Tokyo Gallery was located, Lee beheld a number of
large paintings covering the walls (Figure 5.1). Their white, monochromatic backgrounds dully reflected the bright lights of the gallery so that
they appeared to disappear, or at least to become one with the white
walls. Given what he had written in the show's catalog, Lee could not
have hoped for more. There he called the color white "the most fundamental single language determining our [Korean] way of thinking," a
description that vividly brought to light his long-standing commitment
to seeing Korean art take its place in the international art world.[5] In
some cases, Lee deliberately bypassed other aspects of a work to make
his point; for example, he neglected to discuss how Kwon Young-woo's
Work 74-1 (Figure 1.20) seemed almost to dramatize the encounter
between the support and the mark-making implement.

Lee did this not out of ignorance or willful neglect but as part of his
attempt to craft a specific identity for Korean art. For Lee, as for many

Korean artists and critics working amid the competing rates of acceleration and delay that defined the internationalization of Korean art, the challenge was to establish a direction. Nam Kwan, the painter whose most important contribution to postwar Korean art was perhaps his ability to put into words the consensus opinion of the Korean art world, stated in 1971, "Unless we [in Korea] stop being directionless, jumping from doing one thing today and another thing the next, we will never be free of foreign influence and in the course of copying others will never be anything more than an artistic colony." He also pointed out the need for a brand identity; how, he asked, could art compete on an international stage if it was "nationally indeterminate?"[6]

Japanese gallerists and critics like Yamamoto Takashi and Nakahara Yusuke seemed to agree with this last assessment, as they too reinforced the link between Korean art and the color white as an incipient means of defining what would come to be known as contemporary Asian art. In shows like the Second Asian Art Show, held at the Fukuoka Art Museum in 1980, tansaekhwa would be hailed as an exemplar of what was newly championed as "contemporary Asian art." Yet despite its freshness as a potential alternative to artistic worldviews revolving around developments taking place in the West, contemporary Asian art was inextricably linked to a diachronic chain of events in which the ideals of cultural, ethnic, and national parity otherwise assumed of the "new" paradigm were not always a priority. Tansaekhwa thus lay at the intersection of two streams of identification: between the desire expressed by some Korean critics and certainly the Korean state to establish a visibly recognizable national identity and the will of certain Japanese commentators to imagine an Asia in contradistinction to the West.

WHITEOUT: COLONIAL RESIDUE AND POSTCOLONIAL ANXIETY

When *Five Korean Artists, Five Kinds of White* opened, monochrome painting had already been identified as a casual trend in Korean art. Oh Kwangsu, for example, speculated as to whether the paintings shown in the exhibition *Modern Art 73,* held at the Myongdong Gallery between August 26 and September 1, 1973, indicated the emergence of such a trend.[7] The artist Lee Kun-yong pointed to the 1972 Indépendants Exhibition in Seoul as the first event where monochromism emerged as a significant trend.[8] Yet it was not long afterward that monochrome painting would take on a previously unknown ideological edge as critics began to link color, especially white, to the notion of a distinct Koreanness. In *Five Korean Artists, Five Kinds of White* those overtones became explicit as Lee Yil made a direct analogy between the artists' use of white and Chosŏn dynasty white porcelain, whose connections to an archetypal notion of Koreanness had been explored, if obliquely, by the paintings of Kim Whanki in the 1950s. Lee openly positioned tansaekhwa as emblematic of Koreanness by linking the color white to Koreanness in the catalog for *Five Korean Artists, Five Kinds of White.* His fellow essayist Nakahara Yusuke reiterated the connection, also focusing his attention on the white monochromatic supports of the works. Nakahara began his essay, written after Lee had finished his, with a disclaimer: "It is almost impossible to summarize the characteristics of the contemporary painting of any country"; he too concluded that Korean paintings could be summed up by a use of white.[9] That this was not just any kind of white was emphasized in the Korean title for the show, which used the word *hinsaek* (*hŭinsaek*) rather than the Chinese transliteration more commonly used to refer to white in both Japan and Korea (*paeksaek* in Korean).[10]

But this was also a time when Korean anxiety vis-à-vis Japan was at its most intense. In his *History of Modern Korean Painting*, the first attempt at explicitly tracking and evaluating modern Korean art according to sociopolitical phenomena rather than style, the critic Kim Yun-su argued that the means through which "modern art" (*kŭndae misul*) emerged in Korea was itself a symptom of its "cultural colonization" by Japan.[11] Modern Korean art, Kim argued, was far too indebted to the Japanese art world's absorption of Western artistic conventions and movements.[12] For him, the anxiety over Japanese influence was a call to reconsider the history of modern art in Korea; he would later argue that in order for Korean art to be treated equally with art from other places, it was up to the Korean art world to first put aside any traces of "anti-Japanese sentiment or a kind of sense of inferiority."[13]

In like manner, art historian Won Kap-hui—who, under the pen name Won Dong-suk, would soon champion a nationalist approach to art premised on the rejection of foreign artistic influences—argued against histories of modern art too closely associated with ideas of newness or progress. These ideas were closely linked to the Japanese colonial era and to preexisting histories of Korean art whose periodization tended to be calibrated according to the introduction of new styles or, more recently, the appearance of sociopolitical phenomena. Won considered existing histories of modern art too myopic in their fixation on the West and on "enlightenment," by which he referred to efforts undertaken by reform-minded Korean politicians and intellectuals in the late nineteenth century to open Korea's borders to the outside world. This, he claimed, obscured efforts to situate modernity's origins in the first half of the eighteenth century, when painters and writers demonstrated a reflexive sense of their surroundings through their work.[14]

Under such discursive circumstances, invoking Chosŏn dynasty white porcelain was likely to trigger other associations—namely, the rhetoric of cultural specificity expounded by Yanagi Muneyoshi. The connection with Yanagi's theories was not coincidence; several art historians have claimed that Yamamoto Takashi, the owner of the Tokyo Gallery, had Yanagi's characterization in mind when he decided to organize *Five Korean Artists, Five Kinds of White*.[15] Yamamoto himself lived in colonial Korea from 1940 to 1943 and was well acquainted with Korean antiques.[16] Additionally, an increasing number of authors criticized Yanagi's descriptions of Korean art, particularly after diplomatic relations between Japan and South Korea were normalized in 1965. The poet Kim Chi-ha denounced what he saw as the feminizing rhetoric of Yanagi, and in Japan Kim Tal-su, the first prominent *zainichi* novelist, condemned Yanagi's interpretation in *Chosen to sono geijutsu* (Chosŏn and her arts) as a gross misreading of "Korean white."[17] Renewed attention was paid to Yanagi's discussion of Korean art in the mid-1970s, after Yi Tae-wŏn's 1974 translation of *Chosŏn and Her Arts* appeared and after critic Park Yong-sook, in the progressive journal *Tari*, severely chided Korean art historians who based their accounts on Yanagi's theories.[18]

LEE YIL AT THE CROSSROADS OF INTERPRETATION

Aware of these debates, Lee Yil nevertheless persisted in comparing the works shown in *Five Korean Artists, Five Kinds of White* to Chosŏn dynasty white porcelain. As he saw it, *Five Korean Artists, Five Kinds of White* was a golden opportunity to challenge international artistic trends, a long-cherished goal perhaps most poignantly discussed in his essay "Korean Art on the World Stage." Originally written in February 1967, at a time when many Korean artists were expressing their discontent with what they knew of movements like gestural abstraction and op art, the essay calls on Korean artists to put themselves in a position that would "challenge" international art.[19] Yet despite the enthusiasm he would express in 1975, Lee had serious misgivings about ascribing a cultural identity to the paintings of artists like Park Seobo, Yun Hyongkeun, and Kwon Young-woo. In his 1971 analysis of Henri Focillon's *Vie des formes* for the *Hongdae nonch'ong*, a magazine published by Hongik University, Lee saw Focillon's writings as a way out of what Lee had come to see as a misleading and even oppressive conflation of history and art history.[20] As he had previously discussed in another article from 1967, nearly all art historical narratives of the time saw certain watershed historical events—namely, Korea's liberation from Japanese imperial rule in 1945 and the outbreak of the Korean War in 1950—as the causes inspiring artists to produce work. In Lee's mind, this kind of thinking ran the risk of diminishing art's own capacity to affect the world around it.[21] Context had to be considered, but the problem was how to do so without suppressing the agency of the work. Lee addressed the issue by upholding Focillon's view of art as an intrinsically contradictory outcome, quoting him:

The problems posed by the interpretation of the work of art arise in the form of nearly obsessive contradictions. The work of art is an attempt at the unique; it is affirmed as a whole, as an absolute; and at the same time, it belongs to a system of complex relations.[22]

These contradictions were often most clearly revealed when the viewer entered what Focillon described as the space of the painting: "the space managed by technique, and defined by matter and movement."[23] By predicating his discussion on the assumption of the artwork being contradictory, Focillon implied that the task of interpretation was doomed from the very start.

Shades of this thinking reappeared in Lee's catalog essay for *Five Korean Artists, Five Kinds of White*, in which he spoke of white as "the field [*madang*] where all possibilities arise."[24] Some of this rhetoric echoed that of Yves Klein, to which Lee may have been exposed when he began attending classes in archaeology and art history at the Sorbonne in 1961.[25] Even before then, Lee had already expressed an interest in visual art and may have been aware of Klein's well-attended lecture at the Sorbonne on June 3, 1959, "The Evolution of Art towards the Immaterial." Klein described monochrome painting as the potential for an escape from his feelings of imprisonment; blue is transcendent, he avowed, "outside any dimension."[26]

But as much as Lee recognized the importance of an avowed non-commitment, he was also well aware of the costs incurred in having to do business with an international art world that, despite its arguments to the contrary, cared less for the life of forms than for the status of nations. U.S. and Western European art worlds seemed ill prepared to include works from its putative margins unless those works were accompanied by extenuating declarations of cultural difference. If Lee deliberately focused on the color white used in some examples of tansaekhwa as ineffable proof of their Koreanness—even as it relied on characterizations linked to fraught histories of imperial domination and colonial subjugation—it was because there was no viable alternative, at least not from where Lee and his colleagues in Korea were situated. Lee seemed to be thinking as much when he took pains to establish the non-Europeanness of white as it was used in *Five Korean Artists, Five Kinds of White*: white, he said, was not merely "a method for experimenting with color, as . . . in Europe" but was also a means of "showing how to absorb the vision of the world."[27]

Not satisfied with this bit of editing, Lee revised his thoughts further in the November–December 1975 issue of the architectural magazine *Kwangjang*, a few months after *Five Korean Artists, Five Kinds of White*. There Lee rejected then-common ideas of a "meeting between East and West," as well as tropes of tradition or "Orientalness" through which to articulate a discourse for contemporary art in Korea. Appealing to the monochrome was in keeping with Lee's conviction of the significance of form: "The problem always resided in the fact that we must discuss our [Korean] art against the essential specificities of contemporary visual art, and more broadly, [against] the [other] arts themselves." He stressed that the use of white was an expression of a particular sensibility belonging to an "us" defined as Korea, in sharp contrast to the way artists like Kwon Young-woo, Ha Chonghyun, and Park Seobo actually treated white in their own works.[28]

Despite the success enjoyed by Kwon, Ha, Park, and other representatives of tansaekhwa, Lee was never really comfortable with the rhetoric employed on their behalf, as if he recognized that such promotion actually foreclosed other possibilities of interpretation outside those framed by cultural or national identity:

When we place the development of Korean contemporary art
within an international context, before we evaluate it according to
the yardsticks of our own reality or history, we cannot help but first

feel a kind of embarrassment. One could call it disharmony. And the reason for this may first of all be the gap between artistic thinking and the systematic implementation of such.[29]

This "disharmony" occurred when there was no "systematic reflection on the act of producing work, or when artists became entangled in the inventions of fast-moving concepts."[30] To Lee, too many artists seemed borne adrift by an accelerated "information culture" that showed too much too quickly. In his view, the objective was not to align the pace of activity according to particular ideas or events but to return to the question of what it meant to make art: "It is only right that our [Korean] contemporary art confront 'contemporary art' itself, without the label of 'our' [Korea]."[31] Real inclusion, Lee implied, could only take place when artworks were no longer primarily received on grounds of representation necessarily framed by invocations of artists' national and cultural backgrounds.

THE LOOK OF CONTEMPORARY KOREAN ART

The concerns that troubled Lee seemed not to have touched tansaekhwa's Japanese supporters, who were encouraged by the positive reception of *Five Korean Artists, Five Kinds of White*. In 1976 Nakahara Yusuke began to plan another exhibition of contemporary Korean art titled *Korea: Facet of Contemporary Art*.[32] Taking place on August 16, 1977, at the Central Museum of Art, located in an office building in the Ginza district of Tokyo, the show featured large abstract paintings based on monochromatic supports of whites, browns, and blacks that lined the museum's walls (Figures 5.2 and 5.3).[33] Though they shared exhibition space with sculptures and other kinds of painting, large examples of tansaekhwa appeared to dominate the space. As one of the participants, Pak Chang-nyŏn, recalled, "The entire space of the exhibition was an intense atmosphere of noncolors."[34]

Part of a deliberate collaboration aimed at promoting contemporary Korean art in Japan, *Korea: Facet of Contemporary Art* was in many respects an extended version of *Five Korean Artists, Five Kinds of White*, even though it included a much broader variety of artists.[35] Save for Heu Hwang, all the artists exhibited in the earlier show were present, along with fifteen others, including Lee Ufan and Yun Hyongkeun. Also present at the show's opening were many of the guests who had

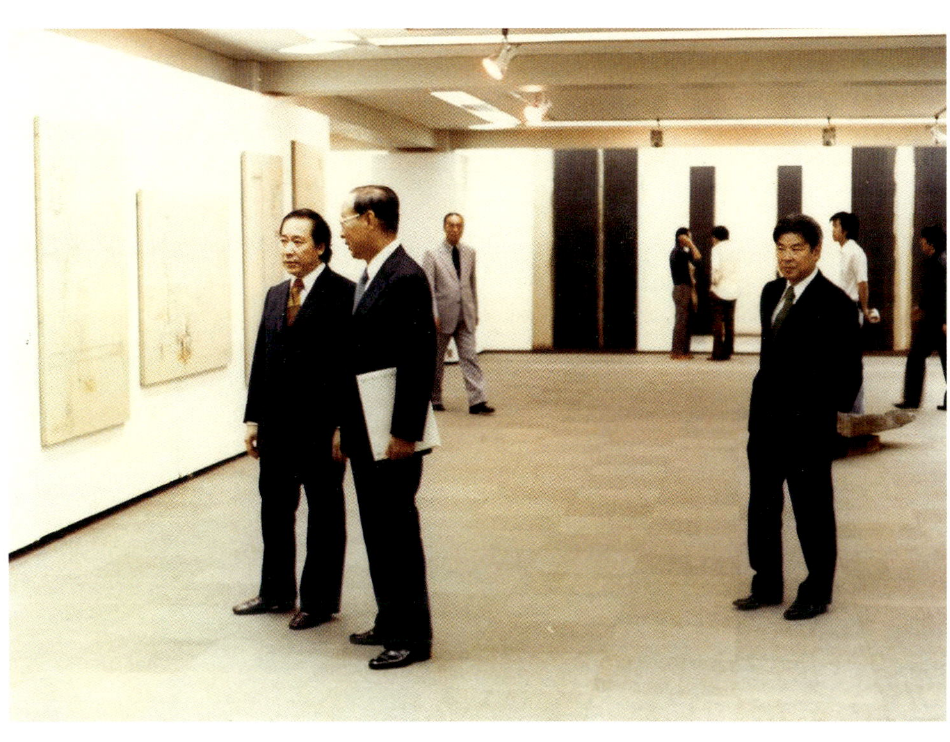

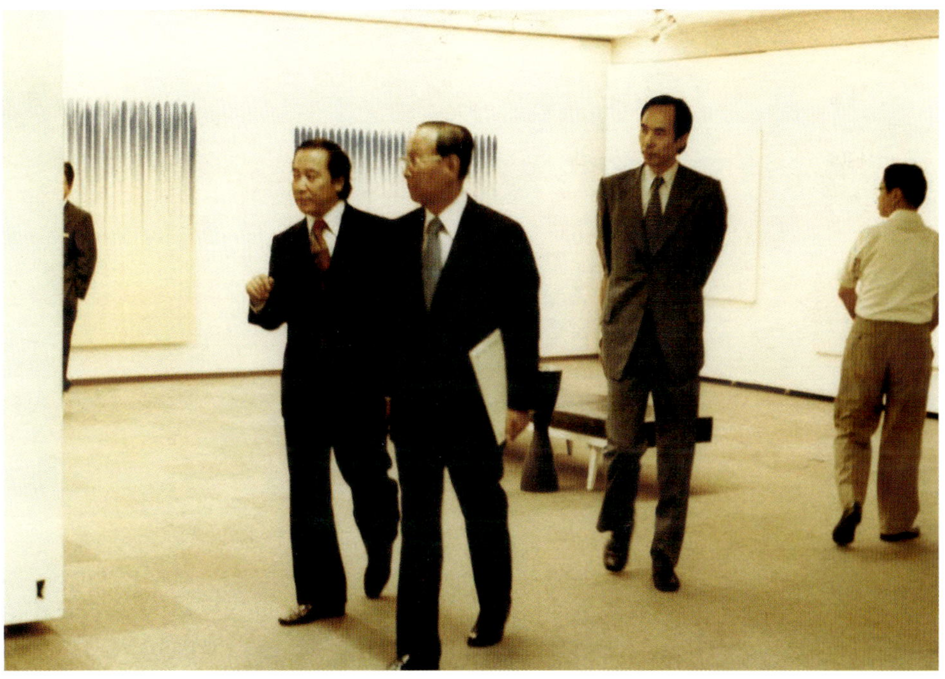

previously attended the opening of the earlier 1975 exhibition. There
was Lee Ufan, now a leading member of the Korean and Japanese art
worlds, his status recently increased by his selection for the exhibition *Documenta VI*. Also present was Lee Yil, who spoke with Tanaka
Tameyoshi, the editor of *Bijutsu techō*.

Summarizing the exhibition in the *Asahi Journal*, Nakahara stressed
the difference between Korean and Japanese art on the basis of what
he described as Korean art's tendency to avoid using color and the "balanced" appearance of its painting surface.[36] Ogawa Masataka, the art
critic and a member of the *Asahi shimbun*'s liberal editorial committee,
who accompanied Nakahara during his trips to Seoul, was interested in
what he saw as a commitment among the artists to explore the basics
of painting. One visit included a trip to the Third École de Seoul, which
by this time was carefully organized so as to showcase monochromatic
work.[37] To Ogawa, the works shown "appeared to investigate a new
departure by returning to a point of origin." They seemed to embrace a
simplicity of method, thus "vigorously" pushing the issues of "materiality" and the "essence of spatial structure."[38]

Korean observers saw the exhibition as a turning point. The newspaper *Kyŏnghyang sinmun* ran a prominent feature on the exhibition in
which journalist Ch'oe No-sŏk heralded the show as the first large-scale
initiative to promote contemporary Korean art in Japan. Although
some artists still considered Japan a portal of access less significant
than Paris or New York, Ch'oe described it as nevertheless crucial for
gaining international visibility. His only objection was the show's focus
on a particular selection of paintings that excluded many ink paintings
and figurative works, not to mention other types of abstraction.[39] The
exhibition was also reviewed in Korea, in the May 1979 issue of the art
magazine *Misul kwa saenghwal*. Clearly bothered by the fact that the
show was organized entirely by a Japanese critic, the discussion moderator Kim Sŭng-gak repeatedly asked whether it was the case that the
show was a protocolonial collaboration with the Japanese.[40] Artist Pak
Chang-nyŏn was frankly enthusiastic about the intervention of a third
party, remarking that if an in-country commissioner had been charged
with selection, it would probably have resulted in a biased view, skewed
in favor of candidates' résumés rather than their work.[41]

Echoing his disclaimer from the catalog of *Five Korean Artists, Five
Kinds of White*, Nakahara asserted that *Korea: Facet of Contemporary Art*
was by no means intended as an expansive representation of contemporary Korean art.[42] But while averse to the idea of a representational

exhibition, he nevertheless embraced the idea of showing the work of "a group of artists" (*ichigun no bijutsuka*) rather than modes of presentation that might emphasize the singularity of an individual artist's practice.[43] Nakahara contended that the works by Korean artists shown in *Korea: Facet of Contemporary Art* distinguished themselves from art made by their counterparts living in the presumed centers of the international art world in Europe, the United States, and Japan.[44] Tanaka Tameyoshi, the editor of *Bijutsu techō*, stated the matter even more directly by extolling Korean art over that of Japan. According to Lee Yil, Tanaka remarked that the works "seemed much more attuned to Asianness than the works of Japanese artists."[45]

THE REGIONALIST ORIGINS OF CONTEMPORARY ASIAN ART

Tanaka's comment touched upon a nascent attempt, beginning in the late 1960s, to promote a distinct body of contemporary Asian art. These efforts drew momentum from another stream of identification based on perceptions of the international art world as a realm defined not by the presumptive exchange among nations but by competition among a set of distinctly different regions, a primary symptom of which was the attempt to stage alternatives to the major biennales held in various European capitals and in São Paulo. An especially illuminating case in point was the Triennale India, established in part to avoid the polarizing dichotomy of communism-versus-anticommunism. Established in 1968, it was first known as the Triennale of Contemporary World Art and echoed the intentions of the Non-Aligned Movement, the loose configuration of mostly non-Euro-American states founded in 1961 on the principle of noninvolvement in the Cold War. The triennale was organized by the state-run national academy of art, the Lalit Kalā Akademi in New Delhi, and benefited from the Indian state's careful negotiation of a fraught political climate in which it aligned itself with neither the Soviet Union nor the United States; it was, for instance, the only major international arts event to include artists from both North and South Korea. Mulk Raj Anand, chairman of the Akademi, wrote in his welcome address to the inaugural triennale,

Though there have been exhibitions of contemporary world art,
every two years through the Venice, the Paris, the São Paulo and the
Tokyo Biennales, yet many Asian, African, and socialist countries

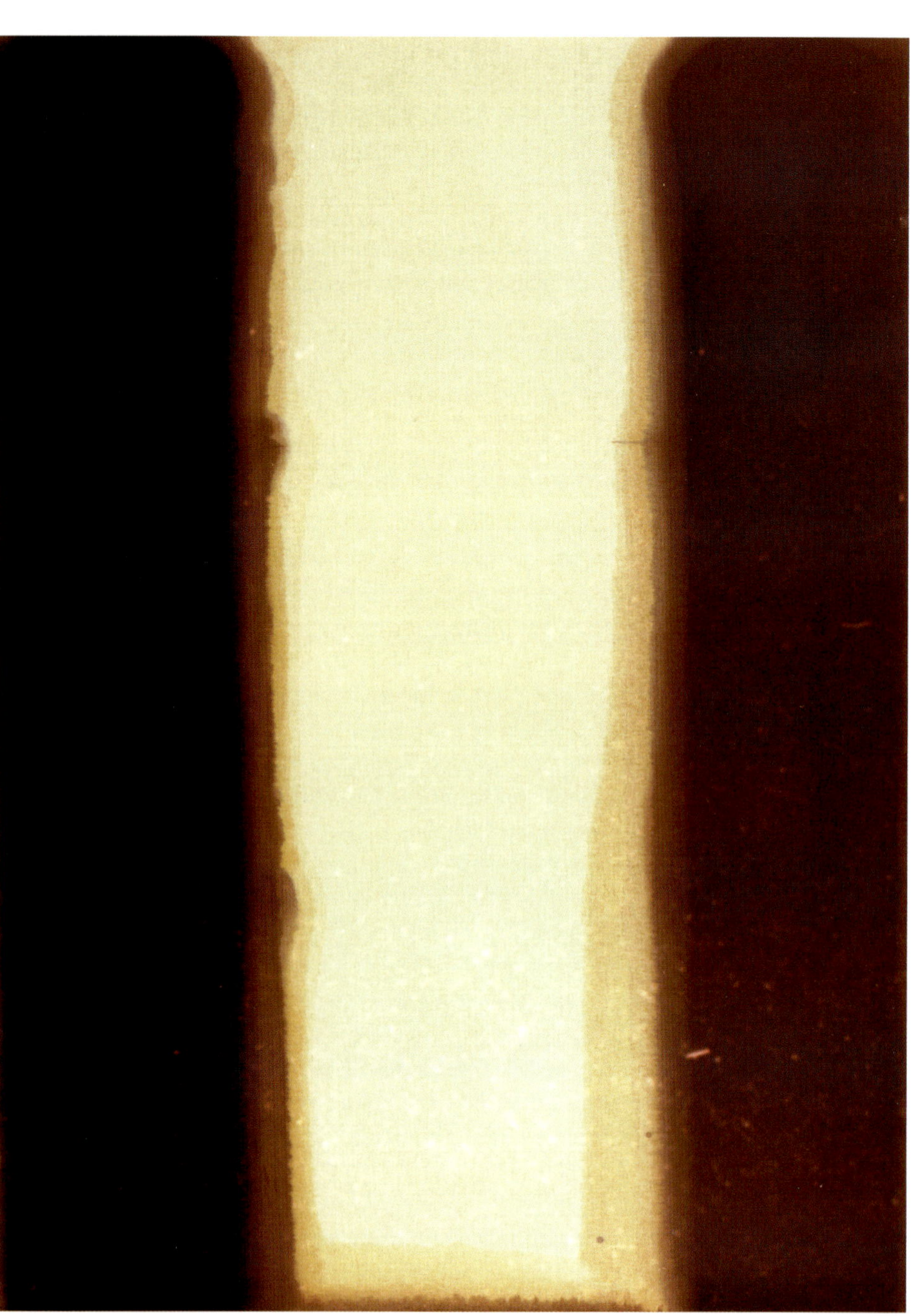

have not been able to establish a platform where the desired images of the oldest and youngest continents (youngest in the sense of secular achievement in the arts) may be seen together with the achievement of the dynamic west.[46]

The curator Honma Masayoshi, who had helped organize *Contemporary Korean Painting*, was a juror for the first Triennale India. He may have been thinking of the triennale's efforts to reframe the world in making selections for his exhibition *Contemporary Art: Dialogue between the East and the West*, held at the National Museum of Modern Art in Tokyo in 1969, just a year after *Contemporary Korean Painting*. Honma declared that "Okakura's saying 'Asia is one' shall have to be changed to 'the World is one' whether one likes it or not."[47]

Other critics, curators, and organizations in Japan regarded events like these as part of a broader call to form and uphold an Asian regionalism. One recalls, for instance, Haryū Ichirō's review of the 1968 show *Contemporary Korean Painting* in which he claimed that the inability of the works on display to break away from the trends of Euro-America was itself a call for viewers to think about the possibility of a distinctly Asian view of contemporary art. The Tokyo Gallery launched an "Asian Art" series, whose first installment in September 1972 was an exhibition of Chosŏn dynasty portraiture and folk paintings and whose later installments included *Five Korean Artists, Five Kinds of White*.[48]

It was not until the mid-1970s, however, that a critical mass of Japanese artists and critics began to map what the features of a distinctly "Asian" contemporary art might look like. In December 1974, three men, Lee Ufan, Joseph Love, and Sekine Nobuo, were specially invited from Japan to view the Seoul Indépendants show. Established in 1972 by the Korean Fine Arts Association as an audition venue from which the association formed delegations to overseas biennials and triennials, the Seoul Indépendants exhibitions had an open-door submission policy, which made them among the best places to see contemporary art in Korea. The visitors from Japan responded positively, often drawing comparisons between what they saw and what they knew of contemporary art in Japan. According to the artist Chŏng Ch'an-sŭng, the guests from Japan described what they saw—namely, the many abstract, monochromatic paintings on display—as being relatively unscathed by what they described pejoratively as "the pollution of civilization."[49]

Attracting special interest from Japanese viewers were the *Umber Blue* works of Yun Hyongkeun (for example, Figure 5.4), which drew more consistent attention than any other tansaekhwa series except Lee Ufan's *From Line* and *From Point*. Yun was invited to exhibit his works at the Muramatsu Gallery in June 1976; the show attracted praise from critics like Segi Shinichi, who called Yun's works "a new frontier of post abstraction."[50] Lee Ufan also wrote that the *Umber Blue* works looked as if they were "filled with the odor of an earthy farmer."[51] Other works were soon celebrated for imparting a natural, unstudied look, as primarily delineated by a limited palette of one or two colors and a perceived absence of deliberation on the part of the artist. Probably encouraged by this positive reception, some artists, including Yun, deliberately associated their works with an idealized concept of nature; *Umber Blue*, for example, celebrated "materials that came directly out of nature."[52]

Some artists saw the association between their works and nature as a virtue. Speaking of *Korea: Facet of Contemporary Art*, Park Seobo stated that the West and its culture of mass production and industrialization led to both literal and figurative pollution. In such a culture, the value of "untainted" and "natural" objects was potentially limitless. Park consequently described these "natural" works as being the result of an intrinsic Asianness.[53] This shift was not so much a jump in logic as a deliberate misframing originating in Park's rejection of the "cosmopolitan" in favor of the "national" in a 1975 discussion organized by the Korean Fine Arts Association. There, he asserted, "The national was the recuperation of philosophies of nature. Through the recuperation of philosophies of nature, we are fundamentally different from people in the West."[54]

Despite being himself one of the staunchest promoters of tansaekhwa's "natural" aspect, Lee Yil also reminded his readers that they should not be "allergic" to foreign influences lest they succumb to a worldview that specifies phenomena in terms of their relationship to trends.[55] Yet Lee recognized that contemporary Korean art would be far more readily accepted if it was framed according to the expectations of the intended audience/consumer, in this case, viewers in Japan already familiar with the idea of a nascent Asian artistic regionalism. Asianness was another name for this difference, whose potential had previously been noted by Lee in his roundup of significant shows of 1977 for the journal *Munye yŏn'gam*. He recounted the remarks of *Bijutsu techō*'s editor, who observed that the examples of tansaekhwa shown in *Korea: Facet of Contemporary Art* were "far more Asian" than their Japanese counterparts. Although Lee understood that "there was no reason to take these words at face value," he felt that the question of an "Asian essence" should be faced, if only to arrive at some way of presenting contemporary Korean art that would enable it to be accepted within a world order of visual art.[56]

Among the best illustrations of the way critics, institutions, and artists tried to visualize a discrete body of contemporary Asian art are the Asian Art Shows, the series of exhibitions sponsored by the Fukuoka Art Museum between 1979 and 1994. The Asian Art Shows were the predecessor to the Fukuoka Asian Art Triennale (which was first established in 1999 at the newly unveiled Fukuoka Asian Art Museum and which still takes place). They belonged to the Fukuoka municipal government's campaign to develop the infrastructure and image of Fukuoka, one of the fastest growing cities in Japan in the first half of the 1970s.[57] In 1976 the city's mayor, Shinto Kazuma, initiated a plan to promote the city, already the largest in western Japan, as an "international cultural exchange city" (*kokusai bunka kōryū tosi*).[58] Intended to raise the status of Fukuoka by framing it as a cosmopolitan site, this campaign tasked the staff of the newly constructed Fukuoka Art Museum to showcase all the nation-states of an "Asia" that stretched from India to Japan. The scale of the proposed undertaking, which curator Yasunaga Koichi recalls as a mandate directly issued from the mayor's office, left several museum staffers "flabbergasted."[59]

Between November 3 and December 2, 1979, the Fukuoka Art Museum held the group show *Asian Artists Exhibition Part I* as its inaugural exhibition. Intended as the first part of a two-part series, it examined how three countries, India, China, and Japan, came to be modern through what the museum's director, Toshihiro Kennoki, described as "the interaction of traditional and modern art."[60] Koike Shinji, adviser to the Fukuoka Art Museum and chairman of the subcommittee for the First Asian Art Show, implied that *Asian Artists Exhibition Part I* was an example of a nascent Asian regionalism by citing Okakura Tenshin's famous declaration "Asia is one" from his influential 1903 book *Ideals of the East*.[61] Koike, a respected scholar of industrial design and a founding sponsor of the Fukuoka Art Museum, invoked Okakura's call in the context of extolling Fukuoka's historical role as a site for cultural exchange, although he may have been influenced by his work for the imperial bureaucracy in the 1940s, when the theory of a Greater East-Asia Co-Prosperity Sphere was employed to help justify imperial expansion.[62] In the decades after Japan's defeat in World War II, when the United States had come to establish what historian Bruce Cumings describes as a "light hold on the Japanese jugular" in matters of both military security and economic development, the imperialist charge of Okakura's statement was less at issue.[63] Some commentators in Korea freely appropriated Okakura's proclamation, the barrage of anxiety over Japan's colonial legacy notwithstanding. In 1968 critic Sŏk To-ryun cited Okakura's proclamation of an Asian "unified body" in his argument for a Korean art that would reflect "an independent and self-conscious national spirit in spite of Korea's political past of invasion and colonial occupation."[64]

By the late 1970s Okakura's axiom was enlisted on behalf of reifying another notion of "Asia," one in which Japan was as much a part as it was its implied center. During its preparations for its First Asian Art Show, the Fukuoka Art Museum followed a model whereby each Asian nation-state was to contribute its own body of work to a larger umbrella institution. One conclusion of the symposium accompanying *Festival: Contemporary Asian Arts Show* of 1980, the second part of the Asian Art Show, was that the Fukuoka Art Museum was promoting a "national consciousness" of the kind advocated by the UNESCO cultural education program initiated between 1973 and 1978. Also significant was the UNESCO-initiated International Association of Art (IAA) congress of May 1973, at which member countries were encouraged to look for national consciousness and identity in art.[65]

In *Festival*, the search for parity implied in the first show shifted somewhat to a more hierarchical model. At issue was the potential of other countries to compensate for Japan's perceived condition of lack. Aoki Shigeru, subcommittee chairman of *Festival*, recalling the writings of commentators like Haryū Ichirō, Lee Ufan, and the visitors to the Second Seoul Indépendants Exhibition, conceived of Asia as an idea predicated on the absoluteness of Japan's lack. Criticizing what he saw as the excess resulting from the modernization of Japan, Aoki contended that there was a need to look for a compensating other that could "reverse" that excess.[66]

This was not a simple matter, especially when the "compensating other" in question was identified in terms of Asianness. The very idea of Asianness was closely associated with views that regarded Japan as distinct and separate from the rest of Asia. Reflecting on the phenomenon of contemporary Asian art, theorist Sakai Naoki notes that evoking Asianness has long been a means for agents to reify the existence of a distinct Japanese national identity.[67] For a Japanese institution to designate itself as a center for Asian art was problematic, even when it was based outside the power center of Tokyo, as in the case of the Fukuoka Art Museum. There was the matter of disparity, expressed in terms of Japan's privileged status in relation to its Asian peers. Artists and institutions in other Asian countries were acutely conscious of the disparity between their own countries and Japan. Discussions of the Triennale India, for instance, often regarded the Tokyo Biennale, established in 1952, as part of a major league of international art exhibitions.[68] Similarly, in a statement published in the catalog for the Second Triennale India, one of the artist-delegates from the Philippines, Virginia Ty-Navarro, observed, "Asian countries have no voice at all in international art congress[es] . . . except for Japan."[69]

More serious was the unresolved legacy of imperial Japan, for which conceptualizations of identity were central. Key among these conceptualizations were theories of essentialism and of Japanese exceptionalism. That these conceptualizations were still in play in the 1970s is evidenced by Joseph Love's characterization of the works in *Five Korean Artists, Five Kinds of White*, which went one step further than the descriptions of either Lee Yil or Nakahara Yusuke. Writing for the English-language daily *Japan Times*, he praised their "sense of isolation, almost sadness."[70] Love's review more explicitly brought to mind Yanagi Muneyoshi's description of Korean art as embodying "the beauty of sorrow."[71]

Yanagi's description was a charged one, particularly in light of the criticisms leveled against Yanagi's theories by Korean intellectuals in both South Korea and Japan from the 1960s through the 1970s. However, there is no published evidence to show that the artists of *Five Korean Artists, Five Kinds of White* objected to Love's review at the time of its publication, or, for that matter, to Lee's essay alluding to Yanagi's characterization. Indeed, many of the artists and commentators involved with the show were more than willing to position tansaekhwa, and Korean art generally, as a normatively superior alternative to both Japanese and Euro-American art, even if it meant tacitly embracing characterizations whose provenance might have been ideologically questionable to their colleagues at the time.

Lee Yil attempted to capitalize on the notion of Asianness on behalf of Korean art in his paper for the symposium accompanying *Festival: Contemporary Asian Arts Show*. Originally drafted in Japanese and later translated into English for the benefit of the other participants, the paper argued for a definition of Korean art that was at once beyond the pale of Euro-American tendencies and a proactive agent in what

its author called "world art."[72] In the discussion that followed, Lee
then characterized Japanese art as an art of precision and meticulous
organization. Korean art, in contrast, was based on an aesthetics of
imperfection; for this reason, Korean art had an unparalleled connection to "nature itself."[73] It was a way of thinking that intersected with
the assertions of tansaekhwa artists such as Yun Hyongkeun, who
stated that "no matter how developed humans become, they can never
make anything to surpass earth, trees, or water."[74]

Lee later stressed the Koreanness of the works by discussing the
"dominant trend to stick to a simple color," an observation supported
by the tendency among some tansaekhwa artists to produce works that
more closely resembled full monochromes than ever before.[75] However,
Lee was also careful to link what he described as the "Korean spirit"
of naturalism to the uniqueness of an "Eastern" way of thinking that
was incommensurable with that of the West.[76] It was a rhetorical tactic
that neatly reframed imperial Japan's imagined monopoly over the
politically charged alterity represented by the notion of Asianness. It
was also a tactic that offered contemporary art from Korea the opportunity to leverage the marginal position of Korean art as being a sign
of its greater proximity to the authentic origins of Asian art. Reviewing
Festival: Contemporary Asian Arts Show, Oh Kwangsu saw Korean art as
a potential vanguard. If the idea of a contemporary Asian art was based
on "overcoming the influence of Euro-American art to form a unique
artistic culture," then the premises laid out for tansaekhwa fit the bill as
a potential "model" for the field.[77]

Not everyone was convinced by these pronouncements. The prominent Malaysian artist and critic Redza Piyadasa immediately took Lee
to task for his inability to break away from a nation-based view of art.
Criticizing Lee's reasoning as an example of what he called the "failure"
of modern art, Piyadasa asked why "we are still on the stage of 'Is my
Minimalism Malaysian? Is your Minimalism Korean?'"[78] His question
took issue with the framing of tansaekhwa as a language that could not
be translated into any other terms but the most simplistic invocations
of cultural identity, a reflection of his own sensitivity regarding the
Malay-versus-non-Malay distinctions that were very much in play at
the university where he taught.[79] Piyadasa might have agreed with Yun
Hyongkeun's statement that "the more one tries to intentionally articulate Koreanness, the more one's work becomes alienated from it."[80]

TANSAEKHWA VENTURES WEST

Although several Korean and Japanese critics and institutions praised what they saw as expressions of Asianness, even going so far as to declare tansaekhwa the most distinctive visual language of 1970s Korea, others had deep reservations about the works, which struck some as both too different and not different enough.[81] Tansaekhwa made its European debut at the Grand Palais in Paris as part of the exhibition *Secondes Rencontres Internationales d'Art Contemporain*, held November 11, 1978–January 29, 1979. Organized by the Association Française d'Action Artistique (AFAA), the quasi-governmental agency that counted among its responsibilities the export of French art shows and the selection of artists to represent France in major international shows, this was the second in an intended series of shows that began in 1977. Five underrepresented countries were selected to grace the Palais: Syria, Venezuela, Tunisia, Greece, and South Korea. Nine artists (Kim Whanki, Yu Kyŏng-ch'ae, Kwon Young-woo, Pyŏn Chong-ha, Yun Hyongkeun, Park Seobo, Ha Chonghyun, Lee Ufan, and Shim Moon-seup) were selected by the AFAA and then approved by the Korean Ministry of Culture and Information to serve as the Korean delegation.[82]

In many respects the organization and purpose of *Secondes Rencontres Internationales d'Art Contemporain* echoed those of *Contemporary Korean Painting*, the 1968 show held at the National Museum of Modern Art in Tokyo. Both were government-sponsored attempts to introduce contemporary Korean art to an overseas audience. But while the artists represented in the 1968 show presented a diverse, if disorganized, array of work ranging from informel-like oils to sculpture, the Korean delegation to *Secondes Rencontres Internationales d'Art Contemporain* focused primarily on examples of tansaekhwa. Works such as *Conjunction 77-15* (Figure 5.5) stood out on walls specially painted dark blue. Most of the artists for this show exhibited works that were considerably larger than those for which they were initially known; for example, Kwon Young-woo's *S 78-72* (Figure 5.6) or Yun Hyongkeun's later versions of *Umber Blue*. Often looking as if they were scaled for a cavernous exhibition hall, these works appeared distinctly at odds with the claims advanced on their behalf; at over two meters tall, *S 78-72* resonated more convincingly with a large industrial building or institutional hall than it did with lyrical descriptions of "nature" or with individual viewers, to whose proportions Kwon's earlier works were often scaled.

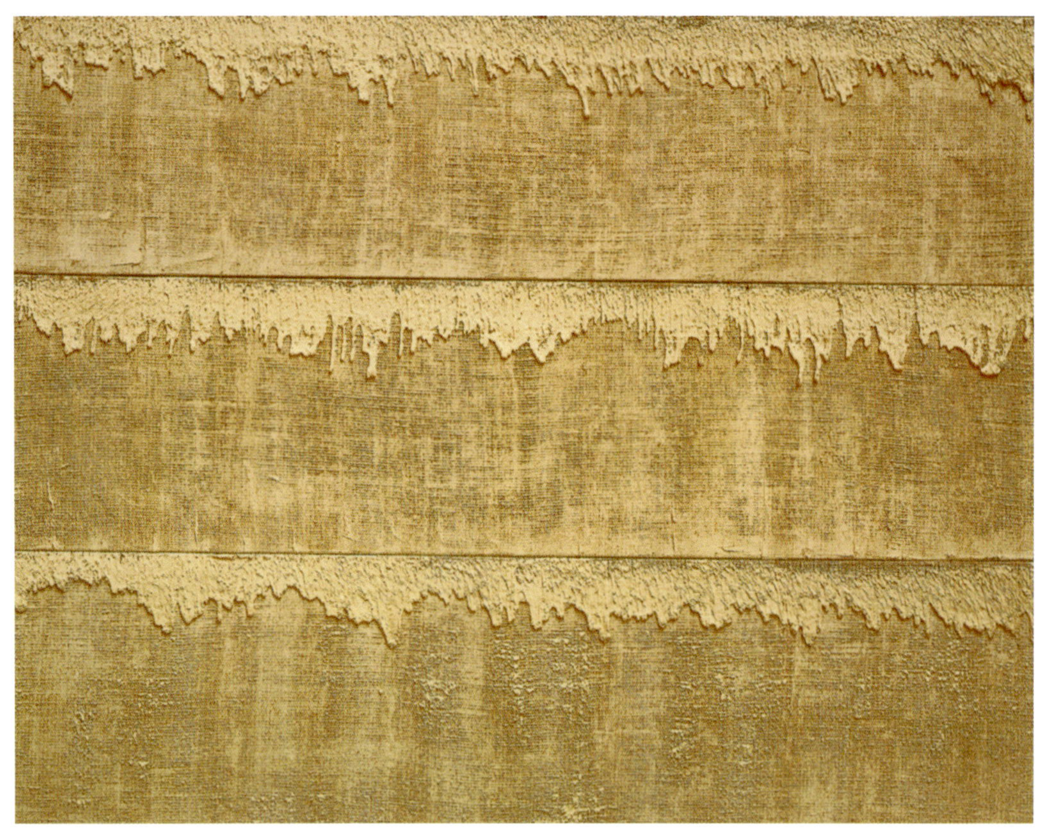

FIGURE 5.5 Ha Chonghyun,
Conjunction 77-15, 1977.
Oil on hemp, 127 × 165 cm.
Collection of the artist.

FIGURE 5.6 Kwon Young-woo,
S 78-72, 1978. Korean paper
on plywood, 227 × 181 cm.
Collection of the artist.

The catalog that accompanied the Korean delegation's works featured a short essay by Lee Yil, who stressed that all twenty-seven works represented what he saw as the crucial problem of reaffirming tradition through the language of the contemporary. Yet despite calling attention to the modernist tactic of the monochrome, Lee made clear that the works "must not solely be understood within the context of international painting."[83] His comments shared much in common with the paper he delivered at the second part of the First Asian Art Show at the Fukuoka Art Museum, in which he argued that any minimalist tendencies "should not be fixed within a context of Euro-American contemporary art but be accepted as part of Korea's unique originary spirit."[84]

Lee Yil tried to stack the deck of interpretation by framing his essay around cultural specificity, but responses to the Korean portion of *Secondes Rencontres Internationales d'Art Contemporain* were mixed at best. In stark contrast to the solo show of Nam June Paik, which took place at the Musée d'Art Moderne de la Ville de Paris at almost the exact same time, *Secondes Rencontres Internationales d'Art Contemporain* received very little published attention in the French media.[85] *Le Figaro* described the exhibition as a rather "arbitrary" attempt to affix "certain specific tendencies"—in this case, monochromaticism—to a particular country.[86] Written by Jeanine Warnod, the review echoed the sentiments of its author's father, André Warnod, who in 1925 first introduced the term "École de Paris" and who, in his description, divided non-French artists into the "great creative artists" and "the rest, the followers, the pasticheurs, the junk merchants whereas others are happy to keep their place and come to France in order to study before going home to put to use what they have acquired."[87]

The reception of the show was a curious riposte to the negative reception of *The Art of the Real: USA 1948–1968*, minimalism's European coming-out party. Also held at the Grand Palais almost a decade earlier, the exhibition had attracted a maelstrom of criticism by French critics eager to downplay American influence.[88] Here tansaekhwa received the opposite reaction, a symptom, perhaps, of the extent to which the French art world was likely to dismiss Asian art not perceived as coming from China or Japan. Some Korean artists, such as Kwon Young-woo, who relocated to Paris in 1978, enjoyed modest success in France. Yet it was negligible in comparison to that of Nam June Paik, whose Korean origins were downplayed in favor of his associations with the emergence of video art, and even Lee Ufan, who was beginning to attract positive notice in Paris and indeed throughout

Western Europe through exhibitions like *Japan: Tradition und Gegenwart*, which took place in Düsseldorf in 1974.[89]

Questions of cultural difference were themselves closely enmeshed with questions about other lines of activity—in particular, the power struggles that increasingly defined the Korean art world. In his review for the *Han'guk ilbo*, Kim Sŏng-u reported that other critics who saw *Secondes Rencontres Internationales d'Art Contemporain* expressed interest in the works of Kim Whanki while chiding artists like Park Seobo, Yun Hyongkeun, and Ha Chonghyun for failing to display their Koreanness.[90] Hardest of all to stomach was an early review by Sin Yong-sŏk, Paris correspondent for the influential *Chosun ilbo*. Sin argued that, except for the "face-saving" paintings of Kwon Young-woo, Ha Chonghyun, Lee Ufan, and Kim Whanki, "the works did not seem as if they hailed from a country with over five thousand years of tradition"; rather, he said, they seemed to come "from a cultural colony of some Western nation."[91] Sin's piece was criticized for its failure to "objectively present the specific reactions of the French audience."[92] Some of the exhibition's participating artists attributed the unexpected harshness of the review to the fact that Sin's mother, Paris-based painter Rhee Seong-ja, had not been invited to participate in the show.[93]

Sin's insinuations of cultural colonization quickly hit home, and a number of the show's participants immediately took issue with the criticisms. Refuting claims that the show merely drew from a group of international show "regulars," Shim Moon-seup vouched for the fairness of the selection process.[94] Park Seobo reacted with characteristic quickness. One rebuttal appeared in the *Chosun ilbo*, a long string of counteraccusations that ended with a contradictory appeal to the approving words of the French organizer ("this international exhibition was, irrefutably, a definite success").[95] Another, more considered response published in *Space* explained the selection process at length, yet the article's plethora of detail betrayed Park's defensiveness.[96]

TANSAEKHWA AT HOME: THE ÉCOLE DE SEOUL

If Park Seobo came across as defensive, it was because he was also defending his own position in the Korean art world. As the vice-chair of the board of directors of the Korean Fine Arts Association, the main organization for visual artists in Korea, Park organized the Seoul

Indépendants series of annual exhibitions. But whether the Seoul Indépendants exhibitions—or any other exhibition in Korea—were truly as open as advertised is a matter of question. In an unsigned article published in the daily *Chungang ilbo*, a writer opined, "For an exhibition that says anyone can join," the Seoul Indépendants have a "contradictory" policy of not allowing any figuration:

Who made this decision, who runs things is not clear. . . . Vice-Chair Park is single-handedly deciding on the glory of Korea in the name of the Fine Arts Association. . . . In order for a truly independent show to occur, the organizers must get rid of any restrictions or dogmatism that influence artistic styles or the works.[97]

Park recognized the success of the Seoul Indépendants, especially their ability to draw more attention than the Kukchŏn, which, due to a much-expanded art world and the proliferation of other exhibition venues, ended in 1981.

Park realized that it was crucial to bestow a distinct identity on any such initiative, as was the case when he established the École de Seoul, an annual series of exhibitions, in 1975. A Francophile of sorts since his first visit to Paris in 1960, Park ostensibly took the name from the École de Paris. In the late 1950s, the appellation was used defensively to recuperate French art in the wake of New York's ascendancy as the world's new epicenter for modern art.[98] Similarly, Park intended the École de Seoul to fulfill two not entirely compatible objectives: chasing both acceptance from an international art world and defending "Korean" values.[99] Park's intentions in establishing the École de Seoul were in line with those of Lee Yil in arguing the idea of a Korean monochrome painting: "In contemporary art, the shared problem is that of co-existence with the international [art world], and the problem of how we [Korean artists] can be different from other countries. . . . This is the *raison d'être* for the École de Seoul."[100] The First École de Seoul took place at the National Museum of Modern Art in Seoul from July 30 to August 5, 1975. Nakahara Yusuke praised it as a progressive force in contemporary Korean art, suggesting the possibility that *Korea: Facet of Contemporary Art* was partly based on what he had seen of the École de Seoul.[101] The Third École de Seoul exhibition was organized around artists tending toward the monochrome.[102] This particular show was lauded by influential critics such as Bang Keun-taek, who in 1977 described the paintings associated with the École

de Seoul as "the very reflection of Korean contemporary art."[103]
Elsewhere he stressed the idea of the white pictorial surface (*paen'myŏn*
as an important component of the works he so esteemed.[104] Whereas
the writings of Lee Yil made a case for the idea of tansaekhwa abroad,
it was the École de Seoul and its supporters that did likewise at
home in Korea.

Many in Korea nevertheless regarded the École as a transparent
attempt on the part of Park to control the contemporary Korean art
world. Ha Chonghyun claims Park's intention was to undermine the
A.G., which drew considerable interest in the Korean art world from
1969 to 1974. Both Ha and another former A.G. member, Lee Kun-
yong, have claimed that Park "could not bear the fact of anyone else
surpassing him, [and] the École de Seoul was kind of a way to reclaim
what he saw as his rightful place of superiority," although Ha was
himself a regular on the École de Seoul roster from 1978 until 1995,
when the shows ended.[105] Park firmly denies any intention of wanting
to deliberately break up the A.G., alleging that the group, which effectively dissolved in 1975, did so of its own accord.[106] Artist Ha In-du,
who had a self-described "love–hate" relationship with Park, described
the École de Seoul in 1975 as a de facto "Park Seobo Association."[107]
Similarly, journalist Pak Mu-il commented in 1977 that some accused
the École de Seoul of being the "Park Seobo gang" (*sadan*).[108] Even
though the École de Seoul had a series of commissioners, Park Seobo
was a member of the exhibition's steering committee that chose the
commissioners, and he remained instrumental in the activities of
the École de Seoul throughout its existence.[109] Even Bang Keun-
taek insinuated that the prominent placement of *Myobŏp* in *Art
International* was the result of Park's having "persuaded" the magazine's
Asia correspondent, Joseph Love.[110] Similarly, art historian Suh Sung-
rok later admitted that "not a few" looked upon the École de Seoul
with suspicion.[111]

With this background in mind, it becomes easier to understand the
alacrity with which Park responded to criticisms of the show in Paris.
Though in no real danger of losing any of the institutional power he
had so carefully accumulated over the course of two decades, he was
nevertheless sensitive to the seismic shifts taking place in the Korean
art world, which were to a degree driven by the changing sociopolitical
terrain of the time. In the fall of 1978, the once-dominant state faced
mounting opposition as students took to the streets of Seoul, Pusan, and
other major cities in protest, and intellectuals continued to rail against

the oppressions of Yushin rule. For some art critics, the promotion of tansaekhwa in state-sponsored exhibitions made it a prime target upon which to project their profound dissatisfaction with the power structure of the Korean art world and with the state itself.

Perhaps the most trenchant criticisms of *Secondes Rencontres Internationales d'Art Contemporain* were those that questioned the reliance on any invocation of cultural difference. In 1978 *Bijutsu techō* hosted a roundtable discussion on the subject of contemporary Korean art as a follow-up to the exhibition *Korea: Facet of Contemporary Art.* Takamatsu Jirō dismissed the idea of ethnic characteristics entirely, arguing that there was "not much meaning" in trying to discuss how a work was "specifically Japanese or Korean."[112] Acting as the roundtable's moderator and translator, Lee Ufan contended that it might be worthwhile to explore the idea of a non-nation-specific or non-ethnic-specific "contemporary art."[113] It was a position for which Lee would be roundly attacked in Korea. To critics such as Won Dong-suk, the shift away from considerations of nationality or ethnicity was shorthand for "Western ways of thinking" that threatened to undermine the validity of Korean art.[114]

Similar were the criticisms of Chŏng Po-wŏn, a young sculptor living in Paris and one of the few Korean critics to have actually visited the show.[115] She treated the obsession with cultural difference as an emperor-without-clothes situation in her remarks on the controversial *Secondes Rencontres Internationales d'Art Contemporain* for the April 1979 issue of *Space.* Why, despite the varied kinds of paintings on display, did the catalog focus only on issues of race and tradition? Chŏng implied that this focus was part of a deeply problematic mind-set that positioned Korean art as having to either refuse or assimilate to the influence of the outside world.[116] Her remarks suggested her restlessness with a discursive situation that put so much emphasis on words like "race" and "tradition" that it became all but impossible to talk about contemporary art in Korea without also invoking cultural difference, an issue that in subsequent decades became a very real problem for artists both in Korea and elsewhere in the so-called non-West.

What Takamatsu, Lee Ufan, and Chŏng had in common was a growing unease with the reification of cultural difference. The insistence on indicating one's national or cultural origins reinforced the idea of the world as a geographical construct divisible into a center and a periphery. As much as the promotion of tansaekhwa appealed to certain Korean nationalist and Japanese regionalist sentiments, it also suggested to some viewers the extent to which notions such as "contemporary Korean art" or "contemporary Asian art" doubled as frames of containment. What were the costs of working under these rubrics? Such was the question that would resound with increasing intensity as artists in Korea found themselves confronted by the global aspirations of what they had once known as an international art world.

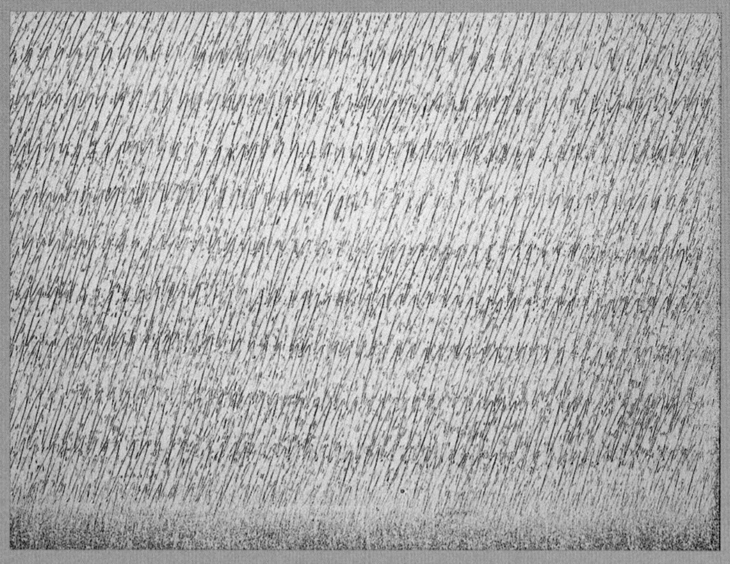

The Contextualist Predicament

Despite the criticisms directed against tansaekhwa and the assumptions underwriting its promotion, the movement continued to flourish. Helped by organizations like École de Seoul, tansaekhwa grew in size and prominence. Tansaekhwa artists featured prominently in highly lucrative private art competitions, many of which were sponsored by newspaper companies, such as the *Han'guk ilbo*, whose 1978 competition saw tansaekhwa artists like Yun Hyongkeun take top honors in the category reserved for invited painters. By the early 1980s tansaekhwa had so dominated group shows of contemporary Korean art that when the critic Yi Kyungsung organized the exhibition *Korean Contemporary Art—A Style of the Second Half of the 1970s* in 1983, he was quoted as saying he wanted to include colorful works lest the exhibition insinuate that Korean art was defined by the "monochrome trend."[1] Tansaekhwa works even gained a foothold in the market: the Fukuoka Art Museum, for insurance purposes, assessed a work from Ha Chonghyun's *Conjunction* series at $12,000, an *Écriture* work for $15,000, and one of Lee Ufan's *From Point* works for $25,000.[2] The 1990s saw the establishment of tansaekhwa's canonical status as many of its representatives came to occupy important university and museum positions, and Yun Hyongkeun was invited to be among those inaugurating Korea's first-ever pavilion at the Venice Biennale in 1995.

Yet the success of tansaekhwa was premised on its rhetoric, which stressed the ineluctable Koreanness and naturalness of its constituent artworks. Such a promotion revealed a chasm between what was said about the works and what could actually be seen, a distinction that might be described as a gap between the realm imagined as internal to the physical artwork and that external to it. Other artists and critics soon raised questions about this gap, most notably in their exploration of art's relationship to various contextual factors, which assumed a

FIGURE E.1 Park Seobo, *Écriture No. 43-78-79-81*, 1981. Oil on canvas, 130 × 162 cm. Collection of National Museum of Contemporary Art, Korea.

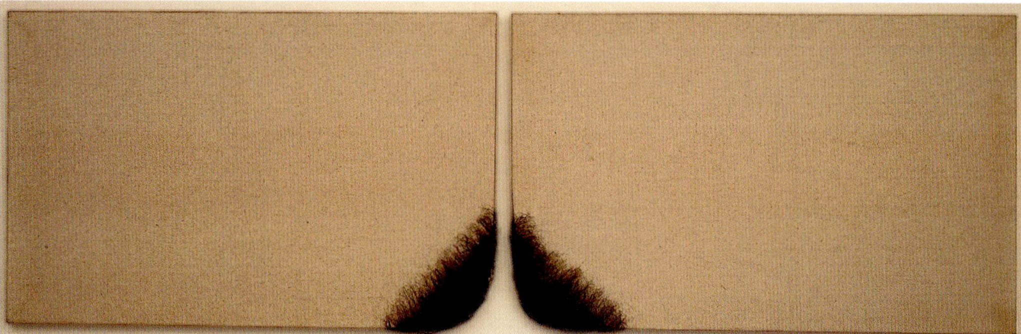

new urgency in the wake of the turbulent political circumstances of the 1980s. Yet this exploration also had its own challenges as the distinction between the internal realm of the artwork and the external domain cohabited by the artwork and viewer was collapsed in the name of "the people" vis-à-vis the rise of Minjung art or of contemporary art's "global turn." The result was the suppression of the dynamic between art and the circumstances of its production and reception. Consequently an untenable standoff arose between form and context, a predicament whose implications continue to reverberate today.

OTHER DIFFERENCES:
LEE SEUNG-TAEK'S *CANVAS WITH HAIR*

In 1976, when tansaekhwa was rapidly gaining prominence in Japan as Korea's leading artistic movement, Lee Seung-taek made *Canvas with Hair* (Figure E.2). Two large rectangular canvases of identical size and shape are directly juxtaposed to one another. The coarsely woven canvas support is left unpainted in order to preserve the fabric's original light brown color. A small thatch of untreated dark brown hair skirts both the bottom right-hand corner of the left canvas and the bottom left-hand corner of the right canvas. Lee, a former member of A.G., had long made use of hair and other everyday materials as part of his artistic repertoire. Yet by placing the canvases in such close proximity that their edges almost touch, the artist compels us to read the hair as a pubic thatch, especially against the somewhat pasty tone of the canvas, which recalls the pallor of the scalp, the underbelly, and other expanses of skin otherwise hidden from view. The gently rounded corners on which the hair is attached suggest the curves of a woman's body, an insinuation supported by Lee's use of female hair and by concurrently produced works in which the artist arranged hair on monochromatic canvases in ways that roughly approximated a woman's pubic area.

Lee's use of hair dated back to the mid-1960s, just prior to his joining the A.G. A sculptor by training, Lee spent much of his career dutifully casting giant effigies of iconic Korean heroes in bronze or chiseling heads out of stone, including one of General Douglas MacArthur, the U.S. general and commander of U.N. forces during the Korean War. But even before his graduation from Hongik University in 1959, Lee had demonstrated a strong interest in working with nontraditional materials, including hair and, earlier, nontangible substances like smoke and water. His interests in such materials eventually converged with those of the A.G., which he joined in 1970. But he was never fully committed to the group's mission, and he left the A.G. two years later.[3]

Yet he seemed to have kept close watch on the activities of his former colleagues, several of whom later emerged as tansaekhwa artists. The canvas in *Canvas with Hair* is of a particularly unremarkable brown, a caricature, perhaps, of both the color and rhetoric associated with the supports used by Ha Chonghyun in his *Conjunction* series (for example, Figure E.3). Although Lee made *Canvas with Hair* before the full onslaught of rhetoric extolling the "naturalness" of tansaekhwa, he seemed to be aware of its excesses. More suggestive still was the use of hair, which "was actually women's hair, sold by poor women for the purpose of making topknots for male actors playing samurai," and the close juxtaposition of the canvases.[4]

In using hair, and human hair at that, Lee imbues the work with a corporeality markedly absent from most examples of tansaekhwa, which, despite the often visceral nature of their facture, tended to be restrained in affect. Alluding to their proclivity for repeating certain strategies of depiction and for organizing their works into series, many Tansaekhwa artists spoke of their work as tantamount to *suryŏn*, a Korean word meaning "practice" of the kind associated with rigorous efforts at self-improvement through meditation, physical labor, and, perhaps above all, denial of the self and of carnal pleasures.[5] *Canvas with Hair* introduced a corporeality best accessed at the level of the erotic, as indicated by the rounded corners of the support and the placement of the hair.

The work also recalls the presence of the female body in such frank terms as to raise the issue of gender difference and its place in the mak-

FIGURE E.3 Ha Chonghyun,
Conjunction 79-99, 1979.
Oil on hemp, 120 × 120 cm.
Collection of the artist.

ing of Korean art. Gender differences were seldom discussed in the Korean art world, and almost never in relation to tansaekhwa, a movement whose key artists, supporters, and commentators were all men. Women far outnumbered men in university art departments, but they had few options, as Yi Kyungsung pointed out in 1963: if there was "not one great woman artist [in Korea]," it was not because female artists lacked talent but because they were routinely denied "opportunities for artistic creation."[6] Magazines and journals paid attention to persons who were specifically identified as "female artists" (*yŏryu hwaga*) in the 1960s, but contemporary art remained under the control of a small coterie of men despite the number of all-women artists' groups that appeared in the 1960s and '70s.[7] Korea's most financially successful gallery, Hyundai Gallery, was owned and operated by a woman, Park Myung-ja; its stable, however, was almost exclusively composed of male artists.[8]

In 1969 Oh Kwangsu observed that "no ordinary woman . . . would dare to go to an art college, unless she had dauntless courage, and of course, the encouragement of an understanding husband."[9] Oh was writing in 1969 of the sculptor Kim Chŏng-suk, one of the first major female sculptors in Korea and one of the first postwar Korean artists to be educated in the United States.[10] Yet he could have very well been talking about the 1970s, when the École de Seoul counted only a single female artist among its list of regulars, Jin Okseon. There was a particular irony in this regard: although tansaekhwa supposedly stood for an essential Koreanness, it was also a movement from which women were absent. At the same time, tansaekhwa's promoters advocated cultural difference as the means through which Korean art should be framed overseas yet excluded from consideration other kinds of difference. *Canvas with Hair* introduced questions of gender in a way that urged viewers to consider other kinds of differences, thus becoming, to some extent, a critique of how gender differences were occluded in the promotion of art otherwise celebrated as exemplary of Korean culture generally. In alluding to such differences, one speculates as to whether *Canvas with Hair* also tried to compromise the idea of a unified Koreanness so earnestly promoted in the 1970s by the state.

TANSAEKHWA'S DISCONTENTS

Harsher criticisms came from another camp, particularly from those artists and commentators interested in foregrounding the differences suppressed in the name of preserving the illusion of equality among all Koreans. Supported by government entities like the Korea Culture and Arts Foundation (now Arts Council Korea), tansaekhwa struck critics such as Kim Yun-su, Won Dong-suk, Sung Wan-kyung, and You Hong-june as suspect, or even complicit with a now morally bankrupt state. Won Dong-suk, who had first risen to prominence in 1977 when he took first prize in the art criticism contest sponsored in *Kyegan misul,* one of the new journals and magazines devoted to visual art that proliferated during the second half of the 1970s, criticized tansaekhwa as essentially irrelevant to the struggles of the people.[11] Such "monochromatic art," he claimed, was disconnected from "the realities and the sensibilities of the people."[12] In referring to what he called "monochromism" (*tansaekchuŭi*), Won made constant reference to terminologies of power ("the establishment," "monopoly"). This was an appeal that recalled his prize-winning essay, in which he had criticized Kim Whanki for willfully distancing himself from the "reality of the people," thus provoking much comment from older critics for whom Kim remained an exemplar of Korean artistic achievement.[13] Writing in the March 1979 issue of *The Deep-Rooted Tree,* a general-interest journal known for its distinctly critical view of the government, Won Dong-suk saw the domestic reception of *Secondes Rencontres Internationales d'Art Contemporain* as evidence further confirming the irrelevance of tansaekhwa.

Fueled by rising discontent toward the Yushin state and later toward the authoritarian regime of Chun Doo-hwan—a military general who seized control of the South Korean government soon after the assassination of Park Chung-hee on October 26, 1979—critics condemned tansaekhwa for having "ignored the political and social circumstances of the seventies" and for running "counter to the democratization movement."[14] By the early 1980s, criticism of tansaekhwa was so heated that for some critics the very idea was itself a byword for multiple sins, including mindless groupthink, social inequity, and apolitical complicity. Chang Sukwon condemned what he saw as the "obliteration" of individual creativity by "tendencies of the group" referred to as the "Korean monochrome."[15]

In 1981 the critic Sung Wan-kyung pointedly declared that the art of the 1970s—a less-than-cryptic reference to tansaekhwa and what some viewers saw as its near-hegemonic grasp on contemporary Korean art—was nothing more than an assertion of cultural and capital privilege.[16] Accusations of elitism coincided with efforts to recast tansaekhwa as

an offshoot of literati painting. "One must first become a scholar [*sŏnbi*]
before becoming an artist," said Park Seobo on the occasion of his solo
exhibition at the Hyundai Gallery in 1981.[17] He later noted, "I don't
paint so much as I move the brush like a scholar paints an orchid or
writes characters."[18] Certainly Park and a number of other tansaekhwa
artists began to paint more refined versions of the works that had first
earned them recognition in the early to middle 1970s. Park's lines
became more orderly (see, for example, Figure E.1), Yun's bleeding was
more controlled, and Ha's lumpy daubs of paint were flattened into
an almost unilaterally smooth surface (as, for example, in Figure E.3).
The overall sense was of painting that was less raw and more mannerly
than before; this shift seemed to anticipate an audience and market
that was beginning to open up to tansaekhwa in a significant way.

But if numerous artists and critics acted upon what critic You
Hong-june described as the "strong instinct to reject the expressionless
monochromes that were the art of the establishment," it was because
it seemed clear to them that tansaekhwa had crystallized into a tele-
graphic style ill-equipped to deal with a society that to them seemed in
need of more explicit, accessible, and even literal forms of depiction.[19]
To critics like Sung Wan-kyung, "the sensibility and form of artistic
activities during the 1970s had utterly failed to escape conservative
frames."[20] To their detractors like Sung, tansaekhwa artists no longer seemed to have a sense of who their audience was or of what this
audience was seeing and thinking. In their relentless pursuit of international recognition, critics wondered, were these artists thinking about
Korean viewers at all, or were they simply producing works for an imagined foreign audience? The question was especially pertinent in the
late 1970s and early 1980s, when university campuses were rife with the
smell of tear gas and when thousands of citizens gathered to protest the
rule of yet another military regime, most notoriously in the Gwangju
Uprising, which occurred shortly after General Chun declared martial
law on May 17, 1980.

Even aside from the dramatic changes in the South Korean sociopolitical landscape, tansaekhwa's detractors had a point. The initial
examples of tansaekhwa work, made prior to the introduction of tansaekhwa rhetoric, had been compelling because they used materials in
ways that enabled viewers to think outside the taxonomic structures
to which painting was subject, especially in Korea. But as tansaekhwa
works were promoted overseas, an increasing number of them gave
the impression that their makers were unable to think about painting

without also thinking about their promotion as exemplars of Koreanness, nature, or tradition. Tansaekhwa rhetoric came to determine the way artists looked at painting, which is why many examples of tansaekhwa made after 1980 lacked the curious potency of their predecessors. Ironically enough, those who criticized tansaekhwa did so in order to sustain the core mission of many tansaekhwa works: the urgency of perpetually reconsidering the assumptions on which the making and reception of artworks were based.

KIM JEONG-HEON ON A LIFE OF PLENTY

The tansaekhwa/anti-tansaekhwa struggle came to a head in such events as the *Works by the Controversial Artists of 1981*, a group exhibition held from January 16 to February 12, 1982, at the Seoul Museum, the first private museum for visual art in Korea.[21] Eleven prominent critics were each invited to select an artist under the age of forty whose works they felt to be especially provocative. By now deeply invested in tansaekhwa, Lee Yil selected a painter named Pak Yong-min, whose past experiences included showing at the École de Seoul, at the A.G.'s Seoul Biennale of 1974, and as part of the Korean delegation for the 1979 São Paulo Biennale. Similarly predictable were the selections of Kim Yun-su and Won Dong-suk. The former chose Kim Kyeong In, a Seoul National University graduate whose solo show at the Korea Culture and Arts Foundation in 1981 demonstrated a "realist spirit" that appeared to counter what Kim decried as excess internationalism and commercialism within the Korean art world.[22] Kim Yun-su described one of Kim Kyeong In's works, a large oil diptych showing two implied scenes of torture, *Double Torture 81-1* (Figure E.4), as an "expression of the anxieties of the present."[23] Similarly, Won picked Yi Ch'ŏng-yun, a painter from Pusan, whose depictions of urban back alleys, covered food stalls, and makeshift houses he praised for their evocation of life in "marginalized areas."[24]

It was up to a less partisan commentator, Park Yong-sook, to make perhaps the most telling selection of all. Park wanted to choose an artist whose work might avoid what he saw as "the excessive congregation of our avant-garde works around the axis of minimalism."[25] Here "minimalism" was code for tansaekhwa, whose pared-down aspect had been greatly emphasized in exhibitions, reviews, and other commentaries. The former *Space* editor chose Kim Jeong-heon, creator of *Lucky*

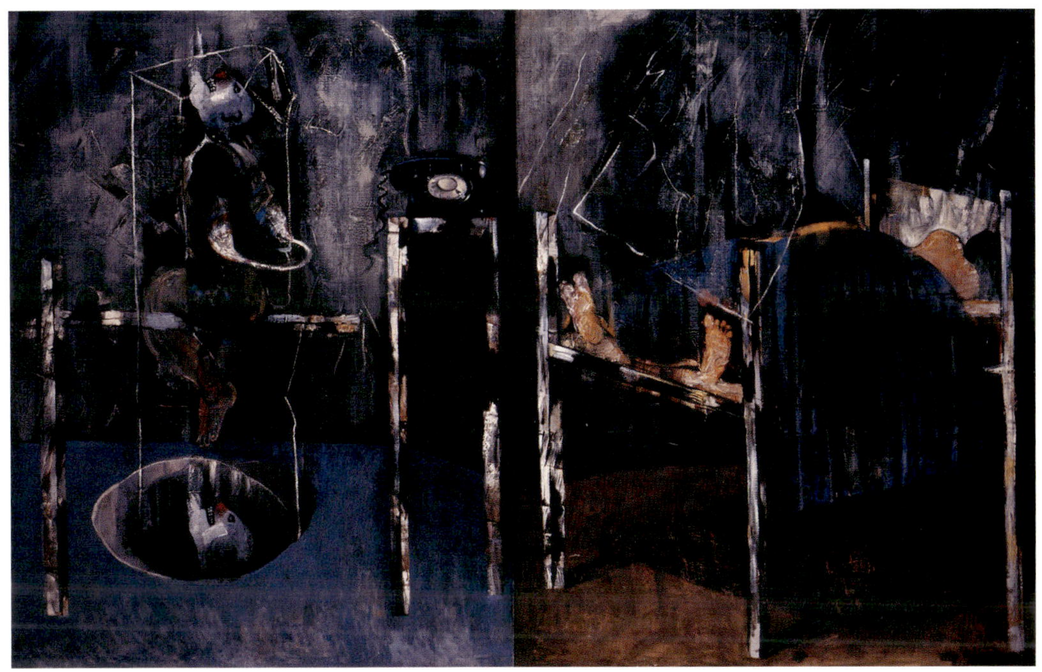

FIGURE E.4 Kim Kyeong In,
Double Torture 81-1, 1981. Oil
on canvas, 162.2 × 260.6 cm.
Collection of National Museum
of Contemporary Art.

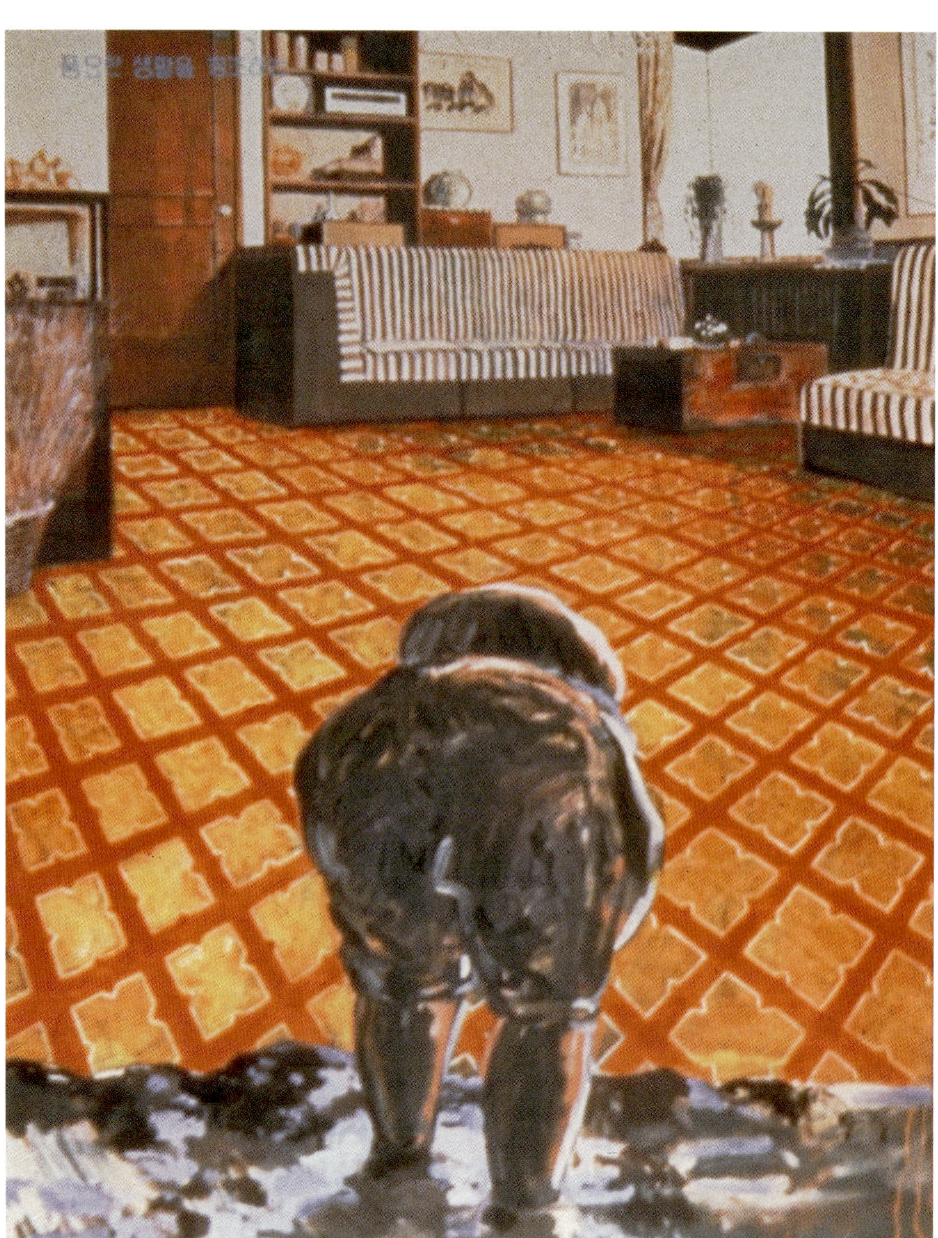

Linoleum—Creating a Life of Plenty (Figure E.5). Born in 1946, Kim was younger than the first tansaekhwa artists, although he too came from a privileged educational background, having received undergraduate and graduate degrees from Seoul National University's art school. In 1980 he took part in the first exhibition of the Reality and Utterance (Hyŏnsil kwa parŏn) group, which was among the most important of the small-scale artists' groups that emerged between 1980 and 1983 and which dealt specifically with the question of art's capacity for sociopolitical intervention. Reality and Utterance was cofounded by O Yun, whose ill-fated painting *1960, Ka* (Figure 4.2) had early established his dissident credentials. The artists of the group, which included critics like Sung Wan-kyung, produced highly figurative woodcuts and paintings that recuperated figuration in tacit contradistinction to the abstraction of tansaekhwa.

First made for a Reality and Utterance exhibition in 1980, *Lucky Linoleum—Creating a Life of Plenty* is based on a magazine advertisement for linoleum produced by Lucky Goldstar, one of the behemoth conglomerates, or *chaebŏl*, that benefited greatly from the support of Park Chung-hee and that came to dominate the South Korean economy. A vast expanse of linoleum is shown amid the trappings of an upper-middle-class living room in a contemporary urban Korean home, presumably to show the linoleum in its most desirable light. Couches with protective striped covers sit at rigidly precise angles, and decorative plants are spaced at regular intervals along a windowsill to the right. Reflecting the tastes of a domestic art market that still favored figurative oils and ink painting, small framed ink paintings festoon the walls, in turn emphasizing the interiority of the living room space. Placed under each of the paintings is a round white porcelain jar long prized by collectors, especially in Japan, as symbols of an ineffable Koreanness. In a further nod to tradition, a low wooden chest from the Chosŏn period (or, more probably, a reproduction) that may once have been used as a wedding chest to carry gifts for the bride (*ham*) is repurposed as a coffee table. A great deal of care has gone into the display of objects, many of which are carefully spaced in order to grant each its proverbial, or in the case of those sitting on the windowsill, its literal moment in the sun. Moreover, the living room is presented in a way intended to show as many of its embellishments as possible. One sees the room not from a purely frontal view but from an oblique angle so that details like a framed calligraphy scroll on the extreme right-hand side are visible. That Kim is well aware of the meticulousness of this arrangement is reflected by his careful brushwork, which verges on preciousness. Like a child reciting a passage from memory in which content seems to matter less than the articulation of the words, he emphasizes each stripe of the sofa covers, each leaf, and even the shadows cast over the bookshelves.

Overall, the depiction comes across as a model of Korean bourgeois living, but one that could be emulated by the advertisement's prospective audience. Spurred by the state's big push for heavy industry, depicted in national documentary paintings such as *Export Frigate* (Figure 4.15), the South Korean economy continued its astonishing growth. But in 1980 the South Korean gross national product declined for the first time in sixteen years, a reflection of what was then a worldwide recession.[26] The artist has repainted the caption of the original advertisement in the upper left-hand corner, a gesture that the artist claims was intended to "make concrete the sheer absurdity of the advertisement, which makes the ludicrous promise that you can actually live a life of plenty once you buy this company's flooring."[27] More evocative, however, is the color, size, and placement of the caption. In grayish-white paint and located at the very top of the work, the tiny letters are barely discernible, fading instead into the background. "Prosperity" is therefore cast into doubt.

Kim reveals this idealized scene to be pure surface by his manipulation of space and his treatment of the lower third of the painting, which shows a faceless, nameless figure toiling in a rice paddy. The viewer cannot tell much about the figure, despite its being in the painting's extreme foreground. That the figure is a farmer one can guess by the stooped pose and specific attire—the loose-fitting clothes, rolled-up pants, and broad-brimmed hat all denote outdoor labor. But *who* the figure is remains a mystery. It is radically foreshortened, and we see only its dappled posterior, hovering above what appears to be a watery field. Rice farmers in Korea during the 1980s tended to be depicted as middle-aged men, but there is no way to guess whether the figure is old or young, male or female. The figure remains anonymous, and perhaps deliberately so, for it leaves open the possibility that the farmer, as in many other examples of Korean cultural production based on matters of social protest, is intended to be an icon, an ur-symbol standing in for all farmers. Compared to both the relatively modest proportions of the actual physical canvas and to the dimensions implied by the depiction of the living-room furnishings, the farmer seems excessively large. Portrayed in isolation in the painting's central foreground, the farmer takes on the valence, if not the function, of a symbol.

The farmer symbolizes a world drastically different from that so
painstakingly spelled out in what is roughly the top third of the work.
The inclusion of such an image, painted in such a way, turns the entire
work into a highly literal allegory of what in the late 1970s and early
1980s was the growing disparity between rich and poor. Despite the
generalizing rhetoric of "one nation, one people" expounded by the
state and visualized in such projects as the national documentary
paintings, the nation was beset by increasingly wide economic and
social disparities. Those working in service occupations and at manual
labor, especially women, bore the brunt of what was frequently a deeply
exploitative system of production in which hours were long and wages
were kept low to ensure the competitive pricing of South Korean
exports. Those in managerial and administrative positions, however,
increasingly enjoyed a more affluent lifestyle, as suggested by Kim's
reproduction of the linoleum advertisement.

The majority of pictorial space is taken up by the linoleum floor that
spans the entire width and almost the entire height of the painting. The
floor is made central to the work in a way that also confirms viewers' weight
and bipedality and what might further be described as their agency in
allowing them to take hold of the work. Here bipedality is configured as
a subject by the stooping farmer placed at the very foot of the painting,
which sets up a viewing experience not unlike that prefigured by the
traditional hanging scroll in the ink painting context. The work takes
the form of a vertical plane divided into implied horizontal bands. In the
uppermost band are the accoutrements of the Korean beau monde, the
radio, books, sofa, paintings, and jars intended to demonstrate the status
of the living room's unseen resident. The floor takes up the middle band,
and its distortion appears to push the living room furnishings into the
far background, thus emphasizing the distance between them and
the farmer toiling at the very bottom of the painting. The exaggerated
distance emphasizes the depiction's allegorical air, so that we might
be induced to read the painting as a series of dyads between the haves
and have-nots, between the farmer working outside and the bourgeois
working indoors (transparently emphasized by the use of two distinctly
different modes of brushwork, the detailed, precise brushstrokes for
the living room versus the loose, rapid interplay used for the farmer and
paddy), or between the stooping farmer and the upright poses of those
who might be expected to sit on the stiff-backed couches.

The contrast between the upright and crouched bodies take on
added effect when we consider the farmer's pose more carefully. Given

the accompanying illustration of the paddy, we might guess that
the farmer is in the midst of planting; however, we cannot see the
figure's hands. In addition, the majority of the farmer's body is silhouetted not by the paddy but by the red-and-yellow grid pattern of the
linoleum. The juxtaposition may accordingly bring to mind what audiences of this time might imagine of the farmer's domestic counterpart,
the maid, who might very well be the farmer's kinswoman or the spouse,
looking to supplement the rural family's income by working in an
affluent urban household. Framed against the linoleum, which, toward
the bottom third of the painting, is tilted upward, the stooped figure
of the farmer begins to resemble that of the maid on her hands and
knees, scrubbing vigorously to make sure that the linoleum floor
never loses its sheen.

Despite its strong allegorical flavor, the work reaches beyond illustration to involve the viewer within the work's narrative of disparity.
The placement of the farmer suggests that the figure is our point of
entry into the work: the vertical configuration of the work, in which
spatial distance is measured by actual distance away from the painting's bottom edge, suggests that this edge is the intermediate threshold
at which the external world of the viewer begins to converge with the
internal world of the work. The paddy water ebbing around the farmer's
ankles distinctly covers part of the linoleum, accordingly highlight-
ing the overlap of one world onto another. That viewers are supposed
to identify with the farmer is suggested by the largeness of the farmer
figure, which is of a size commensurate with viewers' own dimensions.

Kim, however, pulls back from letting viewers ease into the painting
as nonparticipant bystanders. In the upper third of the painting, spatial
perspective conforms to what viewers expect of a mimetic representation of a living room: the floor stays on the ground, dutifully bearing the
weight of the bookcase, sofas, cabinets, and chest. Toward the middle
of the painting, demarcated by the decorative woven planter filled with
dried blond stalks sitting in front of the cabinet situated on the far left,
the floor appears to drop away as if pushed off an invisible precipice.
This is the point at which the imagined, ideal world portrayed in the
advertisement merges with the world in which the linoleum floor no
longer serves a decorative purpose but takes on a material heft embodying other kinds of visions. As the eye travels downward, the viewer sees
the yellow squares getting bigger and the red contour lines encasing
them becoming wider. What once appeared distant now floods viewers'
optical horizon so that all they see is the linoleum pattern, magnified.

Here the figure of the female maid returns, as viewers now see what she sees: the floor at close range.

By the time viewers' eyes reach the juncture at which the swirling waters of the paddy meet the linoleum squares—which they observe as having indentations on all four sides—the squares are so tilted as to be almost parallel with the vertical plane of the painting. The red-and-yellow pattern on the linoleum floor is nonspecific enough that it might pass for wallpaper or textile patterning, consequently leading viewers to revise their initial apprehension of what first appeared as solid ground. Tilted in this way, the floor begins to act as a curtain or screen, one subject to being pulled down or aside. The static constellation of luxury goods exemplifying bourgeois repose at the top of the painting rests on fundamentally unstable ground. It could very well be as Kim Jeong-heon would later describe of the aims of Minjung art, the movement that came to prominence during the turbulent 1980s. "Minjung" can be roughly translated as "the people"; Minjung art picked up what artists like O Yun and those of the ill-fated Reality Group were forced to abandon, an emphasis on art's capacity for social activism in an explicitly Korean context. Despite the privileged educational and social backgrounds of many of its representative artists, the majority of whom were graduates of Seoul National University or Hongik University, Minjung art, as Kim asserted, tried "to pull art into the field of reality and culture."[28]

Lucky Linoleum is a reflection of a particular time. That the floor is tilted upward so as to seem almost parallel with viewers' faces only enhances the painting's function as a mirror. *Lucky Linoleum* does more than reflect back onto viewers the inequities lurking beneath the surface of life in 1980s Korea, where materiality no longer meant painting on tent canvas or on concrete but buying color television sets and stiff-backed sofas. Survival now yielded to consumption, of which visual art was a critical indication; by 1981 the Korean art market had grown enough to include abstraction.[29] If *Lucky Linoleum* can be believably pitted against tansaekhwa, it has very little to do with differences in formal appearance or even the contexts of creation and almost everything to do with what tansaekhwa represented to many: an approach to materiality based on the consumption of nonnecessary things—in a word, the pursuit of luxury.

Kim tries to show viewers as much as possible, cramming the relatively limited amount of pictorial space with as many allusions to the extra-artistic world as possible. But if one feels tempted to read the painting as a scene being literally pulled down by the farmer toiling below, it may be due to the fact that the painting is overwhelmed by a surfeit of references to the world outside the painting. The work anticipates Minjung intentions to undermine the idea of the work as having its own internal and imagined domain. This was further stressed in the 1980s as groups of Minjung artists literally removed painting from the gallery and reinstalled it outside, in public plazas and on university buildings. Similarly, murals were painted on the sides of homes and rural community centers. In these works was an implied will to do away completely with the distinction between the artwork and its viewers, a distinction that Minjung adherents regarded as elitist.

ON GLOBAL POSITIONING SYSTEMS

For many tansaekhwa artists, however, this distinction was still productive as a means of keeping painting fresh. Around 1978 it struck Lee Ufan that his points and lines looked too constitutive of a signature style and were thus potentially fatal to his attempts to disavow artistic creation. His response was to break up his points and lines, whether by pausing his brush as it traveled down the canvas or by disrupting the order he had used in the earliest versions of *From Line* and *From Point*. In *From Line (81021)* of 1981 (Figure E.6), lines are recast as abbreviated traces of a brush that was dipped in paint and then allowed to linger momentarily on the canvas. Scattered over the canvas, these traces— now points—turn surrounding pictorial space atmospheric. Taking a cue from his *Relatum* works, which he continued throughout the 1970s and 1980s, Lee took care to emphasize the relationship between each pair of marks so that the pictorial space looks as if it is held together by a force field generated by the energy stemming from the interaction between one point and another.

Despite explorations like these, tansaekhwa continued to be attacked as a movement. The criticisms became especially heated as artists like Lee Ufan, Park Seobo, Yun Hyongkeun, and Ha Chonghyun assumed leadership roles in the domains that mattered most in the Korean art world: academia, government institutions, and the market. As more Korean artists exhibited work overseas, particularly in the 1990s, tansaekhwa was criticized by some art historians and critics anxious to promote Minjung art as a more ethically qualified representative of contemporary Korean art to overseas audiences. In the catalog

for the 1993 exhibition *Across the Pacific: Contemporary Korean and Korean American Art*, the first major show of contemporary Korean art to take place in the United States since 1958, the critic and curator Lee Young Chul wrote that despite being "the most prominent art movement in Korea during the past twenty years," tansaekhwa was an "art of 'silence'" that failed to reflect in any serious way upon "the [prevailing] system of values."[30] According to Lee, the primary task for Korean artists was to "free themselves from the culture of the West." Minjung art, despite certain shortcomings, was proposed as a more viable response to this challenge than tansaekhwa, which "merely" blended universalist thinking with clichéd views of Korean culture.[31]

Lee's strenuous objection to tansaekhwa rhetoric was partly motivated by what at the time was increasing appreciation for tansaekhwa works overseas as part of growing receptivity on the part of Euro-American institutions to questions of cultural difference. The renewed emphasis on the so-called margins helped propel what Hal Foster has described as an ethnographic turn in contemporary art, the apotheosis of which may have been the much-discussed *Magiciens de la Terre*, the 1989 exhibition at the Centre Georges Pompidou intended to replace the Paris Biennale.[32] Non-Western cultural difference became a putative alternative center around which to restructure the notion of a supranational art world, and a notable illustration in point was *Working with Nature: Traditional Thought in Contemporary Art from Korea*, the first major exhibition of contemporary Korean art in Great Britain. Arranged in part by the National Museum of Contemporary Art of Korea and held at the Tate Liverpool in England in 1992, the show was composed exclusively of the work of tansaekhwa artists, including Park Seobo, Lee Ufan, and Yun Hyongkeun.[33] Despite the show's positive reception, certain reviews seemed to prove Lee Young Chul's point about clichés and cultural difference: the *Times* reviewer John Russell Taylor spoke enthusiastically of the respect shown for the "natural order of things in a distinctively non-Western, specifically Korean, fashion."[34] Yet as demonstrated in such exhibitions as *Magiciens de la Terre*, cultural difference was often construed through the vehicle of metaphor, framed as allegorical representations of sociopolitical circumstances in the home country of the makers of the displayed artworks.

Other exhibitions introducing non-Euro-American art to a largely Euro-American audience adhered to similar logic. This recalled the fears anticipated some two decades earlier by critics like Geeta Kapur, who in 1971 had condemned the 1968 Triennale India—and by implication other large-scale international exhibitions—for encouraging a "cult of internationalism" that "encourages art that has no contact with reality."[35] Perhaps matters had changed little since Nam Kwan had visited the Parisian art world in the early 1960s:

My task was to make something singular that could not be seen in French society. It had to be rooted in the Asia I had lived in as an Asian. Rephrased, my work had to have Asian singularity. I had to forge a world of creation separate from that of Euro-Americans by whatever means possible. Hence it had to address fundamental questions latent in Korean history and not sate foreign touristic tastes for the "exotic." But [I found that] this is a very difficult thing to do.[36]

As the case of tansaekhwa's reception in late 1970s Paris indicates, there was a downside to looking too much like certain examples of Euro-American abstraction.

Yet the situation circa 1990 was not the same as it had been thirty, twenty, or even ten years earlier, as Korean artists well understood. Some fifteen years earlier, only "forty or so artists" were able to travel to Europe and North America; now there were hundreds, perhaps thousands, of artists studying and working overseas.[37] Richer, better informed, more physically mobile, and well accustomed to grappling with multiple cultures and political systems in a way that many of their predecessor counterparts had not been, the younger generation of Korean artists realized that the world was something that could actually be shaped, or in a word, practiced. Here the word "world" deserves closer attention, for it was a word that enjoyed special visibility in early 1990s South Korea. Under its first democratically elected civilian president, Kim Young-sam, South Korea eagerly promoted *segyehwa*, a process that is literally translated as "worldization" but that is more accurately understood as reciprocal convergence between Korea and the rest of the world, an idea anticipated by the oft-repeated slogan of the 1988 Seoul Olympics: "From Seoul to the world, and from the world to Seoul." That the state considered itself an active participant in this convergence was reflected by the establishment of institutions and events like the Gwangju Biennale. Established in 1995, the biennale symbolized government ambition having an average budget of US$12 million, which far surpassed that of any other large-scale visual arts event except for Documenta.[38] The idea of the world as practice

FIGURE E.7 Yun Hyongkeun, *Untitled 93-117*, 1993. Oil on linen, 180.3 × 259.1 inches. Collection of Chinati Foundation, Marfa, Texas. Photograph courtesy of the Chinati Foundation.

extended to exhibitions in both Korea and elsewhere as exhibitions became increasingly utopian in their embrace of themes such as mobility, nomadism, and diasporic movement. One exemplar was *Cities on the Move*. One of the most ambitious shows of contemporary Asian art ever held, it took place in multiple venues in the United States, Western Europe, and Asia from 1997 to 2000 and emphasized the importance of being "in between geographies" and "global connectivity."[39]

As much as the international, or rather, global, art world appeared to embrace artistic production without regard to national or cultural origin, it also had its limits. When asked in 1993 about his opinions of showing in exhibitions organized specifically around themes of race and ethnicity, artist and critic Bahc Mo—a participant in *Across the Pacific* and one of the Korean critics most involved in assessing the relationship between theory and artistic practice—remarked simply, "It was better to show than not show." His comment was later interpreted by critic Alice Yang as a symptom of a broader "failure" in the New York art world to integrate Asian artists into a discursive system able to "cut across racial boundaries."[40]

More instructive still was the reception of Yun Hyongkeun in the New York press. In September 1995 a work from the *Umber Blue* series was shown in the first of a series of multipage layouts featuring well-known U.S. fashion and lifestyle firm Calvin Klein's new line of home furnishings. The advertisement was shot at the Chinati Foundation founded by Donald Judd, which had acquired two untitled works by Yun, including *Untitled 93-117* (Figure E.7), prior to hosting a small show of other *Umber Blue* works in 1994. The advertisement showed another of Yun's paintings displayed above a low platform bed whose dark frame echoed the painting's dark expanses.[41] In a subsequent *New York Times* mention of the advertisement, veteran arts reporter Carol Vogel singled out the work, which was not part of the Chinati Foundation's collection and was photographed without Yun's knowledge.[42]

Vogel wrote about Yun's work because it confused "some contemporary art experts who have seen the ad, because the work is so eerily derivative of Richard Serra and Barnett Newman."[43] The "confusion," born of an absence of any sustained looking, might be explained by the circumstances under which such "contemporary art experts" beheld such work. By this time, tansaekhwa graced the walls of the government-run National Museum of Contemporary Art of Korea, while its representatives held some of the Korean art world's most important positions as museum directors, foundation heads, and university professors. Yun Hyongkeun himself had been a university president: from 1988 to 1989 he had presided over Kyungwon University. Yet the sixty-seven-year-old Yun, whose works had adorned the permanent national pavilion for Korea at the 1995 Venice Biennale, was mistakenly identified in Vogel's short article as a "young Korean artist."[44] Being culturally different mattered, but only in certain situations, and sometimes it was not enough to override old assumptions about originality and who could lay claim to such.

FOLD, CREASE, BUNDLE: THE *BOTTARI* WORKS OF KIMSOOJA

To artists for whom constructions of mobility defined their position in an art world newly configured as "global," the actual experience of moving from one place to another was internalized in their works as a distinctly problematic condition. Theirs was not an experience that could be simply folded into the kinds of global-versus-local discourses then becoming popular in contemporary art circles. On the contrary, the works produced in apparent response to the experience of being newly mobile tried to assuage as much as possible the psychological disjunction arising out of having to mediate between multiple scales of operation. Visual languages tended to cohere around allegories and metaphors of circulation and movement using objects rooted in very particular cultural contexts. An especially memorable example is Kimsooja's bundles of jewel-toned fabric, derived from the cloth bundles known in Korean as *bottari* (Figure E.8). Playing upon idiomatic uses of the word *bottari*, which, depending on the context, can refer to forced expulsion ("to pack up one's *bottari* and leave") or to less involuntary movements, Kimsooja's works attempted to convey patterns of movement in the most visceral way possible.

But while her *bottari* works have been considered primarily through the lenses of diaspora, migration, and the global turn in shows like *Cities on the Move*, their actual genesis might date back to the artist's early engagement with tansaekhwa. Her undergraduate studies took place at Hongik University from 1976 to 1980, and at that time the university was ground zero as far as the promotion of tansaekhwa went. Park Seobo and Suh Seung-won vigorously expounded on the white monochrome, an insistence that caused the young student of what was (and is) still known as "Western painting" to "push back" against

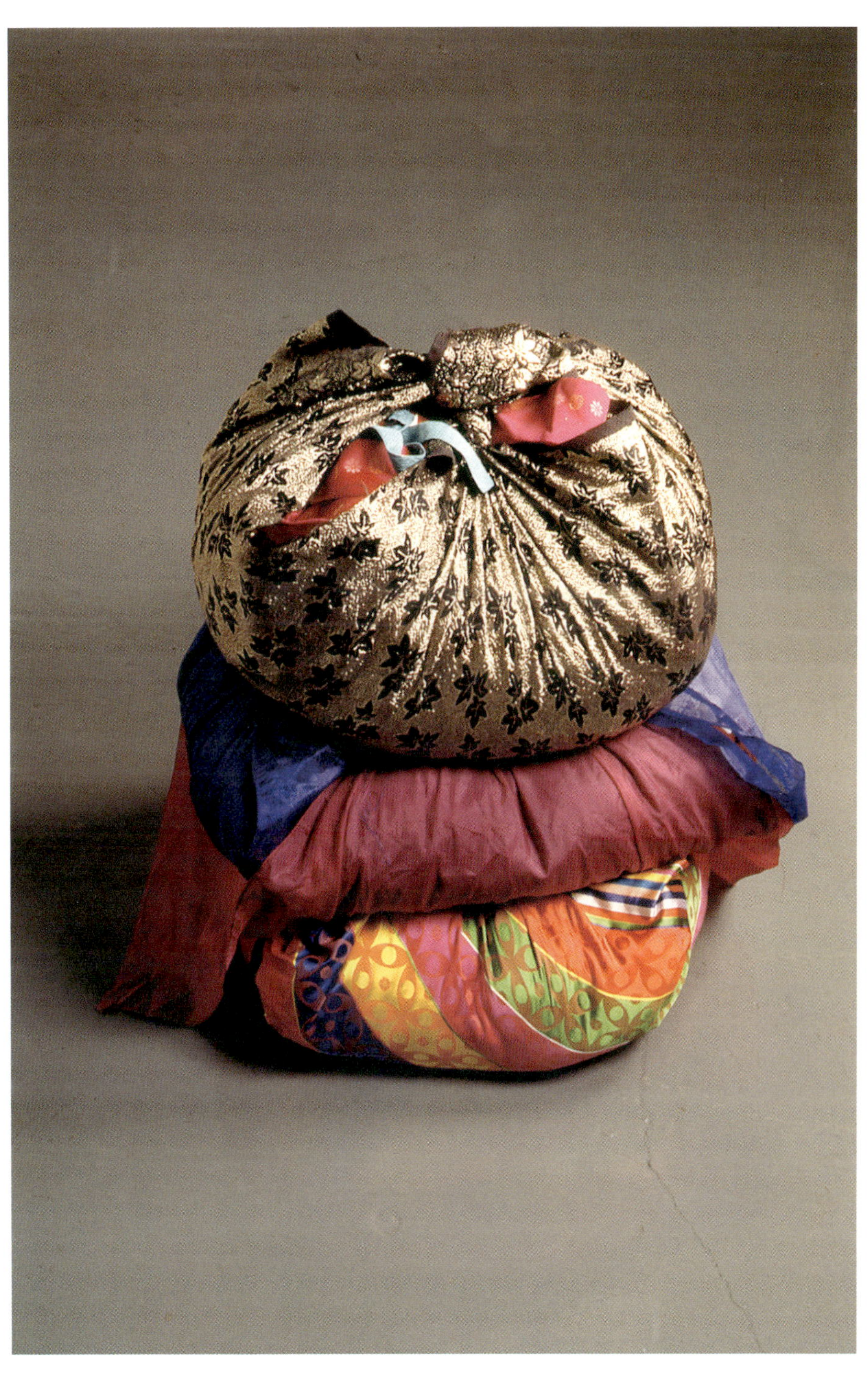

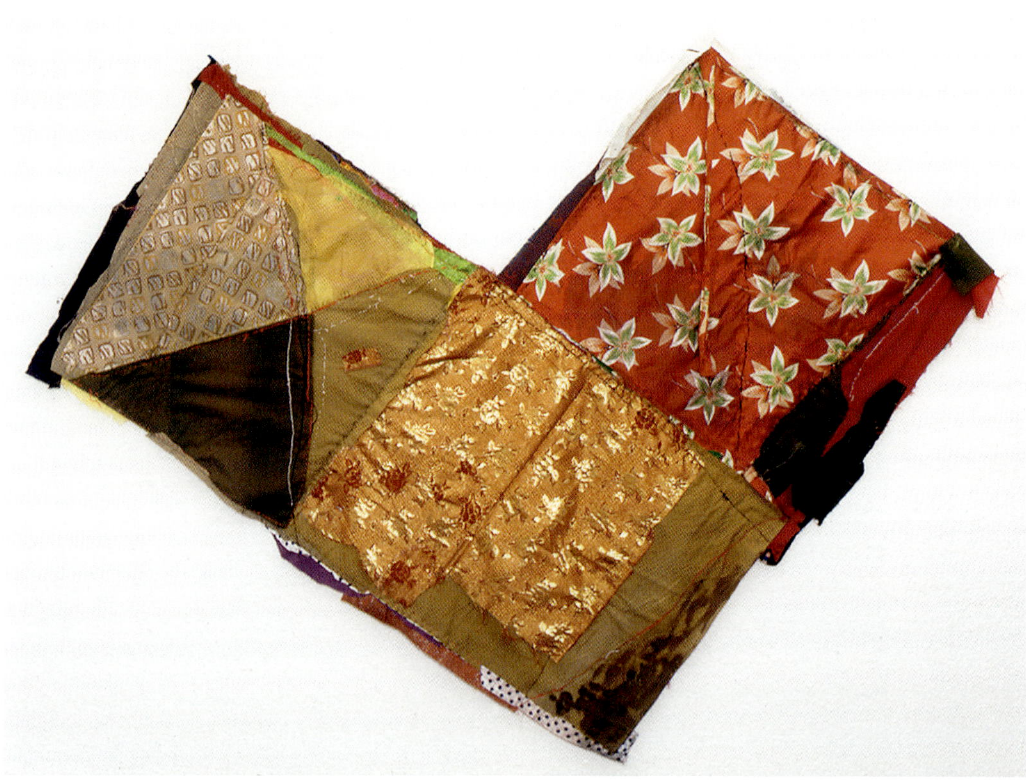

FIGURE E.9 Kimsooja,
L'Automne, 1984. Used cloth
and thread, 189 × 210 cm.
Photograph courtesy of
Kimsooja Studio.

tansaekhwa.[45] Kimsooja does recall being intrigued by the dialogue between flatness and volume, a critical aspect of other tansaekhwa works such as the early versions of *Conjunction*. Her interest subsequently found an outlet through her approach to fabric, with which she started working while sewing with her mother in 1983. Her initial approach, however, was concerned not with fabric's domestic associations but with fabric as itself a plane that could be folded, creased, and bundled.[46] In works like *L'Automne* (Figure E.9), squares of fabric were laid flat and mounted on a frame or sewn together to create a larger frame. She thought of fabric as a "boundary between the two- and three-dimensional" that could be folded or wrapped into a distinct volume.[47] For this reason, the artist gave her earliest *bottari* works the title *Deductive Object*, to emphasize that these objects, though bundled into volumes, could also be unfurled into flat planes.

Despite these interests, Kimsooja's works were quickly absorbed into what from the late 1980s onward was a mounting campaign to stake out a larger place for women artists in the highly patriarchal Korean art world. In the fall of 1989, her works were exhibited in *Women's Art of the 1980s* (*80 nyŏndae yŏsŏngmisul*), a large-scale exhibition that took place at the Kumho Museum in Seoul, one of the few institutions in Korea willing to host potentially controversial shows.[48] Writing for the *Hankyoreh sinmun*, a progressive newspaper newly formed in 1988, Ko Chong-sŏk quoted the museum as stating, "Monochromatic abstract works leave hardly any room in which to express a feminine, as opposed to a male, sensibility." Ko went on to criticize the show, remarking that its choices, including the works of Kimsooja, merely reflected "traditional views of femininity."[49]

Kimsooja's use of fabric and the corollary emphasis on sewing could be read as a rejoinder to tansaekhwa, a movement of "monochromatic abstract works" almost entirely dominated by male artists who often likened the making of their works to building walls, tilling fields, and, especially, literati painting, all modes of labor from which women were traditionally excluded. That Kimsooja also uses bedcovers and takes them from the inside of the house out into the gallery (as well as the street, the plaza, the café, and even the forest) also suggests an effort to invert the interior/exterior or home/public venue distinctions that had traditionally characterized the separation of women from men. She folds these distinctions over themselves and thus claims as her medium the notion of the private as construed through images suggesting domesticity.

THE ROUND AND THE FLAT

Kimsooja's *bottari*, however, was soon used as a means through which to articulate a particular worldview that had little room for extended considerations of form outside its illustrative potential. Comprising colors and patterns readily indicative of a certain foreignness, images of Kimsooja's *bottari* were swiftly incorporated into what might be described as an iconography of the global turn. Beginning in the mid-1990s, her works were especially associated with "contemporary Asian women's art," a notion whose fullest realization occurred in the wake of this turn.[50] It renewed the urgency of the question over which Lee Yil had agonized in 1975: how can the artwork be reconciled to the social and physical domains external to its physical boundaries without collapsing the distinction between it and the "outside world"? Some artists have responded by making work that recognized its viewers and the worlds in which they lived but without being determined by that recognition, and without having it serve as the primary basis upon which such work attempted to claim entry into the global art world. More recently, others have moved away from this by urging a *flattened* view of the world through works that seem as if they could have been made by anyone, anywhere.

In 2007 Yang Haegue exhibited *DIN A4/DIN A3/DIN A2 Whatever Being* at the Galerie Barbara Wien in Basel (Figure E.10). Six rectangular fiberboard monochromes appear to protrude from a wall into the open space of the gallery. Each monochrome leans far enough into space that we understand them as objects with edges, corners, and mass. Moreover, they are placed far enough apart from each other that we see each work as a discrete object and not necessarily as part of a series, as in the case of Byron Kim's similarly proportioned panels titled *Synecdoche* (Figure E.11). At the tail end of multiculturalism's heyday in early 1990s New York, Kim was reconsidering a particular kind of formalism from which any consideration of cultural origins or differences was summarily purged.[51] The title of Yang's work tells viewers that the monochromes are sized according to standard paper measurements, designated "A4," "A3," and "A2." Vertically oriented and modestly sized, they recall the shapes and dimensions of small windowpanes. The architectural connotation is underscored by the whiteness of these monochromes, which almost perfectly replicate the whiteness of the archetypal "white cube" gallery. Somewhere between two-dimensional flatness and three-dimensional plasticity, the monochromes recall the second part of Yang's title. "Whatever being" directly refers back to

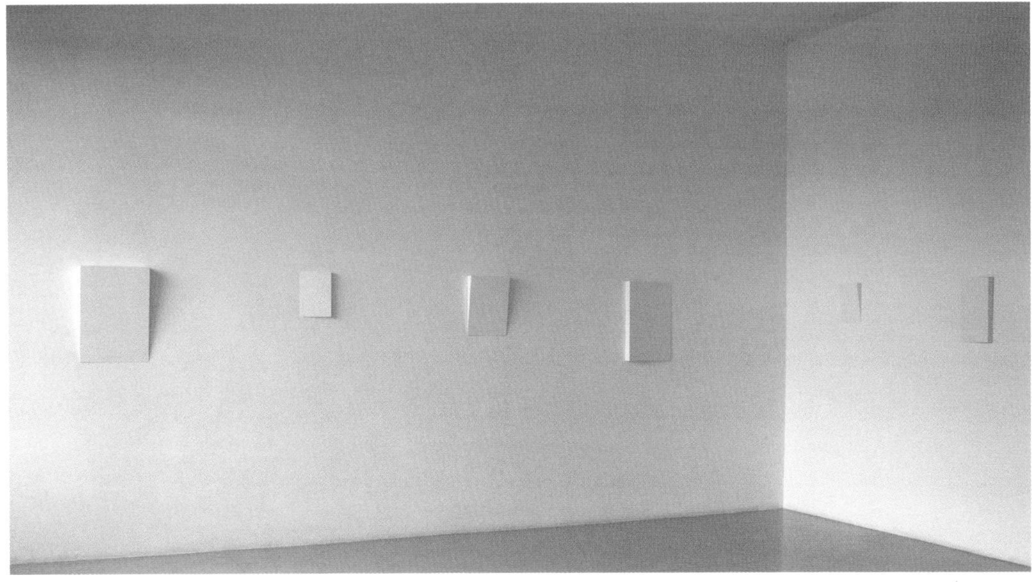

Giorgio Agamben's conception of community as something based on the acceptance of all beings, such as they are.[52] A being is reclaimed from "its having this or that property, which identifies it as belonging to this or that set . . . not for another class nor for the simple generic absence of any belonging, but for its being-*such*, for belonging itself."[53]

Yang graduated in 1999 from the Städelschule in Frankfurt. The school's master's program in architectural design was once characterized by the artist Matthew Ritchie as "fucking hardcore," and her works belie an engagement with the spirit, if not the letter, of the new objectivity movement.[54] Yang's series opens onto a viewing experience best described as a process of dissection in which the monochrome lies naked, awaiting inspection. All six monochromes are angled differently. Some turn laterally, others tilt downward or upward. All are shown slightly off-kilter so that we are not only looking at the front of the monochromatic panel but above it, below it, and around it. The different yet standardized sizes of the panels indicate that we are looking at particular objects, *specimens*. One is always brought back to the certainty generated by the hardness of the panels, the sharpness of their edges, and the starkness of white. *DIN A4/DIN A3/DIN A2 Whatever Being* so insistently emphasizes questions of form that it runs the risk of literalism, as if to treat Frank Stella's dictum ("What you see is what you see") as dogma.

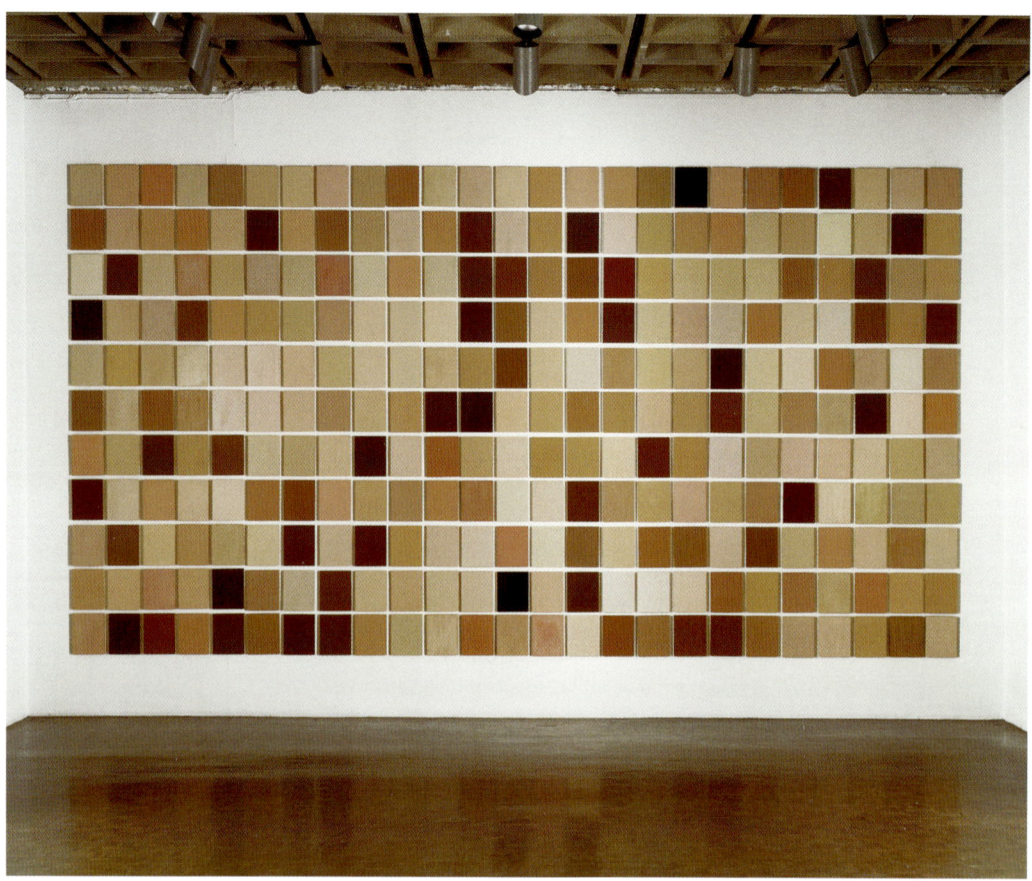

FIGURE E.11 Byron Kim, *Synecdoche*, 1991–present. Oil and wax on wood; each panel 25.4 × 20.32 cm; overall installed, 305.44 × 998.64 cm. Collection of National Gallery of Art, Washington D.C. Installed at Whitney Museum of American Art, New York. Photograph by Dennis Cowley. Courtesy of James Cohan Gallery, New York/Shanghai. Copyright Byron Kim.

This is not, however, an arbitrary return to the questions of flatness and plasticity raised so provocatively by minimalism, although it is a curious throwback that provokes question. It is more analogous to Byron Kim's questioning of how art history—in his case, the history of modernist abstraction—has been written. Kim, who came to the attention of the Korean art world in the mid-1990s after both *Across the Pacific* and the 1993 Whitney Biennial shows traveled to Korea, redresses the exclusion of artists of color by reworking the monochrome, a strategy evocatively described by art historian Ann Gibson, via Gilles Deleuze and Félix Guattari, as "fearfully self-sufficient, refusing congress with the world."[55] Also working within the parameters of the monochrome, *DIN A4/DIN A3/DIN A2 Whatever Being* reads like a return to a context governed by formalist assessments. Yang's decision to make work that resembled, but was not actually based on, the white monochrome alludes to tansaekhwa, which for some time had been described as white monochromes. This characterization was reinforced in the early 1990s, at the time Yang attended Seoul National University. But the whiteness of *DIN A4/DIN A3/DIN A2 Whatever Being* is not the transcendent whiteness seen in tansaekhwa. Its whiteness looks as if it is the same as the wall's, a chalky, opaque whiteness that fights actively against suppositions of transcendentalism. That these monochromes protrude from the wall into the viewers' space also insists that they are presentational as opposed to representational. The order of experience is rooted in the here and now.

In 2007 Yang was still aware of the way the contemporary art world remained deeply circumscribed by the extent to which globalization is often coded, as Saskia Sassen has pointed out, in national terms.[56] In this world, an artwork's value is pegged to its perceived capacity to visibly reflect the origins and location of its maker. Looking "to be engaged without dogma," Yang seeks to carve out a space for herself by preventing her position from being "fully definable or cultivated, therefore [preventing it from being] instrumentalized by anyone else."[57] Her response, ironically, is to barricade herself within the confines supposed of the white monochrome, whose apparent blankness also invites the viewer to project any number of interpretations onto its expressionless face. In many ways, the white monochrome is an ideal response to the situation Yang describes, for it lends itself to being both excessively closed and open to the world around it.

Yang is not alone in her insistence—or more accurately, her stubbornness. Even artists whose works are conceived around the stratification of viewers through disparate levels of knowledge demonstrate an intense attention to color, size, scale, detail, and composition. Their almost formalist aspect appears calculated to push back against the contextualist frameworks to which these works are subject, by virtue of their maker's national origin, so that the question turns on whether it is possible to have an identity outside identitarian politics. The easy, if overly cynical, answer is that such attention to form is the direct result of a heightened consciousness of domestic and international art markets newly receptive to works whose finish and demonstration of technical mastery render them collectible, a speculation made credible by the dramatic rise in prices for contemporary Asian art, especially Chinese art, in the past ten to fifteen years. But the sheer number of non-Western artists whose works appear to champion a kind of neo-formalism suggests a more fundamental reason for this highly visible emphasis, one based in the efforts of such artists to signal their unique-ness without reverting back to frameworks of national or cultural identity. They seek to differentiate themselves, but without resurrect-ing old boundaries rooted in particular views of nationality, ethnicity, and race that might lead to an unjustified foreclosure of possibilities.

The challenge artists like Yang Haegue face is that though they do not wish to be seen primarily as Korean or non-Western, they realize they will always be regarded to some extent as such. However, in making works that all but compel viewers to discuss them in terms bordering on formalism, Yang reflects upon the history of contemporary art thus far as an impasse: non-Western artists are forced to think of the world in terms of a distinction between form defined by a polemical, willful refusal of any metaphorical interpretation of formal qualities and form defined by context. In such cases, the act of contextualization is no lon-ger a function of thinking through the distinction between artworks and their social circumstances; rather, it is a matter of thinking about the former only through the latter. For Yang, and for many others, it is clear that the revisionist project furthered by movements like tansaekhwa and Minjung have failed in the sense that they force artists into an unpalatable bind where form and context are cast as antinomies, unable to be productively conjoined. Such is the challenge facing Yang and other artists for whom the practice of a world art history must necessar-ily be regarded through the demands it makes of its subjects.

ACKNOWLEDGMENTS

The basic premise of this book arose out of my dissertation at the Institute of Fine Arts at New York University. It benefited greatly from the advisement of Jonathan Hay and, at a later stage, of Miwon Kwon at UCLA. The transition from dissertation to book was greatly assisted by the financial and intellectual support of the Center for the Advanced Study for Visual Arts at the National Gallery in Washington, D.C., where I spent one year in residence as a predoctoral fellow. Helping the process further was the generous support of the University of Michigan, and particularly my home department, the Department of the History of Art, many of whose members took precious time from their busy schedules to read the draft of this book in full. In this regard I especially thank Alex Potts and Matt Biro for their extensive comments. Colleagues outside Michigan also contributed enormously to helping me refine my thinking and improve the book's overall structure, including Christine Hahn, Charlotte Horlyck, and Gill Perry. Ed Dimendberg deserves special mention for his sagacious advice on improving the book's readability.

My deep appreciation goes to Richard Morrison of the University of Minnesota Press for his unwavering support of this project. For copyediting I thank Michelle Alumkal, John Alan Farmer, and especially Kathy Delfosse. I am grateful to audiences at the University of Toronto, the University of California at Berkeley, the British Museum, the University of Chicago, and the Museum of Fine Arts, Houston for their interest in and comments on various aspects of this manuscript. Regarding archival materials, I am deeply appreciative of the time and effort spent on my behalf by staff members in numerous libraries, archives, museums, and other institutions in Korea, Japan, England, and the United States. Particular thanks are due Yoon So-hee, formerly of the Archives of Korean Art of the Samsung Foundation; Tae Hyunsun and Lim Jungeun of the Leeum Museum; and Sen Uesaki of Keio University.

In many respects, this book is a case for thinking about form, one that could only be argued with full-color plates. I am indebted to subvention funds from the University of Michigan, both from my home department and from the Nam Center for Korean Studies. Also deserving recognition for assistance with subvention costs is the Academy for Korean Studies.

I owe a considerable debt to the many galleries and museums that generously allowed me to reproduce images of works in their collections, frequently at no cost, as well as to their staffs. Of particular note is Jang Yop, head of collections at the National Museum of Contemporary Art, Korea, without whose assistance this book would never have been possible. I thank his staff, who were tireless in bringing out countless artworks from storage as well as generous in granting me permission to consult museum archives. Special appreciation to photographers Kwon Boo-Moon, Jaey Yong Rhee, Lee Man-Hong, and Kim Sang-tae for their efforts in bringing to life works notoriously difficult to reproduce.

Above all, I thank the artists and critics who gave so generously and freely of their time in answering a relentless barrage of questions, sometimes on very short notice. Their families too must be mentioned for their extraordinary kindness, patience, and support, especially Mina Lee, Suh Do-Ho, Kwon Ohyup, Yun Seong Ryeol, and Park Mi-ja. Other friends and associates helped me pick through various strains of thought, including Chin-Sung Chang, Kevin Chua, Eleanor Hyun, Kenji Kajiya, Chungwoo Lee, Michele Matteini, Tsz Yan Ng, Nadja Rottner, Emma Son, and the members of the Humanities Reading Group of the Institute of East Asian Studies at the University of California at Berkeley during the fall 2011 term.

Although I owe an incalculable debt to my family and friends, this book is dedicated to three persons: my father, Woo Sik Kee, whose own canny grasp of the world enriched mine in ways I could have never imagined; my mother, Hie Jean Rim, whose empathy, tact, and love for the artwork in all its capacities sustained me throughout; and her mother, Yoo Hyun-juh, whose passion for the historicity of things in relation to places is what eventually led me to study art history in the first place.

APPENDIX: KOREAN NAMES AND TERMS

Bahc Mo (birth name: Pak Ch'ŏl-ho, known as Bahc Yiso from 1997) (박 모/박이소, 1957–2004)

Bando Gallery (반도화랑)

Bang Keun-taek (방근택, 1929–1992)

Chang Woo-sung (pen name: Wŏlchŏn) (장우성, 1912–2005)

Ch'oe Su-nu (최순우, 1916–1984)

Choi Tae-shin (최태신, born 1943)

Choi Youl (최 열, born 1956)

Chŏng Ch'an-sŭng (정찬승, 1942–1994)

Chŏng Po-wŏn (정보원, born 1947)

Chu Kyŏng (주 경, 1905–1979)

Chun Doo-hwan (전두환, born 1931)

Chun Young-Paik (전영백, born 1965)

Chung Chang-sup (정창섭, 1927–2011)

Chung Moo-jeong (정무정, born 1962)

Chung Sang Hwa (정상화, born 1932)

Contemporary Art, magazine (현대미술)

Ha Chonghyun (하종현, born 1935)

Ha In-du (하인두, 1930–1989)

Heu Hwang (허 황, born 1946)

Hong Sun-pyo (홍선표, born 1949)

Hongik University (홍익대학교)

Hwarang, magazine (화랑)

Hyundai Gallery (현대화랑)

Invitational Exhibition of Contemporary Artists (현대작가 초대전)

Jin Okseon (진옥선, born 1950)

Kim Byung-ki (김병기, born 1916)

Kim Chi-ha (김지하, born 1941)

Kim Chong-hak (김종학, born 1937)

Kim Hong-hee (김홍희, born 1948)

Kim Hyangan (김향안, 1916–2004)

Kim In-hwan (김인환, 1937–2011)

Kim In-kyŏm (김인겸, born 1945)

Kim Jeong-heon (김정헌, born 1946)

Kim Jong-pil (김종필, born 1926)

Kim Ku-lim (김구림, born 1936)

Kim Kyeong In (김경인, born 1941)

Kim Kyu-jin (김규진, 1868–1933)

Kim Mi-kyung (김미경, born 1958)

Kim Mun-ho (김문호, 1930–1982)

Kim Sang-yu (김상유, 1926–2002)

Kim Swoogeun (김수근, 1931–1986)

Kim Tschang-yeul (김창렬, born 1929)

Kim Whanki (pen name: Su-hwa) (김환기, 1913–1974)

Kim Yŏng-ju (김영주, 1920–1995)

Kim Young Ki (김영기, 1911–2003)

Kim Youngna (김영나, born 1951)

Kim Yun-su (김윤수, born 1936)

Kimsooja (김수자, born 1957)

Kukchŏn (국전)

Kwak Duk-jun (곽덕준, born 1937)

Kwon Ok-yeon (권옥연, 1923–2011)

Kwon Young-woo (권영우, born 1926)

Kyegan misul, journal (계간미술)

Lee Dong Youb (이동엽, born 1946)

Lee Kangso (이강소, born 1943)

Lee Se-duk (이세득, 1921–2001)

Lee Seungjio (이승조, 1941–1990)

Lee Seung-taek (이승택, born 1932)

Lee Ufan (이우환, born 1936)

Lee Ungno (이응노, 1904–1989)

Lee Wan Suk (이완석, 1915–1969)

Lee Yil (이 일, 1932–1997)

Lee Young Chul (이영철, born 1957)

Minjung (민중)

Misul kwa saenghwal, magazine (미술과 생활)

Modern Artists' Association (현대미술가협회)

Moon Myung-dae (문명대, born 1940)

Mungnimhoe (묵림회)

Myongdong Gallery (명동화랑)

Na Hye-sok (나혜석, 1896–1948)

Nam Kwan (남 관, 1911–1990)

national documentary paintings
(민족기록화)

O Yun (오윤, 1946–1986)

Oh Sang-gyel (오상길, born 1957)

Paik Nam June (백남준, 1932–2006)

Pak Chang-nyŏn (박장년, 1938–2009)

Pak Pong-su (박봉수, 1916–1991)

Park Carey (박계리, born 1968)

Park Chung-hee (박정희, 1917–1979)

Park Myung-ja (박명자, born 1943)

Park Rae-kyung (박래경, born 1935)

Park Seobo (birth name: Park Chae-hong)
(박서보, born 1931)

Park Yong-sook (박용숙, born 1935)

Quac Insik (곽인식, 1919–1989)

Reality and Utterance (현실과 발언)

segyehwa (세계화)

Shim Moon-seup (심문섭, born 1942)

simultaneity (동시성)

Sin misul, magazine (신미술)

Sinsegye Gallery (신세계화랑)

Sŏk To-ryun (석도륜, 1923–2011)

Space, journal (공간)

Suh Se-ok (Sanjŏng) (서세옥, born 1929)

Suh Seung-won (서승원, born 1942)

Sun misool, journal (선미술)

Sung Wan-kyung (성완경, born 1944)

tansaekhwa (단색화)

Won Dong-suk (원동석, born 1938)

Won Kap-hui (원갑희, see above)

Yang Haegue (양혜규, born 1971)

Yi Hŭng-u (이홍우, 1928–2003)

Yi Ku-yŏl (이구열, born 1932)

Yi Kyungsung (이경성, 1919–2009)

Yi Pong-sang (이봉상, 1916–1970)

Yi Tae-wŏn (이대원, 1921–2005)

Yim Setaik (임세택, born 1947)

Yoo June-sang (유준상, born 1932)

Yoo Youngkuk (유영국, 1916–2002)

Yoon Jin-sup (윤진섭, born 1955)

You Hong-june (유홍준, born 1949)

Yun Hi-sun (윤희순, 1902–1947)

Yun Hyongkeun (윤형근, 1928–2007)

Yun Myeong-ro (윤명로, born 1936)

Yushin (유신)

NOTES

1. Although numerous artists have been identified as tansaekhwa artists, the usual roster includes Park Seobo, Lee Ufan, Yun Hyongkeun, Ha Chonghyun, Heu Hwang, Kwon Young-woo, Lee Dong Youb, Suh Seung-won, Chung Sang Hwa, Choi Myong Young, Chung Chang-sup, and Kim Tschang-yeul.

2. The problem of what to call tansaekhwa has provoked considerable debate. Yoon Jin-sup, an artist and critic, has argued for the use of *tansaekhwa* (or *dansaekhwa* in the revised romanization system introduced in 2000 by the Korean government), claiming that indigenous Korean words should be used to refer to Korean art, much as indigenous Japanese words refer to groups such as the Gutai (Concrete) group, whose gestural abstractions, events, and performances of the mid-1950s allowed them entry into mainstream histories of postwar art, and the Mono-ha (School of Things). See Yoon Jin-sup, *Han'guk hyŏndae misul tasi ilkki* [Re-reading contemporary Korean art] (Seoul: ICAS, 2001), 415–17. Oh Sang-gyel argues that neither "tansaekhwa" nor "monochrome painting" accurately describes the works on view. He notes their refusal of flatness and what appears to be a concurrent embrace of plasticity; such art exists between media and should instead be referred to as *tansaekjo misul*, or "monotone art." Oh Sang-gyel, "70 nyŏndae tansaekjo misul ŭi pipy'ŏngjŏk ohaedŭl" [Critical misunderstandings of 1970s monotone art], *Art and Discourse*, no. 25 (2007), http://www.artndiscourse.net/no25/contents.php (accessed February 1, 2008). I use "tansaekhwa" partly because of the general prevalence of this term and partly to avoid the confusion likely to arise in connection with its English translation, "[Korean] monochrome painting."

3. The first contemporary Korean art shows were mostly organized by U.S. organizations or individuals. In 1957 the University of Minnesota exhibited the works of students and faculty members from Seoul National University. Malcolm M. Willey, introduction to *Korean Art: Faculty and Students, Seoul National University*, exhibition catalog (Minneapolis, Minn.: University Gallery, 1957), unpaginated. The 1957 Minnesota exhibition was related to the Minnesota Project, in which the International Cooperation Administration contracted the University of Minnesota in 1954 to provide Seoul National University with various forms of scientific and technical knowledge. The exhibition was part of an international exchange project designed to remodel the country's flagship institution of higher learning in the mold of a U.S. institution.

Not all attempts to promote Korean art overseas were driven by a state's political or ideological interests. In 1958, *Contemporary Korean Paintings*, which took place at the World House Galleries in New York, was curated by Ellen Conant, a historian of Japanese art. For a concise summary of the exhibition's reception in Korea, see Choi Youl, *Han'guk hyŏndae misul ŭi yŏksa 1945–1961 II* [The history of Korean modern art] (Seoul:

Youlhwadang, 2006), 502–4, 586–87. See also Chung Moo-jeong, "1950 nyŏndae miguk e sogae toen han'guk misul" [Introductions of Korean art in fifties America], *Han'guk kŭndae misul sahak* 14 (2005): 25–31.

4. Kim Yersu, *Cultural Policy in the Republic of Korea* (Paris: UNESCO, 1976), 16.

5. One major instance was the exhibit *Korean Art—The Methods of Today*. Held May 21–June 10, 1979, at the Art Center of the Korea Culture and Arts Foundation, it surveyed contemporary Korean artistic production. It featured the works of forty-four artists, a large percentage of whom were associated with tansaekhwa.

6. Yi Kyungsung, "'Han'guk misul—onŭl ŭi pangbŏp' ŭi chŏn'gae" [The development of 'Korean art—the methods of today'], *Space* 14, no. 7 (July 1979): 53.

7. Ibid., 51.

8. Lee Yil, "Hoehwa ŭi saeroun pusang kwa kisangdo '76 nyŏn" [The new rise of painting and an artistic weather map for 1976], *Space* 11, no. 9 (September 1976): 42.

9. For an overview of the diversity of works produced in Japan in the 1920s and '30s, see Gennifer Weisenfeld, *MAVO: Japanese Artists and the Avant-Garde, 1905–1931* (Berkeley: University of California Press, 2002), and Alicia Volk, *In Pursuit of Universalism: Yorozu Tetsugoro and Japanese Modern Art* (Berkeley: University of California Press, 2010).

10. On the Free Artists' Association and other groups receptive to abstraction, see John Clark, "Artistic Subjectivity in the Taishō and Early Shōwa Avant-Garde," in *Japanese Art after 1945: Scream against the Sky*, ed. Alexandra Munroe (New York: Abrams, 1994), 41–53. On the activities of Korean artists in 1930s Japan, see Kim Youngna, "1930 nyŏndae ŭi chŏnwi kŭrupjŏn yŏn'gu" [A study of avant-garde groups in the 1930s], in *20 segi ŭi han'guk misul* [20th century Korean art] (Seoul: Yegyŏng, 1998), 63–114.

11. While some have credited *Rondo* with being the first example of Korean abstraction, others, including the National Museum of Contemporary Art, bestow this distinction upon Chu Kyŏng's *Disruption (Pa'ran)*, a small rectangular oil painting whose abrupt changes of direction and repetition of geometric form strongly allude to futurist works. The exact date of *Disruption* ranks among the great conundrums of modern Korean art historical connoisseurship. The fourth son of a privileged family, Chu Kyŏng began studying art in earnest in 1921 under the tutelage of Ko Hui-dong, Korea's first professional Western oil painter. Chu claims that he painted *Disruption* in the wake of his family's financial troubles and that at that time he had no knowledge of abstraction. Quoted in "Hwasil pangmungi" [Studio visit], *Space* 9, no. 9 (September 1974): 21. Chu is cited as claiming that he first saw an example of "Western abstraction" in 1928 when he went to Japan and came across a book of Wassily Kandinsky's works. Chu himself claimed that *Disruption* was made in 1923, but the signature in the painting's lower left-hand corner, the name "Chu Kyŏng" written in Roman letters, indicates that it may have been created in the 1930s. According to his heirs, the artist, whose real name is Chu Chae-kyŏng, began to sign his works in this manner from the 1930s. "Chu Kyŏng: Artist File," unpublished records of the National Museum of Contemporary Art, Korea. It is difficult to ascertain the date as there are no other works attributed to Chu during this time to which this work might be usefully compared, and close examination of the signature is similarly inconclusive, showing what appears to be a garbled "1926" in the lower left-hand corner of the painting. Kim Yong-ch'ŏl, an art historian who has researched the life and works of Chu Kyŏng, avers that the signature was added some time after the painting was actually made, thus suggesting that

the date recorded was not the date of the painting's actual execution. Ibid. The critic Yi Ku-yŏl speculates that the artist might have been encouraged to paint his futurist-like work through articles published in journals like *New Citizen Public Discourse* (*Shinmin kongnon*), which published a feature on futurism by the poet and writer No Cha-yŏng in its inaugural issue in 1923. Yet the treatment of light and color, along with the composition, which shows a constellation of vectorial shapes that pull the eye in multiple directions, indicates a confidence far greater than might be expected of a teenage painter with only two years of formal artistic training.

12. The June 2002 issue of *Wŏlgan misul* devoted several pages to these propaganda painters working in South Korea.

13. Kwon recalls being sent to the front lines to document the war and remembers that an American purchased one of the works he made during this time. Kwon Young-woo, "Na ŭi kŭrim iyagi: P'yehŏ ŭi 6.25 hyŏnjangesŏ" [About my painting story: From the ruins of the Korean War], *Wŏlgan misul* 5, no. 6 (June 1993): 67.

14. Kim Yŏng-ju, "'Hyŏndae' wa han'guk misul" [The "contemporary" and Korean art], *Chosun ilbo*, November 23, 1957.

15. Nam Kwan, in conversation with O Yŏng-jin, "Kukchemisuljŏnŭl chungsimŭro" [On international exhibitions], *Sinch'ŏnji* 8, no. 5 (August 1953): 259.

16. "Chŏlmŭn hwagadŭl ŭi kwangjang—Yi Pong-sang hoehwa yŏn'guso" [A meeting place for young artists—Yi Pong-sang's studio], *Tonga ilbo*, April 17, 1959.

17. Nam Kwan, "A, pamŭl tto saewŏtguna" [Ah, another all-nighter], *Chungang*, April 1971: 200.

18. Yi Pong-sang, "Sasile taehan ch'ugurŭl" [In pursuit of truth], *Sudo py'ŏngnon* 1 (June 1953): 65.

19. One of the most influential applications of the idea of "chaotic input" in relation to creole formation is Derek Bickerton's study of Hawaiian creoles in *Roots of Language* (Ann Arbor, Mich.: Karoma, 1981).

20. Chung Moo-jeong, "Chŏnhu ch'usangmisulgye ŭi esŭp'erant'o, 'aengp'orŭmel' kaenyŏm ŭi hyŏngsŏng kwa chŏngae" [The Esperanto of the postwar world of abstraction, informel's formation and development], *Misulsahak* 17 (August 2003): 25.

21. Syngboc Chon, "Young Artists Hold Third Group Show," *Korean Republic*, May 20, 1958.

22. Park Seobo, in conversation with Kim Yŏng-ju, "Ch'usang undong 10 nyŏn kŭ yusan kwa chŏnmang" [The legacy and outlook for a decade of abstraction], *Space* 2, no. 12 (December 1967): 88.

23. Yi Ku-yŏl, "Hyŏndae han'guk misulsa ŭi aengp'orŭmel yŏlp'ung" [The rage for informel in contemporary Korean art history], *Space* 19, no. 7 (July 1984): 49.

24. Han Sang-jin, "Ch'usangjuŭi misul ŭi nanmujangŭro toego innŭn Nam Chosŏn hwadan" [The South Korean art world becoming a mess of abstract art], *Chosŏn misul* 4 (April 1963): 41.

25. Yi Kyungsung, "Hwansang kwa hyŏngsang: Che 3 hoe hyŏndaejŏn" [Fantasy and form: The third exhibition of the Modern Artists' Association], *Han'guk ilbo*, May 20, 1958.

26. Park Seobo, "'Chŏnjaeng ŭi woemadi sorirŭl . . .': Sŏyang hwaga Pak Sŏ-bo" ["The sounds of war's lone cry . . .": Oil painter Park Seobo], *Chosun ilbo*, February 18, 1965.

27. Park Seobo, "Jaeksŭn P'ollok" [Jackson Pollock], *Tonga ilbo*, August 26, 1960.

28. Chung Moo-jeong, "Chŏnhu ch'usangmisulgye ŭi esŭp'erant'o, 'aengp'orŭmel' kaenyŏm ŭi hyŏngsŏng kwa chŏngae," 32. Chung argues that it is more likely that artists obtained information about informel through Korean-language summaries of the movement. Ibid.

29. Other students included Pak Pong-su, who briefly attended the National Beiping Art College (now the Central Academy of Fine Arts in Beijing) from 1936 to 1937 and whose semiabstract paintings of the late 1940s capitalize on Qi's grasp of linear flow.

30. Kim Mi-jung, "Han'guk aengpo'rŭmel kwa taehan min'guk misul chŏllamhoe—1960 nyŏndae ch'oban chŏngch'ijŏk pyŏnhyŏkkirŭl chungsimŭro" [Korean informel and the Kukchŏn—Focusing on the political turning-point of the early 1960s], *Han'guk kŭnhyŏndae misul sahak*, 2004: 321.

31. Chung Hyungmin, "Sŏ-hwa ŭi ch'usanghwa kwajŏng e kwanhan si" [Examining the move toward abstraction in calligraphy and ink painting], *Chohyŏng* 23 (2000): 17.

32. Kim Byung-ki, "Kukchejŏn ch'amyŏ wa kŭ twi e onŭn kŏt" [Participation in international exhibitions and its consequences], *Sinsegye*, June 1963: 260; Bang Keun-taek, "Kukchŏn kaehyŏge taehan siŏn" [Remarks on Kukchŏn reforms], *Sinsegye*, October 1963: 269.

33. Bang Keun-taek, "Haewoero kanŭn uri hoehwa" [Korean paintings overseas], *Sedae*, August 1963: 240.

34. Oh Kwangsu, "Kukchejŏn chinch'ulp'um chakka sŏnjŏng ŭi chŏnmal" [The circumstances of selecting artists for international exhibitions], *Sedae*, September 1968: 362.

35. Thomas Crow, "Modernism and Mass Culture in the Visual Arts," in *Modernism and Modernity*, ed. Benjamin H. D. Buchloh, Serge Guilbaut, and David Solkin (Halifax: Press of the Nova Scotia College of Art and Design, 1983), 244, 251.

36. Kim Ku-lim, interview with the author, June 2, 2010.

37. Kim Y. B., quoted in Alice Amsden, *Asia's Next Giant: South Korea and Late Industrialization* (New York: Oxford University Press, 1989), 67.

38. As recounted by Lee's daughter, Lee Jieun; interview with the author, June 29, 2010.

39. Ibid.

40. Kim states that *Death of the Sun II* was originally exhibited without a frame but that one was later added. Interview with the author, June 2, 2010.

41. Kim Yŏng-ju, "Kukchejŏn, misulgwan, misul chaeryo" [International exhibitions, the museum, art materials], *Sinsegye*, February 1963: 289.

42. As stated by Kim Mun-sik, a reporter for the daily newspaper *Kyŏnghyang sinmun*, in "Misul kija such'ŏp" [Memo of an art reporter], *Hwarang* 1, no. 1 (Fall 1973): 53.

43. For a survey of the South Korean economy from 1960 to 1980, see Dani Rodrik, Gene Grossman, and Victor Norman, "Getting Interventions Right: How South Korea and Taiwan Grew Rich," *Economic Policy* 10, no. 20 (April 1995): 53–107.

44. Bang Keun-taek, "Musang ŭi yesul" [Art without compensation], *Sinsegye*, September 1963: 238.

45. Mun Sŏn-ho, owner of the Munhwa Gallery, estimated that 70 percent of artists taught art for a living. "Hwarang hyŏp'oega haeya hal il" [What the Galleries Association must do], *Hwarang* 5, no. 1 (Spring 1977): 36.

46. Bang Keun-taek, "Misul ŭi pijinesŭ" [The business of art], *Pijinesŭ* 143 (September 1972): 84–85.

47. Oh Kwangsu, "Hwarangga iyagi" [News of the galleries], *Sedae*, December 1973: 196.

48. Oh Kwangsu, "Myŏngdong hwarang" [Myongdong Gallery], *Misul ch'unch'u* 5 (Summer 1980): 55.

49. Park Yong-sook, "Ch'oegŭn ŭi chŏnwimisul kwa uridŭl, chwadamhoe" [Recent avant-garde art and us, a roundtable discussion], *Space* 10, no. 3 (March 1975): 65.

50. Cited in "Chŏnwi hwaganŭn joeropta" [The avant-garde is lonely], *Kyŏnghyang sinmun*, May 23, 1975. Kim Ku-lim was among the many artists who would donate work to a fund-raising show held July 8–12, 1975. The proceeds of this show would later help reestablish the gallery in a new home at 74 Kwanhun-dong, not far from its former An'guk-dong location.

51. Choi Tae-shin, interview with Oh Sang-gyel, in *Han'guk hyŏndae misul tasi ilkki II* [Rereading Korean contemporary art II], ed. Oh Sang-gyel (Seoul: ICAS, 2001), 269.

52. *Nam June Paik: Edited for Television*, videocassette (Electronic Arts Intermix, 1975).

53. As published on the inside leaf of each issue of the group's magazine, *A.G.*

54. The original members, along with Ha, were Kim Han, Suh Seung-won, Lee Seung-jio, Pak Sŏk-wŏn, Ch'oe Pong-hyŏn, Ch'oe Myŏng-yŏng, Yi T'ae-hyŏn, Kim Tchasup, Kwak Hoon, and Kim Ku-lim.

55. See, for example, Bang Keun-taek's citation of McLuhan in "Misul ŭi pijinesŭ," 88.

56. Ha Chonghyun, "Han'guk misul 1970 nyŏndaerŭl majŭmyŏnsŏ" [Korean art, on entering the 1970s], *A.G.* 2 (1970): 3.

57. Ibid., 61.

58. Suh Seung-won, in "Ilbon chŏnsihoe chakkajwadam" [Roundtable with artists exhibiting work in Japan], *Hyŏndae misul* 1, no. 1 (1974): 27.

59. Lee Ufan, "Y ssie ŭi p'yŏnji: Han'guk chakkadŭl ŭi ilbonjŏnsihoerŭl pogo" [A letter to Y: On seeing Korean artists' exhibitions in Japan], *Hyŏndae misul* 1, no. 1 (1974): 37.

60. Shim Moon-seup, in "Ilbon chŏnsihoe chakka chwadam," 19.

61. Park Seobo, in "Ilbon chŏnsihoe chakka chwadam," 22.

62. There is no exact date when the term *hyŏndae* was first used; however, the comprehensive record of newspaper accounts compiled by Choi Youl show that it appeared with regularity in the 1920s. See Choi Youl, *Han'guk kŭnhyŏndae misul ŭi yŏksa (1800–1961)* [The history of Korean modern and contemporary art] (Seoul: Youlhwadang, 1998), 121–36.

63. Yi Ku-yŏl, "Chwadam" [Roundtable], *Space* 4, no. 10 (October 1969): 30.

64. Lee Ufan, in ibid.

65. Ch'oe Su-nu, "Han'guk misulsa" [History of Korean art], *Kyŏnggi t'oji* 3 (1957): 199.

66. Kim Mun-ho, "Insamal" [Greetings], in *Ch'usang = sanghwang: Chohyŏng kwa panjohyŏng* [Abstraction = situation: Plasticity and anti-plasticity], exhibition catalog (Seoul: Myongdong Gallery, 1973), unpaginated.

67. Lee Yil, "Kwangbok 30 nyŏn ŭi han'guk misul" [Thirty years of Korean art after independence], *Simunhak* 5, no. 8 (August 1975): 73.

68. Ibid.

69. Lee Dong Youb, "Chwadam: Han'gukchŏk modŏnijŭm ŭi chŏngch'ak" [The establishment of a Korean modernism], *Wŏlgan misul* 8, no. 3 (March 1996): 68.

70. Franco Moretti, *Graphs, Maps, Trees: Abstract Models for a Literary Theory* (London and New York: Verso, 2005), 2.

71. Lee Ufan, *Deai o motomete: Gendai no bijutsu no shigen* [Search for encounter: The origins of contemporary art] (Tokyo: Tabata Shoten, 1971), 85.

72. Kang Tae-hi, "Yi U hwan kwa 70 nyŏndae tansaekhoehwa" [Lee Ufan and 1970s tansaekhwa], in *Han'guk hyŏndae misul 197080* [Korean contemporary art, 1970–1980], ed. Han'guk hyŏndae misul yŏn'guhoe (Seoul: Hagyŏn munhwasa, 2004), 157.

73. Lee Yil, "Haebang samsimnyŏn ŭi munjejak munje chakka" [Controversial artists and artworks during the thirty years since 1945], *Chungang ilbo*, January 4, 1975.

74. Oh Kwangsu, interview with the author, October 18, 2008.

75. Jean-Luc Nancy, *The Ground of the Image* (New York: Fordham University Press, 2005), 20.

ONE: KWON YOUNG-WOO AND YUN HYONGKEUN RETHINK PAINTING

1. Bang Keun-taek, "Putjagukŏmnŭn kŭrim ŭi Kwon Yŏng-u ssi" [Kwon Young-woo of the paintings without brushstrokes], *Han'guk ilbo*, June 23, 1966. The work *65-9* appeared in "Kaesŏng innŭn chakp'um segye" [Art with personality], *Chungang ilbo*, June 28, 1966; other reproduced works from this exhibition included *66-12* (present whereabouts unknown) in the *Han'guk ilbo*, and *66-14* in the June 21, 1966, issue of *Sŏul sinmun*, a reproduction of which appears in *Kwon Young-woo* (Seoul: Image Art Research Institute, 2007), 268.

2. Kwon Young-woo, interview with Yi T'ae-ho, "Ponjilhwahan kodokhan chakmi" [The essentialization of a lonesome beauty of making], *Kyegan misul* 7, no. 22 (Summer 1982): 144–45.

3. An image of Kwon cutting into the paper with scissors was reproduced in "Hwap'ane chohyŏng ŭi mi" [The beauty of plasticity on supports for painting], *Taehan ilbo*, October 4, 1966.

4. Yi Ku-yŏl, "Hwasŏnji ŭi 'tŭrama'" [The drama of Korean paper], *Kyŏnghyang sinmun*, June 25, 1966.

5. "Oryŏbuch'in hwasŏnji ŭi kudodo" [Compositions of attached Korean paper], *Chosun ilbo*, April 1, 1965.

6. Kwon Young-woo, interview with Kim Ch'ŏl-hyo, *Archives of Korean Art Journal* 1 (2003): 90.

7. Yi Ku-yŏl, "Hwasŏnji ŭi 'tŭrama.'"

8. Ibid.

9. Hong Sun-pyo, "Myŏngch'ŏngdae sŏhaksŏ ŭi kyŏnhakjisik kwa Chosŏnhugi hoehwaron ŭi pyŏndong" [Optical knowledge in books from the West and developments in painting theory of the late Chosŏn era], *Misulsahak yŏn'gu* 248 (December 2005): 148–68.

10. Hong Sun-pyo, *Han'guk kŭndaemisulsa* [The history of modern art in Korea] (Seoul: Sigong Art, 2009), 31.

11. Ibid., 65.

12. On the introduction of *nihonga* to Korea, see Kang Minki, "Kŭndaejŏnhwangi han'gukhwadane ŭi ilbonhwa yuip kwa han'guk hwagadŭl ŭi ilbonch'ehŏm" [The introduction of *nihonga* into Korea at the turn of the modern era and the experiences of Korean artists in Japan], *Misulsahak yŏn'gu* 235 (March 2007): 217–39.

13. See Choi Youl, "1940 nyŏndae—sumukch'aesaek'wa" [The 1940s—ink and color painting], in *Han'guk kŭndae misul sahak* [The study of modern Korean art history], ed. Han'guk kŭndae misul sahakhoe (Seoul: Ch'ŏngnyŏnsa, 2010), 530.

14. Kwon Young-woo, interview with Kim Ch'ŏl-hyo, *Archives of Korean Art Journal* 1 (2003): 85.

15. Ibid, 86.

16. Kwon Young-woo, interview with Yi T'ae-ho, "Ch'ejilhwahan kodokhan changmi" [Embodying the solitary beauty of artmaking], *Kyegan misul* 7, no. 22 (Summer 1982): 144.

17. Bert Winther-Tamaki, "The Asian Dimensions of Postwar Abstract Art: Calligraphy and Metaphysics," in *The Third Mind: American Artists Contemplate Asia, 1860–1989*, ed. Alexandra Munroe (New York: Guggenheim Museum, 2009), 147–48.

18. Nam Kwan, in conversation with O Yŏng-jin, "Kukchemisuljŏnŭl chungsimŭro" [On international exhibitions], *Sinch'ŏnji* 8, no. 5 (August 1953): 264.

19. "Misurin ŭi tangmyŏn kwaje" [The challenges artists face], *Sin misul* 2 (November 1956): 27. For further discussion of Korean artists' interest in the works of Mark Tobey, see Chung Moo-jeong, "Ch'usangp'yohyŏnjuŭi wa han'guk aengp'orŭmel" [Abstract expressionism and Korean informel], *Misulsa yŏn'gu* 15 (2001): 259.

20. "Chŏnt'ongjŏk tongyanghwae sae tolp'agurŭl chesi" [Presenting a new breakthrough for traditional Oriental painting], *Sŏul sinmun*, June 21, 1966. Of his painting *Fantasy of the Seashore,* which won a special citation at the 1955 Kukchŏn and was arguably his most famous work prior to those shown in his 1966 show, Kwon notes, "This work on initial encounter looks unquestionably like a realistic painting. However even if the expression is realistic, the contents are already surrealistic." Ibid.

21. The idea of "Korean informel" appeared in such articles as Kim Yŏng-ju's "Angp'orŭmel kwa uri misul," [Informel and Korean art], *Chosun ilbo*, December 13, 1958; and Bang Keun-taek's "Hwadan ŭi saeroun seryŏk" [A new force in the art world], *Sŏul sinmun*, December 8, 1958.

22. Yi Tae-wŏn, "Hwarang sigam: Pando hwarangŭl chungsimŭro" [Thoughts on the gallery: The Bando Gallery], *Misul*, June 1964: 44.

23. Suh Se-ok, "Tongyanghwa ŭi subŏp kwa chŏngsin" [The principles and spirit of Oriental painting], *Space* 3, no. 6 (June 1968): 53.

24. Suh Se-ok, interview with Song Hwa-young and Yun Hye-jun, *Archives of Korean Art Journal* 1 (2003): 122. Several of the group's members recall meeting at Suh Se-ok's suggestion in December 1959. "Chwadamhoe" [Roundtable discussion with Min Kyung-kap, Song Young-bang, Chun Young-hwa, and Chung Tak-young], *Archives of Korean Art Journal* 1 (2003): 146–47.

25. The group's last exhibition together took place at the Central Information Center in Seoul in December 1964.

26. Kim Ch'ŏng-gang, "Tongyanghwa poda han'guk'warŭl" [Korean painting instead of Oriental painting], *Kyŏnghyang sinmun*, February 20, 1959. The call to rename "Oriental

painting" as "Korean painting" can be dated even earlier, to the years immediately following Korea's liberation. See Kim Hwa-gyŏng, "Tongyanghwarosŏ ŭi hanhwa" [Korean painting as Oriental painting], *Kyŏnghyang sinmun*, January 14, 1949.

27. Song Young-bang, in "Chwadamhoe," 146.

28. Kwon Young-woo, interview with Kim Ch'ŏl-hyo, 90.

29. Kim Ch'ŏl-hyo, "Mungnimhoe hwagadŭri malhanŭn Mungnimhoe" [The Ink Forest Society on the Ink Forest Society], *Han'guk kŭnhyŏndae misul sahak* 12 (2011): 121.

30. Kwon Young-woo, interview with Kim Ch'ŏl-hyo and Yun Hye-jun, October 13, 2000. The full interview transcript is located in the Samsung Museum of Art, Leeum Library.

31. Chang Woo-sung, interview with Kim Ch'ŏl-hyo, *Archives of Korean Art Journal* 1 (2003): 69.

32. Ibid.

33. Kwon Young-woo, interview with Yi T'ae-ho, "Ponjilhwahan kodokhan chakmi," 145.

34. Kim Ki-chang, "Parŏn kwa haengdonge kidae" [Expectations from declarations and actions], *Sŏul sinmun*, April 1, 1960.

35. Kang Min-ki, "1930–1940 nyŏndae han'guk tongyanghwaga ŭi ilbonhwap'ung" [The popularity of *nihonga* in Korean ink painting during the 1930s and '40s], *Misulsa nondan* 29 (December 2009): 226.

36. Suh Se-ok and Song Young-bang participated in the 1963 and 1969 editions, respectively, of the São Paulo Bienal.

37. Suh Se-ok, in "Kukchejŏn ch'amyŏ ŭiŭi wa kŭ chŏnmang" [The significance and future prospects of participating in international exhibitions], *Sŏul midae hakbo* 1, no. 1 (1966): 42.

38. Bang Keun-taek, "'Oriental' Abstract Painting," *Korea Journal* 3, no. 6 (June 1963): 21.

39. Ibid., 22.

40. Ibid.

41. Ibid.

42. Kwon Young-woo, interview with Kim Ch'ŏl-hyo, *Archives of Korean Art Journal*, 90.

43. Ibid.

44. Kwon Young-woo, interview with Kim Mikyung, "Soye—Kwŏn Yŏng-u" [The art of "so": Kwon Young-woo], in *Kwon Young-woo* (Seoul: Gana Art Center, 2002), unpaginated.

45. "Che 9 hoe hyŏndaemijŏn tongyanghwabu Kwŏn Yŏng-u" [Kwon Young-woo in the ink painting section of the Ninth Contemporary Art exhibition], *Chosun ilbo*, April 1, 1965.

46. "Kaesŏng innŭn chakp'um segye."

47. Hong Sun-pyo, *Han'guk kŭndaemisulsa*, 31.

48. "At'ŭrie t'ambang: Kukchŏnŭl apdun Kwŏn Yŏng-u" [Studio visit: Kwon Young-woo preparing for the Kukchŏn], *Min'guk ilbo*, September 9, 1960. An image of Kwon standing next to *Old Moon* was published in the article.

49. Kwon Young-woo, interview with Kim Bok-young, "Haengwirŭl t'onghan chongi ŭi kaehyŏnsŏng" [The revelatoriness of the paper as seen through gesture], *Space* 17, no. 6 (June 1982): 49.

50. Ch'ŏt kaeinjŏnŭl kannŭn Kwŏn Yŏng-u hwabaek" [The first solo exhibition of Kwon Young-woo], *Sŏul sinmun*, June 21, 1966.

51. Kwon Young-woo, interview with Kim Bok-young, "Haengwirŭl t'onghan chongi ŭi kaehyŏnsŏng," 49.

52. Yi Ku-yŏl, "Hwasŏnji ŭi 'tŭrama.'"

53. Lee Ungno, untitled preface to *Lee Ungno*, exhibition catalog (Paris: Galerie Facchetti, 1962), unpaginated.

54. Kim Hyangan, "Kusang kwa ch'usang ŭi tu panghyang" [The two directions of figuration and abstraction], *Han'guk ilbo*, June 16, 1962.

55. Jacques Massol, untitled preface, *Kwon Young-woo*, exhibition catalog (Paris: Galerie Jacques Massol, 1976), unpaginated.

56. The inaugural issue was published in September 1969.

57. For this edition of the Kukchŏn, Kwon submitted *70-21*, a square panel turned forty-five degrees that he covered with *hanji*, then divided in half with a horizontal rip that stretched from the painting's left corner to the right. A seal was impressed just below the rip. Although there are no high-quality reproductions of this work, a low-resolution reproduction can be found in the catalog of the 1971 Kukchŏn.

58. Kwon Young-woo, "Ch'ejilhwahan kodokhan changmi," 145.

59. Kim In-hwan, "Kwon Yŏng-u kaeinjŏn" [The solo exhibition of Kwon Young-woo], *Sin-a ilbo,* April 30, 1974.

60. Oh Kwangsu, "Idal ŭi chŏnsi" [This month's exhibitions], *Sindonga* 133 (September 1975): 263.

61. Min Kyung-kap, quoted in "Chŏnt'ongtoech'annŭn tongyanghwa" [Oriental painting rediscovers tradition], *Kyŏnghyang sinmun*, May 18, 1974.

62. Yi Kyungsung, "70 nyŏndae hwagaron: Han'gukhwadan 'chŏlmŭn hwaga' rŭl chaep'yŏngkkahanda" [A theory of 1970s artists: Reevaluating the "emerging artists" of the Korean art world], *Chosun ilbo*, June 21, 1978.

63. Denis Roger, "Dans les galeries," *Carrefour*, January 22, 1976, 10.

64. Alain Bosquet, "Les Papiers repoussés de Kwon Young-woo," *Le Figaro*, January 26, 1976.

65. Unsigned review, "Kwon Yŏng-u ssi hŭinbit ch'uguhan tobuljŏn" [Kwon Young-woo explores white in his farewell exhibition], *Chungang ilbo*, May 20, 1977.

66. Kwon Young-woo, interview with Kim Chŏng-hwa, "Kwon Yŏng-u hwabaek kwa hamkke" [Talking with Kwon Young-woo], *P'ari han'gu 7* (December 1987): unpaginated.

67. Barbara Thoren, "The Week in Art," *Japan Times*, August 21, 1977, 9.

68. Yi Hŭng-u, in conversation with Lee Yil, "Idal ŭi misul" [Exhibitions this month], *Chosun ilbo*, August 31, 1976.

69. O To-gwang, "Kwŏn Yŏng-u ŭi chakp'um" [The works of Kwon Young-woo], *Ilgan sŭp'och'ŭ*, August 26, 1977.

70. Oh Kwangsu, "Chŏnt'ong maejae wa sŏgujŏk chohyŏng chŏngsin" [Traditional media and Western design thought], *Space* 12, no. 6 (June 1977): 95.

71. Park Rae-kyung, "Kwon Yŏng-u," *Yŏsŏng donga* 130 (August 1978): 216.

72. Ibid.

73. Oh Kwangsu, "Chŏnt'ong maejae wa sŏgujŏk chohyŏng chŏngsin," 95.

74. You Hong-june, "T'eksŭch'yŏ wa hunyŏm ŭi mihak" [The aesthetics of texture and illumination], *Kyegan misul* 9 (Spring 1979): 127.

75. Bang Keun-taek, "Anjŏnggam chunŭn 'kigae ŭi punbal'" [A sense of stability produced by "an eruption of moral high-mindedness"], *Ilyo sinmun*, May 20, 1973. On Yun's explanation of what he called his "rage," see Kim Ch'ŏl, "Hwaga Yun Hyŏng-gŭn" [The artist Yun Hyongkeun], *Deep-Rooted Tree*, June–July 1980: 97. Yun has referred to his "rage" in his interviews with artist Choi Jong-t'ae, "Yun Hyŏng-gŭn ŭi kŏmjŏng pit kŭrim" [The black paintings of Yun Hyongkeun], in *Na ŭi misul, arŭmdaumŭl hyanghan saesaek* [My art, a contemplation of beauty] (Seoul: Youlhwadang, 1998), 168 (originally published in *Kyŏngje chŏngŭi*, Winter 1996).

76. Yi Kyungsung, *Yun Hyŏng-gŭn: Han'guk hyŏndae misul taep'yo chakka 100 inkwŏnjip* [Yun Hyongkeun: Selected works of 100 modern Korean painters and sculptors] (Seoul: Kumsong, 1979), vol. 99, unpaginated.

77. Yun Hyongkeun, interview with the author, July 5, 1995.

78. Lee Yil, "Yun Hyŏng-gŭn non" [On Yun Hyongkeun], *Sun misool* 11, no. 7 (Fall 1990): 12.

79. Bang Keun-taek, "Anjŏnggam chunŭn 'kigae ŭi punbal.'"

80. Yoo June-sang, "Siwŏnsŭrŏn chingnip ŭi chase" [A refreshingly upright attitude], *Tonga ilbo*, May 24, 1973.

81. Yun Hyongkeun, interview with Kim Eŭn-a, Samsung Culture Foundation, March 23, 1999, unpaginated. The full transcript is located in the Samsung Museum of Art.

82. Yi Kyungsung, "T'ugihan chohyŏng kamgak ŭi kyŏnghŏm" [Experiencing of a unique plastic sensibility], *Space* 11, no. 12 (December 1976): 82.

83. Yun Hyongkeun, interview with Kim Eŭn-a, Samsung Culture Foundation, March 23, 1999, unpaginated. Yun recounted having been early exposed to the process of making small ink paintings and to calligraphic exercises. Yun Hyongkeun, interview with Kim Yisoon, Samsung Culture Foundation Oral History Program, November 16, 2006, 2.

84. Kim Hyangan, *Kim Whanki: Vie et oeuvre* (Paris: Maeght Éditeur, 1992), 38.

85. Excerpt from the diary of Kim Whanki, November 13, 1963, cited by Kim Yun-su, "Kim Hwan'ginon" [On Kim Whanki], *Ch'angjak kwa pip'yŏng* 12, no. 2 (June 1977): 662.

86. As cited in a diary entry from January 23, 1968. Kim Whanki, *Ŏdisŏ muŏssi toeŏ tasi mannarya* [Where, and in what form, will we meet again?] (Seoul: Munye Madang, 1995), 304.

87. Gordon Brown, "Whanki Kim," *Arts Magazine* 49, no. 6 (February 1975): 18.

88. Yi Kyungsung, "T'ugihan chohyŏng kamgak ŭi kyŏnghŏm," 82.

89. Ibid.

90. Yun Hyongkeun, interview with Kim Yisoon, *Samsung Culture Foundation Oral History Program*, December 2, 2006, 8.

91. Yun Hyongkeun, "Chint'ong mannŭng . . . chakp'umi naogikkaji" [A multitude of pains . . . until the work is finished], *Kyŏnghyang sinmun*, February 3, 1977.

92. Ibid.

93. Joseph Love, untitled essay, in *Yun Hyong-gun*, exhibition catalog (Seoul: Munheon Gallery, 1976), unpaginated.

94. Carol Mancusi-Ungaro, "Material and Immaterial Surface: The Paintings of Rothko," in *Mark Rothko*, ed. Jeffrey Weiss (Washington D.C.: National Gallery of Art; New Haven and London: Yale University Press, 1998), 282–301; and Mary Bustin, "Rothko's Painting Technique," in *The Rothko Book*, ed. Bonnie Clearwater (London: Tate, 2006), esp. 172.

95. Lee Yil, "T'eksŭch'yŏ ŏrosŏ ŭi yŏbaek" [The void as texture], in *Yun Hyongkeun*, exhibition catalog (Seoul: Munheon Gallery, 1975), unpaginated.

96. "Yun Hyŏng-gŭn ch'usanghwajŏn" [A show of Yun Hyongkeun's abstraction], *Kyŏnghyang sinmun*, December 2, 1975; "Yun Hyŏng-gŭn kaeinjŏn" [Yun Hyongkeun's solo show], *Tonga ilbo*, December 2, 1975.

97. Yoo June-sang was apparently the critic who told Yun of Love's response, adding that the critic seemed "transfixed." Kim Yŏng-suk, interview with the author, January 3, 2009.

98. Joseph Love, "Tekusuchya no zenei: Ruppo 'dai ni kai kankoku Andepandang'" [The avant-garde of texture: Report on the Second Korean Indépendants Exhibition], *Mizue* 840 (March 1975): 78–83.

99. Lee Ufan, "Yun Hyong-gun no shigoto" [The works of Yun Hyongkeun], in *Yun Hyongkeun*, exhibition catalog (Tokyo: Muramatsu Gallery, 1976), unpaginated.

100. Kim Chŏng-su, "1975 nyŏn che 14 ch'a sangp'aullo piennale" [The 14th São Paulo Bienal in 1975], *Space* 10, no. 12 (December 1975): 79.

101. Kim Yŏng-suk, interview with the author, January 3, 2009. Some earlier versions of *Umber Blue* were framed, particularly those made for the May 1973 show at the Myongdong Gallery. The artist's son speculates that this was "a concession" to audience expectations. Interview with the author, January 3, 2009.

TWO: RATES OF EXCHANGE IN HA CHONGHYUN'S *CONJUNCTION*

1. Yun Myeong-ro, in "Kukchejŏn ch'amyŏ ŭiŭi wa kŭ chŏnmang" [The significance and future prospects of participating in international exhibitions], *Sŏul midae hakbo* 1, no. 1 (1966): 41.

2. Suh Se-ok, in ibid., 41.

3. Held in April 1956, the show displayed twenty-nine paintings. A full list of works appeared in "Kim Hwan-gi hwabaek P'ariesŏ kaeinjŏn kaech'oe" [Kim Whanki to have a solo show in Paris], *Sin misul* 2 (November 1956): 34. Also see "Kim Hwangi kyosu p'arisŏ kaeinjŏn kaemak" [Professor Kim Whanki to have solo show in Paris], *Hongdae hakbo*, October 19, 1956.

4. "Kim Hwan-gi hwabaek P'ari esŏ kaeinjŏn kaech'oe," 34.

5. "Hwadan Terebi" [Art world television], *Sin misul* 8 (March 1958): 38.

6. Oh Kwangsu, "12th Annual Invitational Exhibition of Contemporary Artists," *Korea Journal* 8, no. 6 (June 1968): 38.

7. Yoo June-sang, "Che 12 hoe hyŏndae chakkajŏnwoe" [The 12th Contemporary Artists' Exhibition and other matters], *Sedae*, June 1968: 197.

8. Oh Kwangsu, "Kukchejŏn ch'ulp'um chakka sŏnjŏng ŭi chŏnmal" [Selection criteria for artists participating in international exhibitions], *Sedae*, September 1968: 364.

9. French artist Étienne Martin won the prize for sculpture in 1966. The international prize for painting was awarded to Julio Le Parc, an Argentine artist represented by a Parisian gallery, Galerie Denise René.

10. The commissioner for the South Korean delegation was painter Kim Byung-ki, who was among the Korean artists who had studied in Tokyo in the 1930s. Artist-delegates included Kim Tschang-yeul, Chung Chang-sup, Jo Yong-ik, and Jeang Song-soum, all closely associated with gestural abstraction in Korea.

11. Tobias Wofford, "Exhibiting a Global Blackness: The First World Festival of Negro Arts," in *New World Coming: The Sixties and the Shaping of Global Consciousness*, ed. Karen Dubinsky, Catherine Krull, Susan Lord, Sean Mills, and Scott Rutherford (Toronto: Between the Lines, 2009), 179–86.

12. "First International Exhibition of Fine Arts of Saigon," in *Catalogue of the First International Exhibition of Fine Arts of Saigon* (Saigon: Tao-Đàn Garden, 1962), 20.

13. The full title of the exhibition was *First International Exhibition of Fine Arts Saigon 1962: An International Exposition by Artists of Vietnam and Friendly Countries*. Among those included in the Korean delegation were Suh Se-ok and Park Seobo.

14. Đào Sī Chu, foreword to *Catalogue of the First International Exhibition of Fine Arts of Saigon*, 75. The five members of this preliminary delegation (Kim Young Ki, Kim Keung Seung, Lee Wan Suk, Kwon Yung Hyu, and Kim Son Nyun) played significant roles in the reconstruction of the South Korean art world both after liberation from Japan in 1945 and after the Korean War. Kim Young Ki, the son of well-known ink painter Kim Kyu-jin, in 1946 helped found the Tangu Academy, one of the first ink painting groups after Korea's liberation. Another important figure was Lee Wan Suk, who owned the Ch'ŏnil Gallery, one of the first postwar commercial art galleries in Seoul, opening in 1954.

15. Park Seobo, letter to Adolf Frohner, February 15, 1962. Republished in its entirety in *Elastic Taboos: Within the Korean World of Contemporary Art*, exhibition catalog (Vienna: Kunsthalle Wien, 2006), 47.

16. Otto Muehl, *Lettres à Erika: Journal de l'actionnisme* (Dijon: Les Presses du Réel, 2004). The comments are extracted from Muehl's letters dated January 18, 1962, and November 10, 1961.

17. Bang Keun-taek, "Haewoerŭl kannŭn uri hwadan" [Korean art overseas], *Sedae*, August 1963: 247.

18. Otto Muehl, *Lettres à Erika*, February 15, 1962.

19. Bang was also an oil painter; his first solo exhibition in October 1955 at the U.S. Information Service Office in Gwangju coincided with his initial exposure to abstract expressionism. Sŏ Yŏng-hui, "Pang Kŭn-t'aek, han'guk aengp'orŭmel misul kwa chŏnwijuŭi pip'yŏng" [Bang Keun-taek, Korean informel, and avant-gardist criticism], *Misul p'yŏngdan* 105 (Summer 2012): 58.

20. Bang Keun-taek, "Uri hyŏndae misul ŭi sori'" [The voice of our contemporary art], *Sŏrabŏl hakbo,* April 23, 1963.

21. Bang Keun-taek, "Mobang ŭi hongsugi: Ch'usang hoehwa ŭi munjejŏm" [A flood of copies: Problems of abstraction], *Min'guk ilbo*, May 28, 1962.

22. On the U.S. role in restoring diplomatic ties between South Korea and Japan, see Ki-jil Yi, "In Search of a Panacea: Japan–Korea Rapprochement and America's 'Far Eastern Problem,'" *Pacific Historical Review* 71, no. 4 (November 2002): 633–62.

23. The Tokyo art market briskly expanded from around 1965 until the OPEC oil crisis of 1973, when the market for domestic Japanese art plummeted approximately 50–80 percent. Thomas R. H. Havens, *Artist and Patron in Postwar Japan: Dance, Music, Theater, and the Visual Arts, 1955–1980* (Princeton: Princeton University Press, 1982), 118–20.

24. Paek U-yŏng, "Han'guk hwaga ŭi haewoejŏn (2)" [Korean artists' overseas exhibitions, part 2], *Han'guk ilbo*, June 19, 1973. It was reported that a midcareer artist might expect to sell, on average, five to six works at a gallery exhibition, but mostly to friends or relatives. "Misul chŏnsihoe rŏsi" [A rush on art exhibitions], *Tonga ilbo*, October 24, 1970.

25. In Korea, painting prices and canvas dimensions are usually quoted as a function of *ho*. Paek U-yŏng, "Han'guk hwaga ŭi haewoejŏn (1)" [Korean artists' overseas exhibitions, part 1], *Han'guk ilbo*, June 15, 1973.

26. Oh Kwangsu, "Hwarangga iyagi" [News of the galleries], *Sedae*, December 1973: 201.

27. Kim Sŏn-ju, "Kŭrimi ilbone p'allinda" [Artworks sell in Japan], *Chosun ilbo*, March 14, 1973.

28. One such example of pre-1965 exchange was the *International Freedom Art Exhibition*, which showed both Japanese and Korean art at Kyŏngbok Palace in downtown Seoul in 1962. The idea for the show came from Yi Tae-wŏn, the proprietor of the Bando Gallery, and Yi Hang-sŏng, the publisher of *Sin misul*, the first postwar art magazine in South Korea. Financial support was provided in part by the U.S.-based Asia Foundation. "Kukche chayu misuljŏn ŭi kyŏlsan" [A look back at the *International Freedom Art Exhibition*], *Misul p'yŏngnon* 12 (1962): 4.

29. "Hwadan ŭi ilbon chinch'ul" [Korean art comes to Japan], *Sŏul sinmun*, January 25, 1966.

30. A small delegation of critics from South Korea attended the symposium, including critics Lim Young-bang, who had completed a doctoral thesis on decorative murals for public buildings erected in Paris during the Third Republic at the Sorbonne in 1964, as well as Bang Keun-taek. Reported in *Yunesŭk'o nyusŭ* [UNESCO news], February 1966: 17–18. UNESCO sponsored numerous other Korea–Japan cultural exchanges in the second half of the 1960s, including children's exhibitions and study tours.

31. Thomas T. Ichinose, "Exhibition by Yoshida, Okyon," *Mainichi Daily News*, March 28, 1965.

32. Yoo June-sang, "Ilboneŏ issŭl han'guk hyŏndae misuljŏn" [*Contemporary Korean Painting* to be held in Japan], *Sedae*, May 1965: 308.

33. Yi Kyungsung, interview with Yi In-bŏm, Oral History of Korean Arts, http://oralhistory.knaa.or.kr (accessed October 31, 2012).

34. Lee Se-duk, "Kankoku gendai bijutsu no haikei" [The background of Korean contemporary art], *Gendai no me* 165 (August 1968): 3.

35. Undated draft facsimile, collection of Yi Ku-yŏl, Samsung Museum of Art.

36. Lee Se-duk, in conversation with Honma Masayoshi, "Kankoku gendai bijutsu no haikei," 3.

37. Ibid., 5.

38. For a collection of excerpted reviews of the show, see "Pip'yŏngch'o: Han'guk hyŏndaehoehwajŏn" [A compilation of reviews of *Contemporary Korean Painting*], *Space* 3, no. 12 (December 1968): 72–73.

39. Alain Delissen, "The Aesthetic Pasts of *Space* (1960–1990)," *Korean Studies* 25, no. 2 (2002): 253.

40. Arima Hiroaki, "Kankoku bijutsu ni kibakuzaio!" [To throw a bomb into Korean art!], *SD*, September 1968: 105.

41. The alleged similarity between *Space* and *SD* (*Space Design*) was reported by Kim Yong-Kwon, "'*Konggan*' Makes Its Debut as Architectural Monthly," *Korea Journal* 7, no. 1 (January 1967): 37.

42. Ishiko Junzō, "Kaiga no gendaika o tōe: Kankoku gendai kaigaten o mite" [Inquiring about the contemporization of painting: On seeing *Contemporary Korean Painting*], *Sansai* 235 (September 1968): 65.

43. Haryū Ichirō, "Ajiateki seikaku wa kireruka?" [Can an Asian sensibility arise?], *Asahi Journal*, August 18, 1968: 47.

44. Lee Yil, "68 nyŏndo habangi misulgye" [The art world in the second half of 1968], *Hongdae hakbo*, December 15, 1968: 2. On the selection of artists for *Contemporary Korean Painting*, see Lee Yil, "Ch'ulp'umjakka sŏnjŏng kyŏngŭi" [Criteria for selecting artists], *Space* 3, no. 7 (July 1968): 51.

45. Lee Yil, "68 nyŏndo habangi misulgye," 2.

46. Yoo Youngkuk and Lee Ufan, "Kankoku gendai bijutsu no haikei," *Gendai no me* 165 (August 1968): 4.

47. Painter Jeon Hyuck Lim, born in 1916 like Yoo, wryly commented that Yoo probably saw him as nothing more than a "country hick." Interview with Kim Chu-wŏn, *Oral History of Korean Arts*, http://oralhistory.knaa.or.kr (accessed October 31, 2012).

48. Yoo Youngkuk and Lee Ufan, "Kankoku gendai bijutsu no haikei," 4.

49. Ibid.

50. Park Seobo, "Yi U-hwan kwa ŭi mannam: 68 nyŏn ihurŭl hoisang handa" [My encounter with Lee Ufan: Remembering the years after 1968], *Hwarang* 12, no. 3 (Fall 1984): 32. Also see Park Seobo, "Yi U-hwan e kwanhan il" [About Lee Ufan], *Space* 10, no. 9 (September 1975): 40.

51. Park Seobo, "Yi U-hwan kwa ŭi mannam," 40. Park adds that his own refusal to acquiesce to Yoo's request that Park "beat Lee into a pulp" sent the older artist into a fury. Conversation with the author, October 6, 2008.

52. Suzuki Yoshinori, "Mitekita kankoku no gendai bijutsu" [What I saw of Korea's contemporary art], *Bijutsu techō* 24, no. 353 (March 1972): 22–23. This review was translated by Lee Yil and republished in the March 15, 1972, issue of *Hongdae hakbo* under the title "Ilbon hwagaga pon 71 nyŏn AG chŏn" [A Japanese artist's take on the 1971 AG exhibition].

53. Lee Ufan, Joseph Love, Nakahara Yusuke, and Tōno Yoshiaki were among the attendees. Lee Yil, "*Han'guk 5 in ŭi chakka* tonggyŏngjŏn" [*Five Korean Artists* show in Tokyo], *Sŏul p'yŏngnon*, May 29, 1975: 50.

54. Kim Mun-ho, untitled notice, collection of Samsung Museum of Art. Donated by Park Seobo.

55. Critic Yoo June-sang excitedly told Yun of Love's response, saying that the critic seemed "transfixed." Kim Yŏng-suk, interview with the author, January 3, 2009. Love expressed his own enthusiasm in "The Roots of Korea's Avant-Garde Art," *Art International* 19, no. 6 (June 15, 1975): 31.

56. Yun Hyongkeun, "Ch'ejiljŏkigo chikkwanjŏgŭro todalhal segye" [A world reached constitutionally and directly], interview with Lee Yil, *Space* 24, no. 11 (November 1989): 133.

57. Some examples included the exchange between Hongik University and the Osaka University of Arts in October 1972 and the joint 1972 and 1974 shows of the Creative Artists' Association (Ch'angjak misulga hyŏp'oe) and Kansai-based members of the Nika-kai, one of the most important pre–World War II associations in Japan. Held at the National Museum of Modern Art in Korea from July 3 to 17, 1974, the second joint show featured twenty-two Korean artists and twenty-seven Japanese artists. Another large-scale exchange was initiated by the Hyundai Gallery with the Yamato Gallery. The first of the series took place from June 20 to 30, 1975, at the Hyundai Gallery; the second (and last) installment at the Yamato Gallery, from June 28 to July 3, 1976. "Hyŏndae hwarang simnyŏn ilji" [A diary of the Hyundai Gallery's last ten years], *Hwarang* 8, no. 1 (Spring 1980): 88–89. See also *Hanil misul kyoryu* [Korea–Japan art exchange] (Seoul: Hyundai Gallery, 1975).

58. Cho Ŭn-jŏng, "Sŏknam Yi Kyŏng-sŏng ŭi misul pip'yŏnge taehan yŏn'gu" [A study of Yi Kyungsung's art criticism], *Misul p'yŏngdan*, no. 104 (Spring 2012): 76.

59. "Han'guk sok ŭi ilbon" [The Japan within Korea], *Sedae*, October 1965: unpaginated.

60. Yoo June-sang, "Ilbonesŏ issŭl han'guk hyŏndae misuljŏn," 308.

61. Ibid., 309.

62. Arima Hiroaki, "Kankoku bijutsu ni kibakuzaio!" 105; and Ishiko Junzō, "Kaiga no gendaika o tōe: Kankoku gendai kaigaten o mite," 65.

63. Kim Chong-hak, "Han'guk hyŏndae hoehwa tonggyŏng chŏnsi" [Exhibition of contemporary Korean painting in Tokyo], *Midae hakbo* 3 (1969): 53.

64. Ibid.

65. Nambata Tatsuoki, "Kankoku gendai bijutsu no haikei," *Gendai no me* 165 (August 1968): 3.

66. Lee Yil, in "Ilbon chŏnsihoe chakkajwadam" [Roundtable with artists exhibiting work in Japan], *Hyŏndae misul* 1, no. 1 (1974): 19.

67. Kim Whanki, "Chŏnwi misul ŭi tojŏn" [The challenge of avant-garde art], *Yesulnonmunjip* 13 (1974): 92.

68. Oh Kwangsu, "Han'guk misul ŭi pip'yŏngjŏk chŏnmang" [A critical outlook on Korean art], *A.G.* 3 (1970): 40.

69. Oh Kwangsu, "Hyŏndae misul kwa singminjisŏng" [Contemporary art and colonial sensibility], *Yesulgye*, Winter 1970: 52–53.

70. Yi Kyungsung, "Hwadan ch'oedae ŭi misul nonjaeng—pip'yŏng pujae ŭi hwadane sae nonjaengkkŏri" [The greatest controversy of the art world—the new subject of debate in an art world devoid of criticism], *Chugan Han'guk*, July 28, 1974.

71. Moon Myung-dae, "Han'guk hoehwa ŭi chillo munje" [The problem of Korean painting's future], *Space* 9, no. 6 (June 1974): 5–6.

72. Ibid., 3.

73. Yun Hi-sun, "Chosǒn misulgye ǔi tangmyǒn munje" [Problems facing the Chosǒn art world], *Sindonga* 2, no. 6 (June 1932): 41, 44–45. Ironically, Yun was much less averse to the idea of a relationship between Korean painting and *nihonga* than were his successors; in 1932 he endorsed the "scientific," by which he meant a self-conscious incorporation of *nihonga*'s methods of coloration in Korean painting. Ibid., 42.

74. Suh Se-ok, quoted by Kim Sǒn-ju, "Hwadane 'ch'angjak pip'yǒng' nonjaeng" [Art world debates over "creation and criticism"], *Chosun ilbo*, July 18, 1974.

75. Suh Se-ok, interview with the author, January 9, 2007.

76. Suh Se-ok, quoted by Kim Sǒn-ju, "Hwadane 'ch'angjak pip'yǒng' nonjaeng."

77. Yi Chong-sǒk and Yi Ku-yǒl, "Han'guk hwadan ǔi kyebo" [The genealogy of the Korean art world], *Chungang*, June 1976: 189.

78. Oh Kwangsu, "Kukchejǒn ch'ulp'um chakka sǒnjǒng ǔi chǒnmal," 360.

79. Park Yong-sook, interview with the author, October 13, 2008.

80. Kim Yun-su, "Hwadan p'ungt'o ǔi pansǒng: Chakka wa pip'yǒngga ǔi chase" [Reflections on the Korean art world: The attitude of artists and critics], *Ch'angjak kwa pip'yǒng* 9 (Fall 1974): 767–79.

81. The Seoul galleries were Myongdong Gallery, Chosun Gallery, Korean Arts Gallery, Hanhwa Gallery, Jean's Gallery, and Hyundai Gallery.

82. Oh Kwangsu, "12th Annual Invitational Exhibition of Contemporary Artists," 36.

83. Lee Ufan, "Sonzai to mu o koete: Sekine Nobuo-ron" [Beyond being and nothingness: On Sekine Nobuo], *Sansai* 245 (June 1969): 51–53.

84. Lee Ufan, "Ilbon hyǒndae misul ǔi tonghyang" [The direction of contemporary Japanese art], *Space* 4, no. 7 (July 1969): 82.

85. Oh Kwangsu, "The 13th Invitational Exhibition of Modern Artists," *Korea Journal* 9, no. 7 (July 1, 1969): 34.

86. Suga Kishio, in a roundtable discussion with Koshimizu Susumu, Sekine Nobuo, Narita Katsuhiko, Yoshida Katsuro, and Lee Ufan, "Mono ga hiraku atarashii sekai" [The new world opened up by the thing], *Bijutsu techō* 22, no. 324 (February 1970): 54.

87. On the development of antiart, see *Geijutsu to nichijyō: Han geijutsu/han geijutsu* [Art and Japan: Antiart/panart], exhibition catalog (Suita: National Museum of Art, Osaka, 1991); Tōnō Yoshiaki, "Neo Dada et Anti-Art," *Japon des avant gardes, 1910–1970* (Paris: Centre Georges Pompidou, 1986), 328–35; and Reiko Tomii, "Geijutsu on Their Minds: Memorable Words on Anti-Art," in *Art, Anti-Art, Non-Art: Experimentations in the Public Sphere in Postwar Japan, 1950–1970*, exhibition catalog (Los Angeles: Getty Research Institute, 2007), 35–62.

88. See "Hatsugen suru shinjintachi—higeijutsu no chihei kara" [Voices of emerging artists—from the realm of nonart], *Bijutsu techō* 22, no. 324 (February 1970): 12–53.

89. Lee Ufan, cited in "'Che sam ǔi chonjae' p'yohyǒn: Kaeinjǒn yǒn 'nolli ǔi hwaga' Yi U-hwan" [The expression of a "third being": The solo exhibition of the "logical artist" Lee Ufan], *Chosun ilbo*, August 26, 1972.

90. For a detailed history of the Tokyo Biennale in 1970, see Reiko Tomii, "Toward Tokyo Biennale 1970: Shapes of the 'International' in the Age of International Contemporaneity," *Review of Japanese Culture and Society* 23 (December 2011): 191–210.

91. Nakahara Yusuke, cited in Shinohara Uchio, *Zen'ei no michi* [Avant-garde road] (Tokyo: Bijutsu Shuppansha, 1968), 232–36.

92. Lee Ufan, interview with the author, September 16, 2011.

93. Lee Ufan, "Obŭje sasang ŭi chŏngch'ewa kŭ haengbang" [The identity and place of *objet* ideology], *Hongik misul*, 1972: 96.

94. Lee Ufan, *Deai o motomete: Atarashii geijutsu no hajimari ni* [Search for encounter: At the dawn of new art] (Tokyo: Tabata Shoten, 1971), 128.

95. Donald Judd, "Specific Objects," *Arts Yearbook* 8 (1965): 74.

96. Oh Kwangsu, "The 18th National Art Exhibition," *Korea Journal* 9, no. 11 (November 1, 1969): 24–25.

97. Ha Chonghyun, interview with the author, August 13, 2007.

98. Kim In-hwan, "Che 9 hoe sang p'aullo biennale e tanyŏwasŏ" [Upon seeing the Ninth São Paulo Bienal], *Yesul wŏnbo* 11 (1967): 157.

99. Lee Yil suggested the work's title. Ha Chonghyun, interview with the author, August 13, 2007.

100. Oh Kwangsu, "The 13th Invitational Exhibition of Modern Artists," 33.

101. Ha Chonghyun, "Ilbon hwadanŭl tullŏbogo" [Thoughts on the Japanese art world], *Hongdae hakbo*, April 15, 1972.

102. Lee Yil, reprinted in "Ha Chong-hyŏn ŭi 'pihoehwajŏk' hoehwa e taehayŏ" [On Ha Chonghyun's "nonpainterly" paintings], in *Ha Chong-hyun*, exhibition catalog (Seoul: Misoolsarang, 2001), 214.

103. Lee Ufan, "Ilbon hyŏndae misul ŭi tonghyang," 71.

104. Ha Chonghyun, quoted in An Yŏng-sin, "Ha Chong-hyŏn: Attŭrie t'ambang" [A visit to the atelier of Ha Chonghyun], *Hwarang* 28 (Summer 1980): 88.

105. Ha Chonghyun, interview with the author, January 10, 2008.

106. Ha Chonghyun, interview with the author, December 24, 2011.

107. Ha Chonghyun, interview with Kim Chin-yŏp, "Sirhŏm, kŭ yŏngwŏn chagi pujŏng" [Experimentation, forever a refusal of the self], *Misul segye* 153 (August 1997): 51.

108. Ha Chonghyun, ibid.

109. An Yŏng-sin, "Ha Chong-hyŏn: Attŭrie t'ambang," 87.

110. Ha Chonghyun, interview with the author, August 13, 2007.

111. Ha Chonghyun, interview with the author, June 5, 2009. "The paint was too thick to dribble on its own accord."

112. Quoted in "Ha Chong-hyŏn ch'ŏt kaeinjŏn" [Ha Chonghyun's first solo show], *Chosun ilbo*, June 8, 1974.

113. Oh Kwangsu, *Han'guk misul ŭi hyŏnjang* [The current situation of Korean art] (Seoul: Chosŏn ilbosa, 1988), 19; Bang Keun-taek, "Panyeusulsŏ muyesullo, segyemisullo" [From antiart to nonart, to world art], *Ilyo sinmun*, September 10, 1972. On the reception of minimalism in Korea, see also Kim Yisoon, *Han'guk ŭi kŭnhyŏndaemisul* [Modern and contemporary art in Korea] (Seoul: Chohyŏng kyoyuk, 2007), 228, 254.

114. Ha Chonghyun, interview with Kim Chin-yŏp, "Sirhŏm, kŭ yŏngwŏn chagi pujŏng," 51.

115. Ha Chonghyun, quoted in An Yŏng-sin, "Ha Chong-hyŏn: Attŭrie t'ambang," 86.

116. Oh Kwangsu, "Apsŏganŭn misul: Ha Chong-hyŏn" [Progressive art: Ha Chonghyun], *Kk'umim* 10 (July 1978): 74.

117. Ha Chonghyun, "Mulchilsŏng kwa hoehwa ŭi chohwa" [Fusing materiality and painting], *Space* 12, no. 12 (December 1977): 25.

118. Ibid.

119. Ibid. Ha wanted to use only colors that would not "overpower" that of the hemp. Ha Chonghyun, interview with the author, June 5, 2009.

120. Yanagi Muneyoshi, "Chosen no bijutsu" [The art of Chosŏn], in *Chosen to sono geijutsu* [Chosŏn and her arts] (Tokyo: Sobunkaku, 1922), 185 (originally published in the January 1922 issue of *Shinchō* and revised in May of that year). In the English translation of the title, I use "her" to reflect Yanagi's own references to Korea, then known as Chosŏn, as a feminine entity.

121. Ibid., 173–74.

122. Yi Kyungsung, "Han'guk ŭi chŏnt'ongmi wa puk'han ŭi yesul" [The traditional aesthetics of Korea and North Korean arts], *Kukt'o t'ongil* 28 (October 1972): 89.

123. Yoo June-sang, "Kwon Yŏng-u kaeinjŏne puch'yŏ" [On Kwon Young-woo's solo exhibition], preface to *Kwon Young-woo*, exhibition catalog (Seoul: Myongdong Gallery, 1974), unpaginated.

124. For a summary of Korean and Japanese responses to Yanagi's theorization of Korean art, see Yūko Kikuchi, *Japanese Modernisation and Mingei Theory: Cultural Nationalism and Oriental Orientalism* (London and New York: Routledge Curzon, 2004), 137–38.

125. Ch'oe Ha-rim, "Haesŏl: Yu Chong-yŏl ŭi han'guk misulgwane taehayŏ" [Analysis: On Yanagi Muneyoshi's view of Korean art], in Yanagi Muneyoshi, *Han'guk kwa kŭ yesul* [Korea and its arts] (Seoul: Jisiksanupsa, 1974), 259–60.

126. Park Carey, "Pak Sŏ-bo ŭi 1970 nyŏndae 'Myobŏp' kwa chŏnt'ongnon: Yanagi Muneyosi wa Pak Sŏbo sai ŭi chido kŭrigi" [Park Seobo's *Myobŏp* series of the 1970s and a discourse of traditionalism: Charting a map between Yanagi Muneyoshi and Park Seobo], *Han'guk kŭnhyŏndae misul sahak*, 2007: 55.

127. Ha Chonghyun, "Mulchilsŏng kwa hoehwa ŭi chohwa," 25.

128. Ha Chonghyun, "Konggan misul daesang susang kinyŏm kaeinjŏnŭl kannŭn Ha Chong-hyŏn" [The commemorative solo exhibition of Ha Chonghyun, recipient of the *Space* art grand prize], *Chosun ilbo*, November 21, 1975.

THREE: ENCOUNTERING LEE UFAN IN KOREA AND JAPAN

1. Lee Ufan, interview with the author, April 9, 2007.

2. Prominent among this commentary are Park Yong-sook, "Lee U hwanŭn uriaegae issŏsŏ nuguinga?" [Who is Lee Ufan to us?], *Space* 10, no. 9 (September 1975): 46–47; Hong Kai, "Yi U-hwan yaesul ŭi silch'erŭl palk'inda" [Revealing the essence of Lee Ufan's art], *Wŏlgan misul* 6 (September 1994): 210; and Tani Arata, "Lee Ufan no sakuhin sekai: Taishō o koete aru" [The works of Lee Ufan: The presence that transcends objectivity], in *Lee U-fan Ten*, exhibition catalog (Tokyo: Hara Museum ARC, 1991), unpaginated.

3. Lee Ufan, "Tōweina shikaku o motomete" [In search of a clear vision], *Gendai shisō*, November 1973: 24.

4. Lee Ufan, interview with the author, September 16, 2011.

5. Ibid.

6. Ibid.

7. Lee also considered white and gray, but "despite the appealing anonymity" of the former, "it was not sufficient for generating a strong visual effect." Likewise, "gray had possibilities, but I wanted to make a strong impression," by which he meant what he regarded as the need to stress the materiality of the mark. Ibid.

8. Fujieda Teruo, "Akushyon to purosesu" [Action and process], *Bijutsu techō* 25, no. 373 (1973): 250.

9. Ibid.

10. Lee Ufan, interview with the author, April 9, 2007.

11. Jean Ladrière, "Système (Épistémologie)," *Encyclopedia Universalis* (Paris: Encyclopedia Universalis France, 1968), 15: 658. Chiba adds that Lee's use of the term "structure" (*kōzō*) in his 1969 essay "Sekai to kōzō" [World and structure] was extracted from Ladrière's use of the term. Chiba Shigeo, *Gendai bijutsu itsudatsushi: 1945–1985* [A history of deviations in contemporary art: 1945–1985] (Tokyo: Shobunsha, 1989), 145.

12. Minemura Toshiaki, "Tokisomuru kaiga" [The painting becoming unbound], *Bijutsu techō* 29, no. 420 (May 1977): 146.

13. Ibid., 169.

14. As translated by Jin Baek, "From the 'Topos of Nothingness' to the 'Space of Transparency': Kitarō Nishida's Notion of Shintai and Its Influence on Art and Architecture (Part I)," *Philosophy East and West* 58, no. 1 (January 2008): 91.

15. Lee Ufan, "Hitaishōsekai e no jikaku" [Self-enlightenment in the nonobjective world], *Miru* 28 (September 1969): unpaginated.

16. For a summary of the show and its circumstances of production, see Ono Masaharu, "'Torikusu ando bijyon nusumareta me,' ten ni tsuite" [On the exhibition *Tricks and Vision: Stolen Eyes*], *Shizuoka Art and Culture Bulletin* 2 (2001): 69–78.

17. Lee Ufan, interview with Tatehata Akira, November 23, 2000. Cited in Tatehata Akira, "Mono-ha and Japan's Crisis of the Modern," trans. Alfred Birnbaum, *Third Text* 16, no. 3 (September 2002): 227.

18. Lee Ufan, "Ilbon hyŏndae misul ŭi tonghyang" [The direction of contemporary Japanese art], *Space* 4, no. 7 (July 1969): 82.

19. Masaaki Morishita, *The Empty Museum: Western Cultures and the Artistic Field in Modern Japan* (Farnham, U.K., and Burlington, Vt.: Ashgate, 2010), 64.

20. Lee Ufan, interview with the author, April 9, 2007.

21. Lee Ufan, "Kannen sūhai to hyōgen no kiki: Obuje shisō no shōtai to yukue" [The worship of ideas and crises of expression: The identity and place of *objet* ideology], in *Deai o motomete: Atarashii geijutsu no hajimari ni* [Search for encounter: Toward a beginning of new art] (Tokyo: Tabata Shoten, 1971), 23.

22. Ibid.

23. Michel Foucault, *The Order of Things* (New York: Vintage Books, 1973), 147.

24. Moon Yeo-song, "Ilbonsok ŭi han'guk yesurin" [A Korean artist in Japan], *Sedae*, April 1967: 246–47.

25. John Lie, *Zainichi (Koreans in Japan): Diasporic Nationalism and Postcolonial Identity* (Berkeley and London: University of California Press, 2008), 93.

26. Lee Ufan, interview with the author, April 9, 2007.

27. Park Seobo, conversation with the author, October 6, 2008.

28. Yamamoto Takashi, "Symposium," in *Tokyo 62*, exhibition catalog (Tokyo: Tokyo Gallery, 1962), unpaginated. Saito, whose later accomplishments would include mentoring some of postwar Japan's most intriguing artists, including key members of the Mono-ha, had belonged to the Avant Garde Western Painting Research Institute (Avangyarudo yōga kenkyūshō) as had Kim Whanki, Saito's former Nika-kai colleague whose reputation in South Korea was comparable to Saito's in Japan. For Korean participation in the institute and other painting associations in Tokyo, see Kim Byung-ki, "1930 nyŏndae tonggyŏng yuhaksaeng kwa abanggarŭdŭ" [Korean students in Tokyo in the 1930s and the avant-garde], *Gana Art* 7, no. 8 (1994): 170–77.

29. Yi Ku-yŏl, "Chopgo p'aeswoejŏgin palp'yo kigwan" [Narrow and closed exhibition spaces], *Yesulgye*, Fall 1970: 126–27.

30. Lee Ufan, "Jika dōchaku no bigaku" [The aesthetics of self-contradiction], *Satō Garō geppo* 128 (March 1967): 2.

31. As Lee recalls, association president Shin Hong-sik wanted something that "wasn't just of the Mindan or the Ch'ongnyŏn, but a new site where the two could exchange views in a much broader perspective." Lee Ufan, interview with Nakai Yasuyuki, December 18, 2008. *Oral History Archives of Japanese Art*, http://www.oralarthistory.org/archives/lee_u_fan/interview_01.php (accessed December 10, 2009).

32. Ibid.

33. Lee's works in this exhibition were titled *Relatum (In a Certain Situation).* Lee Ufan stated that Tōnō solicited his advice about the selection of works for *Aspects of New Japanese Art*. Lee Ufan, interview with Okyang Chae-Duforge, in *Lee Ufan* (Saint-Etienne: Musée d'Art Moderne, 2005). Two other younger artists, conceptualist Kawaguchi Tatsuo and Tanaka Shintarō, also exhibited works titled *Relatum*.

34. Significant Korean artists based in Japan included Kyoto-based conceptual artist and painter Kwak Duk-jun, and fellow Kansai resident Chung Sang Hwa, himself subsequently known as a tansaekhwa painter. Chung had a solo show at Osaka's Shinanobashi Gallery in 1970, then one of the few galleries in Japan to consciously promote experimental work. Also prominent was Lee's acquaintance Quac Insik. Based in Tokyo since 1937, Quac showed works that ranged from informel-type paintings to perforated metal sheets reminiscent of the works of Lucio Fontana. These latter works were featured in a multipage photo shoot for the July 1969 issue of *Bijutsu techō*. See Quac Insik, "Mono no kotoba o kiku" [Listening to the language of the thing], *Bijutsu techō* 21, no. 314 (July 1969): 45. Also see Minemura Toshiaki, "Aru genten" [Origins], in *Insik Quac Exhibition*, exhibition catalog (Tokyo: Osaka Formes Gallery, 1975), unpaginated.

35. Yoshikata Aso, chief director of the Japan Art Festival, memorandum to Thomas Messer, director of the Guggenheim Museum, May 7, 1970, Guggenheim Museum Library

and Archives, New York. Over twelve hundred artists submitted works in a nationwide search. Twenty-nine artists were initially chosen, and four additional artists (Matsuzawa Yukata, Takamatsu Jirō, Narita Katsuhiko, and Nagasawa Hidetoshi) were chosen at the discretion of the selection committee. See Joan Kee, "Points, Lines, Encounters: The World according to Lee Ufan," *Oxford Art Journal* 31, no. 3 (October 2008): 412.

36. Kee, "Points, Lines, Encounters," 412.

37. Haryū Ichirō, "Gendai bijutsu no yushutsu kanōka" [Is the export of contemporary art possible?], *Asahi Journal* 12, no. 29 (July 19, 1970): 49.

38. Lee Ufan, "Overcoming the Modern," in *The Art of Encounter*, trans. Stanley N. Anderson (London: Lisson Gallery, 2004), 193. The text was originally written in 1971.

39. The other major venue for avant-garde, blue-chip art was the Minami Gallery. Owned by Shimizu Kusuo, who founded it in 1952, the Minami Gallery featured established or otherwise prominent members of the European and U.S. art worlds. Its 1973 lineup presented the works of Louise Nevelson and Isamu Noguchi. See *Shimizu Kusuo to Minami Garō* [Shimizu Kusuo and the Minami Gallery] (Tokyo: Shimizu Kuso to Minami Garō Kankōkai, 1985).

40. Even though Lee was an ad hoc addition, he, along with fellow Japan expatriate Quac Insik, was selected to be part of the Korean delegation to the Tenth São Paulo Bienal in 1969. "Sangp'aullo piennale ch'ulp'umjak kyŏljŏng" (Selection of entries for the São Paulo Bienal), *Tonga ilbo*, May 1, 1969.

41. Shim Moon-seup, interview with Park Yong-sook, "1970 nyŏndae ŭi hyŏndae misul," [Contemporary art of the 1970s], in *Sim Mun-sŏp: Hyŏnjŏnesŏ chesiro* [Shim Moon-seup: From *Opening Up* to *Presentation*] (Seoul: Hakgojae, 2008), 273. The interview originally took place in 1979.

42. Lee's other nominations included Lee Kun-yong, Lee Dong Youb, and Heu Hwang. Of these, only Shim and Lee Kun-yong were chosen by the final selection committee of the Paris Biennale to participate in the exhibition. Shim was also nominated as a Korean delegate for the 1971 Paris Biennale.

43. Park Yong-sook, "Hyŏndae misul e taehan ihae" [Understanding contemporary art], *Kyegan misul* 12, no. 43 (Fall 1987): 123–24.

44. Park Seobo, "Yi U-hwan e kwanhan il" [About Lee Ufan]; also included were essays by Kim Chong-hak (a painter, and a former classmate of Lee's at Seoul National University), critic Park Yong-sook, and Lee Ufan, whose essay "Mannam ŭi hyŏnsanghakchŏk sogae" [A phenomenological introduction to encounter] was translated from Japanese into Korean. The original essay was published in Lee Ufan's *Deai o motomete*. Park Yong-sook, "Hyŏndae misule taehan ihae," 123–24.

45. Lee Yil, "'Chŏm' kwa 'sŏn' i ŭimihanŭn kŏt" [What the point and the line mean], in *Yi U-hwan*, exhibition catalog (Seoul: Hyundai Gallery, 1978), unpaginated.

46. The artist Chang Sukwon claimed that there was a "substantial lessening" of interest in the so-called Lee Ufan boom, which allegedly peaked after the September 1975 feature in *Space*. Chang Sukwon, in conversation with Park Seobo, "Chungsŏng kujo wa nolli ŭi chongmal" [A neutral structure and the end of logic], *Space* 13, no. 2 (February 1978): 8.

47. "Ilbonsŏ hwalgi ttwinŭn uri chŏnwi chakkadŭl" [Avant-garde Korean artists active in Japan], *Chosun ilbo*, April 11, 1972. Lee is still a citizen of South Korea. Interestingly

enough, many of his younger Mono-ha colleagues, including Enokura Kōji, Koshimizu Susumu, and Yoshida Katsuro, were Japanese delegates to the same biennale.

48. Nam Kwan, "A, pamŭl tto saewŏtkuna" [Ah, another all-nighter], *Chungang*, April 1971: 203.

49. Lee Ufan, "T'umyŏnghan sigagŭl ch'ajasŏ" [In search of transparent vision], *Space* 13, no. 9 (September 1978): 45. This statement was particularly aimed at Korean readers. The feature in *Space* was nominally based on "Tōmeina sigaku motomete nōtō (1961–1977) yori" [In search of transparent vision, notes from 1961–1977], *Bijutsu techō* 29, no. 420 (May 1977): 170–73. However, the statement expressing Lee's feelings of alienation as a Korean was not included in the text published in *Bijutsu techō*.

50. Lee Ufan, "Han'guk hyŏndae misul ŭi munjechŏm" [The problems of Korean contemporary art], *Kyegan misul* 2, no. 2 (Summer 1977): 147.

51. Lee Ufan, "P'yohyŏn ŭi sŏngnibŭl murŭmyŏ" [On questioning the formation of expression], in *Yŏbaek ŭi yaesul* [Art of the void], trans. Kim Choon-mie (Seoul: Hyŏndae munhak, 2002), 8–9. The preface to this collection of writings was specially written to commemorate the book's Korean translation. Lee's use of the word "traitor" may have been in reference to Hong Kai's 1994 article in which Hong speaks of his "feeling betrayed" by what he saw as Lee's beholdenness to Western cultural paradigms. Hong Kai, "Yi U-hwan yaesul ŭi silch'erŭl palk'inda," 208.

52. Lee Ufan, "Hitaishōsekai e no jikaku."

53. Lee Ufan, in roundtable discussion with Koshimizu Susumu, Sekine Nobuo, Narita Katsuhiko, Yoshida Katsuro, and Suga Kishio, "Mono'ga hiraku atarashii sekai" [The new world opened up by the object], *Bijutsu techō* 22, no. 324 (February 1970): 53.

54. Ibid., 52.

55. First published in 1977, *The Age of Uncertainty* was translated into Japanese by the economist Tsuru Shigeto in 1978 (Tokyo: Tibīesu Buritanika, 1978). A key proponent of the idea that economics could never be separated from politics, Galbraith argued that the enormous expenditures incurred by the Vietnam War and the concurrent arms race with the Soviet Union were central to the deep economic woes suffered by the United States, and the world generally, during the 1970s.

56. Recounted by Tono Yoshiaki, "Japan," *Artforum* 5, no. 5 (January 1967): 53. The original wording was "Down with AMPO" and "Down with AMFO."

57. Lee Ufan, interview with the author, April 9, 2007.

58. Lee Ufan, in conversation with Takamatsu Jirō, "Burankusi, Poloku, minimaru ato" [Brancusi, Pollock, minimal art], *Bijutsu techō* 25, no. 317 (September 1973): 206.

59. Lee Ufan, interview with Nakai Yasuyuki, December 18, 2008, *Oral History Archives of Japanese Art*, http://www.oralarthistory.org/archives/lee_u_fan/interview_02.php (accessed October 29, 2011).

60. Lee Ufan, "Han'guk hyŏndae misul ŭi munjechŏm," 148.

61. The only real difference between *washi* and *hanji* is in their methods of production, which result in differently oriented fibers; in *washi* the fibers only run in one direction, whereas in *hanji* the fibers run in all directions.

62. Lee Ufan, "Kankoku gendai bijutsu no haikei" [The background of Korean contemporary art], *Gendai no me* 165 (August 1968): 4. The critic Jeong Biong Kwan also

observed the possibility of this connection, noting both the former student–teacher connection and the amicable relationship between the two. Jeung Biong Kwan, "Hyŏndae misul kwa uyŏn ŭi pŏbch'ik" [Contemporary art and the principle of coincidence], *Kyegan misul* 2, no. 7 (1978): 164. Suh claims that Lee was inspired to address the point and line after seeing his work, a contention Lee denies. Suh Se-ok, interview with the author, January 7, 2009; and Lee Ufan, interview with the author, April 9, 2007.

63. Lee Ufan, cited in Lee Yil, "'Chŏm' kwa 'sŏn' i ŭimihanŭn kŏt"; the quotation was taken from Lee's interview with Nakahara Yusuke, published in the February 1978 issue of *Mizue*.

64. Lee Ufan, interview with the author, April 9, 2007.

65. Lee Ufan, interview with Nakai Yasuyuki, December 19, 2008, *Oral History Archives of Japanese Art*, http://www.oralarthistory.org/archives/lee_u_fan/interview_02.php (accessed October 29, 2011).

66. Alexandra Munroe, "Stand Still a Moment," in *Lee Ufan: Marking Infinity*, exhibition catalog (New York: Solomon R. Guggenheim Museum, 2011), 28.

67. Lee Ufan, interview with Oh Kwangsu, "Chŏm kwa sŏni haengwi hanŭn segyesŏng" [A sense of the world as enacted by the point and the line], *Space* 13, no. 9 (May 1978): 40.

68. Hikosaka Naoyoshi, "Ri U hwan hyŏron: 'Hyŏgen' no naitek ikikini chyokumen suru huashizumu" [A critique of Lee Ufan: The fascism confronted by the internal crisis of "expression"], *Dezain hihyō* 10 (November 1970). *Dezain hihyō* was published by the publishing house Fudosha in collaboration with art critic Ichirō Haryū, architectural critic Noboru Kawazoe, design critic Shinya Izumi, architect Hiroshi Hara, and artist Kiyoshi Awazu. Covering a wide array of subjects, including visual art and architecture, the magazine was particularly known for its critical stance against the 1970 World's Fair (Expo) at Osaka, which eventually led to the discontinuation of the magazine.

69. Lee Ufan, interview with the author, September 16, 2011.

70. Barthes traveled to Japan at the invitation of Maurice Pinguet, then director of the Franco-Japanese Institute in Tokyo. While there he gave a lecture titled "The Structural Analysis of Narrative." Barthes would travel to Japan three times between 1966 and 1967, during which time he worked on his well-known book *Empire of Signs*. Louis-Jean Calvet, *Roland Barthes: A Biography*, trans. Sarah Wykes (Bloomington: Indiana University Press, 1994), 153.

71. Roland Barthes, "The Death of the Author," in *Image Music Text*, trans. Stephen Heath (New York: Hill and Wang, 1977), 142.

72. Ibid., 143.

73. Ibid., 147.

74. Lee Ufan, interview with the author, September 16, 2011.

75. Kang Taehi, "Yi U hwan ŭi sinch'e" [The body of Lee Ufan], *Hyŏndae misul nonjip* 10 (March 2000): 107–8.

76. In 1970 Galerie Yvon Lambert staged solo exhibits of Toroni's works on April 21–28 and then on July 1–10. The next show took place the following year, in 1972, well after Lee had left Europe.

77. Lee, "Mugen ni tuite" [On infinity], in *Lee Ufan* (Kamakura: Museum of Modern Art, 2003), 87.

78. Lee prefaced his theory by drawing an explicit connection to the idea of economic production by extensively discussing the rapid increase of Japan's gross national product throughout the 1960s. Lee Ufan, interview with Kim Yong-ik and Moon Beom, *Space* 25, no. 9 (September 1990): 88–89.

79. Kim Yun-su, "Chŏnsihoe ribyu" [Exhibition review], *Kyegan misul* 2, no. 7 (July 1978): 197.

FOUR: READING PARK SEOBO'S *ÉCRITURE* IN AUTHORITARIAN KOREA

1. Joseph Love, "The Roots of Korea's Avant-Garde Art," *Art International* 19, no. 6 (June 15, 1975): 31.

2. Park Seobo, "'Myobŏpchŏn kajin sirhŏm chakka Pak Sŏ-bo kyosu" [Professor Park Seobo, the experimental artist, and his exhibition of the *Myobŏp* works], *Toksŏ sinmun*, October 21, 1973.

3. Bang Keun-taek, "Pak Sŏ-bo ŭi myobŏpiran!" [What Park Seobo's *Myobŏp* is!], *Simunhak* 5, no. 12 (December 1976): 116.

4. The dating of the first *Myobŏp* works has stirred some controversy in Korean art historical circles, as none of the works made prior to 1972 was publicly exhibited during that time, highly unusual for an artist renowned for his flamboyant self-promotion and with a demonstrated record of showing his latest works as soon as they were made. Park stated that he had decided not to exhibit the earlier, pre-1972 works because he felt they were "not fit for public display. I did show them at the Tongin Gallery [in Seoul in 1976], as the ceilings were quite low and I thought these earlier, smaller works would fit well within that limited space." Park Seobo, interview with the author, August 23, 2010.

5. Park Seobo, interview with the author, October 6, 2008; Okyang Chae-Duporge, "Chronology," in *Lee Ufan: The Search for Encounter*, exhibition catalog (Seoul: Samsung Museum of Modern Art, 2003). On KCIA suspicion of *zainichi*, see Namhee Lee, *The Making of Minjung: Democracy and the Politics of Representation in South Korea* (Ithaca, N.Y., and London: Cornell University Press, 2007), 105.

6. For a succinct discussion of this incident, see Yun Pŏm-mo, "Chŏnt'ong ŭi mukchuk'waesŏ minjok ŭi t'ongilmukkaji" [From traditional ink bamboo painting to portraying the people's dance for unity], in *Ungno Lee*, exhibition catalog (Seoul: Gana Art Center, 1994), 21–23, 27–28. Several French artists and critics, including Zao Wou-ki, petitioned for Lee's release. Eventually Lee was released from prison in 1969 for health reasons.

7. Yi Ku-yŏl, "Chwadam: Konggan pip'an" [Discussion: Critical views of *Space*], *Space* 2, no. 11 (November 1967): 12.

8. Kim Swoogeun's own studio had recently merged with the Korean Engineering Consulting Corporation, a firm created by Park's government in 1965 to advise the state on large-scale engineering and urban development projects, funded, incidentally, by foreign capital obtained from Japan. Hyungmin Pai, "Modernism, Development, and the Transformation of Seoul: A Study of the Development of Sae'oon Sang'ga and Yoido," in *Culture and the City in East Asia*, ed. Wonbae Kim, Clyde Michael Douglass, Sang-Chuel Choe, and Kong Chong Ho (Oxford: Oxford University Press, 1997), 120.

9. Kim Hong-bae, "Konggan'i t'aeŏnan naeryŏk" [The origins of *Space*], in *Tangsini yumyŏnghan kŏnch'ukka Kim Su-gŭnimnikka?* [Are you the famous architect Kim Swoogeun?], ed. Kim Swoogeun Culture Foundation (Seoul: Space, 2006), 206.

10. Kim Yong-Kwon, "'*Konggan*' Makes Its Debut as Architectural Monthly," *Korea Journal* 7, no. 1 (January 1967): 37. However, the magazine was financially troubled, and Kim Swoogeun considered shutting it down in 1970. Oh Kwangsu, "Na ŭi *Konggan* p'yŏnjip chang sijŏl" [My days as *Space* editor in chief], *Space* 10, no. 9 (September 1975): 5.

11. Alain Delissen, "The Aesthetic Pasts of Space (1960–1990)," *Korean Studies* 25, no. 2 (2002): 253–54.

12. Kim Chi-ha, *Hin kŭnŭl ŭi kil* [The path of white clouds] (Seoul: Hakgojae, 2003), 2: 158.

13. *Ka* is a placeholder that in English might translate to *A*, the first letter of the alphabet.

14. O Yŏng-a, interview with the author, December 28, 2011.

15. O studied the works of David Alfaro Siqueiros, whose work he happened to see in a downtown Seoul café, as an example of how to resuscitate tradition as a force with contemporary relevance. Oh Kyung-hwan, telephone conversation with the author, May 3, 2007; Yi Sŏk-u, "Saengmyŏng ŭi him kwa maegŭl hyŏngsangŭro ttŏnaen sŏn'guja" [A pioneer that presented the force and pulse of life through form], *Misul segye* 40 (January 1988): 130.

16. Kim Chi-ha, *Hin kŭnŭl ŭi kil*, 158.

17. Bang, however, seems not to have been found guilty; no sentence followed the report of his alleged violation. Ch'oe Tae-hyŏn, "Pukgwoe ŭi taejungdongwŏn kongjak chŏnsul kwa ie kwallyŏn toen pan'gukkasabŏm chaep'an'gyŏl kwa punsŏk koch'al" [An analytic investigation of the operation tactics of North Korea to co-opt the public and the related sentencing of antistate criminals], *Kŏmch'al* 44 (December 1971): 54.

18. Kim Sang-hyun, "Ch'immukŭl kangyohanŭn sidae ŭi ŭngdap" [A response to an age that enforces silence], *Tari*, January 1972: 12. A month after Kim's article, the editor, the publisher, and a writer for *Tari* were arrested and tried for violating the Anti-Communist Law. The real grounds of scrutiny was the magazine's support of leading opposition politician Kim Dae-jung. *Wŏlgan Tari: Taehwa ŭi kagyo* [The monthly journal *Tari*: A bridge of dialogue] (Seoul: Pŏmusa, 2004), 16–49.

19. Kim Sung-hwan, quoted in Son Sang-ik, *Han'guk manhwa t'ongsa ha: 1945 nyŏn ihu* [A comprehensive history of cartoons in Korea: Post-1945] (Seoul: Sigongsa, 1998), 142. Born in 1932 and largely self-taught, Kim Sung-hwan is the author of *Kobau*, the longest-running four-panel cartoon in Korean history, which appeared in newspapers from 1950 to 2000.

20. Sung Neung-kyung, interview with the author, December 15, 2011.

21. Sung Neung-kyung, interview with the author, December 15, 2011. For a discussion of S.T. and its history, see Kang Tae-hi, "1970 nyŏndae ŭi haengwi misul ibent'ŭ" [The performance art events of the 1970s], *Hyŏndaemisulsa yŏn'gu* 13 (2001): 7–33.

22. Sung Neung-kyung, interview with the author, December 15, 2011.

23. Ibid.

24. Sung Neung-kyung, "Hyŏnjang" [The scene], artist's statement dated August 8, 1986, published in *Tangsinŭn na ŭi t'aeyang: Tongsidae han'guk misurŭl wihan sŏngch'aljŏk not'ŭ* [You are my sunshine: Notes of reflection for a contemporary Korean art], exhibition catalog (Seoul: Total Museum of Art, 2004), 267.

25. Sung Neung-kyung, interview with the author, December 15, 2011.

26. Choi Tae-shin, interview with the artist, June 15, 2010.

27. Ibid.

28. Ibid.

29. Kim Bok-young, *Nun kwa chŏngsin: Han'guk hyŏndae misul iron* [Eye and mind: A theory of contemporary Korean art] (Seoul: Hangil Art, 2006), 369.

30. Ibid.

31. Ibid., 372–73.

32. Ibid., 370.

33. Park Seobo, "Yi U-hwan kwa ŭi mannam" [My encounter with Lee Ufan], *Hwarang* 12, no. 3 (Fall 1984): 33.

34. Park Seobo, interview with the author, August 23, 2010.

35. Park Seobo, in conversation with Maeda Josaku, "Kankoku no bijutsu" [Korean art], *Bijutsu techō* 25, no. 370 (August 1973): 159.

36. Joseph Love, "Travel Diary of the Hand—The Paintings of Park Seobo," in *Travel Diary of the Hand—The Paintings of Park Seobo*, exhibition catalog (Seoul: Tongin Gallery, 1976), unpaginated.

37. Agnes Martin, "The Untroubled Mind," in *Agnes Martin*, exhibition catalog (Philadelphia: Institute of Contemporary Art, 1973), 17. The original remarks were delivered as part of a talk given at Cornell University in 1972.

38. Park Seobo, interview with the author, August 23, 2010.

39. Love, "Travel Diary of the Hand—The Paintings of Park Seobo."

40. Park Seobo, quoted in "Hyŏnjae hwaga chisangjŏn" [Virtual shows of today's artists], *Chugan Han'guk* 443 (March 25, 1973): 15.

41. The exact origins of the national documentary paintings project are not known, but some commentators speculate that the project was inspired by the commemorative paintings made during the Korean War at the state's behest, and even by those paintings commissioned by the Japanese imperial government during what was then referred to as the "Fifteen Year War," or "sacred war" (the Sino–Japanese War and World War II) from 1930 to 1945. Kim Myŏng-hwan, "3 kongttae chejak'han minjok kirok'wa changgoesŏ mudŏgiro ssŏkko itta" [Piles of national documentary paintings made during the Third Republic languish in warehouse], *Chugan Chosŏn* 1119 (September 23, 1990): 70.

42. Ministry of Culture and Information, "Minjok kirok'wa (kyŏngjep'yŏn) kuip alsŏn mit hwaktae chejak kyehoek kungmuhoe ŭi puŭi" [State Council meeting agenda regarding the procurement and the plan for expanded production of national documentary paintings (economic edition)], April 1, 1974, unpaginated. National Archives of Korea. Of note is the exclusion of ink painting from the project, a slight that Lee Jong-sang, one of the few ink painters to participate in the project, attributes to the state's narrow understanding of realistic representation but that could also be read as further indication of ink painting's waning status as a medium for contemporary art. Pak Hye-sŏng, "1960–1970 nyŏndae minjok kirok'wa yŏn'gu" [A study of national documentary paintings in the 1960s and '70s] (M.A. thesis, Seoul National University, 2002), 58.

43. One less-prominent artist invited to participate was Yun Hyongkeun, who in 1967 became involved with the national documentary paintings project even though his professional credentials at the time were much less illustrious than those of other artists tapped to participate. Yun's widow Kim Yŏng-suk claims that Yun was invited to participate after Kim Jong-pil heard of Yun's works. Interview with the author, January 3, 2009.

44. The project distributed about 10 million won in artist's fees (which came out to about 50,000 won per artist) and materials, which were imported from Japan. Bang Keun-taek, "Misul haengjŏng ŭi nanmaeksang," 214.

45. "Minjok kirok'wa chejak chŏnsi" [Production and exhibition of national documentary paintings], *Munye chinhŭng* 1, no. 1 (May 1974): 36. *Munye chinhŭng* was the official publication of the state-run Korea Culture and Arts Foundation (Han'guk munhwa yesul chinhŭngwŏn).

46. Ministry of Culture and Information, "Minjok kirok'wa (kyŏngjep'yŏn) kuip alsŏn mit hwaktae chejak kyuhoek kungmuhoe ŭi puŭi," unpaginated. In 1974 the average price had reached about 1.2 million won per painting. *Han'guk munhwa yesul chinhŭngwŏn 15 nyŏnsa* [Fifteen years of the Korea Culture and Arts Foundation] (Seoul: Korea Culture and Arts Foundation, 1988), 199.

47. See *Munye chinhŭng* 2, no. 6 (June 1975): 11.

48. Park Chung-hee, "Kyŏngnyŏsa" [Congratulatory words], in *Minjok kirok'wajŏn* [Exhibition of national documentary paintings], exhibition catalog (Seoul: Kyŏngbok Palace Museum, 1967), unpaginated.

49. Kang Sŏn-hak, "Sahoejŏk saengsanŭrosŏ ŭi misul: 70 nyŏndae kirok'wa wa 80 nyŏndae minjung misul" [Art as social production: The documentary paintings of the seventies and Minjung art of the eighties], in *Hyŏndae misul ŭi kujo: Hwanwŏn kwa hwaksan* [The structure of contemporary art: Reduction and expansion], ed. Yi Il kyosu hwagap kinyŏm munjip kanhaengwiwŏnhoe (Seoul: Editions API, 1992), 76.

50. Kim Jeong-heon, "30 dae chakka ŭi taehwa" [Conversation with artists in their thirties], *Misul kwa saenghwal* 1, no. 6 (June 1977): 28.

51. Chŏng Ch'an-sŭng, "Ch'oegŭn ŭi chŏnwi misul kwa uridŭl" [Recent avant-garde art and us], *Space* 10, no. 3 (March 1975): 65.

52. "Minjok kirok'warŭl chejak" [Producing heritage paintings], *Chosun ilbo*, March 15, 1973.

53. As reported in "Kyŏngje kaebal sŏngkwarŭl kirok" [Commemorating the fruits of economic development], *Maeil kyŏngje*, March 8, 1973. The committee was chaired by Yi Pyŏng-do, a leading nationalist historian.

54. Park Seobo, interview with the author, August 23, 2010.

55. As reported on the front page of the *Kyŏnghyang sinmun*, March 14, 1974.

56. Ministry of Culture and Information, "Insa malssŭm" [Welcome remarks], in *Minjok kirok'wa (kyŏngjep'yŏn)* [National documentary paintings (economic edition)], exhibition catalog (Seoul: Kwangmyŏng, 1973), unpaginated.

57. Ministry of Culture and Information, "Minjok kirok'wa (kyŏngjep'yŏn) kuip alsŏn mit hwaktae chejak kyuhoek kungmuhoe ŭi puŭi," unpaginated.

58. Alice Amsden, *Asia's Next Giant: South Korea and Late Industrialization* (New York: Oxford University Press, 1989), 118.

59. Figures quoted in Han'guk chosŏnkongŏphyŏp'oe, ed., *Han'guk ŭi chosŏnsanŏp: Sŏngjang kwa kwaje* [The Korean shipbuilding industry: Growth and tasks] (Seoul: Han'guk chosŏnkongŏphyŏp'oe, 2005), 422.

60. On labor unrest in the 1970s South Korea in English, see Jang Jip Choi's classic study *Labor and the Authoritarian State: Labor Unions in South Korean Manufacturing Industries, 1961–1980* (Honolulu: University of Hawaii Press, 1990), and Chun Soonok, *They Are Not Machines: Korean Women Workers and Their Fight for Democratic Trade Unionism in the 1970s* (Burlington, Vt.: Ashgate, 2003).

61. "Sŏltŭn'nyŏk ŏmnŭn minjok kirok'wa" [Unconvincing national documentary paintings], *Chosun ilbo*, December 1, 1976. Nineteen artists, including Park Seobo, showed their works in this exhibition, which took place November 27–December 12, 1976.

62. "Minjok ŭi ŏrŭl toesaeginŭn minjok kirok'wa chŏnsihoe" [Recalling the spirit of the nation: The exhibition of national documentary paintings], *Korea Life* 2, no. 12 (August 1967): unpaginated.

63. Park Seobo, interview with the author, October 14, 2008.

64. Yŏm Mu-ung, "Kyŏnsu samsimnyŏn" [Thirty years of following a superior], in *Minjok ŭi kil, yesul ŭi kil* [The path of the people, the path of art], ed. Kim Yun-su kyosu chŏngnyŏn kinyŏm kihoek kanhaeng wiwŏnhoe (Seoul: Ch'angjak kwa pip'yŏng, 2001), 336. Kim was subsequently sentenced to two years' imprisonment with one year's probation.

65. Yi Ka-rim, "Kisul ŭi yŏngdo" [The zero of writing], *Yesulgye* 2, no. 4 (Fall 1970): 188–202. Structuralism was first introduced in Korea in the July 1968 issue of the political opinion journal *Sasanggye*. Kim Chun-o, "Kujojuŭi pipy'ŏng ŭi suyongyangsang" [The reception of structuralism], *Munhak kwa pipy'ŏng* 1, no. 2 (Summer 1987): 223. Barthes's other works were made available in Korean translation in the September and October 1968 issues of *Sasanggye*. "The Structuralist Activity" (1963) and "Critique and Truth" (1966) were translated by Kim Kwang-nam under the pseudonym Kim Hyŏn, and Kim Hwa-yŏng translated "Language as Criticism," originally written in 1963.

66. Roland Barthes, *Writing Degree Zero*, trans. Annette Lavers and Colin Smith, (New York: Hill and Wang, 1968), 14, 16.

67. Bang Keun-taek, "Hŏgu wa muŭimi: Uri chŏnwimisul ŭi pip'yŏng kwa silche" [Fiction and nonsense: Critique and reality of our avant-garde], *Space* 9, no. 9 (September 1974): 26.

68. Park Seobo, "Hyŏndae misul ŭi wigi" [The crisis of contemporary art], *Wŏlgan chungang* 56 (November 1972): 342.

69. Park Seobo, "Tansang not'ŭ" [Random notes], *Space* 12, no. 11 (November 1977): 46.

70. Roland Barthes, "The Wisdom of Art," in *Cy Twombly: Paintings and Drawings, 1954–1979*, exhibition catalog (New York: Whitney Museum of American Art, 1979), 9.

71. Rosalind Krauss, "Cy's Up," *Artforum* 33, no. 1 (September 1994): 118. Krauss takes this quotation from Barthes, *The Responsibility of Forms*, trans. Richard Howard (Berkeley: University of California Press, 1985), 187.

72. Joseph Love, "Two Korean Exhibitions, Korean White and Japanese Blue," *Japan Times*, May 18, 1975.

73. Park Seobo, "'Myobŏpchŏn kajin sirhŏm chakka Pak Sŏ-bo kyosu" [Professor Park Seobo, the experimental artist, and his exhibition of *Myobŏp* works], *Toksŏ sinmun*, October 21, 1973.

74. Nakahara Yusuke, "Park Seobo no kaiga" [The paintings of Park Seobo], in *Park Seobo,* exhibition catalog (Tokyo: Tokyo Gallery, 1978), unpaginated.

FIVE: TANSAEKHWA AND THE IDEALIZATION OF ASIAN ART

1. Lee Yil, "'Han'guk 5 in ŭi chakka' Tonggyŏngjŏn" [*Five Korean Artists* show in Tokyo], *Sŏul p'yŏngnon,* May 29, 1975: 50.

2. Doi Miho, gallery manager of the Tokyo Gallery, e-mail to the author, February 5, 2007.

3. Yamamoto Takashi's son, Yamamoto Hozu, the current director of the Tokyo Gallery, recalls that although Lee Ufan helped bring the show together, most notably in translating Lee Yil's catalog essay from Korean to Japanese, the actual conceptualization and production of *Five Korean Artists, Five Kinds of White* was done by his father and Nakahara Yusuke. Doi Miho, manager of the Tokyo Gallery, e-mail to the author, February 5, 2007.

4. Lee Yil, "'Han'guk 5 in ŭi chakka' Tonggyŏngjŏn," 50.

5. Lee Yil, "Paeksaegŭn saenggakhanda" [The color white thinks], in *5 tsu no hinsaeku* [Five kinds of white], exhibition catalog (Tokyo: Tokyo Gallery, 1975), unpaginated.

6. Nam Kwan, "Nanŭn wae p'arirŭl tt'ŏnanna?" [Why did I leave Paris?], *Chungang,* December 1971, 357, 356.

7. Oh Kwangsu, "Three Exhibitions," *Korea Journal* 13, no. 10 (October 1973): 59.

8. Lee Kun-yong, "Chŏnwi hwaltong" [Avant-garde activities], *Hwarang* 19 (Spring 1978): 48.

9. Nakahara Yusuke, "Five Korean Artists, Five [Kinds of] White," in *5 tsu no hinsaeku,* unpaginated.

10. Suh Seung-won notes that the Japanese title still used the characters for *paeksaek.* Interview with Kim Chi-ye and Sim Chi-ŏn, in Young-Paik Chun, *22 myŏng ŭi yesulga, sidae wa sot'onghada: 1970 nyŏndae ihu han'guk hyŏndaemisul ŭi chahwasang* [22 artists, communicating with their time: A portrait of contemporary Korean art in the 1970s and after] (Seoul: KungRee, 2010), 114.

11. Kim Yun-su, *Han'guk hyŏndae hoehwasa* [History of modern Korean painting] (Seoul: Ch'unch'u mungo, 1975).

12. Kim Yun-su, "Misul ŭi sahoejŏk kinŭng" [The social function of art], *Taehwa* 81 (September 1977): 274.

13. Kim Yun-su, "Ilbon hyŏndae misurŭl ŏttŏk'e pol kŏsinga" [How are we to view contemporary Japanese art?], *Kyegan misul* 20 (Winter 1981): 162.

14. Won Kap-hui, "Han'guk kŭndae misul ŭi chwap'yo" [The coordinates of modern Korean art], *Ilbon yŏn'gu* 20 (January 1975): 66.

15. Park Carey, "1970 nyŏndae han'guk monok'ŭrom ŭi kiwon kwa chŏnt'ongsŏng" [The origins and traditionalism of 1970s tansaekhwa], *Misulsa nondan* 15 (2002): 295–323.

16. *Document 40: Tokyo Gallery* (Tokyo: Tokyo Gallery, 1990), unpaginated.

17. For a summary of Korean and Japanese responses to Yanagi's theorization of Korean art, see Yūko Kikuchi, *Japanese Modernisation and Mingei Theory: Cultural Nationalism and Oriental Orientalism* (London and New York: Routledge Curzon, 2004), 137–38.

18. Park Yong-sook, "Singminji sidae ŭi mihak pip'an" [A critique of colonial-era aesthetics], *Tari* 3, no. 3 (May 1972): 116–18.

19. Lee Yil, "Segye mudae sok ŭi han'guk misul" [Korean art on the world stage], *Hyŏndae misul ŭi kwyejŏk* [The locus of Korean art] (Seoul: Tonghwa, 1974), 221.

20. Lee Yil, "Yesul hyŏngt'aenon: P'osiyong ŭi 'hyŏngt'ae ŭi saengmyŏng' ŭi chungsimŭro" [A theory of artistic form based on Focillon's *Vie des formes*], *Hongdae nonch'ong* 3 (1971): 37–38.

21. Lee Yil, "Uri nara misul ŭi tonghyang" [The direction of Korean art], *Ch'angjak kwa pip'yŏng* 2, no. 1 (Spring 1967): 60–68.

22. Lee Yil, "Yesul hyŏngt'aenon: P'osiyong ŭi 'Hyŏngt'ae ŭi saengmyŏng' ŭl chungsimŭro," 39, quoting Henri Focillon, *Vie des formes* (Paris: Librairie Ernest Leroux, 1934), 7.

23. Lee Yil, "Yesul hyŏngt'aenon: P'osiyong ŭi 'Hyŏngt'ae ŭi saengmyŏng' ŭl chungsimŭro," 40, quoting Focillon, *Vie des formes*.

24. Lee Yil, "Paeksaegŭn saenggakhanda," unpaginated.

25. For an account of Lee's years in Paris from 1957 to 1965 from Lee's own recollections, see Yi Chu-hŏn, "Han'guk modŏnijŭm pip'yŏng ŭi sŏn'gu" [A pioneer in the critique of Korean modernism], *Gana Art* 34 (November–December 1993): 122–24.

26. Yves Klein, "The Evolution of Art towards the Immaterial," republished in *Yves Klein: Air Architecture*, ed. Peter Noever and Francois Perrin (Ostfildern and Los Angeles: Hatje Cantz and MAK Center for Art and Architecture, 2004), 40.

27. Lee Yil, "'Han'guk 5 in ŭi chakka' Tonggyŏngjŏn," 51.

28. Lee Yil, "Segyesok ŭi han'guk hyŏndae misul" [Korean contemporary art in the world], *Kwangjang*, November–December 1975: 36, 37.

29. Lee Yil, "Hoehwa ŭi saeroun pusang kwa kisangdo '76 nyŏn" [The new rise of painting and an artistic weather map for 1976], *Space* 11, no. 9 (September 1976): 43.

30. Ibid.

31. Ibid., 43, 44.

32. Suenaga Terukazu praised the "high quality" of the works shown. "Tenpyō" [Reviews], *Bijutsu techō* 27, no. 397 (August 1975): 253. It was reported that the planning process for *Korea: Facet of Contemporary Art* took eighteen months. "Ilsŏ 'han'guk hyŏndae misul' pum" [A boom in "contemporary Korean art" in Japan], *Chosun ilbo*, June 18, 1977.

33. Nineteen artists showed works in *Korea: Facet of Contemporary Art*. Those whose works were associated with tansaekhwa were Kwon Young-woo, Lee Ufan, Kim Guiline, Park Seobo, Pak Chang-nyŏn, Lee Dong Youb, Yun Hyongkeun, Jin Okseon, and Suh Seung-won. Several other artists presented works or objects that alluded to tansaekhwa, including Lee Kangso, Ch'oe Pyŏng-so, Shim Moon-seup, Kim Yong-ik, and Kim Chin-sŏk. Other artists in the show were sculptors Quac Insik and Kim Ku-lim and painters Kim Tschang-yeul, Lee Sang Nam, and Yi Sŭng-jo.

34. Pak Chang-nyŏn, "Han'guk misul tanmyŏnjŏn ŭi kŭ sŏngkwarŭl arabonda" [Unpacking the achievements of the exhibition *Korea: Facet of Contemporary Art*], *Misul kwa saenghwal*, May 1979: 129.

35. The Muramatsu Gallery hosted a small group show of eight artists, and the Kaneko Gallery in the central Nihonbashi area organized a solo show of the works of Kim Ku-lim. The Tokyo Gallery held a small retrospective of the works of Kim Whanki, who had

died three years earlier and whom gallery owner Yamamoto Takashi would describe as "Korea's best artist." Yamamoto Takashi, quoted in "Int'ŏbyu" [Interview], *Chungang ilbo*, March 5, 1979.

36. Nakahara Yusuke, "Kankoku no gendai bijutsu no dōkō" [The direction of Korean contemporary art], *Asahi Journal*, July 1, 1977: 73.

37. Suh Sung-rok, "'Ekkol tŭ sŏul' 20 nyŏn ŭi palchach'wi" [The vestiges of twenty years of the École de Seoul] in *Ekkol tŭ sŏul 20 nyŏn, monok'ŭrom 20 nyŏn* [Twenty years of the École de Seoul, 20 years of monochromes], exhibition catalog (Seoul: Kwanhun at'ŭ tijain yŏnguso, 1995), unpaginated.

38. Ogawa Masataka, "Shizukesano nakani mosaku no shisei" [The attitude of a search within stillness], *Asahi shimbun*, August 23, 1977. The article was translated into Korean as "Konggan kujo ŭi ponjil—kangyŏlhago himch'age chŏksorŭl tchirŭn p'yohyŏn" [The essence of spatial structure—expression that simply and forcefully hits the spot], *Misul kwa saenghwal*, May 1979: 121.

39. Ch'oe No-sŏk, "Han'guk hyŏndae misul ire taegŏ sangnyuk" [The large-scale arrival of contemporary Korean art in Japan], *Kyŏnghyang sinmun*, August 11, 1977.

40. Kim Sŭng-gak, "Han'guk misul tanmyŏnjŏn ŭi kŭ sŏngkwarŭl arabonda" [Unpacking the achievements of the exhibition *Korea: Facet of Contemporary Art*], *Misul kwa saenghwal*, May 1979, 127.

41. Pak Chang-nyŏn, in ibid., 128.

42. Nakahara Yusuke, "Gendai bijutsu e appirusuru ichigun—kankoku gendai bijutsu no danmenten" [A group that appeals to contemporary art—on the exhibition *Korea: Facet of Contemporary Art*], *Bijutsu techō* 29, no. 424 (September 1977): 124.

43. Nakahara Yusuke, untitled foreword to *Kankoku gendai bijutsu no danmenten* [Korea: Facet of Contemporary Art], exhibition catalog (Tokyo: Central Museum of Art, 1977), unpaginated. This preface was dated July 1977.

44. Nakahara Yusuke, "Gendai bijutsu e appirusuru ichigun—kankoku gendai bijutsu no danmenten," 124.

45. Tanaka Tameyoshi, quoted by Lee Yil, "Han'guk hyŏndae misul ŭi tanmyŏnjŏn" [The exhibition *Korea: Facet of Contemporary Art*], *Space* 12, no. 9 (September 1977): 84.

46. Mulk Raj Anand, "Chairman's Welcome Address," *Lalit Kalā Contemporary* 36 (September 1990): 12.

47. Honma Masayoshi, "Shyo" [Introduction], *Gendai sekai bijutsuten: Tō to sei no taiwa* [An exhibition of contemporary world art: A dialogue between East and West], (Tokyo: National Museum of Modern Art, 1969), 6. The English title of the exhibition was *Contemporary Art: Dialogue between the East and the West.*

48. *Document 40: Tokyo Gallery.*

49. Chŏng Ch'an-sŭng, "Ch'oegŭn ŭi chŏnwimisul kwa uridŭl, chwadamhoe" [Recent avant-garde art and us, a roundtable discussion], *Space* 10, no. 3 (March 1975): 63.

50. Segi Shinichi, "Gyakkyōwa yūrini sayō siteiru" [Adversity working advantageously], *Nihon bijutsu* 19, no. 11 (November 1976): 42.

51. Lee Ufan, "Yun Hyong-gun no shigoto" [The works of Yun Hyongkeun], in *Yun Hyongkeun*, exhibition catalog (Tokyo: Muramatsu Gallery, 1976), unpaginated.

52. Yun Hyongkeun, "Chint'ong mannŭng . . . chakp'umi naogikkaji" [A multitude of pains . . . until the work is finished], *Kyŏnghyang sinmun*, February 3, 1977.

53. Park Seobo, "Han'guk misul tanmyŏnjŏn ŭi kŭ sŏngkwarŭl arabonda" [Unpacking the achievements of the exhibition *Korea: Facet of Contemporary Art*], *Misul kwa saenghwal*, May 1979: 128, 129.

54. Park Seobo, "Irŏk'e wasŏ ŏdiro kal kŏsinga?" [Now that we're here, where do we go?], *Han'guk misul* 1, no. 1 (1975): 67.

55. Lee Yil, "Hyŏndae misul kwa onŭl ŭi han'guk misul" [Contemporary art and Korean art today], *Han'guk munhak*, January 1977: 204.

56. Lee Yil, "Sŏyanghwa" [Western painting], *Munye yŏn'gam* (1977): 281.

57. In terms of population growth, Fukuoka was only surpassed by Yokohama and Sapporo. Some of the initiatives in Fukuoka's development campaign were nationally mandated; the extension of the high-speed *shinkansen* trains to Fukuoka in 1975 stemmed directly from the 1969 New Comprehensive National Development Plan. The city initiated the construction of a subway system as well as a number of major structures by architect and Kyūshū native Isozaki Arata.

58. Backed by the ruling Liberal Democratic Party (LDP), Shinto Kazuma was elected in 1972. The city underwent a vigorous series of building projects, in part due to the LDP's efforts to recuperate its former electoral dominance. Andre Sorensen, *The Making of Urban Japan: Cities and Planning from Edo to the Twenty-First Century* (London and New York: Routledge, 2002), 212–13. Also see Kishi Seikō, "Bijutsukanga 'ajia' to deautoki" [When the museum encountered "Asia"], in *Sengo nihon no kokusai bunka kōryū* [International cultural exchange in postwar Japan], ed. Hirano Kenichirō (Tokyo: Keiso Shobo, 2005), 246–47.

59. Yasunaga Koichi, interview with the author, February 15, 2008.

60. Toshihiro Kennoki, "Acknowledgement," in *Asian Artists Exhibition Part I*, exhibition catalog (Fukuoka: Fukuoka Art Museum, 1979), 6.

61. Koike Shinji, "Ajia bijutsuten dai i bu: 'Kindai ajia no bijutsu—Indo, Chukuoku, Nihon' kōsei" [*Asian Art Exhibition Part I*: Organization of "modern Asian art—India, China, Japan"], in *Asian Artists Exhibition Part I*, 11. *Ideals of the East* was published just before the onset of Russo–Japanese War, which erupted over competing claims to the Korean peninsula. The book is notable for its martial language. In one instance, the text refers to Japan's burden of having to defend the Asian self following its victory in the Sino–Japanese War (1894–95). Urs Matthias Zachmann, "Blowing Up a Double Portrait in Black and White: The Concept of Asia in the Writings of Fukuzawa Yukichi and Okakura Tenshin," *Positions: East Asia Cultures Critiques* 15, no. 2 (Fall 2007): 358. For another look at Okakura's deliberate martial inflections, see Miya Elise Mizuta, "'Fair Japan': On Art and War at the Saint Louis World's Fair, 1904," *Discourse* 28, no. 1 (Winter 2006): 28–52.

62. Koike Shinji, "Ajia bijutsuten dai i bu: 'Kindai ajia no bijutsu—Indo, Chukoku, Nihon' kōsei," 8, 11. Born in 1901 in Tokyo, Koike spent his early youth in Beijing. He returned to study art history and literature at Tokyo Imperial University. After graduating in 1927, he began to conduct research on Asian design, including a report for the Greater East-Asia Cooperation Trading Strategy Committee.

63. Bruce Cumings, "Japan and Northeast Asia in the Twenty-First Century," *Network Power: Japan and Asia*, ed. Peter Katzenstein and Takashi Shiraishi (Ithaca, N.Y.: Cornell University Press, 1997), 155.

64. Sŏk To-ryun, "The Fine Arts and National Spirit," *Korea Journal* 8, no. 4 (April 1968): 23.

65. Lee Yil, "What Must Be Done for the Future of Asian Tradition and Art Which Have Been Changed under the Influence of Western Art?," summary to *Festival: Contemporary Asian Art Show, 1980 II*, exhibition catalog (Fukuoka: Fukuoka Art Museum, 1980), 40–41.

66. Aoki Shigeru, "Acknowledgement," in *Festival: Contemporary Asian Art Show, 1980 II*, 7.

67. Sakai Naoki, "Asia: Co-figurative Identifications," in *International Symposium 2002: Asia in Transition. Representation and Identity Report* (Tokyo: Japan Foundation Arts Center, 2003), 226–27.

68. An unsigned review for the journal *The Hindu* praised the inaugural version of the Triennale India as "rightfully" claiming "rank with international art exhibitions of the type that take place in Venice or Tokyo." Republished in *Lalit Kalā Contemporary* 36 (September 1990): 19.

69. Virginia Ty-Navarro, untitled statement, in *Second Triennale-India*, exhibition catalog (New Delhi: Lalit Kalā Akademi, 1971), 86. Japanese artist Yoshihara Jirō won one of six gold medals awarded for artistic excellence at this edition of the triennale.

70. Joseph Love, "Two Exhibitions, Korean White and Japanese Blue," *Japan Times*, May 18, 1975.

71. Yanagi Muneyoshi, "Chosen no bijutsu" [The art of Chosŏn], in *Chosen to sono geijutsu* [Chosŏn and her arts] (Tokyo: Sobunkaku, 1922), 173–74.

72. Lee Yil, "What Must Be Done for the Future of Asian Tradition and Art Which Have Been Changed under the Influence of Western Art?," in *Festival: Contemporary Asian Art Show, 1980*, as reproduced in *Space* 16, no. 1 (January 1981): 55.

73. Lee Yil, "What Must Be Done for the Future of Asian Tradition and Art Which Have Been Changed under the Influence of Western Art?," in *Festival: Contemporary Asian Art Show, 1980 II*, 39.

74. Yun Hyongkeun, "Yojŭm muŏsŭl?" [What are you doing these days?], *Toksŏ sinmun*, September 16, 1979.

75. Lee Yil, "What Must Be Done for the Future of Asian Tradition and Art Which Have Been Changed under the Influence of Western Art?," in *Festival: Contemporary Asian Art Show, 1980 II*, 32.

76. Ibid., 37.

77. Oh Kwangsu, "Asia chiyŏke issŏsŏ ŭi sŏgumisul ŭi yŏnghyang kwa kŭkbok" [The influence of Western art in the Asian region and how to overcome it], *Space* 16, no. 1 (January 1981): 58.

78. Lee Yil, "What Must Be Done for the Future of Asian Tradition and Art Which Have Been Changed under the Influence of Western Art?," in *Festival: Contemporary Asian Art Show, 1980 II*, 34.

79. T. K. Sabapathy, *Piyadasa: An Overview, 1962–2000* (Kuala Lumpur: Balai Seni Lukis Negara, 2001), 124–25. Piyadasa's comment may have also been motivated by his interest in

looking at art outside of its relationship to the ethnic and racial origins of its maker. Redza Piyadasa, "Art as Art Becomes Art as Art" (M.F.A. thesis, University of Hawaii, 1977), 4–5.

80. Yun Hyongkeun, quoted in You Hong-june, "T'eksŭch'yŏ wa hunyŏm ŭi mihak" [The aesthetics of texture and illumination], *Kyegan misul* 9 (Spring 1979): 128.

81. Nakahara Yusuke, "Onŭldaun chŏnch'esangŭl ch'uguham" [Pursuing an image of the whole relevant to the present], *Space* 18, no. 9 (September 1983): 76.

82. Park Seobo, "Han'guk hyŏndae misul ŭi sinsŏnhan segyegwan" [The fresh worldview of Korean contemporary art], *Chosun ilbo*, February 2, 1979.

83. Lee Yil, "Hyŏndae han'guk hoehwa" [Contemporary Korean painting], *Secondes Rencontres Internationales d'Art Contemporain: Corée 9 Peintures*, exhibition catalog (Paris: AFAA, 1978), unpaginated.

84. Lee Yil, "What Must Be Done for the Future of Asian Tradition and Art Which Have Been Changed under the Influence of Western Art?," as reproduced in *Space* 16, no. 1 (January 1981): 55.

85. Paik's show took place November 22, 1978–January 8, 1979.

86. Jeanine Warnod, "Cinq nations confrontées," *Le Figaro*, January 16, 1979.

87. André Warnod, "L'École de Paris," *Comoedia*, January 27, 1925.

88. On the French reception of *The Art of the Real*, see James Meyer, *Minimalism: Art and Polemics in the Sixties* (New Haven and London: Yale University Press, 2001), 256–58.

89. For examples of Lee Ufan's reception in France, see René Michà, "Lettre de Paris," *Art International* 23 (Summer 1979): 52; and Sylvie Dupuis, "Lee Ufan," *Art Press*, May 1980: 36.

90. Kim Sŏng-u, "P'arisŏ chumok motkk'ŭn han'guk hwagadŭl" [Korean artists fail to attract attention in Paris], *Han'guk ilbo*, February 2, 1979.

91. Sin Yong-sŏk, "Sŏgu hyungnaeman naen 'han'guk ch'ulp'umjak'" [The "Korean entrants" that only copy the West], *Chosun ilbo*, December 28, 1978.

92. Yi Ku-yŏl, "Uri ŭi hyŏndae misul kwa segye ŭi nun" [Our contemporary art and the views of the world], *Ch'um*, March 1979: 53.

93. Ha Chonghyun, interview with the author, March 17, 2008.

94. Shim Moon-seup, "Kwanchŏm ŭi ch'agoilppun, chakp'um sŏnjŏng kongjŏng haetda" [The approach was wrong but the selection process was fair], *Chungang ilbo*, February 19, 1979.

95. Park Seobo, "Han'guk hyŏndae misul ŭi sinsŏnhan segyegwan."

96. Park Seobo, "Ododanghan chinsil kwa han'guk hyŏndae misul ŭi chuch'esŏng" [Truth perverted and the subjectivity of contemporary Korean art], *Space* 15, no. 4 (April 1979): 49–52.

97. "Munhwa sanch'aek" [A stroll through culture], *Chungang ilbo*, September 1, 1975.

98. An example with which Park would probably have been familiar was Michel Ragon's speech at the Bridgestone Museum in Tokyo in August 1957 to accompany the exhibition *The New École de Paris,* which ran from August 20 to September 8, 1957. Ragon's speech emphasized the "international" character of the École de Paris. "Atarashii ekōru do pari ni tsuite: Pari ni okeru chūshō kaiga" [On the new École de Paris: Abstract painting in Paris], *Bijutsu techō* 9, no. 10 (October 1957): 7. Abstract expressionism, he implied, was included within internationalism, a point that was not lost on Japanese readers like painter Imai

Toshimitsu, who commented on the "nationalism" paradoxically involved in the promotion of abstract expressionism. "Anforumeru o megutte seiyō to tōyō, dentō to gendai" [About informel, East and West, traditional and the modern], *Bijutsu techō* 9, no. 10 (October 1957): 23.

99. Park Seobo, interview with Sŏ Sang-suk, "Wŏllo hwagarŭl ch'ajasŏ: Saeroun chilsŏnŭn ŏnjena p'agwoega chŏnjetoenŭn kŏt" [A visit with master artists: New order is always a prelude to destruction], *Ch'ungch'ŏng ilbo*, May 31, 1986.

100. Yi Hŭng-u, "Pak Sŏboron" [On Park Seobo], *Hwarang* 5, no. 3 (Fall 1977): 69–70.

101. Nakahara Yusuke, "Kankoku no gendai bijutsu no dōkō," 73.

102. Suh Sung-rok, "'Ekkol tŭ sŏul' 20 nyŏn ŭi paljach'wi."

103. Bang Keun-taek, "Editorial Afterword," *Hyŏndae yesul* 1, no. 5 (July 1977): 154.

104. Bang Keun-taek, "Pul punnŭn 'naengsohan myŏng' kwa 'ch'agaun yŏlgi'" ["Stark transparency" and "cold heat" on fire], *Hyŏndae yesul* 1, no. 5 (July 1977): 36–37.

105. Ha Chonghyun, interview with the author, August 13, 2007. Lee Kun-yong recalled that Park felt threatened by the A.G. Lee Kun-yong, interview with Lee Young Chul, *Tangsinŭn na ŭi t'aeyang* [You are my sunshine] (Seoul: Total Museum, 2005), 309.

106. Park Seobo, interview with the author, October 14, 2008. Interestingly, core A.G. members like Ha Chonghyun and Kim Ku-lim participated in École de Seoul exhibitions.

107. Ha In-du, "Aejŭng ŭi pŏt, kŭ wa samsimnyŏn" [A love–hate relationship of thirty years], *Sun misool* 27 (Winter 1975): 28.

108. Pak Mu-il, "Han'guk hwadan ŭi kyebo wa inmaek" [The genealogies and networks of the Korean art world], *Han'guk munhak*, January 1977: 220.

109. After 1983 Park was the lone committee member.

110. Bang Keun-taek, "Pak Sŏ-bo ŭi myobŏpiran!" [What Park Seobo's *Myobŏp* is!], *Simunhak* 6, no. 12 (December 1976): 116.

111. Suh Sung-rok, "'Ekkol tŭ sŏul' 20 nyŏn ŭi palchach'wi."

112. Takamatsu Jirō, in "Gendai kaiga no sikisai o megutte" [On color in contemporary painting], roundtable discussion, *Bijutsu techō* 29, no. 425 (1978): 171. The discussion was translated into Korean and later published in the May 1979 issue of *Misul kwa saenghwal*, May 1979: 89–120.

113. Lee Ufan, in "Gendai kaiga no sikisai o megutte," 169.

114. Won Dong-suk, "70 nyŏndae misul ŭi hyŏndaesŏng kwa kwannyŏm yuhi," *Wŏlgan toksŏ*, October 1978: 21, 23.

115. In 1975 it was estimated that only about twenty Korean artists had lived in Paris since the painter and novelist Na Hye-sok first traveled there in 1927. Kim Sŏng-u, "Chaebul han'guginhwadan ŭi kaŭlmaji" [The Korean art world of Paris greets the fall], *Han'guk ilbo*, September 10, 1975.

116. Chŏng Po-wŏn, "Uri tokch'angsŏng p'yohyŏn ŭi ŏryŏun kwaje" [The difficult process of expressing our uniqueness], *Space* 15, no. 4 (April 1979): 30.

EPILOGUE

1. Quoted in Nakahara Yusuke, "Onŭldaun chŏnch'esangŭl ch'uguham" [Pursuing a presentist image of the whole], *Space* 18, no. 9 (September 1983): 76. *Korean Contemporary Art—A Style of the Second Half of the 1970s* traveled to five public institutions in Japan: the Tokyo Metropolitan Art Museum, the Tochigi Prefectural Museum of Fine Arts, the National Museum of Art in Osaka, the Hokkaido Museum of Modern Art, and the Fukuoka Art Museum.

2. "Ajia bijutsu ten dai ni bu, zen shyutpin mokuroku" [Comprehensive list of works for the second part of the Asian art show], Fukuoka Asian Art Museum archive.

3. Kim Mi-kyung, *Han'guk ŭi sirhŏm misul* [Experimental art in Korea] (Seoul: Sigongart, 2003), 76.

4. Lee Seung-taek, interview with the author, May 25, 2010.

5. Yun Hyongkeun, interview with the author, July 5, 1995; Park Seobo, interview with the author, October 6, 2008.

6. Yi Kyungsung, "Han'guk yŏryu misulga chonghoen'gi" [The odyssey of Korean women artists], *Yŏsang*, April 1963: 240–41. Yi goes on to examine a number of Korean women artists who, "no matter how unfavorable their situations," managed to produce notable work.

7. For a brief history of women artists and artist groups in Korea, see Kim Hong-hee, "Misuresŏ ŭi p'eminijŭm kwa han'guk ŭi yŏsŏngjuŭi misul" [Feminism in art and Korean women's art], in *Yŏsong, kŭ tarŭm kwa him* [Woman, the difference and the power], ed. Kim Hong-hee (Seoul: Samsingak, 1994), 197–205.

8. One of the Hyundai Gallery's most successful artists was the female artist Chun Kyung-ja, whose pastel-hued figurative paintings were widely popular.

9. Oh Kwangsu, "Sculpturess Kim Chŏng-suk," *Korea Journal* 9, no. 12 (December 1969): 29.

10. Kim attended the Cranbrook Academy of Art from 1955 to 1957 and the Cleveland Institute of Art in 1958.

11. Important publications of this time included *Hwarang* (Gallery), which was begun by the Hyundai Gallery in 1973; *Kyegan misul* (Quarterly art), by the publications arm of the Samsung conglomerate in 1976; *Hyŏndae yesul* (Modern art); *Misul kwa saenghwal* (Art and life); *Ch'ŏngnyŏn misul* (Youth art); and *Misul p'yŏngnon* (Art criticism). All appeared in 1977. Short-lived but important publications that appeared in the 1970s were *Hyŏndae misul* (Contemporary art), published by the Myongdong Gallery in 1974, and *Han'guk misul* (Korean art), which appeared in 1975, courtesy of the Korean Fine Arts Association. General publications also featured visual art. Arguably the most balanced coverage was that of the cultural journal *Ppurigip'ŭn namu* (The deep-rooted tree), which featured a wide, sometimes disjointed, range of orientations, from the so-called modernists Yun Myeong-ro, Lee Yil, and Kim Bok-young to the so-called realists Won Dong-suk, Kim Yun-su, and Sung Wan-kyung. Among these, only *Kyegan misul* exists today. Established in November 1976 by the Chungang ilbo newspaper company, a subsidiary of Korean conglomerate Samsung, the journal was part of the newspaper's expansion into magazines, which began in 1968. Relaunched as *Wŏlgan misul* in January 1989, it continues to be one of Korea's leading visual arts publications.

12. Won Dong-suk, "Malssŏng kwa pyŏnmyŏng" [Controversy and excuses], *Deep-Rooted Tree*, March 1979: 21.

13. Commenting on Won's contribution, juror Oh Kwangsu complimented the author's "fresh perspective." Yet Oh harbored deep reservations over what he saw as Won's limited understanding of the artwork; he felt that Won's approach was far too "conceptual" and not attentive enough to the problems of painting. Oh Kwangsu, "Kyegan misul p'yŏngnonsang simsa sŏnhup'yŏng" [Afterthoughts on judging the *Kyegan misul* art criticism competition], *Kyegan misul* 3 (Summer 1977): 170.

14. Kim Yun-su, "Han'guk misul ŭi sae tan'gye" [A new phase of Korean art], in *Han'guk munhak ŭi hyŏn tan'gye II* [The present situation of Korean literature], ed. Paik Nak-chung and Yŏm Mu-ung (Seoul: Ch'angjak kwa pip'yŏng, 1983), 370.

15. Chang Sukwon, "Chiptanchŏk chugŭm" [Collective death], *Space* 15, no. 5 (May 1980): 106.

16. Sung Wan-kyung, quoted in "Hyŏndae misul wŏk'ŭshyop" [Workshop on contemporary art], *Han'guk ilbo*, July 2, 1981.

17. Park Seobo, quoted in Chŏng Chung-hŏn, "Sŏnbiga nanch'och'idŭt kojipsŭrŏpke 'myobŏp' ch'ugu" [Like a scholar paints an orchid, Park presses on with *Myobŏp*], *Chosun ilbo*, November 4, 1981.

18. "'Myobŏp' kaeinjŏn kannŭn Pak Sŏ-bo ssi" [Park Seobo's solo exhibition of *Myobŏp*], *Han'guk ilbo*, November 3, 1981.

19. You Hong-june, "Riŏllijŭm kwa minjok misul—80 nyŏndae saeroun misul undong ŭi inyŏm chŏngnipŭl wihae" [Realism and national art—toward the establishment of an ideology for a new artistic movement in the 1980s], in *Sidae sanghwang kwa misul ŭi nolli* [The present situation and the logic of art], ed. Son Chang-sŏp and Kim Jeong-heon (Seoul: Hankyoreh, 1986), 70. Originally published in *Minjok minjung misullon* [A theory of an art for the nation and the people], ed. Urimadang misulp'ae (Seoul: Uri madang, 1986).

20. Sung Wan-kyung, in "Hyŏndae misul wŏk'ŭshyop."

21. The Seoul Museum, located slightly north of the city center in Kugi-dong, was established in 1981 by Yim Setaik, a classmate of O Yun and a fellow member of the short-lived Reality Group of 1969. The museum was best known for its exhibitions of works associated with the Minjung movement.

22. Kim Yun-su, quoted in *81 nyŏn munje chakka chakp'umjŏn* [Works by the controversial artists of 1981], exhibition catalog (Seoul: Seoul Museum, 1982), unpaginated. The exhibition was held January 16–February 12, 1982.

23. Quoted in You Hong-june, "Kim Kyŏng-in ŭi 'munmaeng kwa konoe'" [Kim Kyeong In's "illiteracy and anguish"], *Madang*, March 1984, unpaginated.

24. Won Dong-suk, in *81 nyŏn munje chakka chakp'umjŏn*, unpaginated.

25. Park Yong-sook, in ibid.

26. Chong-sik Lee, "South Korea in 1980: The Emergence of a New Authoritarian Order," *Asian Survey* 21, no. 1 (January 1981): 139.

27. Kim Jeong-heon, interview with the author, June 2, 2010.

28. Kim Jeong-heon, "Kim Chŏng-hŏn misul" [The art of Kim Jeong-heon], roundtable discussion with Kim Jeong-heon, Im Chŏng-hui, Bahc Mo, and Park Chan-kyong, in

Kim Chŏng-hŏn misul [The art of Kim Jeong-heon] (Seoul: Hakkojae, 1997), 27. *Lucky Linoleum—Creating a Life of Plenty* was prominently reproduced in the exhibition catalog accompanying the large-scale retrospective of Minjung art at the National Museum of Contemporary Art in Korea in 1994.

29. Established artists' prices were very high, a phenomenon aggravated by the competitiveness among senior artists. Kim Yun-su, "Chŏnsihoe ribyu" [Exhibition review], *Kyegan misul* 2, no. 3 (August 1978): 190. Works by a major inkbrush painter like Yi Sang-bŏm commanded prices that were one hundred times those of the mid-1960s; between 1977 and 1978 prices would go up by an additional 50 percent. Pak Mu-il, "Rŭp'o: Tonŭro munhwarŭl sanŭn saramdŭl" [Report: Those who buy culture with cash], *Journalism,* August 1978: 167.

30. Lee Young Chul, "Culture in the Periphery and Identity in Korean Art," in *Across the Pacific: Contemporary Korean and Korean American Art*, exhibition catalog (New York: Queens Museum of Art, 1993), 11. The exhibition later traveled to the Kumho Museum of Art in Seoul.

31. Ibid., 10.

32. Hal Foster, "The Artist as Ethnographer?," in *Global Versions: Towards a New Internationalism in the Visual Arts*, ed. Jean Fisher (London: Kala Press and INIVA, 1994), 12–19.

33. Other artists included Chung Chang-sup, Kim Tschang-yeul, and Lee Kangso.

34. John Russell Taylor, "The Art of Man in Natural Harmony," *Times*, March 8, 1995.

35. Geeta Kapur, quoted in *Link*, February 7, 1971: 38.

36. Nam Kwan, "A, pamŭl tto saewŏtkuna" [Ah, another all-nighter], *Chunang*, April 1971, 201.

37. Lee Ufan, "Han'guk hyŏndae misul ŭi munjechŏm" [The problems of Korean contemporary art], *Kyegan misul* 2, no. 3 (Summer 1977): 150.

38. As noted by the Asia Art Archive, http://www.aaa.org.hk/onlineprojects/bitri/en/ didyouknow.aspx#fn1 (accessed January 13, 2012). The budget of the inaugural Gwangju Biennale was reported to be an astounding US$23 million. Eleanor Heartney, "Into the International Arena," *Art in America* 84, no. 4 (April 1996): 50. By comparison, that of the 1997 Venice Biennale was US$4.6 million.

39. Hou Hanru and Hans Ulrich Obrist, "Cities on the Move," in *Cities on the Move*, exhibition catalog (Ostfildern-Ruit: Verlag Gerd Hatje, 1997), unpaginated.

40. Bahc Mo quoted in Alice Yang, *Why Asia? Essays on Contemporary Asian and Asian American Art*, ed. Jonathan Hay and Mimi Young (New York: New York University Press, 1998), 94, 95.

41. The work shown as part of the Calvin Klein advertisement is not currently part of the Chinati collection. E-mail correspondence with Grace Davis, January 13, 2012. Currently the foundation has *Untitled 93-117* and *Untitled 93-98*. Calvin Klein Incorporated unfortunately denied permission to reproduce the advertisement for this book.

42. Yun Seong Ryeol, interview with the author, January 3, 2009.

43. Carol Vogel, "Klein Shifts from Sexy to Minimal," *New York Times*, October 6, 1995.

44. The mischaracterization of Yun was openly criticized by the South Korean press. Chŏng Chae-suk, "K'aelbin k'ŭlain kwango e woen han'guk hwaga kŭrim?" [Why is there

work by a Korean artist in a Calvin Klein advertisement?], *Hangyŏreh sinmun*, October 23, 1995. I thank Chungwoo Lee for this reference.

45. Kimsooja, interview with the author, December 21, 2011.

46. Tae Hyunsun, "Kim Sooja: A Needle Woman," in *Kim Sooja: A Needle Woman*, exhibition catalog (Seoul: Rodin Gallery, 2000), 20.

47. Kimsooja, interview with the author, December 21, 2011.

48. The exhibition took place from August 30 to October 10, 1989.

49. Ko Chong-sŏk, "Yŏsŏngmisul ŏdikkaji wanna?" [How far has women's art come?], *Hangyoreh sinmun*, August 23, 1989.

50. See Joan Kee, "What Is Feminist about Contemporary Asian Women's Art?," in *Contemporary Art in Asia: A Critical Reader*, ed. Melissa Chiu and Benjamin Genocchio (Cambridge and London: MIT Press, 2011), 347–69.

51. Kim is perhaps the most eloquent commentator in this regard. See, especially, Byron Kim, "Ad and Me," *Flash Art* 172 (October 1993): 122.

52. Giorgio Agamben, *The Coming Community*, trans. Michael Hardt (Minneapolis: University of Minnesota Press, 1993), 1.

53. Ibid., 2.

54. Joe Fig, *Inside the Painter's Studio* (Princeton: Princeton Architectural Press, 2009), 167.

55. Ann Gibson, "Color and Difference in Abstract Painting: The Ultimate Case of Monochrome," *Genders* 13 (Spring 1992): 137.

56. Saskia Sassen, "The Many Scales of the Global: Implications for Theory and for Politics," in *The Postcolonial and the Global*, ed. Revathi Krishnaswamy and John C. Hawley (Minneapolis and London: University of Minnesota Press, 2008), 82.

57. Yang Haegue, interview with Binna Choi, "Community of Absence: Conversation with Haegue Yang," *BAK Newsletter* 2 (March 2006): unpaginated.

INDEX

Deleuze, Gilles, 289
Dezain hihyō (magazine), 319n68
DIN A4/DIN A3/DIN A2 Whatever Being
    (Yang Haegue installation), 286, 287,
    289–90
Disruption (Pa'ran) (Chu Kyŏng painting),
    298n11
Documenta (visual art event), 279
Documenta VI (Lee Ufan exhibit), 242
Dongguk University, 112
Double Torture 81-1, 268, 269
Dubuffet, Jean, 58
Dynamics of Expansion and Reduction, The
    (exhibition), 61–62

École de Paris, 330n98
École de Seoul, 255–59, 261, 268
Écriture No. 3-78 (Park Seobo), 229, 230
Écriture No. 5-73 (Park Seobo).
    See Myobŏp C (Park Seobo)
Écriture No. 5-78 (Park Seobo), 221, 222
Écriture No. 6-74 (Park Seobo), 207–8
Écriture No. 8-67 (Park Seobo), 199, 200,
    201–2, 205
Écriture No. 21-72 (Park Seobo), 206, 207
Écriture No. 31-77-78 (Park Seobo), 2–4
Écriture No. 41-75 (Park Seobo), 225–26, 233
Écriture No. 41-78 (Park Seobo), 222, 223
Écriture No. 42-73 (Park Seobo), 202, 203,
    207–8
Écriture No. 43-78-79-81 (Park Seobo), 260
Écriture No. 62-78 (Park Seobo), 226,
    227, 228
Écriture No. 71-74 (Park Seobo), 210, 211
Écriture No. 72-74 (Park Seobo), 204,
    205, 221
Écriture series (Park Seobo), 31–32, 224–31,
    233, 261
Eight American Artists (exhibition), 10
elitism: tansaekhwa linked to, 266–68
EM-66 (Yun Hyongkeun painting), 77–78
Emergency Decrees (*Kin'gŭp choch'i*), 196
Enlightenment period: in Korean art, 40
essentialism: Japanese imperialism and,
    249–50
ethnic identity: tansaekhwa movement
    and, 31–32
everyday materials: in ink paintings,
    35–36; Korean artists' use of, 15–24

"Evolution of Art towards the Immaterial,
    The" (Klein), 238
exceptionalism: Japanese imperialism
    and, 249–50
Export Frigate (Park Seobo), 213–21, 272
Exultation (Lee Ungno painting), 13, 14

Fantasy of the Seashore (Kwon Young-woo
    painting), 303n20
Festival: Contemporary Asian Arts Show,
    248–50
"Fiction and Nonsense" (Bang Keun-taek),
    2225
Fifth Japan Art Festival, 160–61
fine art (yesul): Korean concepts of, 18
finger painting (*chiduhwa*), 37
"Five Bandits" (Kim Chi-ha poem), 194
Five Korean Artists, Five Kinds of White
    (exhibition), 2, 26, 28, 107, 233–40,
    245, 249
Focillon, Henri, 238
folk paintings (*minhwa*), 149
Foster, Hal, 278
Foucault, Michel, 155, 158
France: influence on Korea artists of, 13,
    17; tansaekhwa in, 31–32, 251–55
Free Artists' Association (Jiyūbijutsuka
    kyōkai), 4, 108
Frohner, Adolf, 98–99
From Cuts (Lee Ufan installation), 167, 168
From Line (81021) (Lee Ufan), 276, 277, 278
From Line (Lee Ufan painting series),
    170, 173, 177; artistic identity in, 180,
    183–84, 186, 189; informel style and,
    167, 169–70; international exhibi-
    tions, 161–65, 246; materiality in,
    205; Mono-ha influences in, 173–76;
    Muramatsu Gallery exhibit, 191–92;
    place in, 151; tansaekhwa and, 31;
    Tokyo Gallery exhibition, 146–49
From Notch (Lee Ufan painting series),
    147, 166, 167, 172
From Point (#76076) (Lee Ufan), 182, 183
From Point (1973) (Lee Ufan), 187, 188, 189
From Point (1975), 184, 185, 187
From Point (Lee Ufan painting series),
    148, 178–79; artistic identity in, 174,
    180, 186; informel style and, 167, 169;
    international exhibitions, 161–65,
    246; materiality in, 205; Muramatsu

Gallery exhibit, 191–92; place in, 151; sale of, 261; tansaekhwa and, 31; Tokyo Gallery exhibition, 146–47

Fry, Edward, 161

Fujieda Teruo, 150

Fukuoka Art Museum, 235, 328n57; Asian Art Shows (exhibition series), 247–49, 254; tansaekhwa at, 261

Fukuoka Asian Art Triennale, 247–48

"Fusing Materiality and Painting" (Ha Chonghyun), 141

Galbraith, John Kenneth, 165

Galerie Barbara Wien, 286

Galerie Bénézit, 97

Galerie Facchetti, 58

Gallery Shinjuku, 160

Garō (journal), 159

Gauguin, Paul, 82

gender: tansaekhwa exploration of, 263, 265

geopolitics: contemporary Korean art and influence of, 24–28; global art world and, 32; tansaekhwa movement and, 1–2

gestural abstraction, 46–47; Ha Chonghyun's work in, 122; international exhibitions of, 95; Kwon Young-woo's work with, 56–64; in postwar Korea, 12

Gibson, Ann, 289

Gin Gallery, 123

Glimpse into the Studio, A (Kwon Young-woo painting), 41, 42–43, 50

Gothic (Tobey painting), 10

Great Britain: Korean art in, 278

Greater East-Asia Co-Prosperity Sphere, 247

Great Kanto Earthquake, 156

Guattari, Félix, 289

Guggenheim Museum (New York), 161, 172

Gutai (Concrete) group, 13, 297n2

Gwangju Biennale, 279

Gwangju Uprising, 267

Ha Chonghyun, 2; abstract art by, 184, 186; *Conjunction* series by, 30–31, 96, 127–45, 263, 265; École de Seoul and, 257; international exhibitions by, 53, 97–100, 251, 255; materiality in work of, 120–27; op art by, 95, 103, 105–6; paintings by, 96; postwar Korean

art and, 22–27; tansaekhwa and, 28, 30–31, 239, 261, 267, 276

Ha In-du, 255

Han'guk ilbo (newspaper), 255, 261

Han'guk Ilbo Grand Prix, 81

hanji (Korean paper), 35–37, 318n61; Kwon Young-woo's work with, 47–49, 57–58, 64–65, 69, 71, 74

Hankyoreh sinmun (newspaper), 285

Han Sang-jin, 11

Haryū Ichirō, 104, 245

Heu Hwang, 234, 240

Hikosaka Naoyoshi, 174

History of Modern Korean Painting (Kim Yun-su), 236–37

Hongdae Nonch'ong (magazine), 238

Hongik University: art department at, 7–8, 24, 81; Osaka University of the Arts exchange with, 311n57; Park Seobo at, 193; rivalry with Seoul National University, 111–12

Hong Sun-pyo, 39

Honma Masayoshi, 103–4, 245

Hyŏndae misul (magazine), 25–27

hyŏndae misul (modern and contemporary art), 7, 26–27, 301n62

Hyundai Gallery, 110–12, 162, 174, 186, 265, 267

Ichinose, Thomas, 102–3

Ideals of the East (Okakura Tenshin), 247, 328n61

Ilgan sŭp'ochŭ (newspaper), 199

illegibility: tansaekhwa and distinction of, 2

illusionism: Lee Ufan's critique of, 152

imperialist ideology: Asian regionalism and, 247–50; tansaekhwa movement in context of, 1–2

Imprints of a No. 50 Brush Repeated at Regular Intervals of 30 cm (Toroni), 180, 181, 183, 186

Indépendants Exhibition (Seoul), 163, 199, 235, 245, 255–59

India: contemporary art in, 243–50

industrialization: Korean artists' response to, 15–24, 271–76

information sources and delivery: Japanese- Korean diplomatic ties and, 101–6; postwar Korean art production and, 8, 10, 24–28

Lee Yil, 3–4, 24, 27–28; art criticism by, 78, 91, 109, 162, 233–34, 236–40, 286; on Asian regionalism, 246–47, 249–50; contemporary Korean art exhibits and, 242–43; on international exhibits of Korean art, 254–55; Japanese exhibits of Korean art and, 103–4, 106, 325n3; tansaekhwa and, 256–57, 268

Lee Young Chul, 278

Le Figaro (newspaper), 254

Léger, Fernand, 17

legibility: tansaekhwa and distinction of, 2

Les Mots et les choses (Foucault), 158

Life magazine, 10

Lim Young-bang, 103

Line Variation (Suh Se-ok painting), 47, 48, 49, 169

literati painting, 13, 21, 40, 47, 56

Love, Joseph, 91–92, 107, 208, 245, 249, 257

Lucky Goldstar company, 271

Lucky Linoleum—Creating a Life of Plenty (Kim Jeong-heon painting), 270, 271–76

MacArthur, Douglas, 263

Maeda Josaku, 106–7, 208

Magiciens de la Terre (exhibit), 278

Mainichi Shimbun, 115

Malevich, Kasimir, 37

Mallarmé, Stéphane, 175

manga comics, 159

Manzoni, Piero, 37

Martin, Agnes, 208, 211, 228

materiality: in Ha Chonghyun's work, 120–27; in paper art, 58, 60–62

Matériologies (Dubuffet series), 58

Mathieu, Georges, 58

McLuhan, Marshall, 25

Merleau-Ponty, Maurice, 116

Metabolism architectural movement, 156

"method" approach to tansaekhwa, 2–4

Mexican social realism, 195

Michaux, Henri, 58

Minami Gallery, 317n39

Mindan (Korean Residents Union in Japan), 160

Minemura Toshiaki, 106, 150

minimalism: international exhibitions of, 254–55; in Japan, 117; Korean contemporary art and, 62

Minjung art, 32, 262, 278

Miru (journal), 152

Misul kwa saenghwal (magazine), 242

Mizue (magazine), 12

Modern Art 73 exhibition, 235

Modern Artists' Association (Hyŏndae misulga hyŏp'oe), 10–11

Monet, Claude, 78

monochromatic art: colonialist influences on, 235–37; Lee Ufan's work in, 151–52; political criticism of, 266–68; resurgence in 1960s of, 36–37, 39; tansaekhwa as form of, 1–4, 238–40. *See also* tansaekhwa painting

Monochrome Malerie (exhibition), 37

Mono-ha (School of Things) (Japanese art group), 30, 96, 112–20, 122–27, 149, 297n2; Lee Ufan and, 155, 160–61, 165, 173–74

Moonlit Night in Kijwa Island (Kim Whanki painting), 81

Moon Myung-dae, 109–12

Moon Yeo-song, 158

Moretti, Franco, 29

Morris, Robert, 62

Mosset, Olivier, 180

Motherwell, Robert, 10

Muehl, Otto, 98–99

Munheon Gallery, 90–91

Munye yŏnggam (journal), 246

Murai Osamu, 116

Muramatsu Gallery, 106–7, 152, 161, 191, 326n35

Musée d'Art Moderne de la Ville de Paris, 254

Museum of Modern Art (New York), 172

Myobŏp (Park Seobo series of paintings), 3, 192–93, 201–13, 220, 224–25, 228, 257, 320n4

Myobŏp A (Park Seobo), 202, 207–8

Myobŏp C (Park Seobo), 190, 191–92, 202, 205, 207

Myongdong Gallery, 20–21, 25–26, 107; Ha Chonghyun paintings in, 131; Kwon Young-woo's exhibit at, 64–74, 140–41, 189; *Modern Art 73* exhibition at, 235; Yun Hyongkeun's work at, 75–81

Na Hye-sok, 331n115

Nakahara Yusuke: on Asian regionalism, 249; Japanese exhibits of Korean art and, 104, 106–7, 160, 233–37, 242–43; Lee Ufan's work and, 152; minimalism in Japan and, 117; Park Seobo's work and, 230

Nambata Tatsuoki, 108

Nam Kwan, 8, 46, 163, 235, 279

Nancy, Jean-Luc, 33

Narita Katsuhiko, 112

narrative structure: tansaekhwa painting and, 28–29

National Documentary Paintings Project (*minjok kirok'hwa*), 193, 213–20, 322n41

nationalist identity: Japanese colonial influences in Korea and, 108–10, 236–37; Japanese exhibition of Korean art and, 106; tansaekhwa movement and, 1–2, 27–29, 31–32

National Museum of Contemporary Art of Korea, 281–82

National Museum of Modern Art (Kungnip hyŏndae misulgwan) (Seoul), 26, 97, 123, 163, 196, 215–16, 219, 256, 278

National Museum of Modern Art (Tokyo), 103–4, 160, 213, 251

NBG (Neo Beaux-Arts Group), 108

Neo-Dada movement, 167

New Citizen Public Discourse (*Shinmin kongnon*) (journal), 298n11

Newman, Barnett, 172–73, 175, 281

Newspaper 74-3 (Choi Tae-shin installation), 199

Newspaper after the First of June 1954 (Sung Neung-kyung performance art), 196, 197, 198

New York Times, 281

nihonga painting, 40, 49–51, 96, 110–11, 125, 147, 149, 170

Nihon University, 165

Nika-kai (art association), 311n57

1960 Artists' Group (1960 nyŏn misulga hyŏp'oe), 11

1960, Ka (O Yun painting), 194–95, 271

Nini's Painting (Twombly), 230

Ninth Contemporary Art Exhibition of Japan, 115, 125, 155, 161

Nishida Kitarō, 151

No. 1 (Park Seobo painting, 1957–58), 9, 10, 12–13, 46, 122, 201

Non-Aligned Movement, 243

"nonfigurative Oriental painting" (*pigu-sang tongyanghwa*): official category of, 54–64

Noon (Suh Se-ok painting), 50, 52, 53

North Korea: art criticism in, 11; wartime artistic production in, 4, 7

Nucleus G-99 (Lee Seung-jio), 17–18, 19, 81, 97

Ogawa Masataka, 242

Oh Kwangsu, 265, 333n13; on colonial influences in Korean art, 235; on Ha Chonghyun's work, 137; on international art world, 97; on Japanese–Korean artistic exchanges, 101, 109; on Kwon Young-woo, 65, 69, 74; Mono-ha group and, 112, 115–16, 120, 122–23; postwar Korean art and, 24; tansaekhwa painting and, 33

Oh Sang-gyel, 297n2

oil painting: Kwon Young-woo's examples of, 41–46; segregation from ink painting, 2, 15, 30, 40; Yun Hyongkeun's work with, 75–81

Okakura Tenshin, 247–48

Old Moon (Kwon Young-woo paper work), 57

On the Way to an Island (Kwon Young-woo painting), 43–44, 45, 50

op art, 96–97, 103–6

Organization of Petroleum Exporting Countries (OPEC), 18

"Oriental" painting (*tongyanghwa*), 36, 39–40, 46

Osaka University of the Arts, 311n57

Ōshima Nagisa, 158

O To-gwang, 72, 74

O Yun, 194–95, 271, 321n15

Paik, Nam June, 24, 27, 254

painting (hoehwa): Ha Chonghyun's frustration with, 126–27

Painting and Sagacity (*Hoehwa wa yeji*) (Yun Hi-sun), 110–11

painting institutes (*hoehwa yŏn'guso*): postwar emergence of, 8

JOAN KEE IS ASSISTANT PROFESSOR OF ART HISTORY AT THE UNIVERSITY OF MICHIGAN AT ANN ARBOR.